DOCTRINE AND COVENANTS.

THE

DOCTRINE AND COVENANTS,

OF THE

CHURCH OF JESUS CHRIST OF LATTER-DAY
SAINTS, CONTAINING THE REVELATIONS

GIVEN TO

JOSEPH SMITH, JUN., THE PROPHET,

FOR THE

BUILDING UP OF THE KINGDOM OF GOD IN
THE LAST DAYS.

———————

DIVIDED INTO VERSES, WITH REFERENCES,

By ORSON PRATT, Sen.

———————

GREENWOOD PRESS, PUBLISHERS
WESTPORT, CONNECTICUT

Originally published in 1880
by Deseret News Company, Salt Lake City, Utah

First Greenwood Reprinting 1971

Library of Congress Catalogue Card Number 69-14082

SBN 8371-4101-X

Printed in the United States of America

DOCTRINE AND COVENANTS.

LECTURES ON FAITH.

LECTURE FIRST.

*On the Doctrine of the Church of Jesus Christ of
Latter-day Saints, originally delivered before a
Class of the Elders, in Kirtland, Ohio.*

1. Faith being the first principle in revealed religion, and the foundation of all righteousness, necessarily claims the first place in a course of lectures which are designed to unfold to the understanding the doctrine of Jesus Christ.

2. In presenting the subject of faith, we shall observe the following order—

3. First, faith itself—what it is.

4. Secondly, the object on which it rests. And,

5. Thirdly, the effects which flow from it.

6. Agreeable to this order we have first to show what faith is.

7. The author of the epistle to the Hebrews, in the eleventh chapter of that epistle and first verse, gives the following definition of the word faith :

8. " Now faith is the substance (assurance) of things hoped for, the evidence of things not seen."

9. From this we learn that faith is the assurance which men have of the existence of things which they have not seen, and the principle of action in all intelligent beings.

10. If men were duly to consider themselves, and turn their thoughts and reflections to the operations of their own minds, they would readily discover that it is faith, and faith only, which is the moving cause of all action in them; that without it both mind and body would be in a state of inactivity, and all their exertions would cease, both physical and mental.

11. Were this class to go back and reflect upon the history of their lives, from the period of their first recollection, and ask themselves what principle excited them to action, or what gave them energy and activity in all their lawful avocations, callings, and pursuits, what would be the answer? Would it not be that it was the assurance which they had of the existence of things which they had not seen as yet? Was it not the hope which you had, in consequence of your belief in the existence of unseen things, which stimulated you to action and exertion in order to obtain them? Are you not dependent on your faith, or belief, for the acquisition of all knowledge, wisdom, and intelligence? Would you exert yourselves to obtain wisdom and intelligence, unless you did believe that you could obtain them? Would you have ever sown, if you had not believed that you would reap? Would you have ever planted, if you had not believed that you would gather? Would you have ever asked, unless you had believed that you would receive? Would you have ever sought, unless you had believed that you would have found? Or, would you have ever knocked, unless you had believed that it would have been opened unto you? In a word, is there anything that you would have done, either physical or mental, if you had not previously believed? Are not all your exertions of every kind, dependent on your faith? Or, may we not ask, what

have you, or what do you possess, which you have not
obtained by reason of your faith? Your food, your
raiment, your lodgings, are they not all by reason of
your faith? Reflect, and ask yourselves if these things
are not so. Turn your thoughts on your own minds,
and see if faith is not the moving cause of all action
in yourselves; and, if the moving cause in you, is it
not in all other intelligent beings?

12. And as faith is the moving cause of all action
in temporal concerns, so it is in spiritual; for the
Saviour has said, and that truly, that "He that *believeth* and is baptized, shall be saved." Mark xvi. 16.

13. As we receive by faith all temporal blessings
that we do receive, so we in like manner receive by
faith all spiritual blessings that we do receive. But
faith is not only the principle of action, but of power
also, in all intelligent beings, whether in heaven or on
earth. Thus says the author of the epistle to the
Hebrews, xi. 3 —

14. "Through faith we understand that the worlds
were framed by the word of God; so that things
which are seen were not made of things which do appear."

15. By this we understand that the principle of
power which existed in the bosom of God, by which
the worlds were framed, was faith; and that it is by
reason of this principle of power existing in the Deity,
that all created things exist; so that all things in
heaven, on earth, or under the earth, exist by reason of
faith as it existed in HIM.

16. Had it not been for the principle of faith the
worlds would never have been framed, neither would
man have been formed of the dust. It is the principle
by which Jehovah works, and through which he exercises power over all temporal as well as eternal things.
Take this principle or attribute—for it is an attribute
—from the Deity, and he would cease to exist.

17. Who cannot see, that if God framed the worlds

by faith, that it is by faith that he exercises power over them, and that faith is the principle of power? And if the principle of power, it must be so in man as well as in the Deity? This is the testimony of all the sacred writers, and the lesson which they have been endeavouring to teach to man.

18. The Saviour says (Matthew xvii. 19, 20), in explaining the reason why the disciples could not cast out the devil, that it was because of their unbelief— "For verily I say unto you" (said he), "if ye have faith as a grain of mustard seed, ye shall say unto this mountain, 'Remove hence to yonder place,' and it shall remove ; and nothing shall be impossible unto you."

19. Moroni, while abridging and compiling the record of his fathers, has given us the following account of faith as the principle of power. He says, page 597, that it was the faith of Alma and Amulek which caused the walls of the prison to be rent, as recorded on the 278th page ; it was the faith of Nephi and Lehi which caused a change to be wrought upon the hearts of the Lamanites, when they were immersed with the Holy Spirit and with fire, as seen on the 443rd page ; and that it was by faith that the mountain Zerin was removed when the brother of Jared spake in the name of the Lord. See also 599th page.

20. In addition to this we are told in Hebrews xi. 32, 33, 34, 35, that Gideon, Barak, Samson, Jephthah, David, Samuel, and the prophets, through faith subdued kingdoms, wrought righteousness, obtained promises, stopped the mouths of lions, quenched the violence of fire, escaped the edge of the sword ; out of weakness were made strong, waxed valiant in fight, turned to flight the armies of the aliens, and that women received their dead raised to life again, &c., &c.

21. Also Joshua, in the sight of all Israel, bade the sun and moon to stand still, and it was done. Joshua x. 12.

22. We here understand, that the sacred writers

say that all these things were done by faith. It was by
faith that the worlds were framed. God spake, chaos
heard, and worlds came into order by reason of the
faith there was in HIM. So with man also ; he spake
by faith in the name of God, and the sun stood still,
the moon obeyed, mountains removed, prisons fell,
lions' mouths were closed, the human heart lost its
enmity, fire its violence, armies their power, the sword
its terror, and death its dominion ; and all this by
reason of the faith which was in him.

23. Had it not been for the faith which was in
men, they might have spoken to the sun, the moon,
the mountains, prisons, the human heart, fire, armies,
the sword, or to death in vain !

24. Faith, then, is the first great governing principle which has power, dominion, and authority over
all things ; by it they exist, by it they are upheld, by
it they are changed, or by it they remain, agreeable to
the will of God. Without it there is no power, and
without power there could be no creation nor existence !

QUESTIONS AND ANSWERS ON THE FOREGOING PRINCIPLES.

What is theology ? It is that revealed science which
treats of the being and attributes of God, his relations
to us, the dispensations of his providence, his will
with respect to our actions, and his purposes with respect to our end. Buck's Theological Dictionary, page
582.

What is the first principle in this revealed science ?
Faith. Lecture i. 1.

Why is faith the first principle in this revealed
science ? Because it is the foundation of all righteousness. Hebrews xi. 6 : " Without faith it is impossible

to please God." 1 John iii. 7 : "Little children, let no man deceive you ; he that doeth righteousness, is righteous, even as he (God) is righteous." Lecture i. 1.

What arrangement should be followed in presenting the subject of faith ? First, it should be shown what faith is. Lecture i. 3. Secondly, the object upon which it rests. Lecture i. 4. And, thirdly, the effects which flow from it. Lecture i. 5.

What is faith ? It is the assurance of things hoped for, the evidence of things not seen (Hebrews xi. 1) ; that is, it is the assurance we have of the existence of unseen things. And being the assurance which we have of the existence of unseen things, must be the principle of action in all intelligent beings. Hebrews xi. 3 : "Through faith we understand the worlds were framed by the word of God." Lecture i. 8, 9.

How do you prove that faith is the principle of action in all intelligent beings? First, by duly considering the operations of my own mind ; and, secondly, by the direct declaration of Scripture. Hebrews xi. 7 : "By faith Noah, being warned of things not seen as yet, moved with fear, prepared an ark to the saving of his house, by the which he condemned the world, and became heir of the righteousness which is by faith." Hebrews xi. 8 : "By faith Abraham, when he was called to go into a place which he should afterwards receive for an inheritance, obeyed, and he went out not knowing whither he went." Hebrews xi. 9 : "By faith he sojourned in the land of promise, as in a strange country, dwelling in tabernacles with Isaac and Jacob, the heirs with him of the same promise." Hebrews xi. 27 : By faith Moses "forsook Egypt, not fearing the wrath of the king, for he endured as seeing him who is invisible." Lecture i. 10, 11.

Is not faith the principle of action in spiritual things as well as in temporal ? It is.

How do you prove it ? Hebrews xi. 6 : "Without faith it is impossible to please God." Mark xvi. 16 :

"He that believeth and is baptized shall be saved."
Romans iv. 16 : " Therefore it is of faith that it
might be by grace ; to the end the promise might bo
sure to all the seed ; not to that only which is of the
law, but to that also which is of the faith of Abraham,
who is the father of us all." Lecture i. 12, 13.

Is faith anything else beside the principle of action ?
It is.

What is it ? It is the principle of power also.
Lecture i. 13.

How do you prove it ? First, it is the principle of
power in the Deity as well as in man. Hebrews xi. 3 :
" Through faith we understand that the worlds were
framed by the word of God, so that things which are
seen were not made of things which do appear." Lecture i. 14, 15, 16. Secondly, it is the principle of
power in man also. Book of Mormon, page 278. Alma
and Amulek are delivered from prison. Ibid. page 443.
Nephi and Lehi, with the Lamanites, are immersed
with the Spirit. Ibid. page 599. The mountain Zerin,
by the faith of the brother of Jared, is removed.
Joshua x. 12 : " Then spake Joshua to the Lord in the
·day when the Lord delivered up the Amorites before
the children of Israel, and he said, in the sight of
Israel, 'Sun, stand thou still upon Gibeon, and thou moon
in the valley of Ajalon.'" Joshua x. 13 : " And the
sun stood still, and the moon stayed, until the people
had avenged themselves of their enemies. Is not this
written in the book of Jasher ? So the sun stood still
in the midst of heaven, and hasted not to go down
about a whole day." Matthew xvii. 19 : "Then came
the disciples to Jesus apart, and said, ' Why could not
we cast him out?'" Matthew xvii. 20 : "And Jesus
said unto them, Because of your unbelief ; for verily I
say unto you, if ye have faith as a grain of mustard
seed, ye shall say unto this mountain, ' Remove hence
to yonder place,' and it shall remove ; and nothing
shall be impossible unto you." Hebrews xi. 32 and

the following verses : " And what shall I say more?
for the time would fail me to tell of Gideon, and of
Barak, and of Samson, and of Jephthah, of David also,
and Samuel, and of the prophets, who through faith
subdued kingdoms, wrought righteousness, obtained
promises, stopped the mouths of lions, quenched the
violence of fire, escaped the edge of the sword ; out of
weakness were made strong, waxed valiant in fight,
turned to flight the armies of the aliens.   Women
received their dead raised to life again, and others were
tortured, not accepting deliverance, that they might
obtain a better resurrection." Lecture i. 16, 17, 18,
19, 20, 21, 22.

How would you define faith in its most unlimited
sense ?   It is the first great governing principle which
has power, dominion, and authority over all things.
Lecture i. 24.

How do you convey to the understanding more
clearly that faith is the first great governing principle
which has power, dominion, and authority over all
things ?   By it they exist, by it they are upheld, by it
they are changed, or by it they remain, agreeable to
the will of God ; and without it there is no power, and
without power there could be no creation nor existence !
Lecture i. 24.

LECTURE SECOND.

1. Having shown in our previous lecture "faith itself—what it is," we shall proceed to show, secondly, the object on which it rests.

2. We here observe that God is the only supreme governor and independent being in whom all fullness and perfection dwell; who is omnipotent, omnipresent, and omniscient; without beginning of days or end of life; and that in him every good gift and every good principle dwell; and that he is the Father of lights; in him the principle of faith dwells independently, and he is the object in whom the faith of all other rational and accountable beings center for life and salvation.

3 In order to present this part of the subject in a clear and conspicuous point of light, it is necessary to go back and show the evidences which mankind have had, and the foundation on which these evidences are, or were, based since the creation, to believe in the existence of a God.

4. We do not mean those evidences which are manifested by the works of creation which we daily behold with our natural eyes. We are sensible that, after a revelation of Jesus Christ, the works of creation, throughout their vast forms and varieties, clearly exhibit his eternal power and Godhead. Romans i. 20 : " For the invisible things of him from the creation of the world are clearly seen, being understood by the things that are made, even his eternal power and Godhead ;" but we mean those evidences by which the first thoughts were suggested to the minds of men that there was a God who created all things.

5. We shall now proceed to examine the situation of man at his first creation. Moses, the historian, has given us the following account of him in the first chapter of the book of Genesis, beginning with the 20th verse, and closing with the 30th. We copy from the new translation :

6. " And I, God, said unto mine Only Begotten, which was with me from the beginning, ' Let us make man in our image, after our likeness ; ' and it was so.

7. " And I, God, said, ' Let them have dominion over the fishes of the sea, and over the fowl of the air, and over the cattle, and over all the earth, and over every creeping thing that creepeth upon the earth.'

8. " And I, God, created man in mine own image, in the image of mine Only Begotten created I him ; male and female created I them. And I, God, blessed them, and said unto them, ' Be fruitful, and multiply, and replenish the earth, and subdue it ; and have dominion over the fish of the sea, and over the fowl of the air, and over every living thing that moveth upon the earth.'

9. " And I, God, said unto man, ' Behold, I have given you every herb bearing seed, which is upon the face of all the earth, and every tree in the which shall be the fruit of a tree yielding seed ; to you it shall be for meat.' "

10. Again, Genesis ii. 15, 16, 17, 19, 20 : " And I, the Lord God, took the man, and put him into the garden of Eden, to dress it and to keep it. And I, the Lord God, commanded the man saying, ' Of every tree of the garden thou mayest freely eat ; but of the tree of the knowledge of good and evil thou shalt not eat of it ; nevertheless thou mayest choose for thyself, for it is given unto thee ; but remember that I forbid it, for in the day thou eatest thereof thou shalt surely die.'

11. " And out of the ground I, the Lord God, formed every beast of the field, and every fowl of the air, and commanded that they should come unto

Adam, to see what he would call them. ＊ ＊ ＊ And
whatsoever Adam called every living creature, that
should be the name thereof. And Adam gave names
to all cattle, and to the fowl of the air, and to every
beast of the field."

12. From the foregoing we learn man's situation at
his first creation, the knowledge with which he was
endowed, and the high and exalted station in which
he was placed—lord or governor of all things on earth,
and at the same time enjoying communion and inter-
course with his Maker, without a vail to separate
between. We shall next proceed to examine the
account given of his fall, and of his being driven out
of the garden of Eden, and from the presence of the
Lord.

13. Moses proceeds—" And they " (Adam and Eve)
" heard the voice of the Lord God, as they were walking in the garden, in the cool of the day ; and Adam
and his wife went to hide themselves from the presence
of the Lord God amongst the trees of the garden.
And I, the Lord God, called unto Adam, and said unto
him, ' Where goest thou ? ' And he said, ' I heard thy
voice in the garden, and I was afraid, because I beheld
that I was naked, and I hid myself.'

14. " And I, the Lord God, said unto Adam, ' Who
told thee thou wast naked ? Hast thou eaten of the
tree whereof I commanded thee that thou shouldst not
eat ? If so, thou shouldst surely die ? ' And the man
said, ' The woman whom thou gavest me, and com-
mandedst that she should remain with me, gave me
of the fruit of the tree, and I did eat.'

15. " And I, the Lord God, said unto the woman,
' What is this thing which thou hast done ? ' And
the woman said, ' The serpent beguiled me, and I did
eat.'

16. And again, the Lord said unto the woman, " ' I
will greatly multiply thy sorrow, and thy conception.
In sorrow thou shalt bring forth children ; and thy

desire shall be to thy husband, and he shall rule over thee.

17. "And unto Adam, I, the Lord God, said, 'Because thou hast hearkened unto the voice of thy wife, and hast eaten of the fruit of the tree of which I commanded thee, saying, Thou shalt not eat of it! cursed shall be the ground for thy sake ; in sorrow thou shalt eat of it all the days of thy life. Thorns also, and thistles shall it bring forth to thee, and thou shalt eat the herb of the field. By the sweat of thy face shalt thou eat bread, until thou shalt return unto the ground—for thou shalt surely die—for out of it wast thou taken : for dust thou wast, and unto dust shalt thou return.'" This was immediately followed by the fulfillment of what we previously said—Man was driven or sent out of Eden.

18. Two important items are shown from the former quotations. First, after man was created, he was not left without intelligence or understanding, to wander in darkness and spend an existence in ignorance and doubt (on the great and important point which effected his happiness) as to the real fact by whom he was created, or unto whom he was amenable for his conduct. God conversed with him face to face. In his presence he was permitted to stand, and from his own mouth he was permitted to receive instruction. He heard his voice, walked before him and gazed upon his glory, while intelligence burst upon his understanding, and enabled him to give names to the vast assemblage of his Maker's works.

19. Secondly, we have seen, that though man did transgress, his transgression did not deprive him of the previous knowledge with which he was endowed relative to the existence and glory of his Creator ; for no sooner did he hear his voice than he sought to hide himself from his presence.

20. Having shown, then, in the first instance, that God began to converse with man immediately after he

"breathed into his nostrils the breath of life," and
that he did not cease to manifest himself to him, even
after his fall, we shall next proceed to show, that
though he was cast out from the garden of Eden, his
knowledge of the existence of God was not lost,
neither did God cease to manifest his will unto him.

21. We next proceed to present the account of the
direct revelation which man received after he was
cast out of Eden, and further copy from the new
translation—

22. After Adam had been driven out of the garden,
he "began to till the earth, and to have dominion over
all the beasts of the field, and to eat his bread by the
sweat of his brow, as I the Lord had commanded him."
And he called upon the name of the Lord, and so did
Eve, his wife, also. "And they heard the voice of the
Lord, from the way toward the garden of Eden, speaking unto them, and they saw him not, for they were
shut out from his presence; and he gave unto them
commandments that they should worship the Lord
their God, and should offer the firstlings of their flocks
for an offering unto the Lord. And Adam was obedient unto the commandments of the Lord.

23. "And after many days an angel of the Lord
appeared unto Adam, saying, 'Why dost thou offer
sacrifices unto the Lord?' And Adam said unto him,
'I know not; save the Lord commanded me.'

24. "And then the angel spake, saying, 'This thing
is a similitude of the sacrifice of the Only Begotten
of the Father, who is full of grace and truth. And
thou shalt do all that thou doest in the name of the
Son, and thou shalt repent and call upon God in the
name of the Son for evermore.' And in that day the
Holy Ghost fell upon Adam, which beareth record of
the Father and the Son."

25. This last quotation, or summary, shows this
important fact, that though our first parents were
driven out of the garden of Eden, and were even sepa-

rated from the presence of God by a vail, they still
retained a knowledge of his existence, and that sufficiently to move them to call upon him.   And further,
that no sooner was the plan of redemption revealed to
man, and he began to call upon God, than the Holy
Spirit was given, bearing record of the Father and
Son.

26. Moses also gives us an account, in the fourth of
Genesis, of the transgression of Cain, and the righteousness of Abel, and of the revelations of God to them.
He says, "In process of time, Cain brought of the
fruit of the ground an offering unto the Lord.   And
Abel also brought of the firstlings of his flock, and of
the fat thereof.   And the Lord had respect unto Abel,
and to his offering ; but unto Cain and to his offering
he had not respect.   Now Satan knew this, and it
pleased him.   And Cain was very wroth, and his countenance fell.   And the Lord said unto Cain, 'Why art
thou wroth ?   Why is thy countenance fallen ?   If thou
doest well, thou shalt be accepted.   And if thou doest
not well, sin lieth at the door, and Satan desireth to
have thee ; and except thou shalt hearken unto my
commandments, I will deliver thee up, and it shall be
unto thee according to his desire.'

27. "And Cain went into the field, and Cain talked
with Abel, his brother.   And it came to pass that
while they were in the field, Cain rose up against Abel,
his brother, and slew him.   And Cain gloried in that
which he had done, saying, 'I am free ; surely the
flocks of my brother falleth into my hands.'

28. "But the Lord said unto Cain, 'Where is Abel,
thy brother ?'   And he said, 'I know not.   Am I my
brother's keeper ?'   And the Lord said, 'What hast
thou done ? the voice of thy brother's blood cries unto
me from the ground.   And now, thou shalt be cursed
from the earth which hath opened her mouth to receive
thy brother's blood from thy hand.   When thou tillest
the ground, it shall not henceforth yield unto thee her

strength. A fugitive and a vagabond shalt thou be in the earth.'

29. " And Cain said unto the Lord, ' Satan tempted me because of my brother's flocks. And I was wroth also ; for his offering thou didst accept and not mine ; my punishment is greater than I can bear. Behold thou hast driven me out this day from the face of the Lord, and from thy face shall I be hid ; and I shall be a fugitive and a vagabond in the earth ; and it shall come to pass that he that findeth me will slay me because of mine iniquities, for these things are not hid from the Lord.' And the Lord said unto him, ' Whosoever slayeth thee, vengeance shall be taken on him sevenfold.' And I the Lord set a mark upon Cain, lest any finding him should kill him."

30. The object of the foregoing quotations is to show to this class the way by which mankind were first made acquainted with the existence of a God ; that it was by a manifestation of God to man, and that God continued, after man's transgression, to manifest himself to him and to his posterity ; and, notwithstanding they were separated from his immediate presence that they could not see his face, they continued to hear his voice.

31. Adam, thus being made acquainted with God, communicated the knowledge which he had unto his posterity ; and it was through this means that the thought was first suggested to their minds that there was a God, which laid the foundation for the exercise of their faith, through which they could obtain a knowledge of his character and also of his glory.

32. Not only was there a manifestation made unto Adam of the existence of a God ; but Moses informs us, as before quoted, that God condescended to talk with Cain after his great transgression in slaying his brother, and that Cain knew that it was the Lord that was talking with him, so that when he was driven out from the presence of his brethren, he carried with him

the knowledge of the existence of a God ; and, through this means, doubtless, his posterity became acquainted with the fact that such a Being existed.

33. From this we can see that the whole human family in the early age of their existence, in all their different branches, had this knowledge disseminated among them ; so that the existence of God became an object of faith in the early age of the world. And the evidences which these men had of the existence of a God, was the testimony of their fathers in the first instance.

34. The reason why we have been thus particular on this part of our subject, is that this class may see by what means it was that God became an object of faith among men after the fall ; and what it was that stirred up the faith of multitudes to feel after him—to search after a knowledge of his character, perfections and attributes, until they became extensively acquainted with him, and not only commune with him and behold his glory, but be partakers of his power and stand in his presence.

35. Let this class mark particularly, that the testimony which these men had of the existence of a God, was the testimony of man ; for previous to the time that any of Adam's posterity had obtained a manifestation of God to themselves, Adam, their common father, had testified unto them of the existence of God, and of his eternal power and Godhead.

36. For instance, Abel, before he received the assurance from heaven that his offerings were acceptable unto God, had received the important information of his father that such a Being did exist, who had created and who did uphold all things. Neither can there be a doubt existing on the mind of any person, that Adam was the first who did communicate the knowledge of the existence of a God to his posterity ; and that the whole faith of the world, from that time down to the present, is in a certain degree dependent

on the knowledge first communicated to them by their common progenitor ; and it has been handed down to the day and generation in which we live, as we shall show from the face of the sacred records.

37. First, Adam was 130 years old when Seth was born. Genesis v. 3. And the days of Adam, after he had begotten Seth, were 800 years, making him 930 years old when he died. Genesis v. 4, 5. Seth was 105 when Enos was born (verse 6) ; Enos was 90 when Cainan was born (verse 9) ; Cainan was 70 when Mahalaleel was born (verse 12) ; Mahalaleel was 65 when Jared was born (verse 15) ; Jared was 162 when Enoch was born (verse 18) ; Enoch was 65 when Methuselah was born (verse 21) ; Methuselah was 187 when Lamech was born (verse 25) ; Lamech was 182 when Noah was born (verse 28).

38. From this account it appears that Lamech, the 9th from Adam, and the father of Noah, was 56 years old when Adam died ; Methuselah, 243 ; Enoch, 308 ; Jared, 470 ; Mahalaleel, 535 ; Cainan, 605 ; Enos, 695 ; and Seth, 800.

39. So that Lamech the father of Noah, Methuselah, Enoch, Jared, Mahalaleel, Cainan, Enos, Seth, and Adam, were all living at the same time, and, beyond all controversy, were all preachers of righteousness.

40. Moses further informs us that Seth lived after he begat Enos, 807 years, making him 912 years old at his death. Genesis v. 7, 8. And Enos lived after he begat Cainan, 815 years, making him 905 years old when he died (verses 10, 11). And Cainan lived after he begat Mahalaleel, 840 years, making him 910 years old at his death (verses 13, 14). And Mahalaleel lived after he begat Jared, 830 years, making him 895 years old when he died (verses 16, 17). And Jared lived after he begat Enoch, 800 years, making him 962 years old at his death (verses 19, 20). And Enoch walked with God after he begat Methuselah 300 years, making him

365 years old when he was translated (verses 22, 23).*
And Methuselah lived after he begat Lamech, 782
years, making him 969 years old when he died (verses
26, 27). Lamech lived after he begat Noah, 595 years,
making him 777 years old when he died (verses 30, 31).

41. Agreeable to this account, Adam died in the
930th year of the world ; Enoch was translated in the
987th,* Seth died in the 1042nd ; Enos in the 1140th ;
Cainan in the 1235th ; Mahalaleel in the 1290th ;
Jared in the 1422nd ; Lamech in the 1651st ; and
Methuselah in the 1656th, it being the same year in
which the flood came.

42. So that Noah was 84 years old when Enos died,
176 when Cainan died, 234 when Mahalaleel died, 366
when Jared died, 595 when Lamech died, and 600
when Methuselah died.

43. We can see from this that Enos, Cainan, Mahalaleel, Jared, Methuselah, Lamech, and Noah, all lived
on the earth at the same time ; and that Enos, Cainan,
Mahalaleel, Jared, Methuselah, and Lamech, were all
acquainted with both Adam and Noah.

44. From the foregoing it is easily to be seen, not
only how the knowledge of God came into the world,
but upon what principle it was preserved ; that from
the time it was first communicated, it was retained in
the minds of righteous men, who taught not only their
own posterity but the world ; so that there was no
need of a new revelation to man, after Adam's creation to Noah, to give them the first idea or notion of
the existence of a God ; and not only of a God, but
the true and living God.

45. Having traced the chronology of the world
from Adam to Noah, we will now trace it from Noah
to Abraham. Noah was 502 years old when Shem was
born ; 98 years afterwards the flood came, being the

---

* According to the Old Testament. For Enoch's age,
see Covenants and Commandments, section 107. 49.

600th year of Noah's age. And Moses informs us
that Noah lived after the flood 350 years, making him
950 years old when he died. Genesis ix. 28, 29.

46. Shem was 100 years old when Arphaxad was
born. Genesis xi. 10. Arphaxad was 35 when Salah
was born (xi. 12) ; Salah was 30 when Eber was born
(xi. 14) ; Eber was 34 when Peleg was born, in whose
days the earth was divided (xi. 16) ; Peleg was 30
when Reu was born (xi. 18) ; Reu was 32 when Serug
was born (xi. 20) ; Serug was 30 when Nahor was born
(xi. 22) ; Nahor was 29 when Terah was born (xi. 24) ;
Terah was 70 when Haran and Abraham were born
(xi. 26).

47. There is some difficulty in the account given by
Moses of Abraham's birth. Some have supposed that
Abraham was not born until Terah was 130 years old.
This conclusion is drawn from a variety of scriptures,
which are not to our purpose at present to quote.
Neither is it a matter of any consequence to us whether
Abraham was born when Terah was 70 years old, or
130. But in order that there may no doubt exist upon
any mind in relation to the object lying immediately
before us, in presenting the present chronology we will
date the birth of Abraham at the latest period, that is,
when Terah was 130 years old. It appears from this
account that from the flood to the birth of Abraham,
was 352 years.

48. Moses informs us that Shem lived after he begat
Arphaxad, 500 years (xi. 11) ; this added to 100 years,
which was his age when Arphaxad was born, makes him
600 years old when he died. Arphaxad lived after he
begat Salah, 403 years (xi. 13) ; this added to 35 years,
which was his age when Salah was born, makes him
438 years old when he died. Salah lived after he begat
Eber, 403 years (xi. 15) ; this added to 30 years, which
was his age when Eber was born, makes him 433 years
old when he died. Eber lived after he begat Peleg,
430 years (xi. 17) ; this added to 34 years, which was

his age when Peleg was born, makes him 464 years old. Peleg lived after he begat Reu, 209 years (xi. 19) ; this added to 30 years, which was his age when Reu was born, makes him 239 years old when he died. Reu lived after he begat Serug 207 years (xi. 21) ; this added to 32 years, which was his age when Serug was born, makes him 239 years old when he died. Serug lived after he begat Nahor, 200 years (xi. 23) ; this added to 30 years, which was his age when Nahor was born, makes him 230 years old when he died. Nahor lived after he begat Terah, 119 years (xi. 25) ; this added to 29 years, which was his age when Terah was born, makes him 148 years old when he died. Terah was 130 years old when Abraham was born, and is supposed to have lived 75 years after his birth, making him 205 years old when he died.

49. Agreeable to this last account, Peleg died in the 1996th year of the world, Nahor in the 1997th, and Noah in the 2006th. So that Peleg, in whose days the earth was divided, and Nahor, the grandfather of Abraham, both died before Noah—the former being 239 years old, and the latter 148 ; and who cannot but see that they must have had a long and intimate acquaintance with Noah ?

50. Reu died in the 2026th year of the world, Serug in the 2049th, Terah in the 2083rd, Arphaxad in the 2096th, Salah in the 2126th, Shem in the 2158th, Abraham in the 2183rd, and Eber in the 2187th, which was four years after Abraham's death. And Eber was the fourth from Noah.

51. Nahor, Abraham's brother, was 58 years old when Noah died, Terah 128, Serug 187, Reu 219, Eber 283, Salah 313, Arphaxad 344, and Shem 448.

52. It appears from this account, that Nahor, brother of Abraham, Terah, Nahor, Serug, Reu, Peleg, Eber, Salah, Arphaxad, Shem, and Noah, all lived on the earth at the same time ; and that Abraham was 18 years old when Reu died, 41 when Serug and his

brother Nahor died, 75 when Terah died, 88 when
Arphaxad died, 118 when Salah died, 150 when Shem
died, and that Eber lived four years after Abraham's
death.   And that Shem, Arphaxad, Salah, Eber, Reu,
Serug, Terah, and Nahor, the brother of Abraham,
and Abraham, lived at the same time.   And that
Nahor, brother of Abraham, Terah, Serug, Reu, Eber,
Salah, Arphaxad, and Shem, were all acquainted with
both Noah and Abraham.

53. We have now traced the chronology of the
world agreeable to the account given in our present
Bible, from Adam to Abraham, and have clearly determined, beyond the power of controversy, that there
was no difficulty in preserving the knowledge of God
in the world from the creation of Adam, and the manifestation made to his immediate descendants, as set
forth in the former part of this lecture : so that the
stud ι ts in this class need not have any doubt resting
on their minds on this subject, for they can easily see
that it is impossible for it to be otherwise, but that the
knowledge of the existence of a God must have continued from father to son, as a matter of tradition at
least ; for we cannot suppose that a knowledge of this
important fact could have existed in the mind of any
of the before-mentioned individuals, without their
having made it known to their posterity.

54. We have now shown how it was that the first
thought ever existed in the mind of any individual
that there was such a Being as a God, who had created
and did uphold all things: that it was by reason of the
manifestation which he first made to our father Adam,
when he stood in his presence, and conversed with him
face to face, at the time of his creation.

55. Let us here observe, that after any portion of
the human family are made acquainted with the important fact that there is a God, who has created and does
uphold all things, the extent of their knowledge respecting his character and glory will depend upon their dili-

gence and faithfulness in seeking after him, until, like Enoch, the brother of Jared, and Moses, they shall obtain faith in God, and power with him to behold him face to face.

56. We have now clearly set forth how it is, and how it was, that God became an object of faith for rational beings ; and also, upon what foundation the testimony was based which excited the inquiry and diligent search of the ancient saints to seek after and obtain a knowledge of the glory of God ; and we have seen that it was human testimony, and human testimony only, that excited this inquiry, in the first instance, in their minds. It was the credence they gave to the testimony of their fathers, this testimony having aroused their minds to inquire after the knowledge of God; the inquiry frequently terminated, indeed always terminated when rightly pursued, in the most glorious discoveries and eternal certainty.

QUESTIONS AND ANSWERS ON THE FOREGOING PRINCIPLES.

Is there a being who has faith in himself, independently ? There is.

Who is it ? It is God.

How do you prove that God has faith in himself independently ? Because he is omnipotent, omnipresent, and omniscient ; without beginning of days or end of life, and in him all fullness dwells. Ephesians i. 23 : " Which is his body, the fullness of him that filleth all in all." Colossians i. 19 : " For it pleased the Father, that in him should all fullness dwell." Lecture ii. 2.

Is he the object in whom the faith of all other

rational and accountable beings center, for life and salvation? He is.

How do you prove it? Isaiah xlv. 22 : "Look
unto me and be ye saved, all the ends of the earth ;
for I am God, and there is none else." Romans xi. 34,
35, 36 : "For who hath known the mind of the Lord ;
or who hath been his counselor? or who hath first
given to him, and it shall be recompensed unto him
again? For of him, and through him, and to him, are
all things, to whom be glory for ever. Amen." Isaiah
xl., from the 9th to the 18th verses : "O Zion, that
bringest good tidings; (or, O thou that tellest good
tidings to Zion) get thee up into the high mountain ;
O Jerusalem, that bringest good tidings ; (or, O thou
that tellest good tidings to Jerusalem) lift up thy
voice with strength ; lift it up, be not afraid ; say unto
the cities of Judah, Behold your God! Behold the
Lord your God will come with strong hand (or,
against the strong) ; and his arm shall rule for him ;
behold, his reward is with him, and his work before
him (or, recompense for his work). He shall feed his
flock like a shepherd ; he shall gather his lambs with
his arms, and carry them in his bosom, and shall gently
lead those that are with young. Who hath measured the
waters in the hollow of his hand, and meted out heaven
with the span, and comprehended the dust of the earth
in a measure, weighed the mountains in scales, and the
hills in a balance? Who hath directed the Spirit of
the Lord, or, being his counselor, hath taught him?
With whom took he counsel, and who instructed him
and taught him in the path of judgment, and taught
him knowledge, and showed to him the way of understanding? Behold, the nations are as a drop of
a bucket and are counted as the small dust of the
balance : behold, he taketh up the isles as a very little
thing. And Lebanon is not sufficient to burn, nor the
beasts thereof sufficient for a burnt offering. All
nations are before him as nothing, and they are counted
to him less than nothing, and vanity." Jeremiah li.

15, 16 : "He (the Lord) hath made the earth by his power, he hath established the world by his wisdom, and hath stretched out the heaven by his understanding. When he uttereth his voice there is a multitude of waters in the heavens, and he causeth the vapors to ascend from the ends of the earth : he maketh lightnings with rain, and bringeth forth the wind out of his treasures. 1 Corinthians viii. 6 : "But to us there is but one God, the Father, of whom are all things, and we in him ; and one Lord Jesus Christ, by whom are all things, and we by him." Lecture ii. 2.

How did men first come to the knowledge of the existence of a God, so as to exercise faith in him ? In order to answer this question, it will be necessary to go back and examine man at his creation ; the circumstances in which he was placed, and the knowledge which he had of God. Lecture ii. 3, 4, 5, 6, 7, 8, 9, 10, 11. First, when man was created he stood in the presence of God. Genesis i. 27, 28. From this we learn that man, at his creation, stood in the presence of his God, and had most perfect knowledge of his existence. Secondly, God conversed with him after his transgression. Genesis iii. from the 8th to the 22nd. Lecture ii. 13, 14, 15, 16, 17. From this we learn that, though man did transgress, he was not deprived of the previous knowledge which he had of the existence of God. Lecture ii. 19. Thirdly, God conversed with man after he cast him out of the garden. Lecture ii. 22, 23, 24, 25. Fourthly, God also conversed with Cain after he had slain Abel. Genesis iv. from the 4th to the 6th. Lecture ii. 26, 27, 28, 29.

What is the object of the foregoing quotation ? It is that it may be clearly seen how it was that the first thoughts were suggested to the minds of men of the existence of God, and how extensively this knowledge was spread among the immediate descendants of Adam. Lecture ii. 30, 31, 32, 33.

What testimony had the immediate descendants of

Adam, in proof of the existence of God? The testimony of their father. And after they were made acquainted with his existence, by the testimony of their father, they were dependent upon the exercise of their own faith, for a knowledge of his character, perfections, and attributes. Lecture ii. 23, 24, 25, 26.

Had any other of the human family, besides Adam, a knowledge of the existence of God, in the first instance, by any other means than human testimony? They had not. For previous to the time that they could have power to obtain a manifestation for themselves, the all-important fact had been communicated to them by their common father; and so from father to child the knowledge was communicated as extensively as the knowledge of his existence was known; for it was by this means, in the first instance, that men had a knowledge of his existence. Lecture ii. 35, 36.

How do you know that the knowledge of the existence of God was communicated in this manner, throughout the different ages of the world? By the chronology obtained through the revelations of God.

How would you divide that chronology in order to convey it to the understanding clearly? Into two parts—First, by embracing that period of the world from Adam to Noah; and secondly, from Noah to Abraham; from which period the knowledge of the existence of God has been so general, that it is a matter of no dispute in what manner the idea of his existence has been retained in the world.

How many noted righteous men lived from Adam to Noah? Nine; which includes Abel, who was slain by his brother.

What are their names? Abel, Seth, Enos, Cainan, Mahalaleel, Jared, Enoch, Methuselah, and Lamech.

How old was Adam when Seth was born? One hundred and thirty years. Genesis v. 3.

How many years did Adam live after Seth was born? Eight hundred. Genesis v. 4.

How old was Adam when he died ?   Nine hundred
and thirty years.   Genesis v. 5.

How old was Seth when Enos was born ?   One
hundred and five years.   Genesis v. 6.

How old was Enos when Cainan was born ?   Ninety
years.   Genesis v. 9.

How old was Cainan when Mahalaleel was born ?
Seventy years.   Genesis v. 12.

How old was Mahalaleel when Jared was born ?
Sixty-five years.   Genesis v. 15.

How old was Jared when Enoch was born ?   One
hundred and sixty-two years.   Genesis v. 18.

How old was Enoch when Methuselah was born ?
Sixty-five years.   Genesis v. 21.

How old was Methuselah when Lamech was born ?
One hundred and eighty-seven years.   Genesis v. 25.

How old was Lamech when Noah was born ?   One
hundred and eighty-two years.   Genesis v. 28.   For
this chronology, see lecture ii. 37.

How many years, according to this account, was it
from Adam to Noah ?   One thousand and fifty-six
years.

How old was Lamech when Adam died ?   Lamech,
the ninth from Adam (including Abel), and father of
Noah, was fifty-six years old when Adam died.

How old was Methuselah ?   Two hundred and forty-
three years.

How old was Enoch ?   Three hundred and eight
years.

How old was Jared ?   Four hundred and seventy
years.

How old was Mahalaleel ?   Five hundred and
thirty-five years.

How old was Cainan ?   Six hundred and five years.

How old was Enos ?   Six hundred and ninety-five
years.

How old was Seth? Eight hundred years. For this item of the account, see lecture ii. 38.

How many of these noted men were cotemporary with Adam? Nine.

What are their names? Abel, Seth, Enos, Cainan, Mahalaleel, Jared, Enoch, Methuselah and Lamech. Lecture ii. 39.

How long did Seth live after Enos was born? Eight hundred and seven years. Genesis v. 7.

What was Seth's age when he died? Nine hundred and twelve years. Genesis v. 8.

How long did Enos live after Cainan was born? Eight hundred and fifteen years. Genesis v. 10.

What was Enos's age when he died? Nine hundred and five years. Genesis v. 11.

How long did Cainan live after Mahalaleel was born? Eight hundred and forty years. Genesis v. 13.

What was Cainan's age when he died? Nine hundred and ten years. Genesis v. 14.

How long did Mahalaleel live after Jared was born? Eight hundred and thirty years. Genesis v. 16.

What was Mahalaleel's age when he died? Eight hundred and ninety-five years. Genesis v. 17.

How long did Jared live after Enoch was born? Eight hundred years. Genesis v. 19.

What was Jared's age when he died? Nine hundred and sixty-two years. Genesis v. 20.

How long did Enoch walk with God after Methuselah was born? Three hundred years. Genesis v. 22.

What was Enoch's age when he was translated? Three hundred and sixty-five years. Genesis v. 23.*

How long did Methuselah live after Lamech was born? Seven hundred and eighty-two years. Genesis v. 26.

---

* For Enoch's age, see Covenants and Commandments, Section 107. 49.

What was Methuselah's age when he died? Nine hundred and sixty-nine years. Genesis v. 27.

How long did Lamech live after Noah was born? Five hundred and ninety-five years. Genesis v. 30.

What was Lamech's age when he died? Seven hundred and seventy-seven years. Genesis v. 31. For the account of the last item see lecture ii. 40.

In what year of the world did Adam die? In. the nine hundred and thirtieth.

In what year was Enoch translated?* In the nine hundred and eighty-seventh.

In what year did Seth die? In the one thousand and forty-second.

In what year did Enos die? In the eleven hundred and fortieth.

In what year did Cainan die? In the twelve hundred and thirty-fifth.

In what year did Mahalaleel die? In the twelve hundred and ninetieth.

In what year did Jared die? In the fourteen hundred and twenty-second.

In what year did Lamech die? In the sixteen hundred and fifty-first.

In what year did Methuselah die? In the sixteen hundred and fifty-sixth. For this account see lecture ii. 41.

How old was Noah when Enos died? Eighty-four years.

How old when Cainan died? One hundred and seventy-nine years.

How old when Mahalaleel died? Two hundred and thirty-four years.

How old when Jared died? Three hundred and sixty-six years.

---

* For Enoch's age, see Covenants and Commandments, Section 107. 49.

How old when Lamech died? Five hundred and ninety-five years.

How old when Methuselah died? Six hundred years. See lecture ii. 42, for the last item.

How many of those men lived in the days of Noah? Six.

What are their names? Enos, Cainan, Mahalaleel, Jared, Methuselah, and Lamech. Lecture ii. 43.

How many of those men were cotemporary with Adam and Noah both? Six.

What are their names? Enos, Cainan, Mahalaleel, Jared, Methuselah, and Lamech. Lecture ii. 43.

According to the foregoing account, how was the knowledge of the existence of God first suggested to the minds of men? By the manifestation made to our father Adam, when he was in the presence of God, both before and while he was in Eden. Lecture ii. 44.

How was the knowledge of the existence of God disseminated among the inhabitants of the world? By tradition from father to son. Lecture ii. 44.

How old was Noah when Shem was born? Five hundred and two years. Genesis v. 32.

What was the term of years from the birth of Shem to the flood? Ninety-eight.

What was the term of years that Noah lived after the flood? Three hundred and fifty. Genesis ix. 28.

What was Noah's age when he died? Nine hundred and fifty years. Genesis ix. 29. Lecture ii. 45.

What was Shem's age when Arphaxad was born? One hundred years. Genesis xi. 10.

What was Arphaxad's age when Salah was born? Thirty-five years. Genesis xi. 12.

What was Salah's age when Eber was born? Thirty-years. Genesis xi. 16.

What was Eber's age when Peleg was born? Thirty-four years. Genesis xi. 14.

What was Peleg's age when Reu was born? Thirty
years. Genesis xi. 18.

What was Reu's age when Serug was born? Thirty-
two years. Genesis xi. 20.

What was Serug's age when Nahor was born?
Thirty years. Genesis xi. 22.

What was Nahor's age when Terah was born?
Twenty-nine years. Genesis xi. 24.

What was Terah's age when Nahor (the father of
Abraham) was born? Seventy years. Genesis xi. 26.

What was Terah's age when Abraham was born?
Some suppose one hundred and thirty years, and others
seventy. Genesis xi. 26. Lecture ii. 46.

What was the number of years from the flood to
the birth of Abraham? Supposing Abraham to have
been born when Terah was one hundred and thirty
years old, it was three hundred and fifty-two years:
but if he was born when Terah was seventy years old,
it was two hundred and ninety-two years. Lecture
ii. 47.

How long did Shem live after Arphaxad was born?
Five hundred years. Genesis xi. 11.

What was Shem's age when he died? Six hundred
years. Genesis xi. 11.

What number of years did Arphaxad live after
Salah was born? Four hundred and three years.
Genesis xi. 13.

What was Arphaxad's age when he died? Four
hundred and thirty-eight years.

What number of years did Salah live after Eber
was born? Four hundred and three years.

What was Salah's age when he died? Four hundred and thirty-three years.

What number of years did Eber live after Peleg
was born? Four hundred and thirty years. Genesis
xi. 17.

What was Eber's age when he died ? Four hundred and sixty-four years.

What number of years did Peleg live after Reu was born? Two hundred and nine years. Genesis xi. 19.

What was Peleg's age when he died? Two hundred and thirty-nine years.

What number of years did Reu live after Serug was born? Two hundred and seven years. Genesis xi. 21.

What was Reu's age when he died? Two hundred and thirty-nine years.

What number of years did Serug live after Nahor was born? Two hundred years. Genesis xi. 23.

What was Serug's age when he died? Two hundred and thirty years.

What number of years did Nahor live after Terah was born? One hundred and nineteen years. Genesis xi. 25.

What was Nahor's age when he died? One hundred and forty-eight years.

What number of years did Terah live after Abraham was born? Supposing Terah to have been one hundred and thirty years old when Abraham was born, he lived seventy-five years ; but if Abraham was born when Terah was seventy years old, he lived one hundred and thirty-five.

What was Terah's age when he died? Two hundred and five years. Genesis xi. 32. For this account, from the birth of Arphaxad to the death of Terah, see lecture ii. 48.

In what year of the world did Peleg die? Agreeable to the foregoing chronology, he died in the nineteen hundred and ninety-sixth year of the world.

In what year of the world did Nahor die? In the nineteen hundred and ninety-seventh.

In what year of the world did Noah die? In the two thousand and sixth.

In what year of the world did Reu die? In the two thousand and twenty-sixth.

In what year of the world did Serug die? In the two thousand and forty-ninth.

In what year of the world did Terah die? In the two thousand and eighty-third.

In what year of the world did Arphaxad die? In the two thousand and ninety-sixth.

In what year of the world did Salah die? In the twenty-one hundred and twenty-sixth.

In what year of the world did Abraham die? In the twenty-one hundred and eighty-third.

In what year of the world did Eber die? In the twenty-one hundred and eighty-seventh. For this account of the year of the world in which those men died, see lecture ii. 49, 50.

How old was Nahor (Abraham's brother) when Noah died? Fifty-eight years.

How old was Terah? One hundred and twenty-eight.

How old was Serug? One hundred and eighty-seven.

How old was Reu? Two hundred and nineteen.

How old was Eber? Two hundred and eighty-three.

How old was Salah? Three hundred and thirteen.

How old was Arphaxad? Three hundred and forty-eight.

How old was Shem? Four hundred and forty-eight.

For the last account see lecture ii. 51.

How old was Abraham when Reu died? Eighteen years, if he was born when Terah was one hundred and thirty years old.

What was his age when Serug and Nahor (Abraham's brother) died? Forty-one years.

What was his age when Terah died? Seventy-five years.

What was his age when Arphaxad died? Eighty-eight.

What was his age when Salah died? One hundred and eighteen years.

What was his age when Shem died? One hundred and fifty years. For this see lecture ii. 52.

How many noted characters lived from Noah to Abraham? Ten.

What are their names? Shem, Arphaxad, Salah, Eber, Peleg, Reu, Serug, Nahor, Terah, and Nahor, (Abraham's brother). Lecture ii. 52.

How many of these were cotemporary with Noah? The whole.

How many with Abraham? Eight.

What are their names? Nahor (Abraham's brother), Terah, Serug, Reu, Eber, Salah, Arphaxad, and Shem. Lecture ii. 52.

How many were cotemporary with both Noah and Abraham? Eight.

What are their names? Shem, Arphaxad, Salah, Eber, Reu, Serug, Terah, and Nahor (Abraham's brother). Lecture ii. 52.

Did any of these men die before Noah? They did.

Who were they? Peleg, in whose days the earth was divided, and Nahor, (Abraham's grandfather). Lecture ii. 49.

Did any one of them live longer than Abraham? There was one. Lecture ii. 50.

Who was he? Eber, the fourth from Noah. Lecture ii. 50.

In whose days was the earth divided? In the days of Peleg.

Where have we the account given that the earth was divided in the days of Peleg? Genesis x. 25.

Can you repeat the sentence? "Unto Eber were born two sons : the name of one was Peleg, for in his days the earth was divided."

What testimony have men, in the first instance, that there is a God? Human testimony, and human testimony only. Lecture ii. 56.

What excited the ancient saints to seek diligently after a knowledge of the glory of God, his perfections and attributes? The credence they gave to the testimony of their fathers. Lecture ii. 56.

How do men obtain a knowledge of the glory of God, his perfections and attributes? By devoting themselves to his service, through prayer and supplication incessantly strengthening their faith in him, until, like Enoch, the brother of Jared, and Moses, they obtain a manifestation of God to themselves. Lecture ii. 55.

Is the knowledge of the existence of God a matter of mere tradition, founded upon human testimony alone, until persons receive a manifestation of God to themselves? It is.

How do you prove it? From the whole of the first and second lectures.

LECTURE THIRD.

1. In the second lecture it was shewn how it was that the knowledge of the existence of God came into the world, and by what means the first thoughts were suggested to the minds of men that such a Being did actually exist ; and that it was by reason of the knowledge of his existence that there was a foundation laid for the exercise of faith in him, as the only Being in whom faith could center for life and salvation ; for faith could not center in a Being of whose existence we have no idea, because the idea of his existence in the first instance is essential to the exercise of faith in him. Romans x. 14 : "How then shall they call on him in whom they have not believed ? and how shall they believe in him of whom they have not heard ? and how shall they hear without a preacher (or one sent to tell them)? So, then, faith comes by hearing the word of God." (New Translation.)

2. Let us here observe, that three things are necessary in order that any rational and intelligent being may exercise faith in God unto life and salvation.

3. First, the idea that he actually exists.

4. Secondly, a *correct* idea of his character, perfections, and attributes.

5. Thirdly, an actual knowledge that the course of life which he is pursuing is according to his will. For without an acquaintance with these three important facts, the faith of every rational being must be imperfect and unproductive ; but with this understanding it can become perfect and fruitful, abounding in righteousness, unto the praise and glory of God the Father, and the Lord Jesus Christ.

6. Having previously been made acquainted with the way the idea of his existence came into the world, as well as the fact of his existence, we shall proceed to examine his character, perfections, and attributes, in order that this class may see, not only the just grounds which they have for the exercise of faith in him for life and salvation, but the reasons that all the world, also, as far as the idea of his existence extends, may have to exercise faith in him, the Father of all living.

7. As we have been indebted to a revelation which God made of himself to his creatures, in the first instance, for the idea of his existence, so in like manner we are indebted to the revelations which he has given to us for a correct understanding of his character, perfections, and attributes ; because, without the revelations which he has given to us, no man by searching could find out God. Job xi. 7, 8, 9. 1 Corinthians ii. 9, 10, 11 : "But as it is written, eye hath not seen, nor ear heard, neither have entered into the heart of man, the things which God hath prepared for them that love him ; but God hath revealed them unto us by his Spirit, for the Spirit searcheth all things, yea, the deep things of God. For what man knoweth the things of a man, save the spirit of man which is in him ? Even so, the things of God knoweth no man but the Spirit of God."

8. Having said so much we proceed to examine the character which the revelations have given of God.

9. Moses gives us the following account in Exodus, xxxiv. 6 : "And the Lord passed by before him, and proclaimed, 'The Lord God, the Lord God, merciful and gracious, long-suffering and abundant in goodness and truth.'" Psalm ciii. 6, 7, 8 : "The Lord executeth righteousness and judgment for all that are oppressed. He made known his ways unto Moses, his acts unto the children of Israel. The Lord is merciful and gracious, slow to anger and plenteous in mercy." Psalm ciii. 17, 18 : "But the mercy of the Lord is from everlasting

to everlasting upon them that fear him, and his right-eousness unto children's children, to such as keep his covenant, and to those that remember his commandments to do them." Psalm xc. 2 : "Before the mountains were brought forth, or ever thou hadst formed the earth and the world, even from everlasting to everlasting, thou art God." Hebrews i. 10, 11, 12 : "And thou, Lord, in the beginning, hast laid the foundation of the earth ; and the heavens are the works of thine hands : they shall perish, but thou remainest ; and they all shall wax old as doth a garment ; and as a vesture shalt thou fold them up, and they shall be changed ; but thou art the same and thy years shall not fail." James i. 17 : "Every good gift and every perfect gift is from above, and cometh down from the Father of lights, with whom is no variableness, neither shadow of turning." Malachi iii. 6 : "For I am the Lord, I change not ; therefore ye sons of Jacob are not consumed."

10. Book of Commandments, Sec. 3, v. 2 : "For God does not walk in crooked paths, neither does he turn to the right hand or the left, or vary from that which he has said, therefore his paths are straight, and his course is one eternal round." Book of Commandments, Sec. 35, v. 1 : "Listen to the voice of the Lord your God, even Alpha and Omega, the beginning and the end, whose course is one eternal round, the same yesterday, to-day, and forever."

11. Numbers xxiii. 19 : "God is not a man that he should lie, neither the son of man that he should repent." 1 John iv. 8 : "He that loveth not, knoweth not God, for God is love." Acts x. 34, 35 : "Then Peter opened his mouth and said, 'Of a truth I perceive that God is no respecter of persons, but in every nation he that feareth God and worketh righteousness is accepted with him.'"

12. From the foregoing testimonies we learn the following things respecting the character of God :

13. First, that he was God before the world was created, and the same God that he was after it was created.

14. Secondly, that he is merciful and gracious, slow to anger, abundant in goodness, and that he was so from everlasting, and will be to everlasting.

15. Thirdly, that he changes not, neither is there variableness with him ; but that he is the same from everlasting to everlasting, being the same yesterday, to-day, and for ever; and that his course is one eternal round, without variation.

16. Fourthly, that he is a God of truth and cannot lie.

17. Fifthly, that he is no respecter of persons : but in every nation he that fears God and works righteousness is accepted of him.

18. Sixthly, that he is love.

19. An acquaintance with these attributes in the divine character, is essentially necessary, in order that the faith of any rational being can center in him for life and salvation. For if he did not, in the first instance, believe him to be God, that is, the Creator and upholder of all things, he could not *center* his faith in him for life and salvation, for fear there should be greater than he who would thwart all his plans, and he, like the gods of the heathen, would be unable to fulfill his promises ; but seeing he is God over all, from everlasting to everlasting, the Creator and upholder of all things, no such fear can exist in the minds of those who put their trust in him, so that in this respect their faith can be without wavering.

20. But secondly ; unless he was merciful and gracious, slow to anger, long-suffering and full of goodness, such is the weakness of human nature, and so great the frailties and imperfections of men, that unless they believed that these excellencies existed in the divine character, the faith necessary to salvation could not exist ; for doubt would take the place of faith, and

those who know their weakness and liability to sin
would be in constant doubt of salvation if it were not
for the idea which they have of the excellency of the
character of God, that he is slow to anger and long-
suffering, and of a forgiving disposition, and does
forgive iniquity, transgression, and sin. An idea of
these facts does away doubt, and makes faith exceedingly strong.

21. But it is equally as necessary that men should
have the idea that he is a God who changes not, in
order to have faith in him, as it is to have the idea
that he is gracious and long-suffering ; for without the
idea of unchangeableness in the character of the Deity,
doubt would take the place of faith. But with the
idea that he changes not, faith lays hold upon the excellencies in his character with unshaken confidence,
believing he is the same yesterday, to-day, and forever,
and that his course is one eternal round.

22. And again, the idea that he is a God of truth
and cannot lie, is equally as necessary to the exercise
of faith in him as the idea of his unchangeableness.
For without the idea that he was a God of truth and
could not lie, the confidence necessary to be placed in
his word in order to the exercise of faith in him could
not exist. But having the idea that he is not man,
that he cannot lie, it gives power to the minds of men to
exercise faith in him.

23. But it is also necessary that men should have
an idea that he is no respecter of persons, for with the
idea of all the other excellencies in his character, and
this one wanting, men could not exercise faith in him ;
because if he were a respecter of persons, they could
not tell what their privileges were, nor how far they
were authorized to exercise faith in him, or whether
they were authorized to do it at all, but all must be
confusion ; but no sooner are the minds of men made
acquainted with the truth on this point, that he is no
respecter of persons, than they see that they have

authority by faith to lay hold on eternal life, the richest
boon of heaven, because God is no respecter of persons,
and that every man in every nation has an equal
privilege.

24. And lastly, but not less important to the exercise of faith in God, is the idea that he is love ; for
with all the other excellencies in his character, without
this one to influence them, they could not have such
powerful dominion over the minds of men ; but when
the idea is planted in the mind that he is love, who
cannot see the just ground that men of every nation,
kindred, and tongue, have to exercise faith in God so
as to obtain eternal life ?

25. From the above description of the character of
the Deity, which is given him in the revelations to
men, there is a sure foundation for the exercise of
faith in him among every people, nation, and kindred,
from age to age, and from generation to generation.

26. Let us here observe that the foregoing is the
character which is given of God in his revelations to
the Former-day Saints, and it is also the character
which is given of him in his revelations to the Latter-
day Saints, so that the saints of former days and those
of latter days are both alike in this respect ; the
Latter-day Saints having as good grounds to exercise
faith in God as the Former-day Saints had, because
the same character is given of him to both.

QUESTIONS AND ANSWERS ON THE FOREGOING PRINCIPLES.

What was shown in the second lecture ? It was
shown how the knowledge of the existence of God
came into the world. Lecture iii. 1.

What is the effect of the idea of his existence among men? It lays the foundation for the exercise of faith in him. Lecture iii. 1.

Is the idea of his existence, in the first instance, necessary in order for the exercise of faith in him? It is. Lecture iii. 1.

How do you prove it? By the tenth chapter of Romans and fourteenth verse. Lecture iii. 1.

How many things are necessary for us to understand, respecting the Deity and our relation to him, in order that we may exercise faith in him for life and salvation? Three. Lecture iii. 2.

What are they? First, that God does actually exist; secondly, correct ideas of his character, his perfections and attributes; and thirdly, that the course which we pursue is according to his mind and will. Lecture iii. 3, 4, 5.

Would the idea of any one or two of the above-mentioned things enable a person to exercise faith in God? It would not, for without the idea of them all faith would be imperfect and unproductive. Lecture iii. 5.

Would an idea of these three things lay a sure foundation for the exercise of faith in God, so as to obtain life and salvation? It would; for by the idea of these three things, faith could become perfect and fruitful, abounding in righteousness unto the praise and glory of God. Lecture iii. 5.

How are we to be made acquainted with the before-mentioned things respecting the Deity, and respecting ourselves? By revelation. Lecture iii. 6.

Could these things be found out by any other means than by revelation? They could not.

How do you prove it? By the scriptures. Job xi. 7, 8, 9. 1 Corinthians ii. 9, 10, 11. Lecture iii. 7.

What things do we learn in the revelations of God respecting his character? We learn the six following

things : First, that he was God before the world was
created, and the same God that he was after it was
created. Secondly, that he is merciful and gracious,
slow to anger, abundant in goodness, and that he was
so from everlasting, and will be so to everlasting.
Thirdly, that he changes not, neither is there
variableness with him, and that his course is one
eternal round. Fourthly, that he is a God of truth,
and cannot lie. Fifthly, that he is no respecter of
persons ; and sixthly, that he is love. Lecture iii. 12,
13, 14, 15, 16, 17, 18.

Where do you find the revelations which give us
this idea of the character of the Deity ? In the bible
and book of commandments, and they are quoted in
the third lecture. Lecture iii. 9, 10, 11.

What effect would it have on any rational being
not to have an idea that the Lord was God, the Creator
and upholder of all things ? It would prevent him
from exercising faith in him unto life and salvation.

Why would it prevent him from exercising faith in
God ? Because he would be as the heathen, not knowing but there might be a being greater and more powerful than he, and thereby he be prevented from fulfilling
his promises. Lecture iii. 19.

Does this idea prevent this doubt? It does ; for
persons having this idea are enabled thereby to exercise
faith without this doubt. Lecture iii. 19.

Is it not also necessary to have the idea that God
is merciful and gracious, long-suffering and full of
goodness? It is. Lecture iii. 20.

Why is it necessary ? Because of the weakness and
imperfections of human nature, and the great frailties
of man ; for such is the weakness of man, and such his
frailties, that he is liable to sin continually, and if God
were not long-suffering, and full of compassion, gracious
and merciful, and of a forgiving disposition, man would
be cut off from before him, in consequence of which he
would be in continual doubt and could not exercise

faith; for where doubt is, there faith has no power; but by man's believing that God is full of compassion and forgiveness, long-suffering and slow to anger, he can exercise faith in him and overcome doubt, so as to be exceedingly strong. Lecture iii. 20.

Is it not equally as necessary that man should have an idea that God changes not, neither is there variableness with him, in order to exercise faith in him unto life and salvation? It is; because without this, he would not know how soon the mercy of God might change into cruelty, his long-suffering into rashness, his love into hatred, and in consequence of which doubt man would be incapable of exercising faith in him, but having the idea that he is unchangeable, man can have faith in him continually, believing that what he was yesterday he is to-day, and will be forever. Lecture iii. 21.

Is it not necessary also, for men to have an idea that God is a being of truth before they can have perfect faith in him? It is; for unless men have this idea they cannot place confidence in his word, and, not being able to place confidence in his word, they could not have faith in him; but believing that he is a God of truth, and that his word cannot fail, their faith can rest in him without doubt. Lecture iii. 22.

Could man exercise faith in God so as to obtain eternal life unless he believed that God was no respecter of persons? He could not; because without this idea he could not certainly know that it was his privilege so to do, and in consequence of this doubt his faith could not be sufficiently strong to save him. Lecture iii. 23.

Would it be possible for a man to exercise faith in God, so as to be saved, unless he had an idea that God was love? He could not; because man could not love God unless he had an idea that God was love, and if he did not love God he could not have faith in him. Lecture iii. 24.

What is the description which the sacred writers give of the character of the Deity calculated to do? It is calculated to lay a foundation for the exercise of faith in him, as far as the knowledge extends, among all people, tongues, languages, kindreds and nations, and that from age to age, and from generation to generation.   Lecture iii. 25.

Is the character which God has given of himself uniform?   It is, in all his revelations, whether to the Former-day Saints, or to the Latter-day Saints, so that they all have the authority to exercise faith in him, and to expect, by the exercise of their faith, to enjoy the same blessings.   Lecture iii. 26.

LECTURE FOURTH.

1. Having shown, in the third lecture, that correct ideas of the character of God are necessary in order to the exercise of faith in him unto life and salvation ; and that without correct ideas of his character the minds of men could not have sufficient power with God to the exercise of faith necessary to the enjoyment of eternal life ; and that correct ideas of his character lay a foundation, as far as his character is concerned, for the exercise of faith, so as to enjoy the fullness of the blessing of the gospel of Jesus Christ, even that of eternal glory ; we shall now proceed to show the connection there is between correct ideas of the attributes of God, and the exercise of faith in him unto eternal life.

2. Let us here observe, that the real design which the God of heaven had in view in making the human family acquainted with his attributes, was, that they, through the ideas of the existence of his attributes, might be enabled to exercise faith in him, and, through the exercise of faith in him, might obtain eternal life ; for without the idea of the existence of the attributes which belong to God the minds of men could not have power to exercise faith in him so as to lay hold upon eternal life. The God of heaven, understanding most perfectly the constitution of human nature, and the weakness of men, knew what was necessary to be revealed, and what ideas must be planted in their minds in order that they might be enabled to exercise faith in him unto eternal life.

3. Having said so much, we shall proceed to examine the attributes of God, as set forth in his revelations to the human family, and to show how necessary

correct ideas of his attributes are to enable men to exercise faith in him; for without these ideas being planted in the minds of men it would be out of the power of any person or persons to exercise faith in God so as to obtain eternal life. So that the divine communications made to men in the first instance were designed to establish in their minds the ideas necessary to enable them to exercise faith in God, and through this means to be partakers of his glory.

4. We have, in the revelations which he has given to the human family, the following account of his attributes :

5. First—Knowledge. Acts xv. 18 : "Known unto God are all his works from the beginning of the world." Isaiah xlvi. 9, 10 : "Remember the former things of old : for I am God, and there is none else ; I am God, and there is none like me, *declaring the end from the beginning*, and from ancient time the things that are not yet done, saying 'My counsel shall stand, and I will do all my pleasure.'"

6. Secondly—Faith or power. Hebrews xi. 3 : "Through faith we understand that the worlds were framed by the word of God." Genesis i. 1 : "In the beginning God created the heaven and the earth." Isaiah xiv. 24, 27 : "The Lord of hosts hath sworn, saying, ' Surely as I have thought, so shall it come to pass : and as I have purposed so shall it stand. For the Lord of Hosts hath purposed, and who shall disannul it ? and his hand is stretched out, and who shall turn it back?'"

7. Thirdly—Justice. Psalm lxxxix. 14 : "Justice and judgment are the habitation of thy throne." Isaiah xlv. 21 : "Tell ye, and bring them near ; yea, let them take counsel together : who hath declared this from the ancient time? have not I the Lord? and there is no God else beside me ; a just God and a Saviour." Zephaniah iii. 5 : "The just Lord is in the midst thereof." Zechariah ix. 9 : "Rejoice greatly,

O daughter of Zion ; shout, O daughter of Jerusalem ;
behold thy King cometh unto thee : he is just and
having salvation."

8. Fourthly—Judgment.   Psalm lxxxix. 14 : "Justice and judgment are the habitation of thy throne."
Deuteronomy xxxii. 4 : " He is the Rock, his work is
perfect ; for all his ways are judgment : a God of
truth and without iniquity, just and right is he."
Psalm ix. 7 : "But the Lord shall endure for ever.
He hath prepared his throne for judgment."   Psalm
ix. 16 : " The Lord is known by the judgment which
he executeth."

9. Fifthly—Mercy.   Psalm lxxxix. 14 : " Mercy
and truth shall go before his face."   Exodus xxxiv. 6 :
" And the Lord passed by before him, and proclaimed,
'The Lord, the Lord God, merciful and gracious.'"
Nehemiah ix. 17 : " But thou art a God ready to par-
don, gracious and merciful."

10. And   sixthly—Truth.   Psalm lxxxix. 14 :
" Mercy and truth shall go before thy face."   Exodus
xxxiv. 6 : " Long-suffering and abundant in goodness
and truth."   Deuteronomy xxxii. 4 : " He is the Rock,
his work is perfect ; for all his ways are judgment : a
God of truth and without iniquity, just and right is
he."   Psalm xxxi. 5 : " Into Thine hand I commit my
spirit : thou hast redeemed me, O Lord God of Truth."

11. By a little reflection it will be seen that the
idea of the existence of these attributes in the Deity is
necessary to enable any rational being to exercise faith
in him ; for without the idea of the existence of these
attributes in the Deity men could not exercise faith
in him for life and salvation ; seeing that without the
knowledge of all things God would not be able to save
any portion of his creatures ; for it is by reason of the
knowledge which he has of all things, from the beginning to the end, that enables him to give that understanding to his creatures by which they are made partakers of eternal life ; and if it were not for the idea

existing in the minds of men that God had all knowledge it would be impossible for them to exercise faith
in him.

12. And it is not less necessary that men should
have the idea of the existence of the attribute power
in the Deity ; for unless God had power over all things,
and was able by his power to control all things, and
thereby deliver his creatures who put their trust in
him from the power of all beings that might seek their
destruction, whether in heaven, on earth, or in hell,
men could not be saved. But with the idea of the
existence of this attribute planted in the mind, men
feel as though they had nothing to fear who put their
trust in God, believing that he has power to save all
who come to him to the very uttermost.

13. It is also necessary, in order to the exercise of
faith in God unto life and salvation, that men should
have the idea of the existence of the attribute justice
in him ; for without the idea of the existence of the
attribute justice in the Deity men could not have confidence sufficient to place themselves under his guidance
and direction ; for they would be filled with fear and
doubt lest the judge of all the earth would not do
right, and thus fear or doubt, existing in the mind,
would preclude the possibility of the exercise of faith
in him for life and salvation. But when the idea of the
existence of the attribute justice in the Deity is fairly
planted in the mind, it leaves no room for doubt to get
into the heart, and the mind is enabled to cast itself
upon the Almighty without fear and without doubt, and
with the most unshaken confidence, believing that the
Judge of all the earth will do right.

14. It is also of equal importance that men should
have the idea of the existence of the attribute judgment in God, in order that they may exercise faith in
him for life and salvation ; for without the idea of the
existence of this attribute in the Deity, it would be
impossible for men to exercise faith in him for life and

salvation, seeing that it is through the exercise of this
attribute that the faithful in Christ Jesus are delivered
out of the hands of those who seek their destruction;
for if God were not to come out in swift judgment
against the workers of iniquity and the powers of
darkness, his saints could not be saved; for it is by
judgment that the Lord delivers his saints out of the
hands of all their enemies, and those who reject the
gospel of our Lord Jesus Christ. But no sooner is the
idea of the existence of this attribute planted in the
minds of men, than it gives power to the mind for the
exercise of faith and confidence in God, and they are
enabled by faith to lay hold on the promises which are
set before them, and wade through all the tribulations
and afflictions to which they are subjected by reason of
the persecution from those who know not God, and
obey not the gospel of our Lord Jesus Christ, believing
that in due time the Lord will come out in swift judgment against their enemies, and they shall be cut off
from before him, and that in his own due time he will
bear them off conquerors, and more than conquerors,
in all things.

15. And again, it is equally important that men
should have the idea of the existence of the attribute
mercy in the Deity, in order to exercise faith in him
for life and salvation; for without the idea of the
existence of this attribute in the Deity, the spirits of
the saints would faint in the midst of the tribulations,
afflictions, and persecutions which they have to endure
for righteousness' sake. But when the idea of the
existence of this attribute is once established in the
mind it gives life and energy to the spirits of the saints,
believing that the mercy of God will be poured out
upon them in the midst of their afflictions, and that
he will compassionate them in their sufferings, and
that the mercy of God will lay hold of them and
secure them in the arms of his love, so that they will
receive a full reward for all their sufferings.

16. And lastly, but not less important to the ex-

ercise of faith in God, is the idea of the existence of
the attribute truth in him ; for without the idea of
the existence of this attribute the mind of man could
have nothing upon which it could rest with certainty
—all would be confusion and doubt. But with the
idea of the existence of this attribute in the Deity in
the mind, all the teachings, instructions, promises, and
blessings, become realities, and the mind is enabled to
lay hold of them with certainty and confidence, believing that these things, and all that the Lord has
said, shall be fulfilled in their time ; and that all the
cursings, denunciations, and judgments, pronounced
upon the heads of the unrighteous, will also be executed in the due time of the Lord : and, by reason of
the truth and veracity of him, the mind beholds its
deliverance and salvation as being certain.

17. Let the mind once reflect sincerely and candidly
upon the ideas of the existence of the before-mentioned
attributes in the Deity, and it will be seen that, as far
as his attributes are concerned, there is a sure foundation laid for the exercise of faith in him for life and
salvation. For inasmuch as God possesses the attribute
knowledge, he can make all things known to his saints
necessary for their salvation ; and as he possesses the
attribute power, he is able thereby to deliver them
from the power of all enemies ; and seeing, also, that
justice is an attribute of the Deity, he will deal with
them upon the principles of righteousness and equity,
and a just reward will be granted unto them for all
their afflictions and sufferings for the truth's sake.
And as judgment is an attribute of the Deity also, his
saints can have the most unshaken confidence that they
will, in due time, obtain a perfect deliverance out of
the hands of all their enemies, and a complete victory
over all those who have sought their hurt and destruction. And as mercy is also an attribute of the Deity,
his saints can have confidence that it will be exercised
towards them, and through the exercise of that attribute towards them comfort and consolation will be

administered unto them abundantly, amid all their afflictions and tribulations. And, lastly, realizing that truth is an attribute of the Deity, the mind is led to rejoice amid all its trials and temptations, in hope of that glory which is to be brought at the revelation of Jesus Christ, and in view of that crown which is to be placed upon the heads of the saints in the day when the Lord shall distribute rewards unto them, and in prospect of that eternal weight of glory which the Lord has promised to bestow upon them, when he shall bring them in the midst of his throne to dwell in his presence eternally.

18. In view, then, of the existence of these attributes, the faith of the saints can become exceedingly strong, abounding in righteousness unto the praise and glory of God, and can exert its mighty influence in searching after wisdom and understanding, until it has obtained a knowledge of all things that pertain to life and salvation.

19. Such, then, is the foundation which is laid, through the revelation of the attributes of God, for the exercise of faith in him for life and salvation; and seeing that these are attributes of the Deity, they are unchangeable—being the same yesterday, to-day, and for ever—which gives to the minds of the Latter-day Saints the same power and authority to exercise faith in God which the Former-day Saints had ; so that all the saints, in this respect, have been, are, and will be, alike until the end of time ; for God never changes, therefore his attributes and character remain forever the same. And as it is through the revelation of these that a foundation is laid for the exercise of faith in God unto life and salvation, the foundation, therefore, for the exercise of faith was, is, and ever will be, the same ; so that all men have had, and will have, an equal privilege.

QUESTIONS AND ANSWERS ON THE FOREGOING
PRINCIPLES.

What was shown in the third lecture? It was
shown that correct ideas of the character of God are
necessary in order to exercise faith in him unto life and
salvation; and that without correct ideas of his character, men could not have power to exercise faith in
him unto life and salvation, but that correct ideas of
his character, as far as his character was concerned in
the exercise of faith in him, lay a sure foundation for
the exercise of it. Lecture iv. 1.

What object had the God of Heaven in revealing
his attributes to men? That through an acquaintance
with his attributes they might be enabled to exercise
faith in him so as to obtain eternal life. Lecture iv. 2.

Could men exercise faith in God without an acquaintance with his attributes, so as to be enabled to
lay hold of eternal life? They could not. Lecture
iv. 2, 3.

What account is given of the attributes of God in
his revelations? First, Knowledge; secondly, Faith or
Power; thirdly, Justice; fourthly, Judgment; fifthly,
Mercy; and sixthly, Truth. Lecture iv. 4, 5, 6, 7, 8,
9 and 10.

Where are the revelations to be found which give
this relation or the attributes of God? In the Old
and New Testaments, and they are quoted in the fourth
lecture, fifth, sixth, seventh, eighth, ninth and tenth
paragraphs.*

Is the idea of the existence of these attributes in
the Deity necessary in order to enable any rational
being to exercise faith in him unto life and salvation?
It is.

---

* Let the student turn and commit these paragraphs
to memory.

How do you prove it? By the eleventh, twelfth, thirteenth, fourteenth, fifteenth and sixteenth paragraphs in this lecture.*

Does the idea of the existence of these attributes in the Deity as far as his attributes are concerned, enable a rational being to exercise faith in him unto life and salvation? It does. How do you prove it? By the seventeenth and eighteenth paragraphs.*

Have the Latter-day Saints as much authority given them, through the revelation of the attributes of God, to exercise faith in him as the Former-day Saints had? They have.

How do you prove it? By the nineteenth paragraph of this lecture.*

---

* Let the student turn and commit these paragraphs to memory.

LECTURE FIFTH.

1. In our former lectures we treated of the being, character, perfections, and attributes, of God. What we mean by perfections is, the perfections which belong to all the attributes of his nature. We shall, in this lecture, speak of the Godhead—we mean the Father, Son, and Holy Spirit.

2. There are two personages who constitute the great, matchless, governing, and supreme, power over all things, by whom all things were created and made, that are created and made, whether visible or invisible, whether in heaven, on earth, or in the earth, under the earth, or throughout the immensity of space. They are the Father and the Son—the Father being a personage of spirit, glory, and power, possessing all perfection and fullness, the Son, who was in the bosom of the Father, a personage of tabernacle, made or fashioned like unto man, or being in the form and likeness of man, or rather man was formed after his likeness and in his image ; he is also the express image and likeness of the personage of the Father, possessing all the fullness of the Father, or the same fullness with the Father ; being begotten of him, and ordained from before the foundation of the world to be a propitiation for the sins of all those who should believe on his name, and is called the Son because of the flesh, and descended in suffering below that which man can suffer ; or, in other words, suffered greater sufferings, and was exposed to more powerful contradictions than any man can be. But, notwithstanding all this, he kept the law of God, and remained without sin, showing thereby that it is in the power of man to keep the

law and remain also without sin; and also, that by
him a righteous judgment might come upon all flesh,
and that all who walk not in the law of God may
justly be condemned by the law, and have no excuse
for their sins. And he being the Only Begotten of the
Father, full of grace and truth, and having overcome,
received a fullness of the glory of the Father, possessing the same mind with the Father, which mind is the
Holy Spirit, that bears record of the Father and the
Son, and these three are one; or, in other words, these
three constitute the great, matchless, governing and
supreme, power over all things; by whom all things
were created and made that were created and made, and
these three constitute the Godhead, and are one; the
Father and the Son possessing the same mind, the same
wisdom, glory, power, and fullness—filling all in all; the
Son being filled with the fullness of the mind, glory, and
power; or, in other words, the spirit, glory, and power,
of the Father, possessing all knowledge and glory, and
the same kingdom, sitting at the right hand of power,
in the express image and likeness of the Father, mediator for man, being filled with the fullness of the mind
of the Father; or, in other words, the Spirit of the
Father, which Spirit is shed forth upon all who believe
on his name and keep his commandments; and all
those who keep his commandments shall grow up from
grace to grace, and become heirs of the heavenly
kingdom, and joint heirs with Jesus Christ; possessing
the same mind, being transformed into the same image
or likeness, even the express image of him who fills all
in all; being filled with the fullness of his glory, and
become one in him, even as the Father, Son and Holy
Spirit are one.

3. From the foregoing account of the Godhead,
which is given in his revelations, the saints have a sure
foundation laid for the exercise of faith unto life and
salvation, through the atonement and mediation of
Jesus Christ; by whose blood they have a forgiveness
of sins, and also a sure reward laid up for them in

heaven, even that of partaking of the fullness of the Father and the Son through the Spirit. As the Son partakes of the fullness of the Father through the Spirit, so the saints are, by the same Spirit, to be partakers of the same fullness, to enjoy the same glory; for as the Father and the Son are one, so, in like manner, the saints are to be one in them. Through the love of the Father, the mediation of Jesus Christ, and the gift of the Holy Spirit, they are to be heirs of God, and joint heirs with Jesus Christ.

QUESTIONS AND ANSWERS ON THE FOREGOING PRINCIPLES.

Of what do the foregoing lectures treat? Of the being, perfections, and attributes of the Deity. Lecture v. 1.

What are we to understand by the perfections of the Deity? The perfections which belong to his attributes.

How many personages are there in the Godhead? Two: the Father and Son. Lecture v. 1.

How do you prove that there are two personages in the Godhead? By the Scriptures. Genesis i. 26. Also lecture ii. 6: "And the Lord God said unto the Only Begotten, who was with him from the beginning, 'Let us make man in our image, after our likeness'—and it was done." Genesis iii. 22: "And the Lord God said unto the Only Begotten, 'Behold, the man is become as one of us: to know good and evil.'" John xvii. 5: "And now, O Father, glorify thou me with thine own self with the glory which I had with thee before the world was." Lecture v. 2.

What is the Father? He is a personage of glory and of power. Lecture v. 2.

How do you prove that the Father is a personage
of glory and of power? Isaiah lx. 19: "The sun
shall be no more thy light by day, neither for brightness shall the moon give light unto thee; but the Lord
shall be unto thee an everlasting light, and thy God
thy glory." 1 Chronicles xxix. 11: "Thine, O Lord,
is the greatness, and the power, and the glory." Psalm
xxix. 3: "The voice of the Lord is upon the waters:
the God of glory thunders." Psalm lxxix. 9: "Help
us, O God of our salvation, for the glory of thy name."
Romans i. 23: "And changed the glory of the incorruptible God into an image made like to corruptible
man." Secondly, of power. 1 Chronicles xxix. 11:
"Thine, O Lord, is the greatness, and the power, and
the glory." Jeremiah xxxii. 17: "Ah! Lord God,
behold thou hast made the earth and the heavens by
thy great power, and stretched-out arm; and there is
nothing too hard for thee." Deuteronomy iv. 37:
"And because he loved thy fathers, therefore he chose
their seed after them, and brought them out in his
sight with his mighty power." 2 Samuel xxii. 33:
"God is my strength and power." Job xxvi., commencing with the 7th verse to the end of the chapter:
"He stretcheth out the north over the empty place,
and hangeth the earth upon nothing. He bindeth up
the waters in his thick clouds; and the cloud is not
rent under them. He holdeth back the face of his
throne, and spreadeth his cloud upon it. He hath
compassed the waters with bounds, until the day and
night come to an end. The pillars of heaven tremble,
and are astonished at his reproof. He divideth the
sea with his power, and by his understanding he smiteth
through the proud. By his Spirit he hath garnished
the heavens; his hand hath formed the crooked serpent. Lo, these are parts of his ways! but how little
a portion is heard of him? But the thunder of his
power who can understand?"

What is the Son? First, he is a personage of
tabernacle. Lecture v. 2.

How do you prove it ? John xiv. 9, 10, 11: "Jesus
saith unto him, ' Have I been so long time with you,
and yet hast thou not known me, Philip? He that
hath seen me hath seen the Father ; and how sayest
thou then, Show us the Father ? Believest thou not
that I am in the Father, and the Father in me ? The
words that I speak unto you I speak not of myself :
but the Father that dwelleth in me he doeth the works.
Believe me that I am in the Father and the Father in
me.' " Secondly,—and being a personage of tabernacle,
was made or fashioned like unto man, or being in the
form and likeness of man. Lecture v. 2. Philippians
ii. 2-8: " Let this mind be in you, which was also in
Christ Jesus ; who, being in the form of God, thought
it not robbery to be equal with God ; but made himself
of no reputation, and took upon him the form of a
servant, and was made in the likeness of man, and
being found in fashion as a man, he humbled himself,
and became obedient unto death, even the death of the
cross." Hebrews ii. 14, 16 : " Forasmuch then as the
children are partakers of flesh and blood, he also himself likewise took part of the same. For verily he
took not on him the nature of angels : but he took on
him the seed of Abraham." Thirdly, he is also in the
likeness of the personage of the Father. Lecture v. 2.
Hebrews i. 1, 2, 3 : " God, who at sundry times and in
divers manners, spake in times past to the fathers, by
the prophets, hath in these last days spoken unto us by
his Son, whom he hath appointed heir of all things, by
whom also he made the worlds ; who being the brightness of his glory, and the express image of his person."
Again, Philippians ii. 5, 6 : " Let this mind be in you,
which was also in Christ Jesus ; who, being in the
form of God, thought it not robbery to be equal with
God."

Was it by the Father and the Son that all things
were created and made that were created and made ?
It was. Colossians i. 15, 16, 17: " Who is the image
of the invisible God, the first born of every creature ;

for by him were all things created that are in heaven
and that are in earth, visible and invisible, whether
they be thrones or dominions, principalities or powers ;
all things were created by him and for him ; and he is
before all things, and by him all things consist." Genesis i. 1 : " In the beginning God created the heavens
and the earth." Hebrews i. 2 : (God) " Hath in these
last days spoken unto us by his Son, whom he hath
appointed heir of all things, by whom also he made the
worlds."

Does he possess the fullness of the Father ? He
does. Colossians i. 19, ii. 9 : " For it pleased the
Father that in him should all fullness dwell." " For
in him dwelleth all the fullness of the Godhead bodily."
Ephesians i. 23 : " Which is his (Christ's) body, the
fullness of him that fills all in all."

Why was he called the Son ? Because of the flesh.
Luke i. 33 : " That holy thing which shall be born of
thee, shall be called the Son of God." Matthew iii.
16, 17 : " And Jesus, when he was baptized, went up
straightway out of the water, and lo, the heavens were
opened unto him, and he (John) saw the Spirit of God
descending like a dove and lighting upon him : and lo,
a voice from heaven saying, 'This is my beloved Son,
in whom I am well pleased.'"

Was he ordained of the Father, from before the
foundation of the world, to be a propitiation for the
sins of all those who should believe on his name ? He
was. 1 Peter i. 18, 19, 20 : " Forasmuch as ye know
that ye were not redeemed with corruptible things, as
silver and gold, from your vain conversation, received
by tradition from your fathers : but with the precious
blood of Christ, as of a lamb without blemish and
without spot ; who verily was foreordained before the
foundation of the world, but was manifested in these
last times for you." Revelations xiii. 8 : " And all
that dwell upon the earth shall worship him (the
beast), whose names are not written in the book of life

of the Lamb slain from the foundation of the world."
1 Corinthians ii. 7 : " But we speak the wisdom of
God in a mystery, even the hidden mystery, which God
ordained before the world, unto our glory."

Do the Father and the Son possess the same mind?
They do.   John v. 30 : " I (Christ) can of my own
self do nothing : as I hear, I judge, and my judgment
is just ; because I seek not my own will, but the will
of the Father who sent me."   John vi. 38 : " For I
(Christ) came down from heaven, not to do my own
will, but the will of him that sent me."   John x. 30 :
" I (Christ) and my Father are one."

What is this mind?   The Holy Spirit.   John xv.
26 : "But when the Comforter is come, whom I will
send unto you from the Father, even the Spirit of
truth, which proceeds from the Father, he shall testify
of me (Christ)."   Galatians iv. 6 : "And because ye
are sons, God hath sent forth the Spirit of his Son into
your hearts."

Do the Father, Son, and Holy Spirit constitute the
Godhead?   They do.   Lecture v. 2.*

Do the believers in Christ Jesus, through the gift of
the Spirit, become one with the Father and the Son,
as the Father and the Son are one?   They do.   John
xvii. 20, 21 : " Neither pray I for these (the apostles)
alone, but for them also who shall believe on me
through their word ; that they all may be one ; as
thou, Father, art in me, and I in thee, that they also
may be one in us, that the world may believe that thou
hast sent me."

Does the foregoing account of the Godhead lay a
sure foundation for the exercise of faith in him unto
life and salvation?   It does.

How do you prove it?   By the third paragraph of
this lecture. *

---

* Let the student commit these paragraphs to memory.

LECTURE SIXTH.

1. Having treated in the preceding lectures of the ideas, of the character, perfections, and attributes of God, we next proceed to treat of the knowledge which persons must have, that the course of life which they pursue is according to the will of God, in order that they may be enabled to exercise faith in him unto life and salvation.

2. This knowledge supplies an important place in revealed religion ; for it was by reason of it that the ancients were enabled to endure as seeing him who is invisible. An actual knowledge to any person, that the course of life which he pursues is according to the will of God, is essentially necessary to enable him to have that confidence in God without which no person can obtain eternal life. It was this that enabled the ancient saints to endure all their afflictions and persecutions, and to take joyfully the spoiling of their goods, knowing (not believing merely) that they had a more enduring substance. Hebrews x. 34.

3. Having the assurance that they were pursuing a course which was agreeable to the will of God, they were enabled to take, not only the spoiling of their goods, and the wasting of their substance, joyfully, but also to suffer death in its most horrid forms ; knowing (not merely believing) that when this earthly house of their tabernacle was dissolved, they had a building of God, a house not made with hands, eternal in the heavens. 2 Corinthians v. 1.

4. Such was, and always will be, the situation of the saints of God, that unless they have an actual knowledge that the course they are pursuing is according to the will of God they will grow weary in their minds, and faint ; for such has been, and always will

be, the opposition in the hearts of unbelievers and
those that know not God against the pure and unadul-
terated religion of heaven (the only thing which insures
eternal life), that they will persecute to the uttermost
all that worship God according to his revelations, receive the truth in the love of it, and submit themselves
to be guided and directed by his will ; and drive them
to such extremities that nothing short of an actual
knowledge of their being the favorites of heaven, and
of their having embraced that order of things which
God has established for the redemption of man, will
enable them to exercise that confidence in him, necessary for them to overcome the world, and obtain that
crown of glory which is laid up for them that fear God.

5. For a man to lay down his all, his character and
reputation, his honor, and applause, his good name
among men, his houses, his lands, his brothers and
sisters, his wife and children, and even his own life
also—counting all things but filth and dross for the
excellency of the knowledge of Jesus Christ—requires
more than mere belief or supposition that he is doing
the will of God ; but actual knowledge, realizing that,
when these sufferings are ended, he will enter into
eternal rest, and be a partaker of the glory of God.

6. For unless a person does know that he is walking according to the will of God, it would be offering
an insult to the dignity of the Creator were he to say
that he would be a partaker of his glory when he should
be done with the things of this life. But when he
has this knowledge, and most assuredly knows that he
is doing the will of God, his confidence can be equally
strong that he will be a partaker of the glory of God.

7. Let us here observe, that a religion that does
not require the sacrifice of all things never has power
sufficient to produce the faith necessary unto life and
salvation ; for, from the first existence of man, the
faith necessary unto the enjoyment of life and salvation never could be obtained without the sacrifice of
all earthly things. It was through this sacrifice, and

this only, that God has ordained that men should enjoy eternal life ; and it is through the medium of the
sacrifice of all earthly things that men do actually
know that they are doing the things that are well
pleasing in the sight of God. When a man has offered
in sacrifice all that he has for the truth's sake, not even
withholding his life, and believing before God that he
has been called to make this sacrifice because he seeks
to do his will, he does know, most assuredly, that God
does and will accept his sacrifice and offering, and that
he has not, nor will not seek his face in vain. Under
these circumstances, then, he can obtain the faith
necessary for him to lay hold on eternal life.

8. It is in vain for persons to fancy to themselves
that they are heirs with those, or can be heirs with them,
who have offered their all in sacrifice, and by this means
obtained faith in God and favor with him so as to
obtain eternal life, unless they, in like manner, offer
unto him the same sacrifice, and through that offering
obtain the knowledge that they are accepted of him.

9. It was in offering sacrifices that Abel, the first
martyr, obtained knowledge that he was accepted of
God. And from the days of righteous •Abel to the
present time, the knowledge that men have that they
are accepted in the sight of God is obtained by offering
sacrifice. And in the last days, before the Lord comes,
he is to gather together his saints who have made a
covenant with him by sacrifice. Psalm l. 3, 4, 5 : "Our
God shall come, and shall not keep silence : a fire shall
devour before him, and it shall be very tempestuous
round about him. He shall call to the heavens from
above, and to the earth, that he may judge his people.
Gather my saints together unto me ; those that have
made a covenant with me by sacrifice."

10. Those, then, who make the sacrifice, will have the
testimony that their course is pleasing in the sight of
God ; and those who have this testimony will have faith
to lay hold on eternal life, and will be enabled, through
faith, to endure unto the end, and receive the crown

that is laid up for them that love the appearing of our Lord Jesus Christ But those who do not make the sacrifice cannot enjoy this faith, because men are dependent upon this sacrifice in order to obtain this faith : therefore, they cannot lay hold upon e⁺ernal life, because the revelations of God do not guarantee unto them the authority so to do, and without this guarantee faith could not exist.

11. All the saints of whom we have account, in all the revelations of God which are extant, obtained the knowledge which they had of their acceptance in his sight through the sacrifice which they offered unto him; and through the knowledge thus obtained their faith became sufficiently strong to lay hold upon the promise of eternal life, and to endure as seeing him who is invisible ; and were enabled, through faith, to combat the powers of darkness, contend against the wiles of the adversary, overcome the world, and obtain the end of their faith, even the salvation of their souls.

12. But those who have not made this sacrifice to God do not know that the course which they pursue is well pleasing in his sight ; for whatever may be their belief or their opinion, it is a matter of doubt and uncertainty in their mind ; and where doubt and uncertainty are there faith is not, nor can it be. For doubt and faith do not exist in the same person at the same time ; so that persons whose minds are under doubts and fears cannot have unshaken confidence ; and where unshaken confidence is not there faith is weak ; and where faith is weak the persons will not be able to contend against all the opposition, tribulations, and afflictions which they will have to encounter in order to be heirs of God, and joint heirs with Christ Jesus ; and they will grow weary in their minds, and the adversary will have power over them and destroy them.

This Lecture is so plain, and the facts set forth so self-evident that it is deemed unnecessary to form a catechism upon it: the student is, therefore, instructed to commit the whole to memory.

LECTURE SEVENTH.

1. In the preceding lessons we treated of what faith was, and of the object on which it rested. Agreeable to our plan, we now proceed to speak of its effects.

2. As we have seen in our former lectures that faith was the principle of action and of power in all intelligent beings, both in heaven and on earth, it will not be expected that we shall, in a lecture of this description, attempt to unfold all its effects; neither is it necessary to our purpose so to do, for it would embrace all things in heaven and on earth, and encompass all the creations of God, with all their endless varieties; for no world has yet been framed that was not framed by faith, neither has there been an intelligent being on any of God's creations who did not get there by reason of faith as it existed in himself or in some other being; nor has there been a change or a revolution in any of the creations of God, but it has been effected by faith; neither will there be a change or a revolution, unless it is effected in the same way, in any of the vast creations of the Almighty, for it is by faith that the Deity works.

3. Let us here offer some explanation in relation to faith, that our meaning may be clearly comprehended. We ask, then, what are we to understand by a man's working by faith? We answer—we understand that when a man works by faith he works by mental exertion instead of physical force. It is by words, instead of exerting his physical powers, with which every being works when he works by faith. God said, "Let there be light, and there was light." Joshua spake, and the great lights which God had created stood still. Elijah

commanded, and the heavens were stayed for the space of three years and six months, so that it did not rain : he again commanded and the heavens gave forth rain. All this was done by faith. And the Saviour says : " If you have faith as a grain of mustard seed, say to this mountain, ' Remove,' and it will remove ; or say to that sycamine tree, ' Be ye plucked up, and planted in the midst of the sea,' and it shall obey you." Faith, then, works by words ; and with these its mightiest works have been, and will be, performed.

4. It surely will not be required of us to prove that this is the principle upon which all eternity has acted and will act ; for every reflecting mind must know that it is by reason of this power that all the hosts of heaven perform their works of wonder, majesty, and glory. Angels move from place to place by virtue of this power ; it is by reason of it that they are enabled to descend from heaven to earth ; and were it not for the power of faith they never could be ministering spirits to them who should be heirs of salvation, neither could they act as heavenly messengers, for they would be destitute of the power necessary to enable them to do the will of God.

5. It is only necessary for us to say that the whole visible creation, as it now exists, is the effect of faith. It was faith by which it was framed, and it is by the power of faith that it continues in its organized form, and by which the planets move round their orbits and sparkle forth their glory. So, then, faith is truly the first principle in the science of THEOLOGY, and, when understood, leads the mind back to the beginning, and carries it forward to the end ; or, in other words, from eternity to eternity.

6. As faith, then, is the principle by which the heavenly hosts perform their works, and by which they enjoy all their felicity, we might expect to find it set forth in a revelation from God as the principle upon which his creatures here below must act in order to

obtain the felicities enjoyed by the saints in the eternal world ; and that, when God would undertake to raise up men for the enjoyment of himself, he would teach them the necessity of living by faith, and the impossibility there was of their enjoying the blessedness of eternity without it, seeing that all the blessings of eternity are the effects of faith.

7. Therefore it is said, and appropriately too, that " Without faith it is impossible to please God." If it should be asked—Why is it impossible to please God without faith? The answer would be—Because without faith it is impossible for men to be saved ; and as God desires the salvation of men, he must, of course, desire that they should have faith ; and he could not be pleased unless they had, or else he could be pleased with their destruction.

8. From this we learn that the many exhortations which have been given by inspired men, to those who had received the word of the Lord to have faith in him, were not mere common-place matters, but were for the best of all reasons, and that was—because without it there was no salvation, neither in this world nor in that which is to come. When men begin to live by faith they begin to draw near to God ; and when faith is perfected they are like him ; and because he is saved they are saved also ; for they will be in the same situation he is in, because they have come to him ; and when he appears they shall be like him, for they will see him as he is.

9. As all the visible creation is an effect of faith, so is salvation also—we mean salvation in its most extensive latitude of interpretation, whether it is temporal or spiritual. In order to have this subject clearly set before the mind, let us ask what situation must a person be in in order to be saved? or what is the difference between a saved man and one who is not saved? We answer, from what we have before seen of the heavenly worlds, they must be persons who can work by faith

and who are able, by faith, to be ministering spirits to
them who shall be heirs of salvation; and they must
have faith to enable them to act in the presence of the
Lord, otherwise they cannot be saved. And what constitutes the real difference between a saved person and
one not saved is—the difference in the degree of their
faith—one's faith has become perfect enough to lay
hold upon eternal life, and the other's has not. But to
be a little more particular, let us ask—Where shall we
find a prototype into whose likeness we may be assimilated, in order that we may be made partakers of life
and salvation? or, in other words, where shall we find
a saved being? for if we can find a saved being, we
may ascertain without much difficulty what all others
must be in order to be saved. We think that it will
not be a matter of dispute, that two beings who are
unlike each other cannot both be saved; for whatever
constitutes the salvation of one will constitute the salvation of every creature which will be saved; and if we
find one saved being in all existence, we may see what
all others must be, or else not be saved. We ask, then,
where is the prototype? or where is the saved being?
We conclude, as to the answer of this question, there
will be no dispute among those who believe the bible,
that it is Christ: all will agree in this, that he is the
prototype or standard of salvation; or, in other words,
that he is a saved being. And if we should continue
our interrogation, and ask how it is that he is saved?
the answer would be—because he is a just and holy
being; and if he were anything different from what he
is he would not be saved; for his salvation depends on
his being precisely what he is and nothing else; for if
it were possible for him to change, in the least degree,
so sure he would fail of salvation and lose all his dominion, power, authority and glory, which constitute
salvation; for salvation consists in the glory, authority,
majesty, power and dominion which Jehovah possesses
and in nothing else; and no being can possess it but
himself or one like him. Thus says John, in his first

epistle, third chapter, second and third verses : "Beloved, now are we the sons of God, and it doth not yet
appear what we shall be ; but we know that, when he
shall appear, we shall be like him, for we shall see him
as he is. And every man that hath this hope in him,
purifieth himself, even as he is pure." Why purify
themselves as he is pure ? Because if they do not they
cannot be like him.

10. The Lord said unto Moses, Leviticus xix. 2 :
"Speak unto all the congregation of the children of
Israel, and say unto them, 'Ye shall be holy : for I the
Lord your God am holy.'" And Peter says, first epistle, i. 15, 16 : "But as he which hath called you is
holy, so be ye holy in all manner of conversation ; because it is written, 'Be ye holy ; for I am holy.'" And
the Saviour says, Matthew v. 48 : "Be ye therefore
perfect, even as your Father which is in heaven is perfect.'" If any should ask, why all these sayings ? the
answer is to be found. from what is before quoted from
John's epistle, that when he (the Lord) shall appear,
the saints will be like him ; and if they are not holy,
as he is holy, and perfect, as he is perfect, they cannot
be like him ; for no being can enjoy. his glory without
possessing his perfections and holiness, no more than
they could reign in his kingdom without his power.

11. This clearly sets forth the propriety of the
Saviour's saying, recorded in John's testimony, xiv. 12 :
"Verily, verily, I say unto you, he that believeth on
me, the works that I do shall he do also ; and greater
works than these shall he do, because I go unto my
Father." This taken in connection with some of the
sayings in the Saviour's prayer, recorded in the seventeenth chapter, gives great clearness to his expressions.
He says in the 20, 21, 22, 23, and 24th verses: "Neither
pray I for these alone, but for them also who shall believe on me through their words ; that they all may be
one ; as thou, Father, art in me, and I in thee, that
they also may be one in us ; that the world may believe
that thou hast sent me. And the glory which thou

gavest me I have given them ; that they may be one,
even as we are one : I in them, and thou in me, that
they may be made perfect in one ; and that the world
may know that thou hast sent me, and hast loved them,
as thou hast loved me.   Father, I will that they also
whom thou hast given me, be with me where I am ;
that they may behold my glory, which thou hast given
me : for thou lovedst me before the foundation of the
world."

12. All these sayings put together give as clear an
account of the state of the glorified saints as language
could give—the works that Jesus had done they were
to do, and greater works than those which he had done
among them should they do, and that because he went
to the Father.   He does not say that they should do
these works in time ; but they should do greater works,
because he went to the Father.   He says in the 24th
verse : " Father, I will that they also, whom thou hast
given me, be with me where I am ; that they may behold my glory."   These sayings, taken in connection,
make it very plain that the greater works which those
that believed on his name were to do were to be done
in eternity, where he was going and where they should
behold his glory.   He had said, in another part of his
prayer, that he desired of his Father that those who
believed on him should be one in him, as he and the
Father were one in each other.   " Neither pray I for
these (the apostles) alone, but for them also who shall
believe on me through their words, that they all may
be one ; " that is, they who believe on him through the
apostles' words, as well as the apostles themselves,
" that they all may be one, as thou, Father, art in me
and I in thee ; that they also may be one in us."

13. What language can be plainer than this ?   The
Saviour surely intended to be understood by his disciples, and he so spake that they might understand him ;
for he declares to his Father, in language not to be
easily mistaken, that he wanted his disciples, even all
of them, to be as himself and the Father, for as he

and the Father were one so they might be one with
them.   And what is said in the 22nd verse is calculated
to more firmly establish this belief, if it needs anything
to establish it.   He says : "And the glory which thou
gavest me, I have given them, that they may be one,
even as we are one." As much as to say that unless
they have the glory which the Father had given him
they could not be one with them ; for he says he had
given them the glory that the Father had given him
that they might be one ; or, in other words, to make
them one.

14. This fills up the measure of information on this
subject, and shows most clearly that the Saviour wished
his disciples to understand that they were to be partakers with him in all things, not even his glory excepted.

15. It is scarcely necessary here to observe what we
have previously noticed, that the glory which the
Father and the Son have is because they are just and
holy beings ; and that if they were lacking in one
attribute or perfection which they have, the glory
which they have never could be enjoyed by them, for
it requires them to be precisely what they are in order
to enjoy it ; and if the Saviour gives this glory to any
others, he must do it in the very way set forth in his
prayer to his Father—by making them one with him as
he and the Father are one.   In so doing he would give
them the glory which the Father has given him ; and
when his disciples are made one with the Father and
Son, as the Father and the Son are one, who cannot see
the propriety of the Saviour's saying—"The works
which I do, shall they do ; and greater works than
these shall they do, because I go to my Father."

16. These teachings of the Saviour most clearly
show unto us the nature of salvation, and what he proposed unto the human family when he proposed to save
them—that he proposed to make them like unto himself, and he was like the Father, the great prototype of

all saved beings; and for any portion of the human
family to be assimilated into their likeness is to be
saved ; and to be unlike them is to be destroyed; and
on this hinge turns the door of salvation.

17. Who cannot see, then, that salvation is the
effect of faith? for, as we have previously observed, all
the heavenly beings work by this principle ; and it is
because they are able so to do that they are saved, for
nothing but this could save them. And this is the
lesson which the God of heaven, by the mouth of all
his holy prophets, has been endeavouring to teach to
the world.   Hence we are told, that " Without faith it
is impossible to please God ;" and that salvation is of
faith, that it might be by grace, to the end the promise
might be sure to all the seed. Romans iv. 16.   And
that Israel, who followed after the law of righteousness, has not attained to the law of righteousness.
Wherefore ? Because they sought it not by faith, but
as it were by the works of the law ; for they stumbled
at that stumbling stone. Romans ix. 32.   And Jesus
said unto the man who brought his son to him, to get
the devil who tormented him cast out : " If thou canst
believe, all things are possible to him that believeth."
Mark ix. 23. These with a multitude of other scriptures
which might be quoted plainly set forth the light in
which the Saviour, as well as the Former-day Saints,
viewed the plan of salvation.   That it was a system of
faith—it begins with faith, and continues by faith ; and
every blessing which is obtained in relation to it is the
effect of faith, whether it pertains to this life or that
which is to come.   To this all the revelations of God
bear witness. If there were children of promise, they
were the effects of faith, not even the Saviour of the
world excepted.   " Blessed is she that believed," said
Elizabeth to Mary, when she went to visit her, " for
there shall be a performance of those things which
were told her from the Lord." Luke i. 45.   Nor was
the birth of John the Baptist the less a matter of faith;
for in order that his father Zacharias might believe he

was struck dumb. And through the whole history of the scheme of life and salvation, it is a matter of faith : every man received according to his faith—according as his faith was, so were his blessings and privileges ; and nothing was withheld from him when his faith was sufficient to receive it. He could stop the mouths of lions, quench the violence of fire, escape the edge of the sword, wax valiant in fight, and put to flight the armies of the aliens ; women could, by their faith, receive their dead children to life again ; in a word, there was nothing impossible with them who had faith. All things were in subjection to the Former-day Saints, according as their faith was. By their faith they could obtain heavenly visions, the ministering of angels, have knowledge of the spirits of just men made perfect, of the general assembly and church of the first born, whose names are written in heaven, of God the judge of all, of Jesus the Mediator of the new covenant, and become familiar with the third heavens, see and hear things which were not only unutterable, but were unlawful to utter. Peter, in view of the power of faith, second epistle, first chapter, second and third verses, says to the Former-day Saints : " Grace and peace be multiplied unto you, through the knowledge of God, and of Jesus our Lord, according as his divine power hath given unto us all things that pertain unto life and godliness, through the knowledge of him that hath called us to glory and virtue." In the first epistle, first chapter, third, fourth and fifth verses he says : " Blessed be the God and Father of our Lord Jesus Christ, which, according to his abundant mercy, hath begotten us again unto a lively hope by the resurrection of Jesus Christ from the dead, to an inheritance incorruptible and undefiled, and that fadeth not away, reserved in heaven for you, who are kept by the power of God through faith unto salvation, ready to be revealed in the last time."

18. These sayings put together show the apostle's views most clearly, so as to admit of no mistake on

the mind of any individual.   He says that all things
that pertain to life and godliness were given unto them
through the knowledge of God and our Saviour Jesus
Christ.   And if the question is asked, how were they
to obtain the knowledge of God ? (for there is a great
difference between believing in God and knowing him
—knowledge implies more than faith.   And notice,
that all things that pertain to life and godliness were
given through the knowledge of God) the answer is
given—through faith they were to obtain this knowledge ; and, having power by faith to obtain the knowledge of God, they could with it obtain all other things
which pertain to life and godliness.

   19. By these sayings of the apostle, we learn that
it was by obtaining a knowledge of God that men got
the knowledge of all things which pertain to life and
godliness, and this knowledge was the effect of faith ;
so that all things which pertain to life and godliness
are the effects of faith.

   20. From this we may extend as far as any circumstances may require, whether on earth or in heaven,
and we will find it the testimony of all inspired men,
or heavenly messengers, that all things that pertain to
life and godliness are the effects of faith and nothing
else ; all learning, wisdom and prudence fail, and every
thing else as a means of salvation but faith.   This is
the reason that the fishermen of Galilee could teach
the world—because they sought by faith, and by faith
obtained.   And this is the reason that Paul counted all
things but filth and dross—what he formerly called his
gain he called his loss ; yea, and he counted all things
but loss for the excellency of the knowledge of Christ
Jesus the Lord.   Philippians iii. 7, 8, 9, and 10.   Because to obtain the faith by which he could enjoy the
knowledge of Christ Jesus the Lord, he had to suffer
the loss of all things.   This is the reason that the
Former-day Saints knew more, and understood more,
of heaven and of heavenly things than all others

beside, because this information is the effect of faith—
to be obtained by no other means. And this is the
reason that men, as soon as they lose their faith, run
into strifes, contentions, darkness, and difficulties ; for
the knowledge which tends to life disappears with faith,
but returns when faith returns ; for when faith comes
it brings its train of attendants with it—apostles, prophets, evangelists, pastors, teachers, gifts, wisdom,
knowledge, miracles, healings, tongues, interpretation
of tongues, etc. All these appear when faith appears
on the earth, and disappear when it disappears from
the earth ; for these are the effects of faith, and always
have attended, and always will, attend it. For where
faith is, there will the knowledge of God be also, with
all things which pertain thereto—revelations, visions,
and dreams, as well as every necessary thing, in order
that the possessors of faith may be perfected, and
obtain salvation ; for God must change, otherwise faith
will prevail with him. And he who possesses it will,
through it, obtain all necessary knowledge and wisdom,
until he shall know God, and the Lord Jesus Christ,
whom he has sent—whom to know is eternal life.
Amen.

COVENANTS AND COMMANDMENTS.

SECTION I.

The Covenants and Commandments of the Lord, to his servants of the Church of Jesus Christ of Latter-day Saints.

1. Hearken, O ye people of [a]my church, saith the voice of him who dwells on high, and whose eyes are upon all men ; yea, verily I say, hearken ye people from afar, and ye that are upon the islands of the sea, listen together.

2. For verily the voice of the Lord is unto [b]all men, and there is none to escape, and there is no eye that shall not see, neither ear that shall not hear, neither heart that shall not be penetrated.

3. And the rebellious shall be pierced with much sorrow, for their iniquities shall be spoken upon the housetops, and their secret acts shall be revealed.

---

a, 1 : 30.   5 : 14.   10 : 53—56.   11 : 16.   18 : 4, 5.   20 : 1—4.   21 : 1—4.   22 : 3   23 : 2—5, 7.   24 : 9, 10.   28 : 12, 13.   30 : 6, 7.   33 : 5.   37 : 3.   38 : 34.   39 : 13.   41 : 3, 9.   42 : 1, 8.   43 : 1, 2.   44 : 1.   45 : 1, 6.   46 : 1—5.   47 : 3.   48 : 6.   49 : 14.   50 : 1, 4.   51 : 4, 5.   52 : 39, 41.   53 : 1, 4.   55 : 2, 4.   56 : 10.   57 : 1.   58 : 1.   60 : 1, 8, 9.   61 : 2.   62 : 1.   63 : 46, 63.   64 : 1, 26, 57.   67 : 1.   68 : 7, 14.   69 : 3, 7.   70 : 1, 5, 6, 10.   71 : 2.   72 : 1, 2, 25.   73 : 1.   75 : 23, 24.   76 : 54.   77 : 5, 11.   78 : 1, 4.   81 : 1.   82 : 18, 21.   83 : 1—6.   84 : 2, 17.   85 : 1, 4, 11.   86 : 3.   88 : 127.   89 : 1.   90 : 13, 15, 16.   93 : 22.   94 : 3.   97 : 5.   98 : 6, 19.   101 : 72, 75.   102 : 1, 2, 3.   103 : 23, 29.   104 : 1, 59.   105 : 2, 7, 8.   106 : 1, 8.   107 : 1, 4, 5.   109 : 72, 73, 79.   112 : 27.   115 : 3, 4.   117 : 13.   119 : 2.   120 : 1.   124 : 84.   128 : 4, 10, 21.   133 : 1, 8, 16.   136 : 2, 41.   *b*, vers. 4, 11, 34, 35.   5 : 5.   18 : 26, 28.   39 : 15.   42 : 58.   43 : 20—28.   45 : 49, 71.   49 : 10.   58 : 9, 10, 11.   68 : 8.   77 : 11.   84 : 74, 75.   88 : 104.   90 : 8—11.   124 : 2.   133 : 7—25.   133 : 63, 64—74, 8, 9, 16, 37.

4. And the voice of warning shall be unto all people, by the mouths of my disciples, whom I have chosen in these last days.

5. And they shall go forth and none shall stay them, for I the Lord have commanded them.

6. Behold, this is mine authority, and the ʿauthority of my servants, and my preface unto the book of my commandments, which I have given them to publish unto you, O inhabitants of the earth.

7. Wherefore, fear and tremble, O ye people, for what I the Lord have decreed in them shall be fulfilled.

8. And verily, I say unto you, that they who go forth, bearing these tidings unto the inhabitants of the earth, to them is power given to ᵈseal both on earth and in heaven, the unbelieving and rebellious ;

9. Yea, verily, to seal them up unto the day when the wrath of God shall be poured out upon the wicked without measure ;

10. Unto the day when the Lord shall come to recompense unto every man according to his work, and measure to every man according to the measure which he has measured to his fellow man.

11. Wherefore the voice of the Lord is unto the ends of the earth, that all that will hear may hear :

12. Prepare ye, prepare ye for that which is to come, for the Lord is ʿnigh ;

13. And the anger of the Lord is kindled, and his sword is ᶠbathed in heaven, and it shall fall upon the inhabitants of the earth ;

c, vers. 4, 5, 6, 17, 18, 19, 23—28.   124 : 123—145.   *d*, 77 : 8, 12.
75 : 18—22.   84 : 74, 92—95.   88 : 84.   128 : 8—11.   68 : 12.   133 : 71—74.
24 : 15.   60 : 15.   103 : 24—26.   124 : 93.   *e*, 1, 35, 36.   20 : 9—11.
33 : 3, 17, 18.   34 : 6—9, 12.   35 : 15, 16, 26, 27.   36 : 8.   38 : 8.   39 : 20, 21,
23, 24.   41 : 4.   43 : 17—19, 28—31.   45 : 36—50, 56—61.   49 : 6, 7, 23—25,
28.   51 : 20.   54 : 10.   61 : 38, 39.   63 : 32—35, 53, 54.   64 : 23, 24.   65 : 5, 6.
68 : 11, 35.   67 : 12.   78 : 20—22.   84 : 118, 110.   87 : 8.   88 : 86—110.
97 : 22—26.   99 : 5.   101 : 3, 22—37, 64—66.   104 : 59.   110 : 16.   112 : 24, 34.
124 : 8, 124.   130 : 14—17.   133 : 2, 3, 10, 11, 17—25, 36—56.   *f*, 1 : 14.
5 : 5, 8, 19, 20.   29 : 14—21.   35 : 14.   43 : 17—27.   45 : 26, 30—33, 45, 47—
50, 63, 60.   63 : 6, 32, 33, 34.   87 : 1—8.   88 : 85, 87—91.   97 : 22—24.   101 :
10, 11.   112 : 23, 24.   133 : 2, 3, 49—51.   Isaiah 34 : 1—8.   66 : 14—16.
Rev. 19 : 11—21.

14. And the arm of the Lord shall be revealed; and the day cometh that they who will not hear the voice of the Lord, neither the voice of his servants, neither give heed to the words of the prophets and apostles, shall be *g*cut off from among the people;

15. For they have strayed from mine ordinances, and have *h*broken mine everlasting covenant;

16. They seek not the Lord to establish his righteousness, but every man walketh in his own way, and after the image of his own God, whose image is in the likeness of the world, and whose substance is that of an idol, which waxeth old and shall perish in Babylon, even Babylon the great, *i*which shall fall.

17. Wherefore I the Lord, knowing the calamity which should come upon the inhabitants of the earth, called upon my servant Joseph Smith, jun., and spake unto him from heaven, and gave him commandments;

18. And also gave commandments to others, that they should proclaim these things unto the world; and all this that it might be fulfilled, which was written by the prophets;

19. The *j*weak things of the world shall come forth and break down the mighty and strong ones, that man should not counsel his fellow man, neither trust in the arm of flesh,

20. But that every man might speak in the name of God the Lord, even the Saviour of the world;

21. That faith also might increase in the earth;

22. That mine *k*everlasting covenant might be established;

---

g, 5 : 19, 20.   29 : 9—11.   35 : 14.   38 : 6, 8, 12.   45 : 30—33, 44, 49, 50, 57, 75.   49 : 6, 10.   50 : 8.   56 : 1, 3, 4.   63 : 6, 32—37.   84 : 92—98.   86 : 7. 87 : 6.   88 : 84, 85.   97 : 7, 22, 25.   99 : 4, 5.   101 : 10, 11.   102 : 23—26. 133 : 2, 49—52, 63, 64, 65—75.   Acts 3 : 22, 23.   *h*, 22 : 1—4.   Isaiah 24 : 5, 6.   *i*, 29 : 21.   35 : 11.   86 : 3—7.   88 : 94, 105.   101 : 65, 66. 133 : 5, 7, 14.   *j*, vers. 23, 24.   35 : 13.   124 : 1.   I. Corinth. 1 : 26—29. *k*, 22 : 1, 3.   39 : 11.   45 : 9.   49 : 0.   66 : 2.   76 : 69, 101.   78 : 11.   82 : 15. 84 : 40, 41, 48, 57, 99.   88 : 131, 133.   98 : 14, 15.   101 : 39.   104 : 4, 5. 107 : 19.   132 : 4, 6, 19, 26, 27, 41, 42.

23. That the fullness of my gospel might be proclaimed by the weak and the simple unto the ends of the world, and before kings and rulers.

. 24. Behold, I am God and have spoken it : these commandments are of me, and were given unto my servants in their weakness, after the manner of their language, that they might come to understanding,

25. And inasmuch as they erred it might be made known :

26. And inasmuch as they sought wisdom they might be instructed :

27. And inasmuch as they sinned they might be chastened, that they might repent :

28. And inasmuch as they were humble they might be made strong, and blessed from on high, and receive knowledge from time to time :

29. And after having received the record of the Nephites, yea, even my servant Joseph Smith, jun., might have power to ᶦtranslate through the mercy of God, by the power of God, the Book of Mormon ;

30. And also those to whom these commandments were given, might have power to lay the foundation of this church, and to bring it ᵐforth out of obscurity and out of darkness, the only true and living church upon the face of the whole earth, with which I, the Lord, am well pleased, speaking unto the church collectively and not individually,

31. For I the Lord cannot look upon sin with the least degree of allowance ;

32. Nevertheless, he that repents and does the commandments of the Lord shall be forgiven ;

33. And he that repents not, from him shall be taken even the light which he has received, for my Spirit shall not always strive with man, saith the Lord of Hosts.

l, 1 : 29. 3 : 12. 5 : 4, 30, 31. 6 : 25, 28. 9 : 12. 10: 1—4, 7, 10, 11, 13, 15, 18, 30, 31, 34, 41, 45. 17 : 6. 20 : 8. 21 : 1. 37 : 1. 77 : 15. 90 : 13. 93 : 53. 107 : 92. 124 : 125. *m*, see *a*.

34. And again, verily I say unto you, O inhabitants of the earth, I the Lord am willing to make these things known unto [n]all flesh,

35. For I am no respecter of persons, and will that all men shall know that the day speedily cometh ; the hour is not yet, but is nigh at hand, when [o]peace shall be taken from the earth, and the [p]devil shall have power over his own dominion ;

36. And also the Lord shall have power over his saints, and shall reign in their midst, and shall come down in judgment upon [q]Idumea, or the world.

37. Search these commandments for they are true and faithful, and the prophecies and promises which are in them shall all be fulfilled.

38. What I the Lord. have spoken, I have spoken, and I excuse not myself: and [r]though the heavens and the earth pass away, my word shall not pass away, but shall all be fulfilled, whether by mine own voice or by the voice of my servants, it is the same ;

39. For behold, and lo, the Lord is God, and the Spirit beareth record, and the record is true, and the truth abideth forever and ever.   Amen.

SECTION 2.

Words spoken by an angel, to Joseph Smith, while in his father's house, in Manchester, Ontario County, New York, on the evening of the 21st of September, 1823.

1. Behold I will reveal unto you the Priesthood, by the hand of [a]Elijah the prophet, before the [b]coming of the great and dreadful day of the Lord ;

n, see b.   o, 87 : 1, 2, 6.   112 : 24.   p, 38 : 11.   q, see f, and g
r, 45 : 23.   57 : 11.

a, 27 : 9.   35 : 4.   98 : 16, 17.   110 : 13, 14.   128 : 17.   133 : 55.   b, see
e. Sec. 1.

2. And he shall plant in the hearts of the children the promises made to the fathers, and the hearts of the children ᶜshall turn to their fathers ;

3. If it were not so, the whole earth would be utterly wasted at its coming.

SECTION 3.

Revelation to Joseph Smith, jun., given in Harmony, Susquehanna County, Pennsylvania, July, 1828, concerning certain Manuscripts on the First Part of the Book of Mormon, which had been taken from the possession of Martin Harris.

1. The works, and the designs, and the purposes of God cannot be frustrated, neither can they come to nought,

2. For God doth not walk in crooked paths, neither doth he turn to the right hand nor to the left, neither doth he vary from that which he hath said, therefore his paths are straight, and his course is ᵃone eternal round.

3. Remember, remember that it is not the work of God that is frustrated, but the work of men ;

4. For although a man may have many revelations, and have power to do many mighty works, yet if he boasts in his own strength, and sets at nought the counsels of God, and follows after the dictates of his own will and carnal desires, he must fall and incur the vengeance of a just God upon him.

5. Behold, you have been intrusted with these things, but how strict were your commandments ; and remember, also the promises which were made to you, if you did not transgress them ;

c, 27 : 9.   110 : 15.   128 : 17.
a, 35 : 1.   l. Nep. 10 : 19.

6. And behold, how oft you have transgressed the commandments and the laws of God, and have gone on in the persuasions of men ;

7. For, behold, you should not have feared man more than God, although men set at nought the counsels of God, and despise his words ;

8. Yet you should have been faithful and he would have extended his arm and supported you against all the fiery darts of the adversary ; and he would have been with you in every time of trouble.

9. Behold, thou art Joseph, and thou wast chosen to do the work of the Lord, but because of transgression, if thou art not aware thou wilt fall ;

10. But remember God is merciful ; therefore, repent of that which thou hast done which is contrary to the commandment which I gave you, and thou art still chosen, and art again called to the work ;

11. Except thou do this, thou shalt be delivered up and become as other men, and have no more gift.

12. And when thou deliveredst up that which God had given thee *b*sight and power to translate, thou deliveredst up that which was sacred into the hands of a wicked man,

13. Who has set at nought the counsels of God, and has broken the most sacred promises which were made before God, and has depended upon his own judgment, and boasted in his own wisdom,

14. And this is the reason that thou hast lost thy privileges for a season,   .

15. For thou hast suffered the counsel of thy director to be trampled upon from the beginning.

16. Nevertheless my work shall go forth, for inasmuch as the knowledge of a Saviour has come unto the world, through the *c*testimony of the Jews, even so shall the knowledge of a Saviour come unto my people,

---

b, see *l*, 1 : 29.   *c*, Rom. 11 : 30, 31.

17. And to the [d]Nephites, and the Jacobites, and the Josephites, and the Zoramites, through the testimony of their fathers—

18. And this testimony shall come to the knowledge of the [e]Lamanites, and the Lemuelites and the Ishmaelites, who dwindled in unbelief because of the iniquity of their fathers, whom the Lord has suffered to [f]destroy their brethren the Nephites, because of their iniquities and their abominations;

19. And for this very purpose are these plates preserved which contain these records, that the promises of the Lord might be fulfilled, which he made to his people;

20. And that the Lamanites might come to the [g]knowledge of their fathers, and that they might know the promises of the Lord, and that they may believe the gospel and rely upon the merits of Jesus Christ, and be glorified through faith in his name, and that through [h]their repentance they might be saved. Amen.

SECTION 4.

Revelation, through Joseph, the Seer, to Joseph Smith, sen., given in Harmony, Susquehanna County, Pennsylvania, February, 1829.

1. Now behold, a [a]marvelous work is about to come forth among the children of men;

---

d, I. Nep. 13 : 30.   Alma 45 : 10—14.   Mor. 9 : 24.   e, Indians, among whom there is a mixture of the Nephites.   f, Near the close of the fourth century of our era.   g, 10 : 48.   28 : 8, 9, 14.   30 : 6. 49 : 24.   54 : 8.   h, 1 : 32.   5 : 19.   6 : 9.   11 : 9.   15 : 6.   18 : 6, 9, 11—15, 22, 41, 42, 44.   19 : 4, 13—17, 20, 21, 31.   20 : 6, 29, 37, 71, 72.   29 : 42, 44, 49. 33 : 10, 11.   34 : 6.   35 : 5.   36 : 6.   39 : 18.`   42 : 20, 21, 23—25, 28, 37, 77. 43 : 20—22.   44 : 3.   49 : 2, 8, 13, 26.   53 : 3.   45 : 2.   56 : 14.   58 : 42, 43, 48. 63 : 15, 63.   64 : 12.   84 : 27, 41, 57.   98 : 41—44, 47.   109 : 21, 29, 50, 53. 124 : 50.   133 : 62.

a, 6 : 1.   13 : 44.   88 : 12.   76 : 114.   121 : 12.

2. Therefore, O ye that embark in the service of
God, see that ye serve him with all your heart, might,
mind and strength, that ye may stand blameless before
God at the last day ;

3. Therefore, if ye have desires to serve God, ye are
called to the work,

4. For behold the field is *white already to harvest,
and lo, he that thrusteth in his sickle with his might,
the same layeth up in store that he perish not, but
bringeth salvation to his soul ;

5. And faith, hope, charity and love, with an eye
single to the glory of God, qualify him for the work.

6. Remember faith, virtue, knowledge, temperance,
patience, brotherly kindness, godliness, charity, humility,
diligence.

7. *Ask and ye shall receive, knock and it shall be
opened unto you.   Amen.

SECTION 5.

*Revelation given through Joseph, the Seer, in Har-
mony, Susquehanna County, Pennsylvania, March,
1829.*

1. Behold, I say unto you, that as my servant
Martin Harris has desired a witness at my hand, that
you, my servant Joseph Smith, jun., have got the plates
of which you have testified and borne record that you
have received of me ;

2. And now, behold, this shall you say unto him,
he who spake unto you, said unto you, I, the Lord, am

b, 11 : 3.   12 : 3. 14 : 3.   33 : 3, 7.   101 : 64.   *c*, 4 : 7.   6 : 5, 11, 14, 15.
7 : 1.   8 : 1, 9, 11.   9 : 7, 8.   11 : 5.   12 : 5.   14 : 5, 8.   18 : 18.   29 : 6, 34.
35 : 9.   42 : 3, 56, 61, 62, 68.   46 : 7, 28, 30.   49 : 26.   50 : 2, 31.   66 : 9.
75 : 27.   88 : 63—65, 83.   101 : 27.   103 : 31, 35.   132 : 40.

God, and have given these things unto you, my servant
Joseph Smith, jun., and have commanded you that
you should stand as a witness of these things,

3. And I have caused you that you should enter
into a covenant with me, that you should *not show
them except to those persons to whom I commanded
you ; and you have no power over them except I grant
it unto you.

4. And you have a *gift to translate the plates
and this is the first gift that I bestowed upon you,
and I have commanded that you should pretend
to no other gift, until my purpose is fulfilled in
this ; for I will grant unto you no other gift until it is
finished.

5. Verily, I say unto you, that *wo shall come unto
the inhabitants of the earth if they will not hearken
unto my words ;

6. For hereafter you shall be *ordained and go forth
and deliver my words unto the children of men.

7. Behold, if they will not believe my words, they
would not believe you my servant Joseph, if it were
possible that you could show them all these things
which I have committed unto you.

8. O ! this unbelieving and stiffnecked generation,
mine anger is kindled against them.

9. Behold, verily I say unto you, I have reserved
those things which I have entrusted unto you, my servant Joseph, for a wise purpose in me, and it shall be
made known unto future generations ;

10. But this generation shall have my word
*through you ;

11. And in addition to your testimony, the *testimony of three of my servants, whom I shall call and
ordain, unto whom I will show these things, and they

a, see testimony of The Eight Witnesses, Book of Mormon.   *b*, see *l*.
1 : 29.   *c*, see *f* and *g*, Sec. 1.   *d*, 20 : 2. 21 : 10, 11. 43 : 7. 113 : 5, 6.
124 : 57, 58, 125.   132 : 7, 19, 44—49.   *e*, see *l*, Sec. 1.   *f*, ver. 15.
Sec. 17 : 2.   27 : 12. Ether 5 : 3, 4. Book of Mor. p. v.

shall go forth with my words that are given through you ;

12. Yea, they shall know of a surety that these things are true, for from heaven will I declare it unto them.

13. I will give them power that they may behold and view these things as they are ;

14. And to none else will I grant this power, to receive this *g*same testimony among this generation, in this the beginning of the rising up and the *h*coming forth of my church out of the wilderness; *i*clear as the moon, and fair as the sun, and terrible as an army with banners.

15. And the testimony of three witnesses will I send forth of my word ;

16. And behold, whosoever believeth on my words them will I *j*visit with the manifestation of my Spirit, and they shall be *k*born of me, even of *l*water and of the *m*Spirit.

17. And you must wait yet a little while, for ye are not yet ordained ;

18. And their testimony shall *n*also go forth unto the condemnation of this generation if they harden their hearts against them ;

19. For a *o*desolating scourge shall go forth among the inhabitants of the earth, and shall continue to be poured out from time to time, if they repent not, until the earth is empty, and the inhabitants thereof are consumed away and utterly destroyed by the *p*brightness of my coming.

---

g, None others, in this generation, to receive a testimony of the same kind as the three : but may receive a knowledge by other manifestations. *h*, see *a*, Sec. 1.   *i*, 105 : 31. 109 : 73.   *j*, 8 : 1. 13 : 2, 18. 39 : 6. 47 : 8—29. 67 : 11. 70 : 12, 13. 75 : 27. 77 : 10—30, 116—118. 79 : 2. 84 : 46, 47, 85.   88 : 3, 13.   90 : 11.   121 : 26—28.   124 : 5.   133 : 59. *k*, Mos. 5 : 7. 27 : 24—27.   Alma 5 : 14, 49. 22 : 15. 36 : 23, 26. 38 : 6. *l*, 19 : 31. 20 : 41. 20 : 73, 74. 33 : 11. 35 : 5, 6. 39 : 6, 10, 20, 23. 42 : 7. 52 :.10. 55 : 1. 84 : 64, 74.   *m*, 19 : 31. 20 : 41, 43. 33 : 15. 35 : 5, 6. 39 : 6, 10, 23. 52 : 10. 55 : 1. 84 : 64, 74.   *n*, testimony of all who are born of the Spirit.   *o*, see *f* and *g*, Sec. 1.   *p*, see *e*, Sec. 1.

20. Behold, I tell you these things, even as I also told the people of the destruction of Jerusalem, and my word shall be ?verified at this time as it hath hitherto been verified.

21. And now I command you my servant Joseph to repent and walk more uprightly before me, and yield to the persuasions of men no more ;

22. And that you be firm in keeping the commandments wherewith I have commanded you, and if you do this, behold I grant unto you eternal life, ʳeven if you should be slain.

23. And now, again, I speak unto you, my servant Joseph, concerning the ˢman that desires the witness.

24. Behold, I say unto him, he exalts himself and does not humble himself sufficiently before me ; but if he will bow down before me. and humble himself in mighty prayer and faith, in the sincerity of his heart, then will I grant unto him a ᵗview of the things which he desires to see.

25. And then he shall say unto the people of this generation, behold, I have seen the things which the Lord has shown unto Joseph Smith, jun., and I know of a surety that they are true, for I have seen them, for they have been shown unto me by the power of God and not of man.

26. And I, the Lord, command him, my servant Martin Harris, that he shall say no more unto them concerning these things, except he shall say I have seen them, and they have been shown unto me by the power of God, and these are the words which he shall say ;

27. But if he deny this, he will break the covenant which he has before covenanted with me, and behold, he is condemned.

28. And now, except he humble himself and acknowledge unto me the things that he has done which are

wrong, and covenant with me that he will keep my commandments, and exercise faith in me, behold, I say unto him, he shall have no such views, for I will grant unto him no views of the things of which I have spoken.

29. And if this be the case, I command you, my servant Joseph, that you shall say unto him, that he shall do no more, nor trouble me any more concerning this matter.

30. And if this be the case, behold, I say unto thee Joseph, when thou hast translated a few more pages, thou shalt stop for a season, even until I command thee again ; then thou mayest translate again.

31. And except thou do this, behold, thou shalt have no more gift, and I will take away the things which I have entrusted with thee.

32. And now, because I foresee the lying in wait to destroy thee, yea, I foresee that if my servant Martin Harris humbleth not himself, and receive a witness from my hand, that he will fall into transgression ;

33. And there are many that lie in wait to destroy thee from off the face of the earth, and for this cause, that thy days may be prolonged, I have given unto thee these commandments ;

34. Yea, for this cause I have said, stop and stand still until I command thee, and I will provide means whereby thou mayest accomplish the thing which I have commanded thee ;

35. And if thou art faithful in keeping my commandments, thou shalt be "lifted up at the last day. Amen.

---

u, 9 : 14.   17 : 8.   27 : 18.   52 : 44.   75 : 16, 22.   I. Nep. 13 : 37.   16 : 2. Alma 26 : 7.   36 : 28.   38 : 5.   III. Nep. 15 : 1.   27 : 14, 15, 22.   Mor. 2 : 19. Ether 4 : 19.

SECTION 6.

Revelation given to Oliver Cowdery and Joseph Smith,
jun., in Harmony, Susquehanna County, Penn-
sylvania, April, 1829.

1. A great and ^amarvelous work is about to come forth unto the children of men.

2. Behold, I am God, and give heed unto my word, which is quick and powerful, sharper than a two-edged sword, to the dividing asunder of both joints and marrow ; therefore give heed unto my words.

3. Behold the field is ^bwhite already to harvest, therefore whoso desireth to reap, let him thrust in his sickle with his might, and reap while the day lasts, that he may treasure up for his soul everlasting salvation in the kingdom of God :

4. Yea, whosoever will thrust in his sickle and reap, the ^csame is called of God ;

5. Therefore, if you will ^dask of me you shall receive ; if you will knock it shall be opened unto you.

6. Now, as you have asked, behold, I say unto you, keep my commandments, and seek to ^ebring forth and establish the cause of Zion,

7. Seek not for riches but for wisdom, and behold, the mysteries of God shall be unfolded unto you, and then shall you be made rich. Behold, he that hath eternal life is rich.

8. Verily, verily, I say unto you, even as you desire of me, so it shall be unto you ; and if you desire, you shall be the means of doing much good in this generation.

9. Say nothing but repentance unto this genera-

---

a, see a, Sec. 4.   b, see b, Sec. 4.   c, 4 : 4. 11 : 3, 4, 27. 12 : 3, 4.
14 : 3, 4. 31 : 5. 33 : 7.   d, see c, Sec. 4.   e, 11 : 6. 12 : 6. 14 : 6.
39 : 13. 84 : 2—5. 101 : 69—71, 75. 103 : 11—24, 34, 35. 105 : 27—29.
113 : 7, 8. 115 : 5, 6. 133 : 9.

tion : keep my commandments, and assist to bring
forth my work, according to my commandments, and
you shall be blessed.

10. Behold thou hast a gift, and blessed art thou
because of thy gift. Remember it is sacred and cometh
from above :

11. And if thou wilt inquire, thou shalt know
mysteries which are great and marvelous : therefore
thou shalt exercise thy gift, that thou mayest find out
mysteries, that thou mayest bring many to the knowledge of the truth ; yea, convince them of the error of
their ways.

12. Make not thy gift known unto any, save it be
those who are of thy faith.   Trifle not with sacred
things.

13. If thou wilt do good, yea, and hold out faithful
to the end, thou shalt be saved in the kingdom of God,
which is the *greatest of all the gifts of God ; for there
is no gift greater than the gift of salvation.

14. Verily, verily, I say unto thee, blessed art thou
for what thou hast done, for thou hast inquired of me,
and behold as often as thou hast inquired, thou hast
received instruction of my Spirit.   If it had not been
so, thou wouldst not have come to the place where thou
art at this time.

15. Behold thou knowest that thou hast inquired
of me, and I did enlighten thy mind ; and now I tell
thee these things, that thou mayest know that thou
hast been enlightened by the Spirit of truth ;

16. Yea, I tell thee, that thou mayest know that
there is none else save God that knowest thy thoughts
and the intents of thy heart :

17. I tell thee these things as a witness unto thee,
that the words or the work which thou hast been writing is true.

18. Therefore be diligent, stand by my servant

Joseph, faithfully, in whatsoever difficult circumstances
he may be for the word's sake.

19. Admonish him in his faults, and also receive
admonition of him. Be patient; be sober; be temperate; have patience, faith, hope and charity.

20. Behold, thou art Oliver, and I have spoken
unto thee because of thy desires; therefore treasure
up these words in thy heart. Be faithful and diligent
in keeping the commandments of God, and I will en-
circle thee in the arms of my love.

21. Behold, I am Jesus Christ, the Son of God.
I am the same that came unto *ᵍ*my own, and my
own received me not. I am the light which *ʰ*shineth
in darkness, and the darkness comprehendeth it
not.

22. Verily, verily, I say unto you, if you desire a
further witness, cast your mind upon the night that
you cried unto me in your heart, that you might know
concerning the truth of these things.

23. Did I not speak peace to your mind concerning
the matter? What greater witness can you have than
from God?

24. And now, behold, you have received a witness,
for if I have told you things which no man knoweth,
have you not received a witness?

25. And, behold, I grant unto you a gift, if you
desire of me, to *ⁱ*translate even as my servant Joseph.

26. Verily, verily, I say unto you, that *ʲ*there are
records which contain much of my gospel, which have
been kept back because of the wickedness of the
people;

27. And now I command you, that if you have
good desires—a desire to lay up treasures for yourself
in heaven—then shall you assist in bringing to light,

g, 10 : 57.   11 : 20.   39 : 3.   45 : 8.   133 : 66.   *h*, 10 : 58.   11 : 11,
28.   12 : 9.   14 : 9.   34 : 2.   39 : 2.   45 : 7, 28, 36.   50 : 24, 25, 27.   84 : 45,
46.   86 : 11.   88 : 6—13, 49, 50, 56—58, 67.   93 : 9.   103 : 9.   *i*, see *l*.
1 : 29.   *j*, vers. 27, 28.

with your gift, those parts of my scriptures which have
been *hidden because of iniquity.

28. And now, behold, I give unto you, and also
unto my servant Joseph, the keys of this gift, which
shall bring to light this ministry ; and in the mouth
of 'two or three witnesses shall every word be established.

29. Verily, verily, I say unto you, if they reject
my words, and this part of my gospel and ministry,
blessed are ye, for they can do no more unto you than
unto me ;

30. And if they do unto you, even as they have
done unto me, blessed are ye, for you shall dwell with
me in glory ;

31. But if they ᵐreject not my words, which shall
be established by the testimony which shall be given,
blessed are they, and then shall ye have joy in the
fruit of your labors.

32. Verily, verily, I say unto you, as I said unto
my disciples, ⁿwhere two or three are gathered together
in my name, as touching one thing, behold, there will
I be in the midst of them, even so am I in the midst
of you.

33. Fear not to do good, my sons, for whatsoever
ye sow, that shall ye also reap ; therefore, if ye sow
good, ye shall also reap good for your reward.

34. Therefore, fear not, little flock, do good; let
earth and hell combine against you, for if ye are built
upon ᵒmy Rock, they cannot prevail.

35. Behold, I do not condemn you, go your ways
and sin no more, perform with soberness the work
which I have commanded you;

36. Look unto me in every thought; doubt not,
fear not ;

---

k, vers. 26, 27.   *l*, 5 : 11, 15.   18 : 34, 36.   42 : 80, 81.   76 : 22.
128 : 3.   *m*, reject not the Book of Mormon.   *n*, 29 : 6.   84 : 1.
o, 10 : 69.   11 : 16, 24.   18 : 4, 17.   33 : 13.   50 : 44.

37. Behold the wounds which pierced my side, and also the prints of the nails in my hands and feet ; be faithful, keep my commandments, and ye shall inherit the kingdom of heaven. Amen.

SECTION 7.

Revelation given to Joseph Smith, jun., and Oliver Cowdery, in Harmony, Pennsylvania, April, 1829, when they desired to know whether John, the beloved disciple, tarried on earth. Translated from parchment, written and hid up by himself.

1. And the Lord said unto me, John, my beloved, what desirest thou ? For if ye shall ask, what you will, it shall be granted unto you.

2. And I said unto him, Lord, give unto me power over death, that I may live and bring souls unto thee.

3. And the Lord said unto me, Verily, verily, I say unto thee, because thou desirest this thou shalt *a*tarry until I come in my glory, and shalt prophesy before nations, kindred, tongues and people.

4. And for this cause the Lord said unto Peter, *b*If I will that he tarry till I come, what is that to thee ? for he desired of me that he might bring souls unto me, but thou desiredst that thou mightest speedily come unto me in my kingdom.

5. I say unto thee, Peter, this was a good desire, but my beloved has desired that he might do more, or a greater work yet among men than what he has before done ;

6. Yea, he has undertaken a greater work, therefore I will make him as flaming fire and a ministering angel:

---

a, 77: 14. III. Nep. 28: 6. John 21: 20--25. Rev. 10: 11. *b*, John 21 : 20—25.

he shall minister for those who ^cshall be heirs of salvation who dwell on the earth:

7. And I will make thee to minister for him and for thy brother James; and unto you three I will give this power and the keys of this ministry until I come.

8. Verily, I say unto you, ye shall both have according to your desires, for ye both joy in that which ye have desired.

SECTION 8.

Revelation given through Joseph, the Seer, in Harmony, Pennsylvania, April, 1829.

1. Oliver Cowdery, verily, verily, I say unto you, that assuredly as the Lord liveth, who is your God and your Redeemer, even so surely shall you receive a knowledge of whatsoever things you shall ask in faith, with an honest heart, believing that you shall receive a knowledge concerning the engravings of ^aold records, which are ancient, which contain those parts of my scripture of which have been spoken by the manifestation of my Spirit;

2. Yea, behold, I will tell you in your mind and in your heart, by the Holy Ghost, which shall come upon you and which shall dwell in your heart.

3. Now, behold, this is the Spirit of revelation; behold, this is the Spirit by which Moses brought the children of Israel through the Red Sea on dry ground';

4. Therefore this is thy gift; apply unto it, and blessed art thou, for it shall deliver you out of the hands of your enemies, when, if it were not so, they would slay you and bring your soul to destruction.

---

c, Heb. 1: 14.

a, see *l*, Sec. 1.

5. O ! remember these words, and keep my commandments. Remember this is your gift.

6. Now this is not all thy gift; for you have another gift, which is the *b*gift of Aaron : behold, it has told you many things ;

7. Behold, there is no other power, save the power of God, that can cause this gift of Aaron to be with you;

8. Therefore doubt not, for it is the gift of God, and you shall hold it in your hands, and do marvelous works ; and no power shall be able to take it away out of your hands, for it is the work of God.

9. And, therefore, whatsoever you shall ask me to tell you, by that means, that will I grant unto you, and you shall have knowledge concerning it :

10. Remember that without faith you can do nothing, therefore ask in faith. Trifle not with these things; do not ask for that which you ought not :

11. Ask that you may know the mysteries of God, and that *c*you may translate and receive knowledge from all those ancient records which have been hid up, that are sacred, and according to your faith shall it be done unto you.

12. Behold, it is I that have spoken it ; and I am the same that spake unto you from the beginning. Amen.

SECTION 9.

Revelation given to Oliver Cowdery, through Joseph, the Seer, in Harmony, Pennsylvania, April, 1829.

1. Behold, I say unto you, my son, that because you did not translate according to that which you desired of me, and did commence again to write for my

---

servant, Joseph Smith, jun., even so I would that ye should continue until you have finished this record, which I have entrusted unto him :

2. And then, behold, ªother records have I, that I will give unto you power that you may assist to translate.

3. Be patient, my son, for it is wisdom in me, and it is not expedient that you should translate at this present time.

4. Behold, the work which you are called to do, is to write for my servant Joseph ;

5. And, behold, it is because that you did not continue as you commenced, when you began to translate, that I have taken away this privilege from you.

6. Do not murmur, my son, for it is wisdom in me that I have dealt with you after this manner.

7. Behold, you have not understood ; you have supposed that I would give it unto you, when you took no thought, save it was to ask me ;

8. But, behold, I say unto you, that you must study it out in your mind ; then you must ask me if it be right, and if it is right I will cause that your bosom shall burn within you ; therefore, you shall feel that it is right ;

9. But if it be not right, you shall have no such feelings, but you shall have a stupor of thought, that shall cause you to forget the thing which is wrong : therefore you cannot write that which is sacred, save it be given you from me.

10. Now if you had known this, you could have translated ; nevertheless, it is not expedient that you should translate now.

11. Behold, it was expedient when you commenced, but you feared and the time is past, and it is not expedient now ;

12. For, do ye not behold that I have given unto

ª, Records kept by the Nephites.

my servant Joseph sufficient strength, whereby it is made up; and neither of you have I condemned.

13. Do this thing which I have commanded you, and you shall prosper. Be faithful, and yield to no temptation.

14. Stand fast in the work wherewith I have called you, and a hair of your head shall not be lost, and you shall be *b*lifted up at the last day. Amen.

SECTION 10.

Revelation given to Joseph Smith, jun., in Harmony, Pennsylvania, May, 1829, informing him of the alteration of the Manuscript of the fore part of the Book of Mormon.

1. Now, behold, I say unto you, that because you delivered up those writings which you had power given unto you to translate, by the means of the Urim and Thummim, into the hands of a wicked man, you have *a*lost them;

2. And you also lost your gift at the same time, and your mind became darkened;

3. Nevertheless, it is now restored unto you again, therefore see that you are faithful and continue on unto the finishing of the remainder of the work of translation as you have begun:

4. Do not run faster, or labor more than you have strength and means provided to enable you to translate; but be diligent unto the end:

5. Pray always, that you may come off conqueror;

---

b, see u, Sec. 5.

---

a, 116 pages of Manuscripts stolen. 10: 1—19, 20—52.

yea, that you may conquer Satan, and that you may escape the hands of the servants of Satan that do uphold his work.

6. Behold, they have sought to destroy you ; yea, even the man in whom you have trusted, has sought to destroy you.

7. And for this cause I said that he is a wicked man, for he has sought to take away the things wherewith you have been entrusted ; and he has also sought to destroy your gift ;

8. And because you have delivered the writings into his hands, behold, wicked men have taken them from you :

9. Therefore, you have delivered them up ; yea, that which was sacred unto wickedness.

10. And, behold, Satan has put it into their hearts to alter the words which you have caused to be written, or which you have translated, which have gone out of your hands.

11. And, behold, I say unto you, that because they have altered the words, they read contrary from that which you translated and caused to be written ;

12. And, on this wise, the devil has sought to lay a cunning plan, that he may destroy this work ;

13. For he has put into their hearts to do this, that by lying they may say they have caught you in the words which you have pretended to translate.

14. Verily, I say unto you, that I will not suffer that Satan shall accomplish his evil design in this thing,

15. For, behold, he has put it into their hearts to get thee to tempt the Lord thy God, in asking to translate it over again ;

16. And then, behold, they say and think in their hearts, we will see if God has given him power to translate, if so, he will also give him power again ;

17. And if God giveth him power again, or if he

translates again, or in other words, if he bringeth forth the same words, behold, we have the same with us, and we have altered them :

18. Therefore, they will not agree, and we will say that he has lied in his words, and that he has no gift, and that he has no power :

19. Therefore, we will destroy him, and also the work, and we will do this that we may not be ashamed in the end, and that we may get glory of the world.

20. Verily, verily, I say unto you, that Satan has great hold upon their hearts ; he stirreth them up to iniquity against that which is good,

21. And their hearts are corrupt, and full of wickedness and abominations, and they love darkness rather than light, because their deeds are evil : therefore they will not ask of me.

22. Satan stirreth them up, that he may lead their souls to destruction.

23. And thus he has laid a cunning plan, thinking to destroy the work of God, but I will require this at their hands, and it shall turn to their shame and condemnation in the day of judgment ;

24. Yea, he stirreth up their hearts to anger against this work ;

25. Yea, he saith unto them, deceive and lie in wait to catch, that ye may destroy : behold, this is no harm, and thus he flattereth them, and telleth them that it is no sin to lie, that they may catch a man in a lie, that they may destroy him ;

26. And thus he flattereth them, and leadeth them along until he draggeth their souls down to hell ; and thus he causeth them to catch themselves in their own snare ;

27. And thus he goeth up and down, to and fro in the earth, seeking to destroy the souls of men.

28. Verily, verily, I say unto you, wo be unto him that lieth to deceive, because he supposeth that

another lieth to deceive, for such are not exempt from the justice of God.

29. Now, behold, they have altered these words, because Satan saith unto them, He hath deceived you: and thus he flattereth them away to do iniquity, to get thee to tempt the Lord thy God.

30. Behold, I say unto you, that you shall not translate again those words which have gone forth out of your hands ;

31. For, behold, they shall not accomplish their evil designs in lying against those words. For, behold, if you should bring forth the same words they will say that you have lied ; that you have pretended to translate, but that you have contradicted yourself :

32. And, behold, they will publish this, and Satan will harden the hearts of the people to stir them up to anger against you, that they will not believe my words.

33. Thus Satan thinketh to overpower your testimony in this generation, that the work may not come forth in this generation :

34. But behold, here is wisdom, and because I show unto you wisdom, and give you commandments concerning these things, what you shall do, show it not unto the world until you have accomplished the work of translation.

35. Marvel not that I said unto you, here is wisdom, show it not unto the world, for I said, show it not unto the world, that you may be preserved.

36. Behold, I do not say that you shall not show it unto the righteous ;

37. But as you cannot always judge the righteous, or as you cannot always tell the wicked from the righteous, therefore I say unto you, hold your peace until I shall see fit to make all things known unto the world concerning the matter.

38. And now, verily I say unto you, that an account of those things that you have written, which have gone

out of your hands, are engraven upon the plates of Nephi;

39. Yea, and you remember it was said in those writings that a more particular account was given of these things upon the plates of Nephi.

40. And now, because the account which is engraven upon the plates of Nephi is more particular concerning the things which, in my wisdom, I would bring to the knowledge of the people in this account;

41. Therefore, you shall translate the engravings which are on the *b*plates of Nephi, down even till you come to the reign of king Benjamin, or until you come to that which you have translated, which you have retained ;

42. And behold, you shall publish it as the record of Nephi, and thus I will confound those who have altered my words.

43. I will not suffer that they shall destroy my work ; yea, I will show unto them that my wisdom is greater than the cunning of the devil.

44. Behold, they have only got a part, or an abridgment of the account of Nephi.

45. Behold, there are many things engraven on the plates of Nephi which do throw greater views upon my gospel ; therefore, it is wisdom in me that you should translate this first part of the engravings of Nephi, and send forth in this work.

46. And, behold, all the remainder of this work does contain all those parts of my gospel which my holy prophets, yea, and also my disciples, *c*desired in their prayers should come forth unto this people.

47. And I said unto them, that it should be granted unto them according to their faith in their prayers ;

48. Yea, and this was their faith, that my gospel

---

b, Small plates of Nephi.   *c*, Enos 1 : 12--18.   Mor. 8 : 24—26.
9 : 36, 37.

which I gave unto them, that they might preach in
their days, might come unto their brethren the Lamanites, and also all that had become Lamanites, because of their dissensions.

49. Now, this is not all—their faith in their prayers
was, that this gospel should be made known also, if
it were possible that other nations should possess this
land ;

50. And thus they did leave a blessing upon this
land in their prayers, that whosoever should believe in
this gospel in this land, might have eternal life ;

51. Yea, that it might be free unto all of whatsoever nation, kindred, tongue, or people they may be.

52. And now, behold, according to their faith in
their prayers will I bring this part of my gospel to the
knowledge of my people. Behold, I do not bring it
to destroy that which they have received, but to build
it up.

53. And for this cause have I said, if this generation
harden not their hearts, I will establish ᵈmy church
among them.

54. Now I do not say this to destroy my church,
but I say this to build up my church ;

55. Therefore, whosoever belongeth to my church
need not fear, for such shall inherit the kingdom of
heaven ;

56. But it is they who do not fear me, neither keep
my commandments, but build up churches unto themselves to get gain, yea, and all those that do wickedly
and build up the kingdom of the devil ; yea, verily,
verily, I say unto you, that it is they that I will dis-
turb, and cause to tremble and shake to the center.

57. Behold, I am Jesus Christ, the son of God. I
came unto ᵉmy own, and my own received me not.

58. I am the light which ᶠshineth in darkness, and
the darkness comprehendeth it not.

---

d, see a, Sec. 1.　　　e, see g, Sec. 6.　　　f, see h, Sec. 6.

59. I am he who said, *g*other sheep have I which are not of this fold, unto my disciples, and many there were that understood me not.

60. And I will show unto this people that I had other sheep, and that they were a branch of the house of Jacob;

61. And I will bring to light their marvelous works, which they did in my name;

62. Yea, and I will also bring to light my gospel which was ministered unto them, and, behold, they shall not deny that which you have received, but they shall build it up, and shall bring to light the *h*true points of my doctrine, yea, and the only doctrine which is in me;

63. And this I do that I may establish my gospel, that there may not be so much contention; yea, Satan doth stir up the hearts of the people to *i*contention concerning the points of my doctrine; and in these things they do err, for they do wrest the scriptures and do not understand them;

64. Therefore, I will unfold unto them this great mystery;

65. For, behold, I will *j*gather them as a hen gathereth her chickens under her wings, if they will not harden their hearts,

66. Yea, if they will come, they may, and partake of the waters of life freely.

67. Behold, this is my doctrine: whosoever repenteth and cometh unto me, the same is *k*my church.

68. Whosoever declareth more or less than this, the same is not of me, but is against me; therefore he is not of my church.

69. And now, behold, whosoever is of my church,

---

g, John 10 : 16. III. Nep. 15 : 16—24.   *h*, I. Nep. 13 : 34—42. 14 :
1, 2.   *i*, III. Nep. 11 : 28—41.   *j*, 29 : 2, 7, 8, 27. 31 : 8.   33 : 6.
38 : 31.   39 : 22.   42 : 36, 64.   43 : 24.   45 : 25, 43.   57 : 1, 15. 58 : 56.
63 : 24.   66 : 11.   77 : 14.   101 : 67, 68.   70 : 74.   84 : 2.   103 : 22.   100 : 58,
59.   110 : 11.   *k*, see *a*, Sec. 1.

and endureth of my church to the end, him will I
establisa upon my rock, and the *l*gates of hell shall not.
prevail against them.

70. And now, remember the words of him who is
the *m*life and light of the world, your Redeemer, your
Lord and your God. Amen.

SECTION 11.

*Revelation given to Hyrum Smith, through Joseph, the
Seer, in Harmony, Pennsylvania, May, 1829.*

1. A great and *a*marvelous work is about to come
forth among the children of men.

2. Behold, I am God, and give heed to my word,
which is quick and powerful, sharper than a two-edged
sword, to the dividing asunder of both joints and marrow; therefore give heed unto my word.

3. Behold, the field is *b*white already to harvest,
therefore, whoso desireth to reap, let him thrust in his
sickle with his might, and reap while the day lasts, that
he may treasure up for his soul everlasting salvation in
the kingdom of God;

4. Yea, whosoever will thrust in his sickle and reap,
the same is called of God;

5. Therefore, if you will *c*ask of me, you shall receive, if you will knock, it shall be opened unto you.

6. Now, as you have asked, behold, I say unto you,
keep my commandments, and seek to *d*bring forth and
establish the cause of Zion.

7. Seek not for riches but for wisdom, and, behold,

---

l, 18 : 5.   21 : 6.   33 : 13.   98 : 22.   *m*, see *h*, Sec. 6.

a, see *a*, Sec. 4.   *b*, see *b*, Sec. 4.   *c*, see *c*, Sec. 4.   *d*, see *e*,
Sec. 6.

the mysteries of God, shall be unfolded unto you, and then shall you be made rich : behold, he that hath eternal life is rich.

8. Verily, verily, I say unto you, even as you desire of me, so it shall be done unto you : and, if you desire, you shall be the means of doing much good in this generation.

9. Say nothing but repentance unto this generation. Keep my commandments, and assist to bring forth my work, according to my commandments, and you shall be blessed.

10. Behold, thou hast a gift, or thou shalt have a gift if thou wilt desire of me in faith, with an honest heart, believing in the power of Jesus Christ, or in my power which speaketh unto thee ;

11. For, behold, it is I that speak ; behold, I am the ᵉlight which shineth in darkness, and by my power I give these words unto thee.

12. And now, verily, verily, I say unto thee, put your trust in that Spirit which leadeth to do good : yea, to do justly, to walk humbly, to judge righteously, and this is my Spirit.

13. Verily, verily, I say unto you, I will impart unto you of my Spirit ; which shall enlighten your mind, which shall fill your soul with joy,

14. And then shall ye know, or by this shall you know all things whatsoever you desire of me, which are pertaining unto things of righteousness, in faith believing in me that you shall receive.

15. Behold, I command you, that you need not suppose that you are called to preach until you are called :

16. Wait a little longer, until you shall have my word, my rock, my church, and my gospel, that you may know of a surety my doctrine ;

17. And then behold, according to your desires, yea, even according to your faith shall it be done unto you.

18. Keep my commandments, hold your peace, appeal unto my Spirit;

19. Yea, cleave unto me with all your heart, that you may assist in bringing to light those things of which have been spoken; yea, the translation of my work; be patient until you shall accomplish it.

20. Behold, this is your work, to keep my commandments, yea, with all your might, mind, and strength;

21. Seek not to declare my word, but first seek to obtain my word, and then shall your tongue be loosed; then, if you desire, you shall have my Spirit and my word, yea, the power of God unto the convincing of men;

22. But now hold your peace, study my word which ᶠhath gone forth among the children of men, and also study my word which shall come forth among the children of men, or that which is ᵍnow translating, yea, until you have obtained all which I shall grant unto the children of men in this generation, and then shall all things be added thereunto.

23. Behold thou art Hyrum, my son, seek the kingdom of God, and all things shall be added according to that which is just.

24. Build upon my rock, which is my gospel;

25. Deny not the Spirit of revelation, nor the Spirit of prophecy, for ʰwo unto him that denieth these things;

26. Therefore, treasure up in your heart until the time which is in my wisdom that you shall go forth.

27. Behold, I speak unto all who have good desires, and have thrust in their sickle to reap.

28. Behold, I am Jesus Christ, the Son of God. I am the ⁱlife and the light of the world.

29. I am the same who came unto ʲmy own and my own received me not;

30. But verily, verily, I say unto you, that as many as receive me, to them will I give *k*power to become the sons of God, even to them that believe on my name. Amen.

SECTION 12.

Revelation given to Joseph Knight, sen., through Joseph, the Seer, in Harmony, Pennsylvania, May, 1829.

1. A great and *a*marvelous work is about to come forth among the children of men.

2. Behold, I am God, and give heed to my word, which is quick and powerful, sharper than a two-edged sword, to the dividing asunder of both joints and marrow ; therefore, give heed unto my word.

3. Behold, the field is *b*white already to harvest, therefore, whoso desireth to reap, let him thrust in his sickle with his might, and reap while the day lasts, that he may treasure up for his soul everlasting salvation in the kingdom of God ;

4. Yea, whosoever will thrust in his sickle and reap, the same is called of God ;

5. Therefore, if you will *c*ask of me you shall receive, if you will knock it shall be opened unto you.

6. Now, as you have asked, behold, I say unto you, keep my commandments, and seek to *d*bring forth and establish the cause of Zion.

7. Behold, I speak unto you, and also to all those who have desires to bring forth and establish this work,

8. And no one can assist in this work, except he shall be humble and full of love, having faith, hope,

---

k, 34 : 3. 39 : 4. 42 : 52. 45 : 8. 76 : 58.

a, see *a*, Sec. 4.   *b*, see *b*, Sec. 4.   *c*, see *c*, Sec. 4.   *d*, see *e*, Sec. 6.

and charity, being temperate in all things, whatsoever
shall be intrusted to his care.

9. Behold, I am the ^elight and the life of the world,
that speak these words, therefore give heed with your
might, and then you are called.   Amen.

SECTION 13.

*Words of the Angel, John, (the Baptist,) spoken to Joseph
Smith, jr., and Oliver Cowdery, as he (the angel)
laid his hands upon their heads and ordained them
to the Aaronic Priesthood, in Harmony, Susquehanna County, Pennsylvania, May 15th, 1829.*

Upon you my fellow servants, in the name of Messiah, I confer the ^aPriesthood of Aaron, which holds
the ^bkeys of the ministering of angels, and of the
gospel of repentance, and of ^cbaptism by immersion for
the remission of sins; and this shall never be taken again
from the earth, until the sons of Levi do offer ^dagain
an offering unto the Lord in righteousness.

SECTION 14.

*Revelation given to David Whitmer, through Joseph, the
Seer, in Fayette, Seneca County, New York, June, 1829.*

1. A great and ^amarvelous work is about to come
forth unto the children of men.

---

e, see m, Sec. 10.

---

a, 20: 46—52, 64, 68, 76, 82, 84. 27: 8. 35: 4, 5. 38: 40. 42: 12, 70.
68: 15—24. 84: 18, 26—28, 30—34, 111. 107: 1, 6, 13—16, 20, 76, 85—88.
124: 142. b, 84: 26. 107: 20. c, 18: 22, 29, 30, 41, 42. 19: 31.
20: 25, 37—42, 72—74. 22: 2. 33: 11. 35: 5, 6. 39: 6, 10, 20, 23. 42: 7.
49: 13. 52: 10. 55: 1, 2. 68: 8, 9, 25—27. 76: 51. 84: 27, 28, 64, 74.
112: 29. d, 84: 26—28. 124: 39. 128: 34.

---

a, see a, Sec. 4.

2. Behold, I am God, and give heed to my word, which is quick and powerful, sharper than a two-edged sword, to the dividing asunder of both joints and marrow ; therefore give heed unto my word.

3. Behold, the field is *b*white already to harvest, therefore, whoso desireth to reap let him thrust in his sickle with his might, and reap while the day lasts, that he may treasure up for his soul everlasting salvation in the kingdom of God ;

4. Yea, whosoever will thrust in his sickle and reap, the same is called of God ;

5. Therefore, if you will *c*ask of me you shall receive, if you will knock it shall be opened unto you.

6. Seek to *d*bring forth and establish my Zion. Keep my commandments in all things ;

7. And, if you keep my commandments and endure to the end, you shall have eternal life, which gift is the *e*greatest of all the gifts of God.

8. And it shall come to pass, that if you shall ask the Father in my name, in faith believing, you shall receive the Holy Ghost, which *f*giveth utterance, that you may stand as a witness of the things of which you shall both *g*hear and see, and also that you may declare repentance unto this generation.

9. Behold, I am Jesus Christ the Son of the living God, who created the heavens and the earth ; a light which cannot be *h*hid in darkness ;

10. Wherefore, I must *i*bring forth the fullness of my gospel from the Gentiles unto the house of Israel.

11. And behold, thou art David, and thou art called to assist ; which thing if ye do, and are faithful, ye

b, see *b,* Sec. 4.　　　*c,* see *c,* Sec. 4.　　　*d,* see *e,* Sec. 6.　　　*e,* see *f,* Sec. 6.　　　*f,* 20 : 26.　24 : 5, 6.　25 : 7.　28 : 1.　33 : 8, 9.　34 : 10.　35 : 18—20.　36 : 2, 3.　39 : 6.　42 : 13—16.　85 : 6.　88 : 137.　90 : 14.　100 : 5—8.　124 : 97.　　　*g,* David Whitmer heard the voice of God, and saw and heard the angel, and saw the golden Plates.　　　*h,* the light shining among the Gentiles is hid in darkness, but when it goes to Israel, it will be seen in its brilliancy.　　*i,* 18 : 26.　19 : 27.　20 : 9.　21 : 12.　32 : 1, 2. 33 : 33.　90 : 9.　107 : 34.　112 : 4.　133 : 8

shall be blessed both spiritually and temporally, and great shall be your reward. Amen.

SECTION 15.

Revelation given to John Whitmer, through Joseph, the Seer, in Fayette, Seneca County, New York, June, 1829.

1. Hearken, my servant John, and listen to the words of Jesus Christ, your Lord and your Redeemer,

2. For behold, I speak unto you with sharpness and with power, for mine arm is over all the earth,

3. And I will tell you that which no man knoweth save me and thee alone,

4. For many times you have desired of me to know that which would be of the most worth unto you.

5. Behold, blessed are you for this thing, and for speaking my words which I have given you according to my commandments.

6. And now, behold, I say unto you, that the thing which will be of the most worth unto you, will be to ᵃdeclare repentance unto this people, that you may bring souls unto me, that you may rest with them in the kingdom of my Father. Amen.

SECTION 16.

Revelation given to Peter Whitmer, jun., through Joseph, the Seer, in Fayette, New York, June, 1829.

1. Hearken my servant Peter, and listen to the words of Jesus Christ, your Lord and your Redeemer,

---

a, see h, Sec. 3.

2. For behold, I speak unto you with sharpness and with power, for mine arm is over all the earth,

3. And I will tell you that which no man knoweth save me and thee alone,

4. For many times you have desired of me to know that which would be of the most worth unto you.

5. Behold, blessed are you for this thing, and for speaking my words which I have given unto you according to my commandments.

6. And now, behold, I say unto you, that the thing which will be of the most worth unto you, will be to *a*declare repentance unto this people, that you may bring souls unto me, that you may rest with them in the kingdom of my Father. Amen.

SECTION 17.

Revelation given through Joseph, the Seer, to Oliver Cowdery, David Whitmer, and Martin Harris, in Fayette, Seneca County, New York, June, 1829, given previous to their viewing the plates containing the Book of Mormon.

1. Behold, I say unto you, that you must rely upon my word, which if you do, with full purpose of heart, you shall have a *a*view of the plates, and also of the *b*breastplate, the *c*sword of Laban, the *d*Urim and Thummim, which were given to the brother of Jared upon the mount, when he talked with the Lord face to face, and the *e*miraculous directors which were given to Lehi while in the wilderness, on the borders of the Red Sea;

---

a, see h, Sec. 3.

---

a, 5 : 15. Testimony of Three Witnesses, Book of Mormon. II. Nep. 11. Ether 5 : 4.   *b,* a sacred plate, having a divine relationship to the Urim and Thummim.   *c,* I. Nep. 4 : 9. 5 : 14. Jacob 1 : 10. Mos. 1 : 16.   *d,* 10 : 1. 17 : 1. 130 : 3, 9. Omni 1 : 20—22. Mos. 8 : 13—19. 21 : 27, 28. 28 : 11—19. Alma 10 : 2. 37 : 21—26. Ether 3 : 23, 28. 4 : 5. *e,* I. Nep. 16 : 10, 16, 26—30. 18 : 12, 21. II. Nep. 5 : 12. Alma 37 : 38—47.

2. And it is by your faith that you shall obtain a view of them, even by that faith which was had by the prophets of old.

3. And after that you have obtained faith, and have seen them with your eyes, you shall testify of them, by the power of God;

4. And this you shall do that my servant Joseph Smith, jun., may not be destroyed, that I may bring about my righteous purposes unto the children of men in this work.

5. And ye shall testify that you have seen them, even as my servant Joseph Smith, jun., has seen them, for it is by my power that he has seen them, and it is because he had faith;

6. And he *f*has translated the book, even that part which I have commanded him, and as your Lord and your God liveth it is true.

7. Wherefore you have received the same power, and the same faith, and the same gift like unto him ;

8. And if you do these last commandments of mine, which I have given you, *g*the gates of hell shall not prevail against you ; for my grace is sufficient for you, and you shall be *h*lifted up at the last day.

9. And I, Jesus Christ, your Lord and your God, have spoken it unto you, that I might bring about my righteous purposes unto the children of men.   Amen.

SECTION 18.

Revelation to Joseph Smith, jun., Oliver Cowdery, and David Whitmer, making known the calling of Twelve Apostles in these last days ; and, also, instructions relative to Building up the Church of Christ, according to the fullness of the gospel. Given in Fayette, New York, June, 1829.

1. Now, behold, because of the thing which you,

f, see *l*, Sec. 1.   *g*, see *l*, Sec. 10.   *h*, see *u*, Sec. 5.

my servant Oliver Cowdery, have desired to know of me, I give unto you these words :

2. Behold, I have manifested unto you, by my Spirit in many instances, that the things which you have written are true ; wherefore you know that they are true ;

3. And if you know that they are true, behold, I give unto you a commandment, that you rely upon the things which are written ;

4. For in them are all things written concerning the foundation of *a*my church, my *b*gospel, and my rock ;

5. Wherefore, if you shall build up my church, upon the foundation of my gospel and my rock, the *c*gates of hell shall not prevail against you.

6. Behold, the world is ripening in iniquity, and it must needs be that the children of men are stirred up unto repentance, both the Gentiles and also the house of Israel :

7. Wherefore, as thou hast been *d*baptized by the hands of my servant Joseph Smith, jun., according to that which I have commanded him, he hath fulfilled the thing which I commanded him.

8. And now marvel not that I have called him unto mine own purpose, which purpose is known in me ; wherefore, if he shall be diligent in keeping my commandments, he shall be blessed unto eternal life, and his name is Joseph.

9. And now, Oliver Cowdery, I speak unto you, and also unto David Whitmer, by the way of commandment ; for, behold, I command all men everywhere to

---

a, see *a*, Sec. 1.   *b*, 18 : 4. 5, 17, 20, 28, 32.   19 : 27.   20 : 9.   24 : 12.   25 : 1.   27 : 5, 13, 16.   28 : 8, 16.   29 : 4.   30 : 5, 9.   32 : 1.   33 : 2, 12. 34 : 5.   35 : 12, 15, 17, 23.   36 : 1, 5.   37 : 2.   39 : 5, 6, 11, 18.   42 : 6, 11, 12, 39. 45 : 28.   49 : 1—4.   50 : 14, 17—27.   52 : 9, 10.   53 : 3, 4.   57 : 10.   58 : 46, 47, 63, 64.   60 : 13—15.   66 : 5—13.   68 : 8—12.   71 : 1—4.   76 : 14—70, 101. 77 : 8.   80 : 1—5.   81 : 2—7.   84 : 10, 26, 27, 60—120.   88 : 77—85, 90, 103, 104.   90 : 10, 11.   93 : 51.   99 : 1—8.   101 : 39.   106 : 2.   107 : 25, 35. 108 : 6.   109 : 65.   111 : 12—16.   112 : 19—21, 28—34.   118 : 3, 4.   124 : 2— 11, 88.   128 : 19.   133 : 36—39, 57.   134 : 12.   135 : 9.   *c*, see *b*, Sec. 10. *d*, as commanded of God, by the angel, John the Baptist.

repent, and I speak unto you, even as unto Paul mine apostle, for you are called even with that same calling with which he was called.

10. Remember the worth of souls is great in the sight of God;

11. For, behold, the Lord your Redeemer suffered death in the flesh; wherefore he suffered ·the *pain of all men, that all men might repent and come unto him.

12. And he hath risen again from the dead, that he might bring all men unto him, on conditions of ʄrepentance;

13. And how great is his joy in the soul that repenteth.

14. Wherefore, you are called to cry repentance unto this people;

15. And if it so be that you should labor all your days in crying repentance unto this people, and bring, save it be one soul unto me, how great shall be your joy with him in the kingdom of my Father?

16. And now, if your joy will be great with one soul that you have brought unto me into the kingdom of my Father, how great will be your joy if you should bring many souls unto me?

17. Behold, you have my ᵍgospel before you, and my rock, and my salvation.

18. ʰAsk the Father in my name, in faith believing that you shall receive, and you shall have the ⁱHoly Ghost, which manifesteth all things which are expedient unto the children of men.

19. And if you have not faith, hope, and charity, you can do nothing.

20. Contend against no church, save it be the ʲchurch of the devil.

e, 86: 41.   18: 11.   19: 18.   II. Nep. 9: 5, 7, 21.   Mos. 3: 7, 14.   15: 10.
Alma 7: 11—13.   11: 40.   22: 14.   34: 8—15.   Hela. 14: 15—17.   III. Nep.
9: 22.   11: 11, 14, 15.   27: 14, 15.   Mor. 9: 13, 14.   *f*, see *h*, Sec. 3.
g, see *b*, Sec. 18.   *h*, see *c*, Sec. 4.   *i*, see *m*, Sec. 5.   *j*, I Nep.
13: 5, 6, 26, 28, 32, 34.   14: 3, 9—17.

21. Take upon you the *kname of Christ, and speak the truth in soberness ;

22. And as many as *lrepent, and are *mbaptized in my name, which is Jesus Christ, and endure to the end, the same shall be saved.

23. Behold, Jesus Christ is the name which is given of the Father, and there is none other name given whereby man can be saved ;

24. Wherefore, all men must take upon them the name which is given of the Father, for in that name shall they be *ncalled at the last day ;

25. Wherefore, if they know not the name by which they are called, they cannot have place in the kingdom of my Father.

26. And now, behold, there are others who are called to declare my gospel, *oboth unto Gentile and unto Jew ;

27. Yea, even *pTwelve, and the Twelve shall be my disciples, and they shall take upon them my name ; and the Twelve are they who shall desire to take upon them my name with full purpose of heart ;

28. And if they desire to take upon them my name with full purpose of heart, they are called to *qgo into all the world to preach my gospel unto every creature ;

29. And they are they who are ordained of me to *rbaptize in my name, according to that which is written ;

30. And you have that which is written before you ; wherefore you must perform it according to the words which are written.

31. And now I speak unto you the Twelve—Behold, my grace is sufficient for you : you must walk uprightly before me and sin not.

k, Mos. 5 : 9—14.   26: 18, 24.   Alma 5: 38.   34 : 38.   III. Nep. 27 : 5—9.
Mor. 8 : 38.   *l*, see *h*, Sec. 3.   *m*, see *l*, Sec. 5.   *n*, see *k*,
Sec. 18.   *o*, 18 : 26.   19 : 27.   21 : 12.   107 : 33.   L Nep. 13 : 42.   Ether
13 : 12.   *p*, 18 : 31— 36.   20 : 38—44.   84 : 63, 64.   95 : 4.   107 : 23—25.
112 : 1, 14, 21.   118.   124 : 127—130.   *q*, 107 : 23, 24, 33, 35, 88, 39, 58.
112: 1, 14, 21.   118.   124 : 127—130.   *r*, see *l*, Sec. 5.

32. And, behold, you are they who are ordained of me to *ordain priests and teachers ; to declare my gospel, according to the power of the Holy Ghost which is in you, and according to the callings and gifts of God unto men ;

33. And I, Jesus Christ, your Lord and your God, have spoken it.

34. These words are not of men, nor of man, but of me ; wherefore, you shall testify they are of me, and not of man ;

35. For it is my voice which speaketh them unto you, for they are given by my Spirit unto you, and by my power you can read them one to another, and save it were by my power, you could not have them ;

36. Wherefore you can testify that you have heard my voice, and know my words.

37. And now, behold, I give unto you Oliver Cowdery, and also unto David Whitmer, that you shall search out the Twelve, who shall have the desires of which I have spoken ;

38. And by their desires and their works you shall know them ;

39. And when you have found them you shall show these things unto them.

40. And you shall fall down and worship the Father in my name ;

41. And you must preach unto the world, saying, you must 'repent and be "baptized, in the name of Jesus Christ ;

42. For all men must repent and be baptized, and not only men, but women, and children who have arrived to the °years of accountability.

43. And now, after that you have received this, you must keep my commandments in all things ;

44. And by your hands I will work a "marvelous

---

*s, 20 : 60. Moro. 3 : 1—4.   t, see h, Sec. 3.   u, see l, Sec. 5.
v, 29 : 47. 78 : 25—27.   w, see a, Sec. 4.

work among the children of men, unto the convincing
of many of their sins, that they may come unto repentance, and that they may come unto the kingdom
of my Father ;

45. Wherefore, the blessings which I give unto you
are *above all things.

46. And after that you have received this, if you
keep not my commandments you cannot be saved in
the kingdom of my Father.

47. Behold, I, Jesus Christ, your Lord and your
God, and your Redeemer, by the power of my Spirit
have spoken it.   Amen.

SECTION 19.

*A Commandment of God, and not of Man, revealed
through Joseph, the Seer, to Martin Harris, given
(Manchester, New York, March, 1830) by Him
who is eternal.*

1. I am Alpha and Omega, Christ the Lord ; yea,
even I am He, the beginning and the end, the Redeemer of the world.

2. I, having accomplished and finished the will of him
whose I am, even the Father, concerning me—having
done this that I might subdue all things unto myself—

3. Retaining *all power, even to the *b*destroying of
Satan and his works at the end of the world, and the
last great day of judgment, which I shall pass upon
the inhabitants thereof, judging every man according
to his works and the deeds which he hath done.

4. And surely every man must *repent or suffer, for
I, God, am *d*endless ;

---

x, fullness of Celestial glory.

a, 20 : 24. 49 : 6. 63 : 59.   b, 29 : 27—30, 44, 45.   i. John 3 : 8
c, see h, Sec. 3.   d, vers. 10, 12. Pearl of Great Price, p. 1.

5. Wherefore, I revoke not the judgments which I shall pass, but woes shall go forth, 'weeping, wailing and gnashing of teeth, yea, to those who are found on my left hand;

6. Nevertheless it is not written that there shall be no end to this torment, but it is written *f*endless torment.

7. Again, it is written *g*eternal damnation; wherefore it is more express than other scriptures, that it might work upon the hearts of the children of men, altogether for my name's glory;

8. Wherefore I will explain unto you this mystery, for it is mete unto you to know even as mine apostles.

9. I speak unto you that are chosen in this thing, even as one, that you may enter into my rest;

10. For, behold, the mystery of Godliness, how great is it? for, behold, I am endless, and the punishment which is given from my hand, is *h*endless punishment, for endless is my name: wherefore—

11. *i*Eternal punishment is God's punishment.

12. *j*Endless punishment is God's punishment.

13. Wherefore I command you to repent, and keep the commandments which you have received by the hand of my servant Joseph Smith, jun., in my name;

14. And it is by my almighty power that you have received them;

15. Therefore I command you to repent—repent, lest I smite you by the rod of my mouth, and by my wrath, and by my anger, and your sufferings be sore—how sore you know not! how exquisite you know not! yea, how hard to bear you know not!

16. For behold, I, God, *k*have suffered these things for all, that they might not suffer if they would repent,

---

e, 101 : 91. 112 : 24. 124 : 8. 134 : 37.   *f*, vers. 7, 10—12. 63 : 77. 76 : 33, 44, 45, 48. 78 : 12. 82 : 21. 104 : 9, 18.   *g*, vers. 10, 11. 29 : 44. 76 : 44.   *h*, vers. 11, 12.   29 : 44. 76 : 44.   *i*, ver. 10. Pearl of Great Price, p. 1.   *j*, ver. 10. Pearl of Great Price, p. 1.   *k*, see *e*, Sec. 18.

17. But if they would not repent, they must suffer even as I,

18. Which suffering caused myself, even God, the greatest of all, to tremble because of pain, and to *bleed at every pore, and to suffer both body and spirit: and would that I might not drink the bitter cup and shrink—

19. Nevertheless, glory be to the Father, and I partook and finished my preparations unto the children of men;

20. Wherefore, I command you again to repent, lest I humble you with my almighty power, and that you confess your sins, lest you suffer these punishments of which I have spoken, of which in the smallest, yea, even in the least degree you have tasted at the time I withdrew my spirit.

21. And I command you, that you preach nought but repentance, and show not these things unto the world until it is wisdom in me.

22. For they cannot ᵐbear meat now, but milk they must receive; wherefore, they must not know these things lest they perish.

23. Learn of me, and listen to my words; walk in the meekness of my Spirit, and you shall have peace in me.

24. I am Jesus Christ; I came by the will of the Father, and I do his will.

25. And again, I command thee that thou shalt not ⁿcovet thy neighbor's wife; nor seek thy neighbor's life.

26. And again, I command thee that thou shalt not covet thine own property, but impart it freely to the printing of the Book of Mormon, which contains the truth and the word of God,

27. Which is my ᵒword to the Gentile, that soon it may go to the Jew, of whom the Lamanites are a ᵖrem-

---

l, see *e*, Sec. 18.　　　*m*, 41: 6.　　　*n*, 42: 24, 80.　43: 16.　66: 10.
132 : 41, 63.　　　*o*, see *o*, Sec. 18.　　　*p*, Omni 1: 14—19.　Mos. 25:
2—4.　Alma 22: 30—32.　Hela. 6: 10.　8: 21.

nant, that they may believe the gospel, and look not for a Messiah to come who has already come.

28. And again, I command thee that thou shalt pray vocally as well as in thy heart; yea, before the world as well as in secret, in public as well as in private.

29. And thou shalt declare 9glad tidings, yea, publish it upon the mountains, and upon every high place, and among every people that thou shalt be permitted to see.

30. And thou shalt do it with all humility, trusting in me, reviling not against revilers.

31. And of tenets thou shalt not talk, but thou shalt declare 'repentance and faith on the Saviour, and 'remission of sins by baptism and by 'fire, yea, even the Holy Ghost.

32. Behold, this is a great and the last commandment which I shall give unto you concerning this matter; for this shall suffice for thy daily walk, even unto the end of thy life.

33. And misery thou shalt receive if thou wilt slight these counsels; yea, even the destruction of thyself and property.

34. Impart a portion of thy property; yea, even part of thy lands, and all save the support of thy family.

35. Pay the debt thou hast contracted with the printer. Release thyself from bondage.

36. Leave thy house and home, except when thou shalt desire to see thy family :

37. And speak freely to all : yea, preach, exhort, declare the truth, even with a loud voice, with a sound of rejoicing, crying—Hosanna, hosanna ! blessed be the name of the Lord God.

38. "Pray always, and I will pour out my Spirit upon you, and great shall be your blessing; yea, even more than if you should obtain treasures of earth and corruptibleness to the extent thereof.

---

39. Behold, canst thou read this without rejoicing and lifting up thy heart for gladness ?

40. Or canst thou run about longer as a blind guide?

41. Or canst thou be humble and meek, and conduct thyself wisely before me ? yea, come unto me thy Saviour. Amen.

SECTION 20.

Revelation on Church Government, given through Joseph the Prophet, in April, 1830.

1. The ^arise of the church of Christ in these last days, being ^bone thousand eight hundred and thirty years since the coming of our Lord and Saviour Jesus Christ in the flesh, it being regularly organized and established agreeable to the laws of our country, by the will and commandments of God, in the fourth month, and on the ^csixth day of the month which is called April ;

2. Which commandments were given to Joseph Smith, jun., who was called of God, and ordained an ^dapostle of Jesus Christ, to be the first elder of this church ;

3. And to Oliver Cowdery, who was also called of God, an ^eapostle of Jesus Christ, to be the second elder of this church, and ordained under his hand ;

4. And this according to the grace of our Lord and Saviour Jesus Christ, to whom be all glory, both now and for ever. Amen.

5. After it was truly manifested unto this first elder that he had received a remission of his sins, he was entangled again in the vanities of the world ;

---

a, see *a*, Sec. 1.   *b*, A.D. 1830. 21 : 3.   *c*, 21 : 3.
d, 1 : 14. 20 : 2, 3. 21 : 1, 10. 27 : 12. 29 : 10, 12. 52 : 36. 63 : 21, 52.
64 : 39. 66 : 2. 84 : 63, 64, 108. 95 : 4. 107 : 23, 33, 35. 112 : 12—16, 21,
30. 124 : 127—129, 139. 133 : 55. 136 : 37.   *e*, see *d*.

6. But after repenting, and humbling himself sincerely, through faith, God ministered unto him by an *f*holy angel, whose countenance was as lightning, and whose garments were pure and white above all other whiteness ;

7. And gave unto him commandments which inspired him ;

8. And gave him power from on high, by the *g*means which were before prepared, to translate the Book of Mormon,

9. Which contains a record of a fallen people, and the *h*fullness of the gospel of Jesus Christ to the Gentiles and to the Jews also,

10. Which was given by inspiration, and is confirmed to *i*others by the ministering of angels, and is declared unto the world by them,

11. Proving to the world that the Holy Scriptures are true, and that God does inspire men and call them to his holy work in this age and generation, as well as in generations of old,

12. Thereby showing that he is the *j*same God yesterday, to-day, and for ever. Amen.

13. Therefore, having so great witnesses, by them shall the world be judged, even as many as shall hereafter come to a knowledge of this work ;

14. And those who receive it in faith, and work righteousness, shall receive a crown of eternal life ;

15. But those who harden their hearts in unbelief, and reject it, it shall turn to their own condemnation,

16. For the Lord God has spoken it ; and we, the elders of the church, have *k*heard and bear witness to the words of the glorious Majesty on high, to whom be glory for ever and ever. Amen.

---

f, 20 : 6, 12, 35. 76 : 67. 77 : 8—11. 84 : 26, 28, 88. 86 : 5. 88 : 92, 94, 99, 103—112. 103 : 20. 110 : 11—13. 128 : 20. 130 : 5. 133 : 17, 36. *g*, see *d*, Sec. 17. *h*, see *b*, Sec. 18. *i*, see *f*, Sec. 5. *j*, ver. 17. 8 : 12. 35 : 1. 38 : 1—4. 39 : 1. 68 : 6. 76 : 4. *k*, 29 : 1. 128 : 21. 130 : 14.

17. By these things we [k]know that there is a God in heaven, who is infinite and eternal, from [m]everlasting to everlasting the same unchangeable God, the framer of heaven and earth, and all things which are in them ;

18. And that he created man, male and female, after his [n]own image and in his own likeness, created he them,

19. And gave unto them commandments that they should love and serve him, the only living and true God, and that he should be the only being whom they should worship.

20. But by the transgression of these holy laws, man became sensual and devilish, and became fallen man.

21. Wherefore the Almighty God gave his Only Begotten Son, as it is written in those scriptures which have been given of him.

22. He suffered temptations but gave no heed unto them ;

23. He was [o]crucified, died, and [p]rose again the third day ;

24. And ascended into heaven, to sit down on the right hand of the Father, to reign with almighty power according to the will of the Father,

25. That as many as would [q]believe and be [r]baptized in his holy name, and endure in faith to the end, should be saved :

26. Not only those who believed after he came in the [s]meridian of time, in the flesh, but all those from the beginning, even as many as were before he came, who believed in the words of the holy prophets, who spake as they were [t]inspired by the gift of the Holy Ghost, who truly testified of him in all things, should have eternal life,

l, 5 : 11—14, 25, 26.   76 : 22, 23.   88 : 49.   93 : 11—17.   110 : 2, 3.   121 : 28. 128 : 23.   133 : 3.   *m*, see *a*, Sec. 39.   Pearl of Great Price, pp. 17, 19. *n*, Pearl of Great Price, pp. 5, 6, 13, 34.   Ether 3 : 16.   *o*, 18 : 11.   21 : 9. 34 : 3.   35 : 2.   45 : 4, 52.   76 : 41.   *p*, 18 : 12.   45 : 52.   133 : 55. *q*, 19 : 23, 24, 31.   20 : 29.   34 : 34.   35 : 2.   38 : 4.   42 : 1.   45 : 5, 8.   49 : 5, 12.   76 : 51.   86 : 50—52, 74, 89.   112 : 19.   *r*, see *l*, Sec. 5. *s*, 39 : 3.   Pearl of Great Price, pp. 16, 20.   *t*, 21 : 2.   6 : 10—12.   8 : 2—4. 11 : 10—21.   18 : 33—35.   20 : 10, 11, 26.   21 : 2.   24 : 5.   111 : 8.   124 : 4, 5.

27. As well as those who should come after, who should believe in the ^ugifts and callings of God by the Holy Ghost, which ^vbeareth record of the Father, and of the Son ;

28. Which Father, Son, and Holy Ghost are ^wone God, ^xinfinite and eternal, without end. Amen.

29. And we ^yknow that all men must repent and believe on the name of Jesus Christ, and worship the Father in his name, and endure in faith on his name to the end, or they cannot be saved in the kingdom of God.

30. And we ^zknow that justification through the grace of our Lord and Saviour Jesus Christ, is just and true ;

31. And we ^{2a}know also, that sanctification through the grace of our Lord and Saviour Jesus Christ, is just and true to all those who love and serve God with all their mights, minds, and strength.

32. But there is a possibility that man may ^{2b}fall from grace and depart from the living God ;

33. Therefore let the church take heed and pray always, lest they fall into temptation ;

34. Yea, and even let those who are sanctified take heed also.

35. And we ^{2c}know that these things are true and according to the revelations of John, neither ^{2d}adding to, nor diminishing from the prophecy of his book, the Holy Scriptures, or the revelations of God, which shall come hereafter by the gift and power of the Holy Ghost, the voice of God, or the ministering of angels.

36. And the Lord God has spoken it ; and honor, power, and glory, be rendered to his holy name, both now and ever. Amen.

37. *And again, by way of* ^{2e}*commandment to the*

u, 5 : 31. 6 : 10—13, 27, 28. 8 : 4—8. 10 : 2, 18. 11 : 10. 14 : 7. 18 : 32. 20 : 27, 60. 136 : 37.   *v*, 1 : 39. 42 : 17. 76 : 23, 26.   *w*, Alma 11 : 44. III. Nep. 11 : 27, 28, 36. 28 : 10. Mor. 7 : 7.   *x*, 20 : 12, 17. 29 : 1, 33. 88 : 1. 39 : 1. 45 : 7. 76 : 4. 121 : 32.   *y*, see *l*. *z*, see *l*.   2*a*, see *l*.   2*b*, 85 : 2, 11. 130 : 23.   2*c*, see *l*. 2*d*, 68 : 34. 93 : 24, 25. 124 : 120.   2*e*, 15 : 6. 16 : 6. 18 : 27. 20 : 37, 72. 88 : 11. 49 : 12, 13. 76 : 51, 52. 84 : 76.

church concerning the manner of baptism.—All those who humble themselves before God, and desire to be baptized and come forth with broken hearts and contrite spirits, and witness before the church that they have truly repented of all their sins, and are willing to take upon them the name of Jesus Christ, having a determination to serve him to the end, and truly manifest by their works that they have received of the Spirit of Christ unto the remission of their sins, shall be received by baptism into his church.

38. *The duty of the elders, priests, teachers, deacons, and members of the church of Christ.*—An [2f]apostle is an elder, and it is his calling to [2g]baptize.

39. And to [2h]ordain other elders, priests, teachers, and deacons,

40. And to administer [2i]bread and wine—the emblems of the flesh and blood of Christ—

41. And to [2j]confirm those who are baptized into the church, by the laying on of hands for the baptism of fire and the Holy Ghost, according to the scriptures;

42. And to teach, expound, exhort, baptize, and watch over the church;

43. And to confirm the church by the laying on of the hands, and the giving of the Holy Ghost,

44. And to take the lead of all meetings.

45. The elders are to conduct the meetings as they are [2k]led by the Holy Ghost, according to the commandments and revelations of God.

46. The priest's [2l]duty is to preach, teach, expound, exhort, and baptize, and administer the sacrament,

47. And visit the house of each member, and exhort them to pray vocally and in secret, and attend to all family duties;

2 *f*, vers. 2, 3, 5, 16, 38.   21: 1, 11, 12.   105: 27.   2 *g*, 18: 29.
2 *h*, 18: 32.   2 *i*, vers. 68, 69, 75—79. 27: 2—5.   2 *j*, ver. 43.
33: 11. 34: 15. 35: 6. 39: 6, 23. 52: 10. 53: 3. 55: 1—3. 68: 25.
2 *k*, 46: 2. i. Nep. 13: 37. Moro. 6: 9.   2 *l*, vers. 46—52. 84: 111.
107: 20, 61.

48. And he may also [2m]ordain other priests, teachers, and deacons.

·49. And he is to take the lead of meetings when there is no elder present ;

50. But when there is an elder present, he is only to preach, teach, expound, exhort, and baptize,

51. And visit the house of each member, exhorting them to pray vocally and in secret, and attend to all family duties.

52. In all these duties the priest is to [2n]assist the elder if occasion requires.

53. The teacher's duty is to [2o]watch over the church always, and be with and strengthen them,

54. And see that there is no iniquity in the church —neither hardness with each other—neither lying, backbiting, nor evil speaking ;

55. And see that the church meet together often, and also see that all the members do their duty ;

56. And he is to take the lead of meetings in the absence of the elder or priest—

57. And is to be [2p]assisted always, in all his duties in the church, by the deacons, if occasion requires ;

58. But neither teachers nor deacons have authority to baptize, administer the sacrament, or lay on hands :

59. They are, however, to warn, expound, exhort, and teach and invite all to come unto Christ.

60. Every elder, priest, teacher, or deacon, is to be [2q]ordained according to the gifts and callings of God unto him ; and he is to be ordained by the [2r]power of the Holy Ghost, which is in the one who ordains him.

61. The several elders, composing this church of Christ are to meet in [2s]conference once in three months, or from time to time as said conferences shall direct or appoint ;

---

2 m, he cannot ordain to an office higher than that of a Priest.   2 n, 107:
5, 14.   2 o, 84 : 111.   2 p, 84 : 111.   2 q, 18 : 32.   Moro.
2 : 1—4.   2 r, 18 : 32.   Moro. 2 : 1—4.   2 s, ver. 62.

62. And said conferences are to do whatever church business is necessary to be done at the time.

63. The elders are to receive their [2t]licenses from other elders, by [2u]vote of the church to which they belong, or from the conferences.

64. Each priest, teacher, or deacon, who is ordained by a priest may take a certificate from him at the time, which certificate when presented to an elder, shall entitle him to a [2v]license, which shall authorize him to perform the duties of his calling, or he may receive it from a conference.

*65. No person is to be ordained to any office in this church, where there is a regularly organized branch of the same, without the [2w]vote of that church;

66. But the presiding elders, traveling bishops, High Counselors, High Priests, and elders, may have the privilege of ordaining, where there is no branch of the church that a [2x]vote may be called.

67. Every President of the High Priesthood (or presiding elder), bishop, High Counselor, and High Priest, is to be ordained by the [2y]direction of a High Council or general conference.

68. *The duty of the members after they are received by baptism.*—The elders or priests are to have a sufficient time to expound all things concerning the church of Christ to their understanding, [2z]previous to their partaking of the sacrament and being confirmed by the laying on of the hands of the elders, so that all things may be done in order.

69. And the members shall manifest before the church, and also before the elders, by a Godly walk and conversation, that they are worthy of it, that there may be works and faith agreeable to the Holy Scriptures—walking in holiness before the Lord.

---

2 t, ver. 64.   2 u, vers. 65, 66.   26 : 2.   104 : 64, 71, 72, 76.
2 v, ver. 63.   2 w, see 2 u, Sec. 20.   2 x, see 2 u, Sec. 20.   2 y, 68 :
15—21. 162: 1—3. 107: 22, 91, 92. 118 : 1.   2 z, ver. 69. 46: 4—6. 69:12.

* Verses 65, 66, and 67 were added sometime after the others.

70. Every member of the church of Christ [3a]having children, is to bring them unto the elders before the church, who are to lay their hands upon them in the name of Jesus Christ, and bless them in his name.

71. No one can be received into the church of Christ, unless he has arrived unto the [3b]years of accountability before God, and is capable of repentance.

72. [3c]Baptism is to be administered in the following manner unto all those who repent :—

73. The person who is called of God, and has authority from Jesus Christ to baptize, shall go down into the water with the person who has presented him or herself for baptism, and shall say, calling him or her by name—Having been commissioned of Jesus Christ, I baptize you in the name of the Father, and of the Son, and of the Holy Ghost. Amen.

74. Then shall he immerse him or her in the water, and come forth again out of the water.

75. It is expedient that the church [3d]meet together often to partake of bread and wine in the remembrance of the Lord Jesus ;

76. And the elder or priest shall administer it ; and after this [3e]manner shall he administer it—he shall kneel with the church and call upon the Father in solemn prayer, saying—

77. O God, the eternal Father, we ask thee in the name of thy Son, Jesus Christ, to bless and sanctify this bread to the souls of all those who partake of it, that they may eat in remembrance of the body of thy Son, and witness unto thee, O God, the eternal Father, that they are willing to take upon them the name of thy Son, and always remember him and keep his commandments which he has given them, that they may always have his Spirit to be with them. Amen.

3a, Mat. 19: 13—15.   Mark 10: 13—16.   III. Nep. 17: 12—24.   26: 14, 16.
3b, see y, Sec. 68.   3c, 5: 16.   20: 73, 74.   76: 51.   128: 12, 13.
3d, III. Nep. 48: 1—14, 28—30.   III. Nep. 20: 8.   Mor. 9: 29.   Moro. 6: 6.
3e, Moro. 4: 1—3.

78. The [3f]manner of administering the wine. He shall take the cup also, and say—

79. O God, the eternal Father, we ask thee in the name of thy Son, Jesus Christ, to bless and sanctify this wine to the souls of all those who drink of it, that they may do it in remembrance of the blood of thy Son, which was shed for them ; that they may witness unto thee, O God, the eternal Father, that they do always remember him, that they may have his Spirit to be with them. Amen.

80. Any member of the church of Christ [3g]transgressing, or being overtaken in a fault, shall be dealt with as the scriptures direct.

81. It shall be the duty of the several churches composing the church of Christ, to send [3h]one or more of their teachers to attend the several conferences held by the elders of the church,

82. With a [3i]list of the names of the several members uniting themselves with the church since the last conference, or send by the hand of some priest, so that a regular list of all the names of the whole church may be kept in a book by one of the elders, whoever the other elders shall appoint from time to time ;

83. And also if any have been expelled from the church, so that their names may be [3j]blotted out of the general church record of names.

84. All members removing from the church where they reside, if going to a church where they are not known, may [3k]take a letter, certifying that they are regular members and in good standing, which certificate may be signed by any elder or priest, if the member receiving the letter is personally acquainted with the elder or priest, or it may be signed by the teachers or deacons of the church.

---

3 f, Moro. 5 : 1, 2.   3 g, 42 : 80, 81.   Mos. 26 : 29—32.   3 h, vers.
61, 62.   3 i, 85 : 3—5.   3 j, 85 : 3—5, 11, 12.   3 k, 72 : 17,
18, 19, 25, 26.

SECTION 21.

Revelation to Joseph Smith, jun., given at Fayette, New York, April 6, 1830.

1. Behold there shall be a *a*record kept among you, and in it thou shalt be called a seer, a translator, a prophet, an apostle of Jesus Christ, an elder of the church through the will of God the Father, and the grace of your Lord Jesus Christ,

2. Being *b*inspired of the Holy Ghost to lay the foundation thereof, and to build it up unto the most holy faith,

3. Which church was organized and established in the year of your Lord *c*eighteen hundred and thirty, in the fourth month, and on the sixth day of the month, which is called April.

4. Wherefore, meaning the church, thou shalt give heed unto all his words and commandments which he shall give unto you as he receiveth them, walking in all holiness before me ;

5. For his word ye shall receive, as if from mine own mouth, in all patience and faith ;

6. For by doing these things the *d*gates of hell shall not prevail against you ; yea, and the Lord God will disperse the powers of darkness from before you, and cause the heavens *e*to shake for your good, and his name's glory.

7. For thus saith the Lord God, him have I inspired to move the cause of *f*Zion in mighty power for good, and his diligence I know, and his prayers I have heard.

8. Yea his weeping for *g*Zion I have seen, and I will cause that he shall mourn for her no longer, for his days

---

a, 47 : 1, 3, 4. 60 : 3—8. 85.   *b*, ver. 7. 20 : 26.   *c*, A.D.
1830. 20 : 1.   *d*, see *l*, Sec. 10.   *e*, 21 : 6. 29 : 23, 24.   43 : 18.
45 : 22, 48.   49 : 22.   183 : 49, 60.   *f*, see *e*, Sec. 6.   *g*, see
Sec. 6

of rejoicing are come unto the remission of his sins, and the manifestations of my blessings upon his works.

9. For, behold, I will bless all those who labor in my vineyard with a mighty blessing, and they shall believe on his words, which are given him through me by the Comforter, which manifesteth that Jesus was crucified by sinful men for the sins of the world, yea, for the remission of sins unto the contrite heart.

10. Wherefore it behoveth me that he should be [h]ordained by you, Oliver Cowdery, mine apostle ;

11. This being an ordinance unto you, that you are an elder under his hand, he being the first unto you, that you might be an elder unto this church of Christ, bearing my name,

12. And the [i]first preacher of this church unto the church, and before the world, yea, before the [j]Gentiles; yea, and thus saith the Lord God, lo, lo ! to the [k]Jews also. Amen.

SECTION 22.

Revelation to the Church of Christ, which was established in these last days, in the year of our Lord one thousand eight hundred and thirty, given through Joseph, the Seer, in Manchester, New York, April, 1830, in consequence of some desiring to unite with the Church without re-baptism, who had previously been baptized.

1. Behold, I say unto you, that all [a]old covenants have I caused to be done away in this thing, and this is a [b]new and an everlasting covenant, even that which was from the beginning.

h, see d, Sec. 5.   i, vers. 10, 11.   28 : 8.   j, ver. 11.
k, 28 : 8.
      a, Isa. 24: 5, 6.   III. Nep. 12: 46, 47.   III. Nep. 9: 17.   b, see k, Sec. 1.

2. Wherefore, although a man should be baptized an hundred times, it availeth him nothing, for you cannot enter in at the straight gate by the law of Moses, neither by your dead works ;

3. For it is because of your dead works, that I have caused this ᶜlast covenant and this ᵈchurch to be built up unto me, even as in days of old.

4. Wherefore, enter ye in at the ᵉgate, as I have commanded, and seek not to counsel your God. Amen.

SECTION 23.

Revelation to Oliver Cowdery, Hyrum Smith, Samuel H. Smith, Joseph Smith, sen., and Joseph Knight, sen., given through Joseph, the Seer, in Manchester, New York, April, 1830.

1. Behold, I speak unto you, Oliver, a few words. Behold, thou art blessed, and art under no condemnation. But beware of pride, lest thou shouldst enter into temptation.

2. Make known thy calling unto the church, and also before the world, and thy heart shall be opened to preach the truth from henceforth and forever. Amen.

3. Behold, I speak unto you, Hyrum, a few words : for thou also art under no condemnation, and thy heart is opened, and thy ᵃtongue loosed ; and thy calling is to exhortation, and to strengthen the church continually. Wherefore thy duty is unto the church for ever, and this because of thy family. Amen.

4. Behold, I speak a few words unto you, Samuel,

c see *k*, Sec. 1.   *d*, see *q*. Sec. 1.   *e*, II. Nep. 9 : 41. 31 : 9, 17, 18. 33 : 9. Alma 37 : 44, 45. Hela. 3 : 29, 30. III. Nep. 14 : 13, 14.

a, III. Nep. 26 : 14, 16.

for thou also art under no condemnation, and thy calling is to exhortation, and to strengthen the church,
and thou art not as yet called to preach before the world.
Amen.

5. Behold, I speak a few words unto you, Joseph,
for thou also art under no condemnation, and thy calling also is to exhortation, and to strengthen the church,
and this is thy duty from henceforth and forever.
Amen.

6. Behold, I manifest unto you, Joseph Knight, by
these words, that you must take up your cross, in the
which you must *b*pray vocally before the world as well
as in secret, and in your family, and among your friends,
and in all places.

7. And, behold, it is your duty to unite with the
true church, and give your language to exhortation
continually, that you may receive the reward of the
laborer. Amen.

SECTION 24.

*Revelation given to Joseph Smith, jun., and Oliver Cow-
dery, in Harmony, Susquehanna Co., Pennsylvania,
July,* 1830.

1. Behold, thou wast called and chosen to write the
Book of Mormon, and to my ministry; and I have
lifted thee up out of thy afflictions, and have counseled
thee, that thou hast been delivered from all thine
enemies, and thou hast been delivered from the powers
of Satan and from darkness!

2. Nevertheless thou art not excusable in thy transgressions; nevertheless, go thy way and sin no more.

3. Magnify thine office; and after thou hast sowed

b, Alma 33: 3—11.

thy fields and secured them, go speedily unto the church which is in Colesville, Fayette and Manchester, and they shall support thee ; and I will bless them both spiritually and temporally ;

4. But if they receive thee not, I will send upon them a *a*cursing instead of a blessing.

5. And thou shalt continue in calling upon God in my name, and *b*writing the things which shall be given thee by the Comforter, and expounding all scriptures unto the church ;

6. And it shall be given thee in the very moment what thou shalt speak and write, and they shall hear it, or I will send unto them a *c*cursing instead of a blessing.

7. For thou shalt devote all thy service in *d*Zion ; and in this thou shalt have strength.

8. Be patient in afflictions, for thou shalt have *e*many ; but endure them, for, lo, I am with thee, even unto the end of thy days.

9. And in temporal labors thou shalt not have strength, for this is not thy calling. Attend to thy calling and thou shalt have wherewith to magnify thine office, and to expound all scriptures, and continue in *f*laying on of the hands and confirming the churches.

10. And thy brother Oliver shall continue in bearing my name before the world, and also to the church. And he shall not suppose that he can say enough in my cause ; and lo, I am with him to the end.

11. In me he shall have glory, and not of himself, whether in weakness or in strength, whether in bonds or free,

12. And at all times, and in all places, he shall open his mouth and declare my *g*gospel as with the voice of a trump, both day and night. And I will give unto him strength such as is not known among men.

---

13. [h]Require not miracles, except I shall command you, except casting out devils, healing the sick, and against poisonous serpents, and against deadly poisons;

14. And these things ye shall not do, except it be required of you by them who desire it, that the scriptures might be fulfilled; for ye shall do according to that which is written.

15. And in whatsoever place ye shall enter, and they receive you not in my name, ye shall leave a cursing instead of a blessing, by [i]casting off the dust of your feet against them as a testimony, and cleansing your feet by the wayside.

16. And it shall come to pass, that whosoever shall lay their hands upon you by violence, ye shall command to be smitten in my name : and, behold, I will smite them according to your words, in mine own due time.

17. And whosoever shall go to law with thee shall be cursed by the law.

18. And thou shalt take no [j]purse nor scrip, neither staves, neither two coats, for the church shall give unto thee in the very hour what thou needest for food and for raiment, and for shoes and for money, and for scrip;

19. For thou art called to [k]prune my vineyard with a mighty pruning, yea, even for the last time. Yea, and also all those whom thou hast [l]ordained, and they shall do even according to this pattern. Amen.

SECTION 25.

Revelation given through Joseph, the Seer, in Harmony, Susquehanna Co., Pennsylvania, July, 1830.

1. Hearken unto the voice of the Lord your God,

---

h, Great miracles to be wrought only by command.   i, see a.
j, 60 : 15.   75 : 18—22.   84 : 78—80.   k, 31 : 45.   33 : 3, 4.   39 : 17.
43 : 23.   6 : 3, 4.   11 : 3.   21 : 9.   Jacob 5 : 61—74.   l, Sec. 24, as a pattern.

while I speak unto you, Emma Smith, my daughter, for verily I say unto you, all those who receive my gospel are ^asons and daughters in my kingdom.

2. A revelation I give unto you concerning my will, and if thou art faithful and walk in the paths of virtue before me, I will preserve thy life, and thou shalt receive an inheritance in ^bZion.

3. Behold, thy sins are forgiven thee, and thou art an elect lady, whom I have called.

4. Murmur not because of the things which thou hast not seen, for they are withheld from thee and from the world, which is wisdom in me in a time to come.

5. And the office of thy calling shall be for a comfort unto my servant, Joseph Smith, jun., thy husband, in his afflictions with consoling words, in the spirit of meekness.

6. And thou shalt go with him at the time of his going, and be unto him for a scribe, while there is no one to be a scribe for him, that I may send my servant, Oliver Cowdery, whithersoever I will.

7. And thou shalt be ordained under his hand to expound scriptures, and to exhort the church, according as it shall be given thee by my Spirit :

8. For he shall lay his hands upon thee, and thou shalt receive the Holy Ghost, and thy time shall be given to writing, and to learning much.

9. And thou needest not fear, for thy husband shall support thee in the church ; for unto them is his calling, that all things might be revealed unto them, whatsoever I will, according to their faith.

10. And verily I say unto thee, that thou shalt lay aside the things of this world, and seek for the things of a better.

11. And it shall be given thee, also, to make a ^cselec-

---

a, 11 : 30. 34 : 3. 35 : 2. 39 : 4. 42 : 52. 45 : 8. 50 : 41. 58 : 17.
76 : 24, 58. 121 : 7.   b, 38 : 19. 45 : 65. 52 : 2, 5, 42. 55 : 5. 57 :
5, 7, 8, 15. 58 : 17, 28, 36, 38, 40, 44, 51, 53. 63 : 29, 31, 48, 49. 64 : 30. 70 :
16. 72 : 17. 85 : 1—3, 7, 9, 11. 99 : 7. 101 : 1, 6, 18. 103 : 11, 14.
c, 1. Cor. 14 : 26. Eph. 5 : 19. Colos. 3 : 16.

tion of sacred hymns, as it shall be given thee, which is pleasing unto me, to be had in my church ;

12. For my soul delighteth in the song of the heart, yea, the *d*song of the righteous is a prayer unto me, and it shall be answered with a blessing upon their heads.

13. Wherefore lift up thy heart and rejoice, and cleave unto the covenants which thou hast made.

14. Continue in the spirit of meekness, and beware of pride. Let thy soul delight in thy husband, and the glory which shall come upon him.

15. Keep my commandments continually, and a crown of righteousness thou shalt receive. And except thou do this, where I am you cannot come.

16. And verily, verily I say unto you, that this is my voice unto all. Amen.

SECTION 26.

Revelation to Joseph Smith, jun., Oliver Cowdery, and John Whitmer, given in Harmony, Pennsylvania, July, 1830.

1. Behold, I say unto you, that you shall let your time be devoted to the studying of the scriptures, and to preaching, and to confirming the church at Colesville, and to performing your labors on the land, such as is required, until after you shall go to the west to hold the next conference ; and then it shall be made known what you shall do.

2. And all things shall be done by *a*common consent in the church, by much prayer and faith, for all things you shall receive by faith. Amen.

d, see c

a, see 2 u, Sec. 20.

SECTION 27.

The first four verses of the following Revelation, were given through Joseph, the Seer, in Harmony, Penn., August, 1830, and the remainder in Fayette, New York, September, 1830.

1. Listen to the voice of Jesus Christ, your Lord, your God, and your Redeemer, whose word is *a*quick and powerful.

2. For, behold, I say unto you, that it *b*mattereth not what ye shall eat, or what ye shall drink, when ye partake of the sacrament, if it so be that ye do it with an eye single to my glory; remembering unto the Father my body which was laid down for you, and my blood which was shed for the remission of your sins :

3. Wherefore, a commandment I give unto you, that you *c*shall not purchase wine, neither strong drink of your enemies :

4. Wherefore, you shall partake of none, except it is made new among you ; yea, in this my Father's kingdom which shall be built up on the earth.

5. Behold, this is wisdom in me : wherefore, marvel not, for the hour cometh that I will *d*drink of the fruit of the vine with you on the earth, and with Moroni, whom I have sent unto you to reveal the Book of Mormon, containing the *e*fullness of my everlasting gospel, to whom I have committed the keys of the record of the *f*stick of Ephraim ;

6. And also with *g*Elias, to whom I have committed the keys of bringing to pass the restoration of all things, spoken by the mouth of all the holy prophets since the world began, concerning the last days :

---

a, 6 : 2.   11 : 2.   12 : 2.   14 : 2.   15 : 2.   16 : 2.   *b*, vers. 3, 4, 5.
89 : 5, 6.   *c*, 89 : 4, 5.   *d*, vers. 6—14.   Mat. 26 : 29.   Mark 14 :
25.   Luke 22 : 18.   *e*, see *b*, Sec. 18.   *f*, Mor. 8 : 14.   Moro.
10 : 2.   *g*, ver. 7.   76 : 100.   77 : 9, 14.   110 : 12.

7. And also [h]John the son of Zacharias, which Zacharias he (Elias) visited and gave promise that he should have a son, and his name should be John, and he should be filled with the spirit of Elias ;

8. Which John I have sent unto you, my servants, Joseph Smith, jun., and Oliver Cowdery, to ordain you unto this [i]first priesthood which you have received, that you might be called and ordained even as Aaron :

9. And also [j]Elijah, unto whom I have committed the keys of the power of turning the hearts of the fathers to the children, and the hearts of the children to the fathers, that the whole earth may not be smitten with a curse :

10. And also with Joseph and Jacob, and Isaac, and Abraham, your fathers, by whom the promises remain ;

11. And also with [k]Michael, or Adam, the father of all, the prince of all, the ancient of days.

12. And also with Peter, and James, and John, [l]whom I have sent unto you, by whom I have ordained you and confirmed you to be apostles, and especial witnesses of my name, and bear the keys of your ministry, and of the same things which I revealed unto them :

13. Unto whom I have committed the keys of my kingdom, and a dispensation of the gospel for the [m]last times ; and for the [n]fullness of times, in the which I will gather together in [o]one all things, both which are in heaven, and which are on earth :

14. And also with all those whom my Father hath given me out of the world :

15. Wherefore, lift up your hearts and rejoice, and gird up your loins, and take upon you my whole armor, that ye may be able to withstand the evil day, having done all ye may be able to stand.

16. Stand, therefore, having your loins girt about

h, Sec. 13.   27 : 8.   i, see Sec. 2.   j, see Sec. 2.   k, 20 :
20, 36, 40, 42.   78 : 16.   84 : 16.   88 : 112—115.   107 : 54—56.   116 : 1.   128 :
18, 20, 21.   l, see d, Sec. 5.   m, 64 : 80, 87.   77 : 15.   n, 76 :
100.   77 : 12.   110 : 14.   112 : 30.   124 : 41.   o, 29 : 11.   84 : 100.

with truth, having on the breastplate of righteousness, and your feet shod with the preparation of the gospel of peace, which I have *p*sent mine angels to commit unto you,

17. Taking the shield of faith wherewith ye shall be able to quench all the fiery darts of the wicked ;

18. And take the helmet of salvation, and the sword of my Spirit, which I will pour out upon you, and my word which I reveal unto you, and be agreed as touching all things whatsoever ye ask of me, and be faithful until I come, and ye shall be caught up, that where I am ye shall be also. Amen.

SECTION 28.

Revelation given through Joseph, the Seer, to Oliver Cowdery, in Fayette, New York, September, 1830.

1. Behold, I say unto thee, Oliver, that it shall be given unto thee, that thou shalt be heard by the church in all things whatsoever thou shalt teach them by the Comforter, concerning the revelations and commandments which I have given.

2. But, behold, verily, verily, I say unto thee, *a*no one shall be appointed to receive commandments and revelations in this church, excepting my servant Joseph Smith, jun., for he receiveth them even as Moses ;

3. And thou shall be obedient unto the things which I shall give unto him, even as Aaron, to declare faithfully the commandments and the revelations, with power and authority unto the church.

4. And if thou art led at any time by the Com-

---

n, vers. 5—14.   128 : 19—21.   Testimony of Three Witnesses, Book of Mormon.

a, vers. 12, 13.   43 : 3—6

forter, to speak or teach, or at all times by the way of commandment unto the church, thou mayest do it.

5. But thou shalt not write by way of commandment, but by wisdom :

6. And thou shalt not command him who is at thy head, and at the head of the church,

7. *b*For I have given him the keys of the mysteries, and the revelations which are sealed, until I shall appoint unto them another in his stead.

8. And now, behold, I say unto you, that you shall go unto the Lamanites and preach my gospel unto them ; and inasmuch as they receive thy teachings, thou shalt cause *c*my church to be established among them, and thou shalt have revelations, but write them not by way of commandment.

9. And now, behold, I say unto you, that it is not revealed, and no man knoweth where *d*the city shall be built, but it shall be given hereafter. Behold, I say unto you, that it shall be on the borders by the Lamanites.

10. Thou shalt not leave this place until after the conference, and my servant Joseph shall be appointed to preside over the conference by the voice of it, and what he saith to thee thou shalt tell.

11. And again, thou shalt take thy brother, Hiram Page, between him and thee alone, and tell him that those things which he hath *e*written from that stone, are not of me, and that Satan deceiveth him ;

12. For, behold, these things have not been appointed unto him, neither shall anything be appointed unto any of this church contrary to the church covenants.

13. For all things must be done in order, and by *f*common consent in the church, by the prayer of faith.

---

b, 35 : 18.   42 : 65.   43 : 4.   64 : 5.   76 : 114.   90 : 2—8.   107 : 18, 19. 112 : 15.   *c*, see *a*, Sec. 1.   *d*, see *q*, Sec. 42.   *e*, Satan's deception detected.   *f*, see 2*u*, Sec. 20.

14. And thou shalt assist to settle all these things according to the covenants of the church before thou shalt take thy journey among the Lamanites.

15. And it shall be given thee from the time thou shalt go, until the time thou shalt return, what thou shalt do.

16. And thou must open thy mouth at all times, declaring my gospel with the sound of rejoicing. Amen.

SECTION 29.

Revelation given through Joseph, the Seer, in the presence of six Elders, in Fayette, New York, September, 1830.

1. Listen to the voice of Jesus Christ, your Redeemer, the Great I AM, whose arm of mercy hath atoned for your sins;

2. Who will ᵃgather his people even as a hen gathereth her chickens under her wings, even as many as will hearken to my voice and humble themselves before me, and call upon me in mighty prayer.

3. Behold, verily, verily, I say unto you, that at this time your sins are forgiven you, therefore ye receive these things; but remember to sin no more, lest perils shall come upon you.

4. Verily, I say unto you, that ye are chosen out of the world to declare my gospel with the sound of rejoicing, as with the ᵇvoice of a trump:

5. Lift up your hearts and be glad, for I am in your midst, and am your advocate with the Father; and it is his good will to give you the kingdom;

---

a, see *f,* Sec. 10.   *b,* 83 : 2.   34 : 6.   36 : 1.   42 : 6.

6. And as it is written, [c]Whatsoever ye shall ask in faith, being united in prayer according to my command, ye shall receive ;

7. And ye are called to bring to pass the [d]gathering of mine elect, for mine elect hear my voice and harden not their hearts ;

8. Wherefore the decree hath gone forth from the Father, that they shall be gathered in unto [e]one place upon the face of this land, to prepare their hearts and be prepared in all things against the day when [f]tribulation and desolation are sent forth upon the wicked ;

9. For the [g]hour is nigh, and the day soon at hand when the earth is ripe : and all the proud, and they that do wickedly, shall be as stubble, and I will [h]burn them up, saith the Lord of Hosts, that wickedness shall not be upon the earth ;

10. For the hour is nigh, and that which was spoken by mine apostles must be fulfilled; for as they spoke so shall it come to pass ;

11. For I will reveal [i]myself from heaven with power and great glory, with all the hosts thereof, and dwell in righteousness with men on earth a [j]thousand years, and the wicked shall not stand.

12. And again, verily, verily, I say unto you, and it hath gone forth in a firm decree, by the will of the Father, that mine apostles, the Twelve which were with me in my ministry at Jerusalem, shall stand at my right hand at the day of my coming in a pillar of fire, being clothed with robes of righteousness, with [k]crowns upon their heads, in glory even as I am, to judge the whole house of Israel, even as many as have loved me and kept my commandments, and none else ;

13. For a [l]trump shall sound both long and loud, even as upon Mount Sinai, and all the earth shall quake,

---

c, see c, Sec. 4.　　　d, see j, Sec. 10,　　　e, see d.　　　f, see f and g, Sec. 1.　　　g, see b, Sec. 4.　　　h, see i, Sec. 1.　　　i, see e, Sec. 1.　　　j, see e, Sec. 1.　　Rev. 20: 4—6.　　　k, Mat. 19: 23.　　Luke 22: 30.　　　l, 20: 13.　　43: 18.　　88: 98, 99.

and they shall come forth : yea, *m*even the dead which died in me, to receive a crown of righteousness, and to be clothed upon, even as I am, to be with me, that we may be one.

14. But, behold, I say unto you, that before this great day shall come, the *n*sun shall be darkened and the moon shall be turned into blood, and the stars shall fall from heaven, and there shall be greater signs in heaven above, and in the earth beneath ;

15. And there shall be *o*weeping and wailing among the hosts of men ;

16. And there shall be a *p*great hailstorm sent forth to destroy the crops of the earth ;

17. And it shall come to pass, because of the wickedness of the world, that I will take *q*vengeance upon the wicked, for they will not repent; for the cup of mine indignation is full ; for behold my blood shall not cleanse them if they hear me not.

18. Wherefore, I the Lord God will send forth *r*flies upon the face of the earth, which shall take hold of the inhabitants thereof, and shall eat their flesh, and shall cause maggots to come in upon them ;

19. And their tongues shall be staid that they shall not utter against me ; and their flesh shall fall from off their bones, and their eyes from their sockets :

20. And it shall come to pass that the *s*beasts of the forest, and the fowls of the air shall devour them up ;

21. And that great and *t*abominable church, which is the whore of all the earth, shall be cast down by devouring fire, according as it is spoken by the mouth of Ezekiel the prophet, who spoke of these things, which have not come to pass, but surely must, as I live, for abominations shall not reign.

22. And again, verily, verily, I say unto you, that

---

m, 45 : 45, 46.   76 : 50—64.   79 : 21.   88 : 96, 97.   133 : 56.   *n*, 34 : 9.   45 : 42.   88 : 87.   133 : 49.   *o*, see *e*, Sec. 19.   *p*, 43 : 25.   63 : 6.   88 : 89, 90.   Ezek. 38 : 22.   *q*, see *f* and *g*, Sec. 1.   *r*, Zech. 14 : 12.   Isaiah 18 : 6.   *s*, Isaiah 18 : 6.   Rev. 19 : 17, 18.   Ezek. 39 : 17 - 20.   *t*, see *j*, Sec. 13.   Ezek. 38 : 22.

when the *u*thousand years are ended, and men again begin to deny their God, then will I spare the earth but for a little season ;

23. And the end shall come, and the heaven and the earth shall be *v*consumed and pass away, and there shall be a new *w*heaven and a new earth,

24. For all *x*old things shall pass away, and all things shall become new, even the heaven and the earth, and all the fullness thereof, both men and beasts, the fowls of the air, and the fishes of the sea ;

25. And not one hair, neither mote, shall be lost, for it is the workmanship of mine hand.

26. But, behold, verily I say unto you, before the earth shall pass away, *y*Michael, mine archangel, shall sound his trump, and then shall all the dead awake, for their graves shall be opened, and they shall come forth ; yea, even all.

27. And the righteous shall be gathered on my right hand unto eternal life ; and the wicked on my left hand will I be ashamed to own before the Father ;

28. Wherefore I will say unto them—*z*Depart from me, ye cursed, into everlasting fire, prepared for the devil and his angels.

29. And now, behold, I say unto you, never at any time, have I declared from mine own mouth that they should return, for where I am they cannot come, for they have no power ;

30. But remember that all my judgments are not given unto men : and as the words have gone forth out of my mouth, even so shall they be fulfilled, that the *2a*first shall be last, and that the last shall be first in all things whatsoever I have created by the word of my power, which is the power of my Spirit ;

---

u. 88 : 101, 110—115.   Rev. 20 : 3—9.   *v*, Rev. 20 : 11.   Ether 13 : 9.
w, Rev. 21 : 1—5.   Ether 13 : 8, 9.   *x*, 77 : 2—4.   Rev. 21 : 5, 6.
Ether 13 : 8, 9.   *y*, 76 : 85.   88 : 100, 101.   *z*, vers. 29, 30, 41.
Matt. 25 : 41.   2*a*, ver. 32.

31. For by the power of my Spirit created I them ; yea, all things both spiritual and temporal :

32. Firstly, spiritual—secondly, temporal, which is the [2b]beginning of my work ; and again, firstly, temporal—and secondly, spiritual, which is the last [2c]of my work :

33. Speaking unto you that you may naturally understand, but unto myself my works have no end, neither beginning ; but it is given unto you that ye may understand, because ye have asked it of me and are agreed.

34. Wherefore, verily I say unto you, that all things unto me are spiritual, and not at any time have I given unto you a law which was temporal ; neither any man, nor the children of men ; neither Adam, your father, whom I created.

35. Behold, I gave unto him that he should be an agent unto himself ; and I gave unto him commandment, but no temporal commandment gave I unto him, for my commandments are spiritual ; they are not natural nor temporal, neither carnal nor sensual.

36. And it came to pass, that Adam being tempted of the devil (for, behold, the [2d]devil was before Adam, for he rebelled against me, saying, Give me thine honor, which is my power : and also a [2e]third part of the hosts of heaven turned he away from me because of their agency ;

37. And they were [2f]thrust down, and thus came the devil and his angels.

38. And, behold, there is a place prepared for them from the beginning, which place is [2g]hell :

39. And it must needs be that the devil should tempt the children of men, or they could not be agents

2b, ver. 30.   2c, ver. 10.   2d, 76 : 25—28.   Pearl of Great Price, p. 7.   2e, Pearl of Great Price, p. 32.   2f, 76 : 25—30. Pearl of Great Price, p. 7.   Jude 1 : 6.   2g, ver. 28.   76 : 33, 36, 44—48, 84, 105, 106.   77 : 8.   83 : 113, 114.   Pearl of Great Price, p. 14.   I. Nep. 15 : 29, 35.   II. Nep. 1 : 3.   2 : 29.   9 : 8—19, 23, 34, 36.   28 : 15, 21, 23. Jacob 6 : 10.   Alma 12 : 16—18.   III. Nep. 27 : 11, 12.   Moro. 8 : 13, 14, 21.

unto themselves, for if they never should have bitter, they could not know the sweet.)

40. Wherefore, it came to pass that the devil tempted Adam, and he partook the forbidden fruit and transgressed the commandment, wherein he became [2h]subject to the will of the devil, because he yielded unto temptation.

41. Wherefore I the Lord God caused that he should be cast out from the Garden of Eden, [2i]from my presence, because of his transgression, wherein he became [2j]spiritually dead, which is the [2k]first death, even that same death, which is the last death, which is spiritual, which shall be pronounced upon the wicked when I shall say—[2l]Depart, ye cursed.

42. But, behold, I say unto you, that I the Lord God gave unto Adam and unto his seed that they should not die as to the temporal death, until I the Lord God should send forth [2m]angels to declare unto them repentance and redemption, through faith on the name of mine Only Begotten Son.

43. And thus did I, the Lord God, appoint unto man the days of his probation; that by his natural death he might be [2n]raised in immortality unto eternal life, even as many as would believe;

44. And they that believe not unto [2o]eternal damnation, for they cannot be redeemed from their spiritual fall, because they repent not;

45. For they will love darkness rather than light, and their deeds are evil, and they receive their wages of whom they list to obey.

46. But, behold, I say unto you, that [2p]little children are redeemed from the foundation of the world through mine Only Begotten:

47. Wherefore, they cannot sin, for power is not

2h, ver. 36.   2i, Pearl of Great Price, p. 9.   2j, Pearl of Great Price, p. 15.   2k, u. Nep. 9: 7—12.   Mos. 3: 26, 27.   16: 4—11.   Alma 11: 45.   12: 18, 26, 26.   42: 6, 9, 14.   Hela. 14: 16, 17.   Mor. 9: 13.   2l, ver. 28.   76: 37.   2m, vers. 43, 46.   Pearl of Great Price, pp. 9, 10, 16, 17.   2n, see m.   2o, see v, Sec. 76.   2p, see l, Sec. 93.

given unto Satan to ²⁹tempt little children, until they
begin to become accountable before me ;

48. For it is given unto them even as I will, according to mine own pleasure, that great things may be required at the hand of their fathers.

49. And, again, I say unto you, that whoso having
knowledge, have I not commanded to repent?

50. And he that hath no understanding, it remaineth in me to do according as it is written. And now I
declare no more unto you at this time. Amen.

SECTION 30.

*Revelation given through Joseph, the Seer, to David
Whitmer, Peter Whitmer, jun., and John Whitmer,
at Fayette, September, 1830.*

1. Behold, I say unto you, David, that you have
feared man and have not relied on me for strength as
you ought :

2. But your mind has been on the things of the
earth more than on the things of me, your Maker, and
the ministry whereunto you have been called ; and you
have not given heed unto my Spirit, and to those who
were set over you, but have been persuaded by those
whom I have not commanded :

3. Wherefore, you are left to inquire for yourself,
at my hand, and ponder upon the things which you
have received.

4. And your home shall be at your father's house,
until I give unto you further commandments. And you
shall attend to the ministry in the church, and before
the world, and in the regions round about. Amen.

5. Behold, I say unto you, Peter, that you shall take

your ^ajourney with your brother Oliver, for the time has come that it is expedient in me that you shall open your mouth to declare my gospel; therefore, fear not, but give heed unto the words and advice of your brother, which he shall give you.

6. And be you afflicted in all his afflictions, ever lifting up your heart unto me in prayer, and faith, for his and your deliverance : for I have given unto him power to build up my church among the Lamanites :

7. And none have I appointed to be his counselor over him in the church, concerning church matters, except it is his brother, Joseph Smith, jun.

8. Wherefore, give heed unto these things and be diligent in keeping my commandments, and you shall be blessed unto eternal life. Amen.

9. Behold, I say unto you, my servant John, that thou shalt commence from this time forth to proclaim my gospel, as with the voice of a trump.

10. And your labor shall be at your brother Philip Burrough's, and in that region round about ; yea, wherever you can be heard, until I command you to go from hence.

11. And your whole labor shall be in ^bZion, with all your soul, from henceforth ; yea, you shall ever open your mouth in my cause, not fearing what man can do, for I am with you. Amen.

SECTION 31.

Revelation to Thomas B. Marsh, given through Joseph, the Seer, September, 1830.

1. Thomas, my son, blessed are you because of your faith in my work.

2. Behold, you have had many afflictions because of

---

a, westward to the Lamanites.   *b*, among the saints.

your family : nevertheless, I will bless you and your family; yea, your little ones, and the day cometh that they will believe and know the truth and be one with you in ^amy church.

3. Lift up your heart and rejoice, for the hour of your mission is come: and your tongue shall be loosed; and you shall declare glad tidings of great joy unto this generation.

4. You shall declare the things which have been revealed to my servant, Joseph Smith, jun. You shall begin to preach from this time forth ; yea, to reap in the field which is ^bwhite already to be burned :

5. Therefore, thrust in your sickle with all your soul, and your sins are forgiven you, and you shall be laden with sheaves upon your back, for the laborer is worthy of his hire. Wherefore, your family shall live.

6. Behold, verily I say unto you, go from them only for a little time, and declare my word, and I will prepare a place for them ;

7. Yea, I will open the hearts of the people, and they will receive you. And I will establish a church by your hand ;

8. And you shall strengthen them and prepare them against the time when they shall be gathered.

9. Be patient in afflictions, revile not against those that revile. Govern your house in meekness, and be steadfast.

10. Behold, I say unto you, that you shall be a physician unto the church, but not unto the world, for they will not receive you.

11. Go your way whithersoever I will, and it shall be ^cgiven you by the Comforter what you shall do, and whither you shall go.

12. ^dPray always, lest you enter into temptation, and lose you^r reward.

a, see a, Sec. 1.   b, see b, Sec. 4.   c, 34: 10. 35: 19. 36: 2. 39: 6. 42: 13, 14, 16, 17. 45: 67. 46: 11, 27—31. 50: 13, 14, 17—22. 61: 27, 28. 72: 24. 75: 10. 76: 12, 86, 116. 88: 137. 105: 36. 121: 26. d, see c, Sec. 4.

13. Be faithful unto the end, and lo, I am with you. These words are not of man nor of men, but of me, even Jesus Christ, your Redeemer, by the will of the Father. Amen.

SECTION 32.

Revelation given through Joseph, the Seer, to Parley P. Pratt and Ziba Peterson, October, 1830.

1. And now concerning my servant Parley P. Pratt, behold, I say unto him, that as I live I will that he shall declare my gospel and learn of me, and be meek and lowly of heart ;

2. And that which I have appointed unto him is, that he shall *a*go with my servants Oliver Cowdery and Peter Whitmer, jun., into the wilderness among the Lamanites ;

3. And *b*Ziba Peterson, also, shall go with them, and I myself will go with them and be in their midst ; and I am their advocate with the Father, and nothing shall prevail.

4. And they shall give heed to that which is written and pretend to no other revelation, and they shall *c*pray always that I may unfold them to their understanding ;

5. And they shall give heed unto these words and trifle not, and I will bless them. Amen.

SECTION 33.

Revelation given through Joseph, the Seer, to Ezra Thayre and Northrop Sweet, at Fayette, October, 1830.

1. Behold, I say unto you, my servants Ezra and

a, West of Missouri.　　b, West of Missouri.　　c, see c, Sec. 4.

Northrop, open ye your ears and hearken to the voice of the Lord your God, whose word is ªquick and powerful, sharper than a two-edged sword, to the dividing asunder of the joints and marrow, soul and spirit; and is a discerner of the thoughts and intents of the heart.

2. For verily, verily, I say unto you, that ye are called to lift up your voices as with the sound of a trump, to declare my ᵇgospel unto a crooked and perverse generation :

3. For behold, the field is ᶜwhite already to harvest: and it is the ᵈeleventh hour, and for the ᵉlast time that I shall call laborers into my vineyard.

4. And my vineyard has become corrupted ᶠevery whit; and there is none which doeth good save it be a few; and they err in many instances, because of ᵍpriestcrafts, all having corrupt minds.

5. And verily, verily, I say unto you, that this church have I established and called forth ʰout of the wilderness :

6. And even so will I ⁱgather mine elect from the four quarters of the earth, even as many as will believe in me, and hearken unto my voice :

7. Yea, verily, verily, I say unto you, that the field is ʲwhite already to harvest; wherefore, thrust in your sickles, and reap with all your might, mind, and strength.

8. Open your mouths and they shall be filled, and you shall become even as Nephi of old, who journeyed from Jerusalem in the wilderness :

9. Yea, open your mouths and spare not, and you shall be laden with sheaves upon your backs, for lo, I am with you:

10. Yea, open your mouths and they shall be filled, saying—-Repent, repent, and ᵏprepare ye the way of the

---

a, see a, Sec. 27.   b, see b, Sec. 18.   c, see b, Sec. 4.   d, see k, Sec. 24.   e, see k, Sec. 24.   f, 35 : 7, 12.   38 : 11.   101 : 44—62. g, II. Nep. 26 : 29—31. III. Nep. 21 : 19—21. 29 : 4--9. Ch. 30.   h, see a, Sec. 1.   i, see j, Sec. 10.   j, see b, Sec. 4.   k, see e, Sec. 1.

Lord, and make his paths straight; for the kingdom of heaven is at hand;

11. Yea, [l]repent and be baptized, every one of you, for a remission of your sins; yea, be baptized even by water, and then cometh the baptism of fire and of the Holy Ghost.

12. Behold, verily, verily, I say unto you, this is my gospel, and remember that they shall have faith in me, or they can in no wise be saved;

13. And upon this [m]rock I will build my church; yea, upon this rock ye are built, and if ye continue, the [n]gates of hell shall not prevail against you;

14. And ye shall remember the church articles and covenants to keep them;

15. And whoso having faith you shall confirm in my church, by the [o]laying on of the hands, and I will bestow the gift of the Holy Ghost upon them.

16. And the Book of Mormon and the Holy Scriptures, are given of me for your instruction; and the power of my Spirit quickeneth all things:

17. Wherefore, be faithful, praying always, having your [p]lamps trimmed and burning, and oil with you, that you may be ready at the coming of the Bridegroom:

18. For behold, verily, verily, I say unto you, that I [q]come quickly. Even so. Amen.

SECTION 34.

Revelation to Orson Pratt, given through Joseph, the Seer, in Fayette, New York, November 4th, 1830.

1. My son Orson, hearken and hear and behold

l, see *h*, Sec. 3. *m*, see *o*, Sec. 6. *n*, see *l*, Sec. 10. *o*, see 2*j*, Sec. 20. *p*, 45: 44–46. 88: 92. *q*, see *e*, Sec. 1.

what I, the Lord God, shall say unto you, even Jesus
Christ your Redeemer ;

2. The [a]light and the life of the world ; a light
which [b]shineth in darkness and the darkness comprehendeth it not ;

3. Who so loved the world that he gave his own
life, that as many as would believe might [c]become the
sons of God : wherefore you are my son,

4. And blessed are you because you have believed ;

5. And more blessed are you because you are [d]called
of me to preach my gospel,

6. To lift up your voice as with the sound of a
trump, both [e]long and loud, and cry [f]repentance unto
a crooked and perverse generation, [g]preparing the way
of the Lord for his second coming ;

7. For behold, verily, verily, I say unto you, the
time is soon at hand, that I shall come in a cloud with
power and great glory,

8. And it shall be a [h]great day at the time of my
coming, for all nations shall tremble.

9. But before that great day shall come, the [i]sun
shall be darkened, and the moon be turned into blood,
and the stars shall refuse their shining, and some shall
fall, and [j]great destructions await the wicked :

10. Wherefore lift up your voice and [k]spare not,
for the Lord God hath spoken ; therefore [l]prophesy,
and it shall be given by the power of the Holy
Ghost ;

11. And if you are faithful, behold, I am with
you [m]until I come :

12. And verily, verily, I say unto you, I [n]come
quickly. I am your Lord and your Redeemer. Even
so. Amen.

---

a, see h, Sec. 6.   b, see h, Sec. 6.   c, see k, Sec. 11.   d, see k,
Sec. 24.   e, see b, Sec. 29.   f, see h, Sec. 3.   g, see e,
Sec. 1.   h, see e, Sec. 1.   i, see n, Sec. 29.   j, see f and
g, Sec. 1.   k, 84 : 87, 94, 117.   l, 42 : 16, 17.   m, see e,
Sec. 1.   n, see e, Sec. 1.

SECTION 35.

*Revelation to Joseph Smith, jun., and Sidney Rigdon,
given December, 1830.*

1. Listen to the voice of the Lord your God, even
Alpha and Omega, the beginning and the end, whose
^acourse is one eternal round, the same to-day as yester-
day, and for ever.

2. I am Jesus Christ, the Son of God, who was
crucified for the sins of the world, even as many as will
believe on my name, that they may become the sons of
God, even ^bone in me as I am in the Father, as the
Father is one in me, that we may be one.

3. Behold, verily, verily, I say unto my servant
Sidney, I have looked upon thee and thy works. I
have heard thy prayers, and prepared thee for a greater
work.

4. Thou art blessed, for thou shalt do great things.
Behold thou wast sent forth, even as John, to prepare
the way before me, and before ^cElijah which should
come, and thou knewest it not.

5. Thou didst baptize by water unto repentance,
but they received not the Holy Ghost;

6. But now I give unto thee a commandment, that
thou shalt ^dbaptize by water, and they shall receive the
Holy Ghost by the ^elaying on of the hands, even as the
apostles of old.

7. And it shall come to pass that there shall be a
great work in the land, even among the Gentiles, for
their folly and their ^fabominations shall be made manifest in the eyes of all people;

8. For I am God, and mine arm is not shortened;
and I will ^gshow miracles, signs, and wonders, unto all
those who believe on my name.

---

a, see *a*, Sec. 3.   *b*, 50 : 43.   76 : 59.   84 : 37, 38.   *c*, see *a*,
Sec. 2.   *d*, see *l*, Sec. 5.   *e*, see 2*j*, Sec. 20.   *f*, 85 : 117.
88 : 94.   *g*, vers. 9—11.   45 : 8.   66 : 9.

9. And whoso shall [h]ask it in my name in faith, they shall cast out devils; they shall heal the sick; they shall cause the blind to receive their sight, and the deaf to hear, and the dumb to speak, and the lame to walk;

10. And the time speedily cometh that great things are to be shown forth unto the children of men;

11. But without faith shall not anything be shown forth except [i]desolations upon Babylon, the same which has made all nations drink of the wine of the wrath of her fornication.

12. And there are none that doeth good, except those who are ready to receive the [j]fullness of my gospel which I have sent forth unto this generation.

13. Wherefore I have called upon the [k]weak things of the world, those who are unlearned and despised, to thresh the nations by the power of my Spirit:

14. And their arm shall be my arm, and I will be their shield and their buckler; and I will gird up their loins, and they shall fight manfully for me; and their [l]enemies shall be under their feet; and I will let [m]fall the sword in their behalf, and by the fire of mine indignation will I preserve them.

15. And the poor and the meek shall have the gospel preached unto them, and they shall be looking forth for the [n]time of my coming, for it is nigh at hand:

16. And they shall learn the parable of the fig tree, for even now already summer is nigh,

17. And I have sent forth the [o]fullness of my gospel by the hand of my servant Joseph; and in weakness have I blessed him,

18. And I have given unto him the [p]keys of the mystery of those things which have been sealed, even

---

h, see g.   i, see i, Sec. 1.   j, see b, Sec. 18.   k, see j, Sec. 1.
l, 96 : 34 – 38.   m, see f, Sec. 1.   n, see e, Sec. 1.   o, see b,
Sec. 18.   p, see b, Sec. 23.

things which were from the *q*foundation of the world, and the things which shall come from this time until the time of my coming, if he abide in me, and if not, another will I plant in his stead.

19. Wherefore, watch over him that his faith fail not, and it shall be given by the Comforter, the Holy Ghost, that *r*knoweth all things:

20. And a commandment I give unto thee, that thou shalt write for him ; and the Scriptures *s*shall be given, even as they are in mine own bosom, to the salvation of mine own elect ;

21. For they will hear my voice, and shall see me, and shall not be asleep, and shall abide the day of my coming, for they shall be purified, even as I am pure.

22. And now I say unto you, tarry with him, and he shall journey with you ; forsake him not, and surely these things shall be fulfilled.

23. And inasmuch as ye do not write, behold, it shall be given unto him to prophesy : and thou shalt preach my gospel and call on the holy prophets to prove his words, as they shall be given him.

24. Keep all the commandments and covenants by which ye are bound ; and I will cause the *t*heavens to shake for your good, and Satan shall tremble and *u*Zion shall rejoice upon the *v*hills and flourish,

25. And Israel shall be saved in mine own due time ; and by the *w*keys which I have given shall they be led, and no more be confounded at all.

26. Lift up your hearts and be glad, your redemption draweth nigh.

27. Fear not, little flock, *x*the kingdom is yours until I come. Behold I *y*come quickly. Even so. Amen.

---

q, Pearl of Great Price, pp. 1—3, 32.   *r*, 39 : 6.   75 : 10.   *s*, 42 : 50.   *t*, see *e*, Sec. 21.   *u*, see *e*, Sec. 6.   *v*, 39 : 13.   49 : 25.   64 : 37.   117 : 7, 8. .   *w*, 15 : 19.   42 : 69.   61 : 24—29.   90 : 2, 7, 9. 111 : 11, 16.   112 : 32.   113 : 6.   *x*, 38 : 9.   50 : 35.   101 : 100, 101. 105 : 32.   *y*, see *e*, Sec. 1.

SECTION 36.

*Revelation to Edward Partridge, given through Joseph,
the Seer, December, 1830.*

1. Thus saith the Lord God, the Mighty One of
Israel, Behold, I say unto you, my servant Edward,
that you are blessed, and your sins are forgiven you,
and you are called to preach my gospel as with the
voice of a trump ;

2. And I will lay my hand upon you by the [a]hand
of my servant Sidney Rigdon, and you shall receive
my Spirit, the Holy Ghost, even the Comforter, which
shall teach you the peaceable things of the kingdom ;

3. And you shall declare it with a loud voice, saying, Hosanna, blessed be the name of the most high God.

4. And now this calling and commandment give I
unto you concerning all men,

5. That as many as shall come before my servants
Sidney Rigdon and Joseph Smith, jun., embracing
this calling and commandment, [b]shall be ordained and
sent forth to preach the everlasting gospel among the
nations,

6. Crying repentance, saying, Save yourselves from
this untoward generation, and come forth out of
the fire, hating even the garments spotted with the
flesh.

7. And this commandment shall be given unto the
elders of my church, that [c]every man which will embrace it with singleness of heart, may be ordained and
sent forth, even as I have spoken.

8. I am Jesus Christ the Son of God : wherefore,
gird up your loins and I will [d]suddenly come to my
temple. Even so. Amen.

---

[a], see 2j, Sec. 20.   [b], see c, Sec. 6.   [c], see c, Sec. 6.
[d], 42: 36. 97: 16. 133: 2.

SECTION 37.

Revelation given to Joseph Smith, jun., and Sidney Rigdon, December, 1830.

1. Behold, I say unto you, that it is not expedient in me that ye should ^atranslate any more until ye shall go to the Ohio, and this because of the enemy and for your sakes.

2. And again, I say unto you, that ye shall not go, until ye have preached my gospel in those parts, and have strengthened up the church whithersoever it is found, and more especially in Colesville ; for, behold, they pray unto me in much faith.

3. And again, a commandment I give unto the church, that it is expedient in me that they should ^bassemble together at the Ohio, against the time that my servant Oliver Cowdery shall return unto them.

4. Behold, here is wisdom, and let every man choose for himself until I come. Even so. Amen.

SECTION 38.

Revelation given through Joseph, the Seer, at Fayette, New York, January 2nd, 1831.

1. Thus saith the Lord your God, even Jesus Christ, the Great I AM, Alpha and Omega, the beginning and the end, the same which looked upon the ^awide expanse of eternity, and all the seraphic hosts of heaven, before the world was made :

---

a, the Scriptures.   *b*, first direct command to gather.

a, ver. 2.   67 : 2.   121 : 2, 24.

2. The same which *b*knoweth all things, for all things are *c*present before mine eyes :

3. I am the same which spake, and the world was made, and all things came by me :

4. I am the same which have taken the *d*Zion of Enoch into mine own bosom ; and verily, I say, even as many as have believed in my name, for I am Christ, and in mine own name, by the virtue of the blood which I have spilt, have I pleaded before the Father for them ;

5. But behold, the residue of the wicked have I kept in *e*chains of darkness until the judgment of the great day, which shall come at the end of the earth ;

6. And even so *f*will I cause the wicked to be kept, that will not hear my voice but harden their hearts, and wo, wo, wo, is their doom.

7. But behold, verily, verily, I say unto you that mine eyes are upon you. I am in your midst and ye cannot see me ;

8. But the day soon cometh that ye shall see me, and know that I am ; for the vail of darkness shall soon be *g*rent, and he that is not purified shall not abide the day :

9. Wherefore gird up your loins and be prepared. Behold, the *h*kingdom is yours, and the enemy shall not overcome.

10. Verily, I say unto you, ye are clean, but not all ; and there is none else with whom I am well pleased,

11. For all flesh is corrupted before me ; and the powers of darkness prevail upon the earth, among the children of men, in the presence of all the hosts of heaven,

12. Which causeth *i*silence to reign, and all *j*eternity

---

b, 93 : 23, 24, 28, 30, 36. 121 : 24.   *c*, see *a*.   *d*, 84 : 99, 100.
e, 88 : 99.   *f*, see *e*.   *g*, see *e*, Sec. 1.   *h*, see *x*, Sec. 35.
i, 88 : 95. Pearl of Great Price, p 20.   *j*, see *i*.

is pained, and the ᵏangels are waiting the great command to reap down the earth, to gather the ᶫtares that they may be burned : and, behold, the enemy is combined.

13. And now I show unto you a mystery, a thing which is had in secret chambers, to bring to pass even your destruction in process of time, and ye knew it not;

14. But now I tell it unto you, and ye are blessed, not because of your iniquity neither your hearts of unbelief ; for verily some of you are guilty before me, but I will be merciful unto your weakness.

15. Therefore, be ye strong from henceforth ; fear not, for the ᵐkingdom is yours :

16. And for your salvation I give unto you a commandment, for I have heard your prayers, and the poor have complained before me, and the rich have I made, and all flesh is mine, and I am no ⁿrespecter of persons.

17. And I have made the earth rich, and behold it is my footstool, wherefore, again I will stand upon it ;

18. And I hold forth and deign to give unto you greater riches, even a ᵒland of promise, a land flowing with milk and honey, upon which there shall be no curse when the Lord cometh :

19. And I will give it unto you for the land of your inheritance, if you seek it with all your hearts :

20. And this shall be my covenant with you, ye shall have it for the land of your inheritance, and for the inheritance of your children forever, while the earth shall stand, and ye shall possess it ᵖagain in eternity, no more to pass away.

21. But, verily, I say unto you, that in time ye shall have no king nor ruler, for I will be your king and watch over you.

22. Wherefore, hear my voice and follow me, and

---

k, 86 : 3—7.　　*l*, 86 : 7.　88 : 04.　101 : 66.　133 : 63, 64.　*m*, see *x*,
Sec. 35.　　*n*, Acts 10 : 34.　*l*. Pet. 1 : 17.　*o*, 52 : 2.　57 : 1, 2, 5, 7.
p, 56 : 20.　57 : 5.　63 : 20, 48, 49.

you shall be a free people, and ye shall have no laws but my laws when I come, for I am your Law-givér, and what can stay my hand ?

23. But, verily, I say unto you, teach one another according to the office wherewith I have appointed you,

24. And let every man esteem ⁱhis brother as himself, and practice virtue and holiness before me.

25. And again I say unto you, let every man esteem his brother as himself ;

26. For what man among you having twelve sons, and is no respecter of them, and they serve him obediently, and he saith unto the one, be thou clothed in robes and sit thou here ; and to the other, be thou clothed in rags and sit thou there, and looketh upon his sons and saith I am just.

27. Behold, this I have given unto you a parable, and it is even as I am : I say unto you, be one ; and if ye are not one, ye are not mine.

28. And again I say unto you, that the enemy in the secret chambers seeketh your lives.

29. Ye hear of wars in far countries, and you say that there will soon be great wars in far countries, but ye know not the ʰhearts of men in your own land.

30. I tell you these things because of your prayers ; wherefore treasure up wisdom in your bosoms, lest the wickedness of men reveal these things unto you by their wickedness, in a manner which shall speak in your ears with a voice louder than that which shall shake the earth ; but if ye are prepared, ye shall not fear.

31. And that ye might escape the power of the enemy, and be ᵘgathered unto me a righteous people, without spot and blameless :

32. Wherefore, for this cause I gave unto you the

---

q, ver. 25. 59 : 6. 88 : 123.   r, 19 : 9. 61 : 8.   s, 5 : 32, 33.
10 : 6, 25.   38 : 13. 42 : 64. 89 : 4. 117 : 11.   t, 45 : 26, 63. 87 :
1—3. 130 : 12.   u, see j, Sec. 10.

commandment that ye should [v]go to the Ohio; and there I will give unto you my [w]law; and there you shall be [x]endowed with power from on high;

33. And from thence, whomsoever I will, shall [y]go forth among all nations, and it shall be told them what they shall do; for I have a great work laid up in store, for Israel shall be saved, and I will lead them whithersoever I will, and no power shall stay my hand.

34. And now I give unto the church in these parts, a commandment that certain men among them shall be appointed, and they shall be appointed by the voice of the church;

35. And they shall look to the poor and the needy, and administer to their relief, that they shall not suffer; and send them forth to the place which I have commanded them;

36. And this shall be their work, to govern the affairs of the property of this church.

37. And they that have farms that cannot be sold, let them be left or rented as seemeth them good.

38. See that all things are preserved; and when men are [z]endowed with power from on high and sent forth, all these things shall be gathered unto the bosom of the church.

39. And if ye seek the riches which it is the will of the Father to give unto you, ye shall be the richest of all people, for ye shall have the [2a]riches of eternity; and it must needs be that the riches of the earth are mine to give; but beware of pride, lest ye [2b]become as the Nephites of old.

40. And again, I say unto you, I give unto you a commandment, that every man, both elder, priest, teacher, and also member, go to with his might, with the labor of his hands, to prepare and accomplish the things which I have commanded.

v, see b, Sec. 37.   w, see Sec. 42.   x, 39: 15.   43: 16.   95: 8.
108: 4.   y, see q, Sec. 18.   z, ver. 32.   39: 15.   95: 8, 9.   105:
18, 33.   110: 9, 10.   124: 36—44.   2a, 11: 7.   68: 31.   78: 18.
2b, the Nephites were destroyed through wickedness.

41. And let your preaching be the warning voice, every man to his neighbor, in mildness and in meekness.

42. And go ye out from among the wicked. Save yourselves. Be ye clean that bear the vessels of the Lord. Even so. Amen.

SECTION 39.

Revelation to James Covill, given through Joseph, the Seer, in Fayette, New York, January 5th, 1831.

1. Hearken and listen to the voice of him who is *a*from all eternity to all eternity, the Great I AM, even Jesus Christ,

2. *b*The light and the life of the world; a light which *c*shineth in darkness and the darkness comprehendeth it not:

3. The same which came in the *d*meridian of time unto my own, and my own received me not;

4. But to as many as received me, gave I *e*power to become my sons, and even so will I give unto as many as will receive me, power to become my sons.

5. And verily, verily, I say unto you, he that receiveth my gospel, receiveth me; and he that receiveth not my gospel receiveth not me.

6. And this is my gospel: *f*repentance and baptism by water, and then cometh the baptism of fire and the Holy Ghost, even the Comforter, which showeth all things, and teacheth the peaceable things of the kingdom.

7. And now, behold, I say unto you, my servant James, I have looked upon thy works and I know thee:

a, 29: 33.   61: 1.   76: 4.   88: 6—13.   93: 8—10.   *b*, see *h*, Sec. 6.
c, see *h*, Sec. 6.   *d*, Pearl of Great Price, pp. 16, 20.   *e*, see *k*, Sec. 11.
f, see *b*, Sec. 18.

8. And verily I say unto thee, thine heart is now right before me at this time, and, behold, I have bestowed great blessings upon thy head :

9. Nevertheless thou hast seen great sorrow, for thou hast rejected me many times because of pride and the cares of the world ;

10. But, behold, the days of thy deliverance are come, if thou wilt hearken to my voice, which saith unto thee, arise and be ⁿbaptized, and wash away your sins, calling on my name, and you shall receive my Spirit, and a blessing so great as you never have known.

11. And if thou do this, I have prepared thee for a greater work. Thou shalt preach the ʰfullness of my gospel which I have sent forth in these last days; the ⁱcovenant which I have sent forth to recover my people, which are of the house of Israel.

12. And it shall come to pass that power shall rest upon thee ; thou shalt have great faith, and I will be with thee and go before thy face.

13. Thou art called to labor in my vineyard, and to build up ʲmy church, and to bring forth ᵏZion, that it may rejoice upon the ˡhills and flourish.

14. Behold, verily, verily, I say unto thee, thou art not called to go into the eastern countries, but thou art called to go to the Ohio.

15. And inasmuch as my people shall assemble themselves to the Ohio, I have kept in store a blessing such as is not known among the children of men, and it shall be poured forth upon their heads. And from thence men shall ᵐgo forth into all nations.

16. Behold, verily, verily, I say unto you, that the people in Ohio call upon me in much faith, thinking I will stay my hand in judgment upon the nations, but I cannot deny my word :

17. Wherefore lay to with your might and call

---

g, see *l*, Sec. 5.   *h*, see *b*, Sec. 18.   *i*, see *k*, Sec. 1.   *j*, see *a*, Sec. 1.   *k*, see *e*, Sec. 6.   *l*, 49 : 25.   64 : 37.   65 : 2.   117 : 8. 128 : 19.   *m*, see *q*, Sec. 18.

*n*faithful laborers into my vineyard, that it may be pruned for the last time.

18. And inasmuch as they do repent and receive the *o*fullness of my gospel, and become sanctified, I will stay mine hand in judgment :

19. Wherefore go forth, crying with a loud voice, saying, the kingdom of heaven is at hand ; crying Hosanna ! blessed be the name of the most high God.

20. Go forth baptizing with water, *p*preparing the way before my face, for the time of my coming ;

21. For the time is at hand ; the *q*day nor the hour no man knoweth ; but it surely shall come,

22. And he that receiveth these things receiveth me ; and they shall be *r*gathered unto me in time and in eternity.

23. And again, it shall come to pass, that on as many as ye shall baptize with water, ye shall *s*lay your hands, and they shall receive the gift of the Holy Ghost, and shall be looking forth for the signs of my coming, and shall know me.

24. Behold, I *t*come quickly.   Even so.   Amen.

SECTION 40.

Revelation to Joseph Smith, jun., and Sidney Rigdon, given in Fayette, New York, January, 1831, explaining why James Covill obeyed not the revelation which was given unto him.

1. Behold, verily I say unto you, that the heart of my servant James Covill was right before me, for he covenanted with me that he would obey my word.

------

n, see *k,* Sec. 24.   *o,* see *b,* Sec. 18.   *p,* see *e,* Sec. 1.   *q,* see *e,* Sec. 1.   *r,* see *j,* Sec. 10.   *s,* see 2*j,* Sec. 20.   *t,* see *e,* Sec. 1.

2. And he received the word with gladness, but straightway Satan tempted him ; and the fear of persecution, and the cares of the world, caused him to reject the word ;

3. Wherefore he broke my covenant, and it remaineth with me to do with him as seemeth me good. Amen.

SECTION 41.

Revelation given through Joseph, the Seer, in Kirtland, Ohio, February 4th, 1831.

1. Hearken and hear, O ye my people, saith the Lord and your God, ye whom I delight to bless with the greatest blessings, ye that hear me ; and ye that hear me not will I curse, that have professed my name, with the ^aheaviest of all cursings.

2. Hearken, O ye elders of my church whom I have called : behold I give unto you a commandment, that ye shall assemble yourselves together to agree upon my word,

3. And by the prayer of your faith ye shall receive my ^blaw, that ye may know how to govern my church, and have all things right before me.

4. And I will be your Ruler when I come ; and behold, I ^ccome quickly, and ye shall see that my law is kept.

5. He that receiveth my ^dlaw and doeth it, the same is my disciple ; and he that saith he receiveth it and doeth it not, the same is not my disciple, and shall be cast out from among you :

6. For it is not meet that the things which belong to the children of the kingdom, should be given to

---

a, 76 : 29—37.   b, Sec. 42.   c, see e, Sec. 1.   d, ver. 6.

them that are not worthy, or to dogs, or the pearls to be cast before swine.

7. And again, it is meet that my servant Joseph Smith, jun., should have a house built, in which to live and translate.

8. And again, it is meet that my servant Sidney Rigdon should live as seemeth him good, inasmuch as he keepeth my commandments.

9. And again, I have called my servant Edward Partridge, and give a commandment, that he should be appointed by the voice of the church, and *ordained a bishop unto the church, to leave his merchandise and to spend all his time in the labors of the church :

10. To see to all things as it shall be appointed unto him, in my laws in the day that I shall give them.

11. And this because his heart is pure before me, for he is like unto Nathaniel of old, in whom there is no guile.

12. These words are given unto you, and they are pure before me ; wherefore beware how you hold them, for they are to be answered upon your souls in the day of judgment. Even so. Amen.

SECTION 42.

Revelation given through Joseph, the Seer, at Kirtland, Ohio, February 9th, 1831.

1. Hearken, O ye elders of my church, who have assembled yourselves together in my name, even Jesus Christ the Son of the living God, the Saviour of the world : inasmuch as they believe on my name and keep my commandments,

---

*, first Bishop in the Church.

2. Again, I say unto you, hearken and hear and obey the *law which I shall give unto you ;

3. For verily I say, as ye have assembled yourselves together according to the commandment wherewith I commanded you, and are agreed as touching this one thing, and have asked the Father in my name, even so ye shall receive.

4. Behold, verily I say unto you, I give unto you this first commandment, that ye shall go forth in my name, every one of you, excepting my servants Joseph Smith, jun., and Sidney Rigdon.

5. And I give unto them a commandment that they shall go forth for a little season, and it shall be given by the power of my Spirit when they shall return ;

6. And ye shall go forth in the power of my Spirit, preaching my gospel, two by two, in my name, lifting up your voices as with the voice of a trump, declaring my word like unto angels of God ;

7. And ye shall go forth baptizing with water, saying—*b*Repent ye, repent ye, for the kingdom of heaven is at hand.

8. And from this place ye shall go forth into the regions westward ; and inasmuch as ye shall find them that will receive you, ye shall build up *c*my church in every region,

9. Until the time shall come when it shall be revealed unto you from on high, when the city of the *d*New Jerusalem shall be prepared, that ye may be gathered in one, that ye may be my people and I will be your God.

10. And again, I say unto you, that my servant Edward Partridge shall stand in the office wherewith I have appointed him. And it shall come to pass, that if he transgress, another shall be appointed in his stead. Even so. Amen.

11. Again, I say unto you, that it shall not be given

---

a, Sec. 42.   b, see h, Sec. 3.   c, see a, Sec. 1.   d, see d, Sec. 28.

to any one to go forth to preach my gospel, or to build
up my church, except he be ordained by some one who
has authority, and it is known to the church that he has
authority, and has been regularly ordained by the heads
of the church.

12. And again, the elders, priests, and teachers of
this church shall teach the principles of my gospel,
which are in the Bible and the Book of Mormon, in the
which is the ʳfullness of the gospel ;

13. And they shall observe the covenants and
church articles to do them, and these shall be their
teachings, as they shall be directed by the Spirit ;

14. And the Spirit shall be given unto you by the
prayer of faith, and if ye ʃreceive not the Spirit, ye
shall not teach.

15. And all this ye shall observe to do as I have
commanded concerning your teaching, until the ᵍfullness
of my scriptures is given.

16. And as ye shall lift up your voices by the Comforter, ye shall speak and prophesy as seemeth me good;

17. For, behold, the Comforter ʰknoweth all things,
and ⁱbeareth record of the Father and of the Son.

18. And now, behold, I speak unto the church.
Thou shalt not kill ; and he that kills shall ʲnot have
forgiveness in this world, nor in the world to come.

19. And again, I say, thou shalt not kill ; but he
that killeth shall die.

20. Thou shalt not steal ; and he that stealeth and
will not repent, shall be cast out.

21. Thou shalt not lie ; he that lieth and will not
repent, shall be cast out.

22. Thou shalt love thy ᵏwife with all thy heart,
and shalt cleave unto her and none else ;

23. And he that looketh upon a woman ˡto lust

---

e, see *b*, Sec. 18.   *f*, 50 : 17, 18.   *g*, vers. 56—58.   *h*, 75 : 10.
88 : 41.   93 : 23—28.   *i*, I. John, 5 : 6—8.   III. Nep. 11 : 32, 35, 36.
j, vers. 19, 79.   *k*, 49 : 15—17.   75 : 28.   83 : 2.   132 : 62.   *l*, 63 : 16.

after her, shall deny the faith, and shall not have the Spirit, and if he repents not he shall be cast out.

24. Thou shalt ^mnot commit adultery ; and he that committeth adultery, and repenteth not, shall be cast out ;

25. But he that has committed adultery and repents with all his heart, and forsaketh it, and doeth it no more, thou shalt forgive ;

26. But if he doeth it again, he shall not be forgiven, but shall be cast out.

27. Thou shalt not speak evil of thy neighbor, nor do him any harm.

28. Thou knowest my laws concerning these things are given in my scriptures; he that sinneth and repenteth not, shall be cast out.

29. If thou lovest me, thou shalt serve me and keep all my commandments.

30. And behold, thou wilt remember the poor, and ⁿconsecrate of thy properties for their support that which thou hast to impart unto them with a covenant and a deed which cannot be broken ;

31. And inasmuch as ye impart of your substance unto the poor, ye will do it unto me, and they shall be laid before the bishop of my church and his counselors, two of the elders,* or High Priests, such as he shall or has appointed and set apart for that purpose.

32. And it shall come to pass, that after they are laid before the bishop of my church, and after that he has received these testimonies concerning the consecration of the properties of my church, that they cannot be taken from the church agreeable to my commandments ; every man shall be made accountable unto me, a ^osteward over his own property, or that which he has

---

m, vers. 25, 26, 80—83.   63: 14—19.   101: 6.   132: 26, 27, 39, 41—44, 52, 54, 61—63, 65.   *n*, 58: 35, 36.   85: 3.   104: 60, 66. 105: 29.   *o*, ver. 53.   51: 3—6.   64: 30.   70: 9—11.   72: 3, 5, 16, 17, 20, 22.   101: 61.   104: 11—44, 54—57, 68—86.

* The words, "or High Priests," were added by the Prophet some years after ; and also the words, "High Council," in the 34th verse.

received by consecration, inasmuch as is sufficient for himself and family.

33. And again, if there shall be properties in the hands of the church, or any individuals of it, more than is necessary for their support, after this first consecration, which is a residue to be consecrated unto the bishop, it shall be kept to administer to those who have not, from time to time, that every man who has need may be amply supplied, and receive according to his wants.

34. Therefore, the residue shall be kept in my storehouse, to administer to the poor and the needy, as shall be appointed by the *p*High Council of the church, and the bishop and his council,

35. And for the purpose of purchasing lands for the public benefit of the church, and building houses of worship, and building up of the *q*New Jerusalem which is hereafter to be revealed,

36. That my *r*covenant people may be gathered in one in that day when I shall *s*come to my temple. And this I do for the salvation of my people.

37. And it shall come to pass, that he that sinneth and repenteth not, shall be cast out of the church, and shall not receive again that which he has consecrated unto the poor and the needy of my church ; or in other words, unto me ;

38. For inasmuch as ye do it unto the least of these, ye do it unto me ;

39. For it shall come to pass, that which I spake by the mouths of my prophets, shall be fulfilled ; for I will consecrate of the riches of those who embrace my gospel among the Gentiles, unto the poor of my people who are of the house of Israel.

40. And again, thou shalt not be proud in thy heart ; let all thy *t*garments be plain, and their beauty the beauty of the work of thine own hands ;

*p,*102: 1—34. 120:1.   *q,* vers. 9, 62, 67. 28: 9. 45: 66—71. 52:43. 57: 2,14. 58: 7, 13.   *r,* the remnant of Joseph.   *s,* see *d,* Sec. 36.   *t,*95: 13

41. And let all things be done in cleanliness before me.

42. Thou shalt "not be idle; for he that is idle shall not eat the bread nor wear the garments of the laborer.

43. And whosoever among you "are sick, and have not faith to be healed, but believe, shall be nourished with all tenderness, with herbs and mild food, and that not by the hand of an enemy.

44. And the elders of the church, two or more, shall be called, and shall pray for and lay their hands upon them in my name; and if they die they shall die unto me, and if they live they shall live unto me.

45. Thou shalt live together in love, insomuch that ᵛthou shalt weep for the loss of them that die, and more especially for those that have not hope of a glorious resurrection.

46. And it shall come to pass that those that die in me, shall ˣnot taste of death, for it shall be sweet unto them;

47. And they that die not in me, ʸwo unto them, for their death is bitter.

48. And again, it shall come to pass that he that hath ᶻfaith in me to be healed, and is not appointed unto death, shall be healed;

49. He who hath faith to see shall see;

50. He who hath faith to hear shall hear;

51. The lame who hath faith to leap shall leap;

52. And they who have not faith to do these things, but believe in me, have power to become my sons; and inasmuch as they break not my laws, thou shalt bear their infirmities.

53. Thou shalt stand in the place of thy stewardship;

u, 60 : 13.   68 : 30, 81.   75 : 3, 29.   88 : 124.   *v*, 42 : 44, 48—52.
59 : 16—22.   89 : 10, 11.   *w*, ver. 47.   84 : 74, 75.   *x*, 63 : 49—52.
y, see *w*.   *z*, vers. 49—52.   85 : 8—11.   46 : 19, 20.   52 : 20.   84 : 65—73.
68 : 10.

54. Thou shalt not take thy brother's garment; thou shalt [2a]pay for that which thou shalt receive of thy brother;

55. And if thou obtainest [2b]more than that which would be for thy support, thou shalt give it into my store-house, that all things may be done according to that which I have said.

56. Thou shalt ask, and my [2c]Scriptures shall be given as I have appointed, and they shall be preserved in safety;

57. And it is expedient that thou shouldst hold thy peace concerning them, and not teach them until ye have received them in full.

58. And I give unto you a commandment that then ye shall teach them unto all men; for [2d]they shall be taught unto all nations, kindreds, tongues and people.

59. Thou shalt take the things which thou hast received, which have been given unto thee in my Scriptures for a law, to be my law to govern my church;

60. And he that doeth according to these things shall be saved, and he that doeth them not shall be damned, if he continues.

61. If thou shalt ask, [2e]thou shalt receive revelation upon revelation, knowledge upon knowledge, that thou mayest know the mysteries and peaceable things —that which bringeth joy, that which bringeth life eternal.

62. Thou shalt ask, and it shall be revealed unto you in mine own due time [2f]where the New Jerusalem shall be built.

63. And behold, it shall come to pass that my servants shall be sent forth to the east and to the west, to the north and to the south;

64. And even now, let him that goeth to the east,

2a, 51 : 10—12.   2b, vers. 83, 34.   51 : 13.   70 : 7.   72 : 10.   82 : 18.
101 : 96.   119 : 1.   2c, the inspired translation of the Bible.   2d, 45 :
60, 61.   94 : 10.   124 : 89.   2e, vers. 65, 67.   59 : 4.   76 : 7.   88 : 77—79.
121 : 26—33.   2f, see g.

teach them that shall be converted to flee to the west, and this in consequence of that which is coming on the earth, and of ^{2g}secret combinations.

65. Behold, thou shalt observe all these things, and great shall be thy reward ; for unto you it is given to ^{2h}know the mysteries of the kingdom, but unto the world it is not given to know them.

66. Ye shall observe the laws which ye have received and be faithful.

67. And ye shall hereafter receive ²ⁱchurch covenants, such as shall be sufficient to establish you, both here and in the New Jerusalem.

68. Therefore, he that lacketh wisdom, let him ask of me, and I will give him liberally and upbraid him not.

69. Lift up your hearts and rejoice, for unto you the ^{2j}kingdom, or in other words, the keys of the church have been given. Even so. Amen.

70. The priests and teachers shall have their stewardships, even as the members ;

71. And the elders,* or High Priests who are appointed to assist the bishop as counselors in all things, are to have their families supported out of the property which is consecrated to the bishop, for the good of the poor, and for other purposes, as before mentioned ;

72. Or they are to receive a just remuneration for all their services, either a stewardship or otherwise, as may be thought best or decided by the counselors and bishop.

73. And the bishop, also, shall receive his support, or a just remuneration for all his services in the church.

74. † Behold, verily I say unto you, that whatever persons among you, having put away their companions for the ^{2k}cause of fornication, or in other words, if they shall testify before you in all lowliness of heart that this is the case, ye shall not cast them out from among you ;

2g, see s, Sec. 38.   2 h, see 2 e.   2 i, Revealed Laws.
2 j, see z, Sec. 35.   2 k, l. Cor. 5 : 9—13.   6 : 9, 13—20.

* The words "or High Priests" were added by the Prophet some years after.
† Verses 74 to 93 inclusive, were given some days after the first 73 verses.

75. But if ye shall find that any persons have left their companions for the [21]sake of adultery, and they themselves are the offenders, and their companions are living, they shall be cast out from among you.

76. And again, I say unto you, that ye shall be watchful and careful, with all inquiry, that ye receive none such among you if they are married ;

77. And if they are not married, they shall repent of all their sins, or ye shall not receive them.

78. And again, every person who belongeth to this church of Christ, shall observe to keep all the commandments and covenants of the church.

79. And it shall come to pass, that if any persons among you shall kill, they shall be delivered up and dealt with according to the laws of the land ; for remember that he hath [2m]no forgiveness, and it shall be proven according to the laws of the land.

80. And if any man or woman shall [2n]commit adultery, he or she shall be tried before two elders of the church, or more, and every word shall be established against him or her by two witnesses of the church, and not of the enemy ; but if there are more than two witnesses it is better.

81. But he or she shall be condemned by the mouth of two witnesses, and the elders shall lay the case before the church, and the church shall lift up their hands against him or her, that they may be dealt with according to the law of God.

82. And if it can be, it is necessary that the bishop is present also.

83. And thus ye shall do in all cases which shall come before you.

84. And if a man or woman shall rob, he or she shall be delivered up unto the law of the land.

85. And if·he or she shall steal, he or she shall be delivered up unto the law of the land.

[2l], ver. 76. See m.   [2m], vers. 18, 19,   [2n], see m.

86. And if he or she shall lie, he or she shall be delivered up unto the law of the land.

87. And if he or she do ²ᵒany manner of iniquity, he or she shall be delivered up unto the law, even that of God.

88. And if thy brother or sister ²ᵖoffend thee, thou shalt take him or her between him or her and thee alone; and if he or she confess, thou shalt be reconciled.

89. And if he or she confess not, thou shalt deliver him or her up unto the church, not to the members, but to the elders. And it shall be done in a meeting, and that not before the world.

90. And if thy brother or sister offend ²ᑫmany, he or she shall be chastened before many.

91. And if any one off*nd openly, he or she shall be rebuked openly, that he or she may be ashamed. And if he or she confess not, he or she shall be delivered up unto the law of God.

92. If any shall ²ʳoffend in secret, he or she shall be rebuked in secret, that he or she may have opportunity to confess in secret to him or her whom he or she has offended, and to God, that the church may not speak reproachfully of him or her.

93. And thus shall ye conduct in all things.

SECTION 43.

Revelation given through Joseph, the Seer, at Kirtland,
Ohio, February, 1831.

1. O hearken, ye elders of my church, and give an ear to the words which I shall speak unto you;

2o, ver. 28.   43 : 11.   2p, 20 : 80.   2q, that all may see
that there is justice in the church.   2r, confession and repentance,
intended to be as extensive as the offence.

2. For behold, verily, verily, I say unto you, that ye have received a commandment for a ^alaw unto my church, through him whom I have appointed unto you, to receive commandments and revelations from my hand.

3. And this ye shall know assuredly that there is ^bnone other appointed unto you to receive commandments and revelations until he be taken, if he abide in me.

4. But verily, verily, I say unto you, that none else shall be appointed unto this gift except it be through him, for if it be taken from him, he shall not have power except to appoint another in his stead ;

5. And this shall be a law unto you, that ye receive not the teachings of any that shall come before you as revelations or commandments ;

6. And this I give unto you that you may not be deceived, that you may know they are not of me.

7. For verily I say unto you, that he that is ^cordained of me shall come in at the gate and be ordained as I have told you before, to teach those revelations which you have received, and shall receive through him whom I have appointed.

8. And now, behold, I give unto you a commandment, that when ye are assembled together, ye shall instruct and edify each other, that ye may know how to act and direct my church, how to act upon the points of my law and commandments, which I have given ;

9. And thus ye shall become instructed in the law of my church, and be sanctified by that which ye have received, and ye shall ^dbind yourselves to act in all holiness before me,

10. That inasmuch as ye do this, glory shall be added to the kingdom which ye have received. Inas-

---

much as ye do it not, it shall be taken, even that which
ye have received.

11. Purge ye out the iniquity which is among you ;
sanctify yourselves before me,

12. And if ye desire the glories of the kingdom,
appoint ye my servant Joseph Smith, jun., and uphold
him before me by the prayer of faith.

13. And again, I say unto you, that if ye desire the
mysteries of the kingdom, provide for him food and
raiment, and whatsoever thing he needeth to accomplish
the work, wherewith I have commanded him ;

14. And if ye do it not, he shall remain unto them
that have received him, that I may reserve unto myself
a pure people before me.

15. Again I say, hearken ye elders of my church,
whom I have appointed ; ye are not sent forth to be
taught, but to teach the children of men the things
which I have put into your hands by the power of my
Spirit ;

16. And ye ᶜare to be taught from on high. Sanctify yourselves and ye shall be ᶠendowed with power,
that ye may give even as I have spoken.

17. Hearken ye, for, behold, the great day of the
Lord is nigh at hand.

18. For the day cometh that the Lord shall ᵍutter
his voice out of heaven ; the heavens shall ʰshake and
the earth shall tremble, and the ⁱtrump of God shall
sound both long and loud, and shall say to the sleeping
nations, Ye saints arise and live ; ye sinners stay and
sleep until I shall call again ;

19. Wherefore gird up your loins lest ye be found
among the wicked.

20. Lift up your voices and spare not. Call upon
the ʲnations to repent, both old and young, both bond

---

e, 46 : 7—33. 50 : 10—36. 52 : 9.   f, see x, Sec. 38.   g, vers.
23—27. 1 : 11. 45 : 49. 63 : 5.   h, see e, Sec. 21.   i, see l,
Sec. 29.   j, see b, Sec. 1.

and free, saying, prepare yourselves for the great day of the Lord ;

21. For if I, who am a man, do lift up my voice and call upon you to repent, and ye hate me, what will ye say when the day cometh when the thunders shall utter their voices from the ends of the earth, speaking to the ears of all that live, saying, *k*Repent, and prepare for the great day of the Lord ;

22. Yea, and again, when the lightnings shall streak forth from the east unto the west, and shall utter forth their voices unto all that live, and make the ears of all tingle that hear, saying these words, *l*Repent ye, for the great day of the Lord is come.

23. And again, the Lord shall *m*utter his voice out of heaven, saying, Hearken, O ye nations of the earth, and hear the words of that God who made you.

24. O, ye nations of the earth, how often would I have *n*gathered you together as a hen gathereth her chickens under her wings, but ye would not ?

25. How oft have I called upon you by the mouth of my servants, and by the ministering of angels, and by mine own voice, and by the *o*voice of thunderings, and by the voice of lightnings, and by the voice of tempests, and by the voice of earthquakes, and great hailstorms, and by the voice of famines and pestilences of every kind, and by the great sound of a trump, and by the voice of judgment, and by the voice of mercy all the day long, and by the voice of glory, and honor, and the riches of eternal life, and would have saved you with an everlasting salvation, but ye would not ?

26. Behold the day has come, when the cup of the wrath of mine indignation is full.

27. Behold, verily I say unto you, that these are the words of the Lord your God ;

28. Wherefore labor ye, *p*labor ye in my vineyard

for the last time—for the last time call upon the inhabitants of the earth,

29. For in my own due time will I come upon the earth in judgment, and my people shall be redeemed and shall *q*reign with me on earth,

30. For the great *r*Millennium, of which I have spoken by the mouth of my servants, shall come ;

31. For *s*Satan shall be bound, and when he is loosed again, he shall only reign for a *t*little season, and then cometh the *u*end of the earth ;

32. And he that liveth in righteousness shall be *v*changed in the twinkling of an eye, and the *w*earth shall pass away so as by fire ;

33. And the wicked shall go away into *x*unquenchable fire, and their end no man knoweth on earth, nor ever shall know, until they come before me in judgment.

34. Hearken ye to these words ; Behold, I am Jesus Christ, the Saviour of the world. Treasure these things up in your hearts, and let the solemnities of eternity rest upon your minds.

35. Be sober. Keep all my commandments. Even so. Amen.

SECTION 44.

Revelation to Joseph Smith, jun., and Sidney Rigdon,
given in Kirtland, Ohio, February, 1831.

1. Behold, thus saith the Lord unto you my servants, it is expedient in me that the elders of my church should be called together, from the east and

---

q, 1 : 36.   66 : 63.   84 : 119.   88 : 17, 26.   r, 29 : 11, 22.   s, 88 : 110.   101 : 28.   t, 29 : 22.   u, see t, Sec. 88.   v, 88 : 20, 23.
w, see t, Sec. 88.   x, 29 : 23.   See s and f, Sec. 19.

from the west, and from the north and from the south, by letter or some other way.

2. And it shall come to pass, that inasmuch as they are faithful, and exercise faith in me, I will pour out my Spirit upon them in the day that they assemble themselves together.

3. And it shall come to pass that they shall go forth into the regions round about, and preach repentance unto the people ;

4. And many shall be converted, insomuch that ye shall obtain power to organize yourselves, *according to the laws of man ;

5. That your enemies may not have power over you, that you may be preserved in all things ; that you may be enabled to keep my laws, that every *band may be broken wherewith the enemy seeketh to destroy my people.

6. Behold, I say unto you, that ye must visit the poor and the needy, and administer to their relief, that they may be kept until all things may be done according to my *law which ye have received.   Amen.

SECTION 45.

Revelation given through Joseph, the Seer, at Kirtland, Ohio, March 7th, 1831.

1. Hearken, O ye people of my church to whom the *kingdom has been given—hearken ye and give ear to him who laid the foundation of the earth, who made the heavens and all the hosts thereof, and by whom all

---

a, with civil officers, elected by themselves.   b, that the civil officers may be good men, and not persecutors.   c, see Sec. 42.

a, see x, Sec. 35.

things were made which live, and move, and have a being.

2. And again, I say, hearken unto my voice, lest death shall overtake you ; in an hour when ye think not the [b]summer shall be past, and the harvest ended, and your souls not saved.

3. Listen to him who is the [c]advocate with the Father, who is pleading your cause before him,

4. Saying, Father, behold the sufferings and death of him who did no sin, in whom thou wast well pleased; behold the blood of thy Son which was shed—the blood of him whom thou gavest that thyself might be glorified ;

5. Wherefore, Father, spare these my brethren that believe on my name, that they may come unto me and have everlasting life.

6. Hearken, O ye people of my church, and ye elders listen together, and hear my voice while it is called to-day, and harden not your hearts,

7. For verily I say unto you that I am Alpha and Omega, the beginning and the end, the [d]light and the life of the world—a light that [e]shineth in darkness and the darkness comprehendeth it not.

8. I came unto my [f]own, and my own received me not ; but unto as many as received me, gave I [g]power to do many miracles, and to become the sons of God, and even unto them that believed on my name gave I power to obtain eternal life.

9. And even so I have sent mine [h]everlasting covenant into the world, to be a light to the world, and to be a [i]standard for my people and for the Gentiles to seek to it, and to be a [j]messenger before my face to prepare the way before me ;

10. Wherefore, come ye unto it, and with him that

---

b, 50: 16.   Jer. 8: 20.   c, vers. 4, 5.   20: 5.   62: 1.   110: 4.
d, see h, Sec. 6.   e, see h, Sec. 6.   f, see g, Sec. 6.   g, see g,
Sec. 6.   h, see k, Sec. 1.   i, ver. 28.   .1: 29.   3: 16—20.   5:
15, 16.   10: 45—53.   20: 8—12.   64: 42.   113: 6.   115: 5.   j, see i.

cometh I will reason as with men in days of old, and I
will show unto you my strong reasoning,

11. Wherefore hearken ye together and let me show
it unto you, even my wisdom—the wisdom of him whom
ye say is the God of Enoch, and his brethren,

12. Who were *k*separated from the earth, and were
received unto myself—a city reserved until a day of
righteousness shall come—a day which was sought for
by all holy men, and they found it not because of
wickedness and abominations ;

13. And confessed they were strangers and pilgrims
on the earth ;

14. But obtained a promise that they should find it
and see it in their flesh.

15. Wherefore, hearken and I will reason with you,
and I will speak unto you and prophesy, as unto men
in days of old ;

16. And I will show it plainly as I showed it unto
my disciples as I stood before them in the flesh, and
spake unto them, saying, as ye have asked of me concerning the signs of my coming in the day when I shall
come in my glory in the clouds of heaven, to fulfill the
promises that I have made unto your fathers,

17. For as ye have looked upon the long absence of
your spirits from your bodies to be a bondage, I will
show unto you how the day of redemption shall come,
and also the *l*restoration of the scattered Israel.

18. And now ye behold this temple which is in
Jerusalem, which ye call the house of God, and your
enemies say that this house shall never fall.

19. But, verily, I say unto you, that desolation shall
come upon this generation as a thief in the night, and
this people shall be *m*destroyed and scattered among all
nations.

20. And this temple which ye now see shall be

k, 84 : 99, 100. 183 : 54.   *l*, vers. 43, 51—53.   *m*, Luke 20 :
16. 21 : 23, 24.

thrown down that there shall not be left *one stone upon another.

21. And it shall come to pass, that this generation of Jews shall not pass away, until every desolation which I have told you concerning them shall come to pass.

22. Ye say that ye know that the end of the world cometh; ye say also that ye know that the heavens and the earth shall pass away;

23. And in this ye say truly, for so it is; but these things which I have told you shall not pass away until all shall be fulfilled,

24. And this I have told you concerning Jerusalem, and when that day shall come, shall a remnant be scattered among all nations;

25. But they shall be gathered again, but they shall remain until the °times of the Gentiles be fulfilled.

26. And in that day shall be heard of wars and rumors of wars, and the ᵖwhole earth shall be in commotion, and men's hearts shall fail them, and they shall say that Christ delayeth his coming until the end of the earth.

27. And the love of men shall wax cold, and iniquity shall abound;

28. And when the times of the Gentiles is come in, a ᵠlight shall break forth among them that sit in darkness, and it shall be the ʳfullness of my gospel;

29. But they receive it not, for they perceive not the light and they turn their hearts from me because of the precepts of men;

30. And in that ˢgeneration shall the times of the Gentiles be fulfilled;

31. And there shall be ᵗmen standing in that generation, that shall not pass, until they shall see an over-

n, Matt. 24 : 2.　Luke 19 : 44.　　*o*, ver. 30.　Luke 21 : 24.　Rom.
11 : 25—27.　　　　*p*, vers. 33, 63, 31, 49, 50.　Luke 21 : 10, 11, 25—27.
q, see *i*.　　*r*, see *b*, Sec. 18.　　*s*, see *o*.　　*t*, 29 : 18—21.　84.
92—97, 114, 115, 117.　87 : 3—7.　97 : 22—26.

flowing scourge ; for a [u]desolating sickness shall cover the land ;

32. But my disciples [v]shall stand in holy places, and shall not be moved ; but among the wicked, men shall lift up their voices, and [w]curse God and die.

33. And there shall be [x]earthquakes also in divers places, and many desolations ; yet men will harden their hearts against me, and they will [y]take up the sword, one against another, and they will kill one another.

34. And, now, when I the Lord had spoken these words unto my disciples, they were troubled :

35. And I said unto them, be not troubled, for when all these things shall come to pass, ye may know that the promises which have been made unto you shall be fulfilled ;

36. And when the light shall [z]begin to break forth, it shall be with them like unto a parable which I will show you :

37. Ye look and behold the fig-trees, and ye see them with your eyes, and ye say when they begin to shoot forth, and their leaves are yet tender, that summer is now nigh at hand ;

38. Even so it shall be in that day when they shall see all these things, then shall they [2a]know that the hour is nigh.

39. And it shall come to pass that he that feareth me shall be looking forth for the great day of the Lord to come, even for the [2b]signs of the coming of the Son of man :

40. And they shall [2c]see signs and wonders, for they shall be shown forth in the heavens above, and in the earth beneath ;

41. And they shall behold blood, and fire, and vapors of smoke ;

u, see ..   *v*, 63 : 24.   64 : 41—43.   87 : 8.   101 : 21, 22, 64.
w, Rev. 16 : 21.   *x*, 43 : 18.   45 : 33, 48.   84 : 118.   88 : 87, 90.
y, see p.   *z*, see *i*.   2*a*, see *e*, Sec. 1.   2*b*, see *e*, Sec. 1.
2*c*, 88 : 83—110. See *e*, Sec. 1.

42. And before the day of the Lord shall come, the [2d]sun shall be darkened, and the moon be turned into blood, and stars fall from heaven ;

43. And the remnant shall be [2c]gathered unto this place,

44. And then they shall look for me, and, behold, I will come ; and [2f]they shall see me in the clouds of heaven, clothed with power and great glory, with all the holy angels ; and he that watches not for me shall be cut off.

45. But before the arm of the Lord shall fall, an [2g]angel shall sound his trump, and the saints that have slept shall come forth to [2h]meet me in the cloud ;

46. Wherefore, if ye have slept in peace, blessed are you, for as you now behold me and know that I am, even so shall ye come unto me and your souls shall live, and your redemption shall be perfected, and the [2i]saints shall come forth from the four quarters of the earth.

47. Then shall the [2j]arm of the Lord fall upon the nations,

48. And then shall the Lord set his [2k]foot upon this mount, and it shall cleave in twain, and the earth shall [2l]tremble, and reel to and fro, and the [2m]heavens also shall shake,

49. And the Lord shall [2n]utter his voice, and all the ends of the earth shall hear it, and the [2o]nations of the earth shall mourn, and they that have laughed shall see their folly,

50. And calamity shall cover the mocker, and the scorner shall be consumed, and they that have watched for iniquity shall be hewn down and cast into the fire.

51. And then shall the Jews look upon me and

2*d*, see *n*, Sec. 20.   2*e*, vers. 17, 25, 44, 61—53.   133 : 13.
2*f*, 34 : 7.   76 : 63, 102.   78 : 21.   84 : 100.   88 : 94--98.   2*g*, see *l*, Sec.
20.   2*h*, see *m*, Sec. 20.   2*i*, see *j*, Sec. 10.   2*j*, see *f* and *g*, Sec. 1.
2*k*, 133 : 20.   2*l*, see *x*.   2*m*, see *e*, Sec. 21.   2*n*, see *y*,
Sec. 43.   2*o*, see *f* and *g*, Sec. 1.

say, [2p]What are these wounds in thine hands and in thy feet ?

52. Then shall they know that I am the Lord ; for I will say unto them, These wounds are the wounds with which I was wounded in the house of my friends. I am he who was lifted up.   I am Jesus that was crucified.   I am the Son of God.

53. And then shall [2q]they weep because of their iniquities ; then shall they lament because they percuted their King.

54. And then shall the [2r]heathen nations be redeemed, and they that knew no law shall have [2s]part in the first resurrection; and it shall be tolerable for them ;

55. And [2t]Satan shall be bound that he shall have no place in the hearts of the children of men.

56. And at that day, when I shall come in my glory, shall the parable be fulfilled which I spake concerning the [2u]ten virgins ;

57. For they that are wise and have received the truth, and have taken the Holy Spirit for their guide, and have not been deceived ; verily I say unto you, they shall not be hewn down and cast into the fire, but shall abide the day,

58. And the earth shall be given unto them for an inheritance ; and they shall [2v]multiply and wax strong, and their children shall grow up without sin unto salvation,

59. For the Lord shall be [2w]in their midst, and his glory shall be upon them, and he will be their King and their Lawgiver.

60. And now, behold I say unto you, it shall not be given unto you to know any further concerning this chapter, until the New Testament be [2x]translated, and in it all these things shall be made known ;

2 p, Zech. 12: 10.   13 : 6.   2 q, Zech. 12: 10—14.   2 r, Ezek.
36 : 23, 36.   37 : 28.   38 : 16, 23.   39 : 7, 21, 23.   2 s, 76 : 71—80.
2 t, 88 : 110.   101 : 28.   2 u, 63 : 54.   2 v, 63 : 51.   101 : 29—31.
132 : 30, 63.   2 w, see e, Sec. 1.   2 x, translated by inspiration.

61. Wherefore I give unto you that ye may now translate it, that ye may be prepared for the things to come ;

62. For verily I say unto you, that great things await you ;

63. Ye hear of wars in foreign lands, but, behold, I say unto you, they are nigh, even at your doors, and not [2y]many years hence ye shall hear of wars in your own lands.

64. Wherefore I, the Lord, have said, [2z]gather ye out from the eastern lands, assemble ye yourselves together ye elders of my church ; go ye forth into the western countries, call upon the inhabitants to repent, and inasmuch as they do repent, build up churches unto me ;

65. And with one heart and with one mind, gather up your riches that ye may purchase an inheritance which shall hereafter be appointed unto you,

66. And it shall be called the [3a]New Jerusalem, a land of peace, a city of refuge, a place of safety for the saints of the most High God ;

67. And the [3b]glory of the Lord shall be there, and the [3c]terror of the Lord also shall be there, insomuch that the wicked will not come unto it, and it shall be called [3d]Zion.

68. And it shall come to pass, among the wicked, that every man that will [3e]not take his sword against his neighbor, must needs flee unto [3f]Zion for safety.

69. And there shall be gathered unto it out of [3g]every

2y, see t, Sec. 38.   2z, see j, Sec. 10.   3a, see q, Sec. 42.
3b, 64 : 41—43.   84 : 4, 5, 31, 32.   97 : 15—20.   3c, see 3b.   3d, 28 :
9.   39 : 13.   42 : 35.   58 : 49, 50.   59 : 3.   61 : 16, 24.   62 : 2, 4.   63 : 24, 25,
29, 36, 39—41, 43, 48.   64 : 18, 22, 26, 34, 35, 38, 41.   66 : 6, 11.   68 : 25, 26,
29—32.   69 : 1, 5, 6, 8.   70 : 1, 8.   72 : 6, 13—15, 17, 18, 24, 26.   78 : 3, 9.
82 : 12—14.   84 : 2—4, 32, 56, 58, 76, 104.   89 : 1.   90 : 32, 34, 36.   97 : 1,
3—5, 10, 12, 18—21, 25.   99 : 6.   100 : 13.   101 : 16—18, 21, 70, 74, 75.   103 :
1, 11, 13, 15, 18, 22, 24, 29, 30, 34, 35.   104 : 47, 48.   105 : 5, 8, 9, 13, 14, 34.
107 : 59, 74.   109 : 51, 59.   111 : 2, 6.   115 : 3, 6.   117 : 9, 14.   118 : 2.
119 : 1, 2, 5, 6, 7.   124 : 36.   133 : 4, 9, 12, 18, 20, 21, 24, 32, 56.   3e, vers.
33, 63, 69.   38 : 29.   63 : 33.   Sec. 87.   3f, see 3d.   3g, see j,
Sec. 10.

nation under heaven; and it shall be the [3h]only people that shall not be at war one with another.

70. And it shall be said among the wicked, [3i]Let us not go up to battle against [3j]Zion, for the inhabitants of Zion are terrible; wherefore we cannot stand.

71. And it shall come to pass that the righteous shall be gathered out from [3k]among all nations, and shall come to Zion, singing with [3l]songs of everlasting joy.

72. And now I say unto you, keep these things from going abroad unto the world, until it is expedient in me that ye may accomplish this work in the eyes of the people, and in the eyes of your enemies, that they may not know your works until ye have accomplished the thing which I have commanded you;

73. That when they shall know it, that they may consider these things;

74. For when the Lord shall appear he shall be [3m]terrible unto them, that fear may seize upon them, and they shall stand afar off and tremble;

75. And [3n]all nations shall be afraid because of the terror of the Lord, and the power of his might. Even so. Amen.

SECTION 46.

Revelation given through Joseph, the Seer, at Kirtland, Ohio, March 8th, 1831.

1. Hearken, O ye people of my church, for verily I say unto you, that these things were spoken unto you for your profit and learning;

2. But notwithstanding those things which are written, it always has been given to the elders of my

---

3h, see o, Sec. 1.   Isa. 13: 4—13.   66: 14—16.   3i, see 3b.
3j, see 3d.   3k, see j, Sec. 10.   3l, 101: 18.   Isa. 35: 10.
3m, see e, Sec. 1.   3n, see e, Sec. 1.

church from the beginning, and ever shall be to ^aconduct all meetings as they are directed and guided by the Holy Spirit;

3. Nevertheless ye are commanded never to cast any one out from your public meetings, which are held before the world;

4. Ye are also commanded not to cast any one, who belongeth to the church out of your sacrament meetings; nevertheless, if any have trespassed, ^blet him not partake until he makes reconciliation.

5. And again I say unto you, ye shall not cast any out of your sacrament meetings, who are earnestly seeking the kingdom : I speak this concerning those who are not of the church.

6. And again I say unto you, concerning your ^cconfirmation meetings, that if there be any that are not of the church, that are earnestly seeking after the kingdom, ye shall not cast them out;

7. But ye are commanded in all things to ask of God, who giveth liberally; and that which the Spirit testifies unto you, even so I would that ye should do in all holiness of heart, walking uprightly before me, considering the end of your salvation, doing all things with prayer and thanksgiving, that ye may not be seduced by evil spirits, or doctrines of devils, or the commandments of men, for some are of men, and others of devils.

8. Wherefore, beware lest ye are deceived; and that ye may not be deceived, ^dseek ye earnestly the best gifts, always remembering for what they are given;

9. For verily I say unto you, they are given for the benefit of those who love me and keep all my commandments, and him that seeketh so to do, that all may be benefited that seeketh or that asketh of me, that asketh and not for a sign that he may consume it upon his lusts.

---

a, I. Nep. 13 : 37. Moro. 3 : 4. 6 : 9.   *b*, 20 : 68, 69. III. Nep. 12 : 23—26. 18 : 28—33.   *c*, see *a*.   *d*, I. Corinth. 12 : 31. 14 : 1.

10. And again, verily I say unto you, I would that ye should always remember, and always retain in your minds ᶜwhat those gifts are, that are given unto the church,

11. For all have not every gift given unto them ; for there are many gifts, and to ᶠevery man is given a gift by the Spirit of God :

12. To some it is given one, and to some is given another, that all may be profited thereby ;

13. To some it is given by the Holy Ghost to ᵍknow that Jesus Christ is the Son of God, and that he was crucified for the sins of the world ;

14. To others it is given to believe on their words, that they also might have eternal life if they continue faithful.

15. And again, to some it is given by the Holy Ghost to know the differences of administration, as it will be pleasing unto the same Lord, according as the Lord will, suiting his mercies according to the conditions of the children of men.

16. And again, it is given by the Holy Ghost to some to know the diversities of operations, whether it be of God, that the manifestations of the Spirit may be given to every man to profit withal.

17. And again, verily I say unto you, to some it is given, by the Spirit of God, the word of wisdom ;

18. To another it is given the word of knowledge, that all may be taught to be wise and to have knowledge.

19. And again, to some it is given to have faith to be healed,

20. And to others it is given to have faith to heal.

21. And again, to some it is given the working of miracles,

22. And to others it is given to prophesy,

23. And to others the discerning of spirits.

24. And again, it is given to some to speak with tongues,

25. And to another it is given the interpretation of tongues :

26. And all these gifts cometh from God, for the benefit of the children of God.

27. And unto the bishop of the church, and unto such as God shall appoint and ordain to watch over the church, and to be elders unto the church, are to have it given unto them to discern all those gifts, lest there shall be any among you professing and yet be not of God.

28. And it shall come to pass that he that asketh in Spirit shall receive in Spirit ;

29. That unto some it may be given to have ʰall those gifts, that there may be a head, in order that every member may be profited thereby :

30. He that asketh in the Spirit, asketh according to the will of God, wherefore it is done even as he asketh.

31. And again, I say unto you, all things must be done in the name of Christ, whatsoever you do in the Spirit ;

32. And ye must give thanks unto God in the Spirit for whatsoever blessing ye are blessed with ;

33. And ye must practice virtue and holiness before me continually. Even so. Amen.

SECTION 47.

Revelation to Joseph Smith, jun., and John Whitmer, given in Kirtland, Ohio, March 8th, 1831.

1. Behold, it is expedient in me that my servant

ʰ, ver. 27.

John should write and keep a regular ᵃhistory, and assist you, my servant Joseph, in transcribing all things which shall be given you, until he is called to further duties.

2. Again, verily I say unto you, that he can also lift up his voice in meetings, whenever it shall be expedient.

3. And again, I say unto you, that it shall be appointed unto him to keep the church record and history continually, for Oliver Cowdery I have appointed to another office.

4. Wherefore it shall be given him, inasmuch as he is faithful, by the Comforter, to write these things. Even so. Amen.

SECTION 48.

Revelation given through Joseph, the Seer, at Kirtland, Ohio, March, 1831.

1. It is necessary that ye should remain for the present time in your places of abode, as it shall be suitable to your circumstances ;

2. And inasmuch as ye have lands, ye shall impart to the ᵃeastern brethren ;

3. And inasmuch as ye have not lands, let them buy for the present time in those regions round about as seemeth them good, for it must needs be necessary that they have places to live for the present time.

4. It must needs be necessary, that ye save all the money that ye can, and that ye obtain all that ye can

---

a, see *a*, Sec. 21.

a, The saints who were coming from the state of N. York.

in righteousness, that in time ye may be enabled to purchase [b]land for an inheritance, even the city.

5. The place is not yet to be revealed, but after your brethren [c]come from the east, there are to be certain men appointed, and to them it shall be given to know the place, or to them it shall be revealed.

6. And they shall be appointed to [d]purchase the lands, and to make a commencement to lay the [e]foundation of the city ; and then shall ye begin to be gathered with your families, every man according to his family, according to his circumstances, and as is appointed to him by the Presidency and the bishop of the church, according to the laws and commandments which ye have received, and which ye shall hereafter receive. Even so. Amen.

SECTION 49.

Revelation through Joseph, the Seer, to Sidney Rigdon, Parley P. Pratt, and Lemon Copley, given at Kirtland, Ohio, March, 1831.

1. Hearken unto my word, my servants Sidney, and Parley, and Lemon, for behold, verily I say unto you, that I give unto you a commandment that you shall go and preach [a]my gospel which ye have received, even as ye have received it, unto the Shakers.

2. Behold, I say unto you, that they desire to know the truth in part, but not all, for they are not right before me and must needs repent ;

b, see *q*, Sec. 42.   45 : 65.   57 : 8.   58 : 37, 51.   63 : 27.   64 : 30.   90 : 29, 30.   101 : 18, 70.   103 : 23.   105 : 29.   *c*, see *a*.   *d*, see *b*. *e*, 57 : 1—5.   84 : 2—4.

a, see *b*, Sec. 18.

3. Wherefore I send you, my servants Sidney and Parley, to preach the gospel unto them ;

4. And my servant Lemon shall be ordained unto this work, that he may reason with them, not according to that which he has received of them, but according to that which shall be taught him by you my servants, and by so doing I will bless him, otherwise he shall not prosper.

5. Thus saith the Lord, for I am God, and have sent mine Only Begotten Son into the world for the redemption of the world, and have decreed that he that receiveth him shall be saved, and he that receiveth him not shall be damned.

6. And they have done unto the Son of man even as they listed; and he has taken his power on the right hand of his glory, and now reigneth in the heavens, and will reign till he *b*descends on the earth to put all enemies under his feet, which time is nigh at hand :

7. I, the Lord God, have spoken it, but the *c*hour and the day no man knoweth, neither the angels in heaven, nor shall they know until he comes ;

8. Wherefore I will that all men shall repent, for all are under sin, except them which I have reserved unto myself, holy men that ye know not of ;

9. Wherefore I say unto you, that I have sent unto you mine *d*everlasting covenant, even that which was from the beginning,

10. And that which I have promised I have so fulfilled, and the nations of the earth shall bow to it ; and, if not of themselves, they shall come down, for that which is now exalted of itself shall be laid low of power ;

11. Wherefore I give unto you a commandment that ye go among this people and say unto them, like unto mine apostle of old, whose name was Peter ;

---

12. Believe on the name of the Lord Jesus, who was on the earth, and is to come, the beginning and the end,

13. ʻRepent and be baptized in the name of Jesus Christ, according to the holy commandment, for the remission of sins;

14. And whoso doeth this shall receive the gift of the Holy Ghost, by the laying on of the hands of the elders of this church.

15. And again, I say unto you, that whoso forbiddeth to marry is not ordained of God, for ʲmarriage is ordained of God unto man;

16. Wherefore it is lawful that he should have one wife, and they twain shall be one flesh, and all this that the earth might answer the end of its creation,

17. And that it might be filled with the measure of man, according to his creation before the world was made.

18. And whoso forbiddeth to abstain from meats, that man should not eat the same, is not ordained of God;

19. For, behold, the beasts of the field and the fowls of the air, and that which cometh of the earth, is ordained for the use of man for food and for raiment, and that he might have in abundance:

20. But it is ᵍnot given that one man should possess that which is above another, wherefore the world lieth in sin;

21. And wo be unto man that sheddeth blood or that wasteth flesh and hath no need.

22. And again, verily I say unto you, that the Son of man cometh not in the form of a woman, neither of a man traveling on the earth;

23. Wherefore be not deceived, but continue in steadfastness, looking forth for the ʰheavens to be

5, 6.   c, see b, Sec. 18.   f, ver. 16. See k, Sec. 42.   g, 51: 9.   78:
        h, see e, Sec. 21.

198 COVENANTS AND [SEC. L.

shaken, and the earth to tremble and to reel to and fro as a drunken man, and for the valleys to be exalted, and for the mountains to be made low, and for the rough places to become smooth; and all this when the angel shall sound his trumpet.

24. But before the great day of the Lord shall come, Jacob shall flourish in the wilderness, and the Lamanites shall blossom as the rose.

25. Zion shall flourish upon the hills and rejoice upon the mountains, and shall be assembled together unto the place which I have appointed.

26. Behold, I say unto you, go forth as I have commanded you—repent of all your sins, ask and ye shall receive, knock and it shall be opened unto you:

27. Behold, I will go before you and be your rearward; and I will be in your midst, and you shall not be confounded;

28. Behold, I am Jesus Christ, and I come quickly. Even so. Amen.

SECTION 50.

Revelation given through Joseph, the Seer, at Kirtland, Ohio, May, 1831.

1. Hearken, O ye elders of my church, and give ear to the voice of the living God, and attend to the words of wisdom which shall be given unto you, according as ye have asked and are agreed as touching the church, and the spirits which have gone abroad in the earth.

2. Behold, verily I say unto you, that there are

i, see *x*, Sec. 45. *j*, 133: 22. Isa. 40: 4. *k*, see *l*, Sec. 29. *l*, Ezek. 20: 33–38. *m*, III. Nep. 21: 22–25. Isa. 35: 1, 2. *n*, see *v*, Sec. 35. *o*, see *v*, Sec. 35. *p*, see *c*, Sec. 4. *q*, see *e*, Sec. 1.

many spirits which are false spirits, which have gone forth in the earth, deceiving the world ;

3. And also Satan hath sought to deceive you, that he might overthrow you.

4. Behold, I the Lord have looked upon you, and have seen abominations in the church that profess my name ;

5. But blessed are they who are faithful and endure, whether in life or in death, for they shall inherit eternal life.

6. But wo unto them that are deceivers and hypocrites, for, thus saith the Lord, I will bring them to judgment.

7. Behold, verily I say unto you, there are hypocrites among you, who have deceived some, which has given the adversary power, but behold such shall be reclaimed ;

8. But the hypocrites shall be detected and shall be cut off, either in life or in death, even as I will ; and ^awo unto them who are cut off from my church, for the same are overcome of the world ;

9. Wherefore, let every man beware lest he do that which is not in truth and righteousness before me.

10. And now come, saith the Lord, by the Spirit, unto the elders of his church, and let us reason together, that ye may understand :

11. Let us reason even as a man reasoneth one with another face to face :

12. Now when a man reasoneth he is understood of man, because he reasoneth as a man, even so will I, the Lord, reason with you that you may understand ;

13. Wherefore I, the Lord, asketh you this question, unto what were ye ordained ?

14. To preach my gospel by the ^bSpirit, even the Comforter which was sent forth to teach the truth ;

---

a, 41: 1. 76: 29—37. 104: 8, 9. 121: 13—25.　　　b, 42: 14

15. And then received ye spirits which ye could not
understand, and received them to be of God, and in
this are ye justified ?

16. Behold ye shall answer this question yourselves;
nevertheless I will be merciful unto you—he that is
weak among you hereafter shall be made strong.

17. Verily I say unto you, he that is ordained of
me and sent forth to preach the word of truth by the
Comforter, in the Spirit of truth, doth he preach it by
the Spirit of truth or some other way ?

18. And if it be by some other way, it be not of
God.

19. And again, he that receiveth the word of truth,
doth he receive it by the Spirit of truth or some other
way ?

20. If it be some other way it be not of God :

21. Therefore, why is it that ye cannot understand
and know that he that receiveth the word by the Spirit
of truth, receiveth it as it is preached by the Spirit of
truth ?

22. Wherefore, he that preacheth and he that receiveth, understandeth one another, and both are
edified and rejoice together ;

23. And that which doth not edify is not of God,
and is darkness ;

24. That which is of God is light ; and he that receiveth light ᶜand continueth in God, receiveth more
light, and that light groweth brighter and brighter
until the perfect day.

25. And again, verily I say unto you, and I say it
that you may know the truth, that you may chase
darkness from among you ;

26. For he that is ordained of God and sent forth
the same is appointed to be the greatest, notwithstanding he is least and the servant of all :

27. Wherefore he is possessor of all things ; for ^dall
things are subject unto him, both in heaven and on
the earth, the life and the light, the Spirit and the
power, sent forth by the will of the Father, through
Jesus Christ, his Son ;

28. But no man is possessor of all things ; except ^ehe be purified and cleansed from all sin ;

29. And if ye are purified and cleansed from all
sin, ye shall ask ^fwhatsoever you will in the name of
Jesus and it shall be done :

30. But know this, it shall be given you what you
shall ask, and as ye are appointed to the head, the
spirits shall be subject unto you.

31. Wherefore it shall come to pass, that if you
behold a spirit manifested that you cannot understand,
and you receive not that spirit, ye shall ask of the
Father in the name of Jesus, and if he give ^gnot unto
you that spirit, then you may know that it is not of
God :

32. And it shall be given unto you power over that
spirit, and you shall proclaim against that spirit with
a loud voice that it is not of God ;

33. Not with railing accusation, that ye be not
overcome, neither with boasting, nor rejoicing, lest you
be seized therewith.

34. He that receiveth of God, let him account it
of God, and let him rejoice that he is accounted of
God worthy to receive,

35. And by giving heed and doing these things
which ye have received, and which ye shall hereafter
receive : and the ^hkingdom is given you of the Father,
and power to overcome all things which are not ordained
of him.

36. And behold, verily I say unto you, blessed
are you who are now hearing these words of mine from

d, 76 : 5—10, 53—60.   93 : 27, 28.   121 : 26—29.   132 : 20.   e, ver.
27.   93 : 27, 28.   f, see c, Sec. 4.   g, vers. 29, 30.   h, see x,
Sec. 35.

the mouth of my servant, for your sins are forgiven you.

37. Let my servant Joseph Wakefield, in whom I am well pleased, and my servant Parley P. Pratt, go forth among the churches and strengthen them by the word of exhortation ;

38. And also my servant John Corrill, or as many of my servants as are ordained unto this office, and let them labor in the vineyard ; and let no man hinder them of doing that which I have appointed unto them :

39. Wherefore in this thing my servant Edward Partridge is not justified, nevertheless let him repent and he shall be forgiven.

40. Behold, ye are little children and ye cannot bear all things now ; ye must grow in grace and in the knowledge of the truth.

41. Fear not, little children, for you are mine, and I have overcome the world, and you are of ʲthem that my Father hath given me ;

42. And none of them that my Father hath given me shall be lost :

43. And the Father and I are ʲone : I am in the Father and the Father in me : and inasmuch as ye have received me, ye are ᵏin me and I in you ;

44. Wherefore I am in your midst, and I am the good ˡShepherd, and the ᵐStone of Israel. He that buildeth upon this ⁿrock shall never fall,

45. And the day cometh that you shall hear my voice and ᵒsee me, and know that I am.

46. Watch, therefore, that ye may be ready. Even so. Amen.

ɩ, John 17 : 2—12. 10 : 27—29.   ʲ, see v., Lecture on Faith. Also 93 : 3. ɪɪɪ. Nep. 11 : 27. 19 : 23, 29. Ether 3 : 14. John 10 : 30.   ᵏ, 88 : 67.   93 : 19—23.   ˡ, Mos. 3 : 14. Alma 5 : 38—60. Hela. 7 : 18. ɪɪɪ. Nep. 15 : 16—24. Psalm 80 : 1—3.   ᵐ, 6 : 34. 10 : 69. 33 : 13. 65 : 2. See o, Sec. 6. Gen. 49 : 24.   ⁿ, see m.   ᵒ, 35 : 21. 67 : 10—14.   76 : 113—119.   84 : 19—25.   88 : 47—50, 68, 75.   93 : 1. 97 : 16. 101 : 38.   107 : 19.   110 : 1—9.

SECTION 51.

Revelation given through Joseph, the Seer, in Thompson,
Geauga County, Ohio, May, 1831.

1. Hearken unto me, saith the Lord your God, and I will speak unto my servant Edward Partridge, and give unto him directions, for it must need be that he receive directions how to organize this people ;

2. For it must needs be that they be organized according to my laws—if otherwise, they will be cut off ;

3. Wherefore let my servant Edward Partridge, and those whom he has chosen, in whom I am well pleased, appoint unto this people their portion, every man *ª*equal according to their families, according to their circumstances, and their wants and needs.

4. And let my servant Edward Partridge, when he shall appoint a man his portion, give unto him a *ᵇ*writing that shall secure unto him his portion, that he shall hold it, even this right and this inheritance in the church, until he trangresses and is not accounted worthy by the voice of the church, according to the laws and covenants of the church, to belong to the church ;

5. And if he shall transgress and is *ᶜ*not accounted worthy to belong to the church, he shall not have power to claim that portion which he has consecrated unto the bishop for the poor and needy of my church ; therefore, he shall not retain the gift, but shall only have claim on that portion that is *ᵈ*deeded unto him.

6. And thus all things shall be made sure, according to the laws of the land.

7. And let that which belongs to this people be appointed unto this people ;

---

a, 49: 20.   70: 14.   78: 5, 6.   82 : 17.   b, ver. 5.   c, 42 :
30—39.   d, vers. 4, 6.   42 : 37.   Sec. 83.

8. And the money which is left unto this people, let there be an agent appointed unto this people, to take the money to provide food and raiment, according to the wants of this people.

9. And let every man deal honestly, and be ᵉalike among this people, and receive alike, that ye may be one, even as I have commanded you.

10. And let that which belongeth to this people not be taken and given unto that of another church;

11. Wherefore, if another church would receive money of this church, let them ᶠpay unto this church again according as they shall agree;

12. And this shall be done through the bishop or the agent, which shall be appointed by the voice of the church.

13. And again, let the bishop appoint a ᵍstorehouse unto this church, and let all things both in money and in meat, which is more than is needful for the want of this people, be kept in the hands of the bishop.

14. And let him also reserve unto himself for his own wants, and for the wants of his family, as he shall be employed in doing this business.

15. And thus I grant unto this people a privilege of organizing themselves according to ʰmy laws;

16. And I consecrate unto them this land for a little season, until I, the Lord, shall provide for them otherwise, and command them to go hence;

17. And the hour and the day is not given unto them, wherefore let them act upon this land as for years, and this shall turn unto them for their good.

18. Behold, this shall be an ⁱexample unto my servant Edward Partridge, in other places, in all churches.

19. And whoso is found a faithful, a just, and a ʲwise

e, see a.   f, 42: 42, 53, 54.   g, 42: 34, 35.   58: 24.   63: 42.
72: 10.   78: 3.   82: 18.   83: 5, 6.   h, 42: 30—39.   i, Sec. 51,
an Example for all branches of the church.   58: 35,36.   72: 19—26.   119: 7.
j, see o, Sec. 42.

steward, shall enter into the joy of his Lord, and shall inherit eternal life.

20. Verily, I say unto you, I am Jesus Christ, who *k*cometh quickly, in an hour you think not. Even so. Amen.

SECTION 52.

Revelation given through Joseph, the Seer, at Kirtland, Ohio, June 7th, 1831.

1. Behold, thus saith the Lord unto the elders whom he hath called and chosen in these last days, by the voice of his Spirit,

2. Saying, I, the Lord, will make known unto you what I will that ye shall do from this time until the next conference, which shall be held in Missouri, upon the land which I will consecrate unto my people, which are a *a*remnant of Jacob, and them who are heirs according to the *b*covenant.

3. Wherefore, verily I say unto you, let my servants Joseph Smith, jun., and Sidney Rigdon take their journey as soon as preparations can be made to leave their homes, and journey to the land of Missouri.

4. And inasmuch as they are faithful unto me, it shall be made known unto them what they shall do;

5. And it shall also, inasmuch as they are faithful, be made *c*known unto them the land of your inheritance.

6. And inasmuch as they are not faithful, they shall be cut off, even as I will, as seemeth me good.

7. And again, verily I say unto you, let my servant

---

k, see *e*, Soc. 1.

a, the Lamanites.　　*b*, the believing Gentiles.　　*e*, see *b*, Sec. 25.

206COVENANTS AND[SEC. LII.

Lyman Wight, and my servant John Corril take their journey speedily :

8. And also my servant John Murdock, and my servant Hyrum Smith, take their journey unto the same place by the way of Detroit.

9. And let them journey from thence preaching the word by the way, saying none other things than that which the prophets and apostles have written, and that which is taught them by the Comforter through the prayer of faith.

10. Let them go two by two, and thus let them preach by the way in every congregation, baptizing by water, and the ^dlaying on of the hands by the water's side ;

11. For thus saith the Lord, I will cut my work short in righteousness, for the days cometh that I will send forth judgment unto victory.

12. And let my servant Lyman Wight beware, for Satan desireth to sift him as chaff.

13. And behold, he that is faithful shall be made ruler over many things.

14. And again, I will give unto you a ^epattern in all things, that ye may not be deceived, for Satan is abroad in the land, and he goeth forth deceiving the nations ;

15. Wherefore he that prayeth whose spirit is contrite, the same is accepted of me if he obey mine ordinances.

16. He that speaketh, whose spirit is contrite, whose language is meek and edifieth, the same is of God if he obey mine ordinances.

17. And again, he that trembleth under my power shall be made strong, and shall bring forth fruits of praise and wisdom, according to the revelations and truths which I have given you.

18. And again, he that is overcome and bringeth

d, see 2j, Sec. 20.   e, vers. 15—19.

not forth fruits, even according to this pattern, is not of me ;

19. Wherefore by this /pattern ye shall know the spirits in all cases under the whole heavens.

20. And the days have come, according to men's faith it shall be done unto them.

21. Behold, this commandment is given unto all the elders whom I have chosen.

22. And again, verily I say unto you, let my servant Thomas B. Marsh, and my servant Ezra Thayre, take their journey also, preaching the word by the way unto this same land.

23. And again, let my servant Isaac Morley, and my servant Ezra Booth take their journey, also preaching the word by the way unto the same land.

24. And again, let my servants Edward Partridge and Martin Harris take their journey with my servants Sidney Rigdon and Joseph Smith, jun.

25. Let my servants David Whitmer and Harvey Whitlock also take their journey and preach by the way unto this same land.

26. And let my servants Parley P. Pratt and Orson Pratt take their journey and preach by the way, even unto this same land.

27. And let my servants Solomon Hancock and Simeon Carter also take their journey unto this same land, and preach by the way.

28. Let my servants Edson Fuller and Jacob Scott also take their journey.

29. Let my servants Levi Hancock and Zebedee Coltrin also take their journey.

30. Let my servants Reynolds Cahoon and Samuel H. Smith also take their journey.

31. Let my servants Wheeler Baldwin and William Carter also take their journey.

32. And let my servants Newel Knight and Selah J. Griffin, both be ordained, and also take their journey ;

33. Yea, verily I say, let all these take their journey unto one place, in their several courses, and one man shall not build upon another's foundation, neither journey in another's track.

34. He that is faithful, the same shall be kept and blessed with much fruit.

35. And again, I say unto you, let my servants Joseph Wakefield and Solomon Humphrey take their journey into the eastern lands :

36. Let them labor with their families, declaring none other things than the prophets and apostles, that which they have seen, and heard, and most assuredly believe, that the prophecies may be fulfilled.

37. In consequence of transgression, let that which was bestowed upon Heman Basset be taken from him, and placed upon the head of Simonds Rider.

38. And again, verily I say unto you, let Jared Carter be ordained a priest, and also George James be ordained a priest.

39. Let the residue of the elders watch over the churches, and declare the word in the regions among them : and let them labor with their own hands that there be no idolatry nor wickedness practised.

40. And remember in all things the poor and the needy, the sick and the afflicted, for he that *doeth not these things, the same is not my disciple.

41. And again, let my servants Joseph Smith, jun., and Sidney Rigdon, and Edward Partridge, take with them a recommend from the church. And let there be one obtained for my servant Oliver Cowdery also ;

42. And thus, even as I have said, if ye are faithful, ye shall assemble yourselves together to rejoice upon the land of Missouri, which is the *land of your inheritance, which is now the land of your enemies.

---

43. But, behold, I the Lord, will hasten the ᶦcity in its time, and will crown the faithful with joy and with rejoicing.

44. Behold, I am Jesus Christ, the Son of God, and I will ʲlift them up at the last day. Even so. Amen.

SECTION 53.

Revelation through Joseph, the Seer, to Sidney Gilbert, given at Kirtland, Ohio, June, 1831.

1. Behold, I say unto you my servant Sidney Gilbert, that I have heard your prayers, and you have called upon me that it should be made known unto you of the Lord your God, concerning your calling and election in this church, which I, the Lord, have ᵃraised up in these last days.

2. Behold, I, the Lord, who was crucified for the sins of the world, give unto you a commandment that you shall forsake the world.

3. Take upon you mine ordinances, even that of an elder, to preach ᵇfaith and repentance, and remission of sins, according to my word, and the reception of the Holy Spirit by the laying on of hands.

4. And also to be an agent unto this church in the place which shall be appointed by the bishop, according to commandments which shall be given hereafter.

5. And again, verily I say unto you, you shall take your journey with my servants Joseph Smith, jun., and Sidney Rigdon.

6. Behold, these are the first ordinances which you

---

i, see *j*, Sec. 10.　　*j*, see *u*, Sec. 5.

a, see *a*, Sec. 1.　　*b*, see *b*, Sec. 18.

shall receive, and the residue shall be known in a time to come, according to your labor in my vineyard.

7. And again, I would that ye should learn that it is he only who is saved that endureth unto the end. Even so. Amen.

SECTION 54.

Revelation through Joseph, the Seer, to Newel Knight, given at Kirtland, Ohio, June, 1831.

1. Behold, thus saith the Lord, even Alpha and Omega, the beginning and the end, even he who was crucified for the sins of the world.

2. Behold, verily, verily I say unto you, my servant Newel Knight, you shall stand fast in the office wherewith I have appointed you ;

3. And if your brethren desire to escape their enemies, let them repent of all their sins, and become truly humble before me and contrite ;

4. And as the covenant which they made unto me *a*has been broken, even so it has become void and of none effect ;

5. And *b*wo to him by whom this offence cometh, for it had been better for him that he had been drowned in the depth of the sea ;

6. But blessed are they who have kept the covenant and observed the commandment, for they shall obtain mercy.

7. Wherefore, go to now and *c*flee the land, lest your enemies come upon you ; and take your journey, and appoint whom you will to be your leader, and to pay monies for you.

---

a, see Sec. 51.   *b,* a wealthy owner of lands in Thompson.   *c,* Saints from Colesville, N. Y., temporarily located at Thompson.

8. And thus you shall take your journey into the regions westward, unto the land of Missouri, unto the borders of the Lamanites.

9. And after you have done journeying, behold, I say unto you, seek ye a living like unto men, until I prepare a place for you.

10. And again, be patient in tribulation until I come ; and, behold, I ^dcome quickly, and my reward is with me, and they who have sought me ^eearly shall find rest to their souls. Even so. Amen.

SECTION 55.

Revelation through Joseph, the Seer, to William W. Phelps, given at Kirtland, Ohio, June, 1831.

1. Behold, thus saith the Lord unto you, my servant William, yea, even the Lord of the whole earth, thou art called and chosen, and after thou hast been ^abaptized by water, which, if you do with an eye single to my glory, you shall have a remission of your sins, and a reception of the Holy Spirit by the laying on of hands ;

2. And then thou shalt be ordained by the hand of my servant Joseph Smith, jun., to be an elder unto this church, to preach repentance and remission of sins by way of baptism in the name of Jesus Christ, the Son of the living God ;

3. And on whomsoever you ^bshall lay your hands, if they are contrite before me, you shall have power to give the Holy Spirit.

---

d, see e, Sec. 1.   e, the Colesville saints were among the first who received the Gospel.

a, sec l, Sec. 5.   b, see 2j, Sec. 20.

4. And again, you shall be ordained to assist my servant Oliver Cowdery to do the work of printing, and of selecting, and writing ᶜbooks for schools in this church, that little children also may receive instruction before me as is pleasing unto me.

5. And again, verily I say unto you, for this cause you shall take your journey with my servants Joseph Smith, jun., and Sidney Rigdon, that you may be planted in the land of your inheritance to do this work.

6. And again, let my servant Joseph Coe also take his journey with them. The residue shall be made known hereafter, even as I will. Amen.

SECTION 56.

Revelation given through Joseph, the Seer, at Kirtland, Ohio, June, 1831.

1. Hearken, O ye people who profess my name, saith the Lord your God, for behold, mine anger is kindled against the rebellious, and they shall know mine arm and mine indignation, in the ᵃday of visitation and of wrath upon the nations.

2. And he that will not take up his cross and follow me, and keep my commandments, the same shall not be saved.

3. Behold, I, the Lord, command, and he that will not obey, shall be cut off in mine own due time, and after that I have commanded, and the commandment is broken ;

4. Wherefore I, the Lord, command ᵇand revoke,

---

c, 88 : 118.   90 : 15.   97 : 3—6.

a, see f and g, Sec. 1.   b, 19 : 5. 56 : 4—6 58 : 32. 61 : 19.

as it seemeth me good; and all this to be answered upon the heads of the rebellious, saith the Lord;

5. Wherefore, I revoke the commandment which was given unto my servants Thomas B. Marsh and Ezra Thayre, and give a new commandment unto my servant Thomas, that he shall take up his journey speedily, to the land of Missouri, and my servant Selah J. Griffin shall also go with him;

6. For behold, I revoke the commandment which was given unto my servants Selah J. Griffin and Newel Knight, in consequence of the stiff-neckedness of my people which are in Thompson, and their rebellions;

7. Wherefore, let my servant Newel Knight remain with them, and as many as will go may go, that are contrite before me, and be led by him to the land which I have appointed.

8. And again, verily I say unto you, that my servant Ezra Thayre must repent of his pride, and of his selfishness, and obey the former commandment which I have given him concerning the place upon which he lives;

9. And if he will do this, as there shall be no divisions made upon the land, he shall be appointed still to go to the land of Missouri;

10. Otherwise he shall receive the money which he has paid, and shall leave the place, and shall be cut off out of my church, saith the Lord God of hosts;

11. And though the heaven and the earth pass away, these words shall not pass away, but shall be fulfilled.

12. And if my servant Joseph Smith, jun., must needs pay the money; behold, I, the Lord, will pay it unto him again in the land of Missouri, that those of whom he shall receive may be rewarded again, according to that which they do;

13. For according to that which they do, they shall receive, even in lands for their inheritance.

14. Behold, thus saith the Lord unto my people, you have many things to do and to repent of; for behold,

your sins have come up unto me, and are not pardoned, because you seek to counsel in your own ways.

15. And your hearts are not satisfied. And ye obey not the truth, but have pleasure in unrighteousness.

16. ^cWo unto you rich men, that will not give your substance to the poor, for your riches will canker your souls; and this shall be your lamentation in the day of visitation, and of judgment, and of indignation—The harvest is past, the summer is ended, and my soul is not saved!

17. ^dWo unto you poor men, whose hearts are not broken, whose spirits are not contrite, and whose bellies are not satisfied, and whose hands are not stayed from laying hold upon other men's goods, whose eyes are full of greediness, who will not labor with your own hands!

18. But ^eblessed are the poor who are pure in heart, whose hearts are broken, and whose spirits are contrite, for they shall see the kingdom of God coming in power and great glory unto their deliverance; for the fatness of the earth shall be theirs.

19. For behold, the Lord shall come, and his recompense shall be with him, and he shall reward every man, and the poor shall rejoice;

20. And ^ftheir generations shall inherit the earth from generation to generation, for ever and ever. And now I make an end of speaking unto you. Even so. Amen.

SECTION 57.

Revelation given through Joseph, the Seer, in Zion, in Jackson County, Missouri, July, 1831.

1. Hearken, O ye elders of my church, saith the

Lord your God, who have assembled yourselves together, according to my commandments, in this land, which is the land of Missouri, which is the land which I have *appointed and consecrated for the gathering of the saints :

2. Wherefore this is the land of promise, and the *place for the city of Zion.

3. And thus saith the Lord your God, if you will receive wisdom, here is wisdom. Behold, the place which is now called Independence, is the center place, and a *spot for the temple is lying westward, upon a lot which is not far from the court house ;

4. Wherefore it is wisdom that the land should be *purchased by the saints ; and also every tract lying westward, even unto the line running directly between Jew and Gentile.

5. And also every tract bordering by the prairies, inasmuch as my disciples are enabled to buy lands. Behold, this is wisdom, that they may obtain it for an *everlasting inheritance.

6. And let my servant Sidney Gilbert stand in the office which I have appointed him, to receive monies, to be an *agent unto the church, to buy land in all the regions round about, inasmuch as can be in righteousness, and as wisdom shall direct.

7. And let my servant Edward Partridge, stand in the office which I have appointed him, to *divide the saints their inheritance, even as I have commanded ; and also those whom he has appointed to assist him.

8. And again, verily I say unto you, let my servant Sidney Gilbert plant himself in this place, and establish a store, that he may sell goods without fraud, that he may obtain money *to buy lands for the good of the

a, see j, Sec. 10.   b, see q, Sec. 42.   c, 58 : 57.   84 : 3—5,
31.   d, see q, Sec. 42.   Also b, Sec. 48.   e, 88 : 16—20.   See b,
Sec. 25.   f, 53 : 4.   57 : 8—10, 14, 15.   g, 41 : 9—11.   42 : 30—39,
71—73.   Sec. 51.   58 : 17, 18.   h, see b, Sec. 48.

saints, and that he may obtain whatsoever things the disciples may need to plant them in their inheritance.

9. And also let my servant Sidney Gilbert obtain a license—(behold here is wisdom, and whoso readeth let him understand)—that he may send goods also unto the 'people, even by whom he will, as clerks employed in his service,

10. And thus provide for my saints, that my gospel may be preached unto those ʲwho sit in darkness, and in the region and shadow of death.

11. And again, verily I say unto you, let my servant William W. Phelps be planted in this place, and be established as a printer unto the church ;

12. And lo, if the world receiveth his writings— (behold here is wisdom)—let him obtain whatsoever he can obtain in righteousness, for the good of the saints.

13. And let my servant Oliver Cowdery, assist him, even as I have commanded, in whatsoever place I shall appoint unto him, to copy, and to correct, and select, that all things may be right before me, as it shall be proved by the Spirit through him.

14. And thus let those of whom I have spoken be planted in the land of ᵏZion, as speedily as can be, with their families, to do those things even as I have spoken.

15. And now concerning the gathering. Let the bishop and the agent make preparations for those families which have been commanded to come to this land, as soon as possible, and plant them in their inheritance.

16. And unto the residue of both elders and members, further directions shall be given hereafter. Even so. Amen.

---

i the Lamanites.   *j,* the Lamanites   *k,* see *b,* Sec. 25.

SECTION 58.

Revelation given through Joseph, the Seer, in Zion, in Jackson County, Missouri, August 1st, 1831.

1. Hearken, O ye elders of my church, and give ear to my word, and learn of me what I will concerning you, and also concerning this land unto which I have sent you :

2. For verily I say unto you, blessed is he that keepeth my commandments, whether in life or in death ; and he that is faithful in tribulation, the reward of the same is greater in the kingdom of heaven.

3. Ye cannot behold with your natural eyes, for the present time, the design of your God concerning those things which shall come hereafter, and the glory which shall follow after much tribulation.

4. For after *a*much tribulation cometh the blessings. Wherefore the day cometh that ye shall be crowned with much glory ; the hour is not yet, but is nigh at hand.

5. Remember this, which I tell you before, that you may lay it to heart, and receive that which shall follow.

6. Behold, verily I say unto you, for this cause I have sent you that you might be obedient, and that your hearts might be prepared to bear testimony of the things which are to come ;

7. And also that you might be honored of laying the foundation, and of bearing record of the land upon which the *b*Zion of God shall stand ;

8. And also that a feast of fat things might be prepared for the poor ; yea, a feast of fat things, of wine on the lees well refined, that the earth may know that the mouths of the prophets shall not fail ;

---

a, 103 : 11—14.   *b*, see *q* Sec 42.

9. Yea a supper of the house of the Lord, well prepared, unto which all nations shall be invited.

10. Firstly, the rich and the learned, the wise and the noble ;

11. And after that cometh the ^cday of my power : then shall the poor, the lame, and the blind, and the deaf, come in unto the marriage of the Lamb, and partake of the supper of the Lord, prepared for the great day to come.

12. Behold, I, the Lord, have spoken it.

13. And that the testimony might go forth from ^aZion, yea, from the mouth of the city of the heritage of God :

14. Yea, for this cause I have sent you hither, and have selected my servant Edward Partridge, and have appointed unto him his mission in this land ;

15. But if he repent not of his sins, which are unbelief and blindness of heart, let him take heed lest he fall.

16. Behold his mission is given unto him, and it shall not be given again.

17. And whoso standeth in his mission is appointed to be a ^ejudge in Israel, like as it was in ancient days, to divide the lands of the heritage of God unto his children,

18. And to judge his people by the testimony of the just, and by the assistance of his counselors, according to the laws of the kingdom which are given by the prophets of God ;

19. For verily I say unto you, my law shall be kept on this land.

20. Let no man think he is ruler, but let God rule him that judgeth, according to the counsel of his own will ; or, in other words, him that counseleth or sitteth upon the judgment seat.

21. Let no man ʳbreak the laws of the land, for he that keepeth the laws of God hath no need to break the laws of the land :

22. Wherefore, be subject to the powers that be, until He reigns whose right it is to reign, and subdues all enemies under his feet.

23. Behold, the laws which ye have received from my hand are the laws of the church, and in this light ye shall hold them forth. Behold, here is wisdom.

24. And now as I spake concerning my servant Edward Partridge, this land is the land of his residence, and those whom he has appointed for his counselors. And also the land of the residence of him whom I have appointed to keep my store-house ;

25. Wherefore let them bring their families to this land, as they shall counsel between themselves and me :

26. For behold, it is not meet that I should command in all things, for he that is compelled in all things, the same is a slothful and not a wise servant ; wherefore he receiveth no reward.

27. Verily I say, men should be anxiously engaged in a good cause, and do ᵍmany things of their own free will, and bring to pass much righteousness ;

28. For the power is in them, wherein they are agents unto themselves. And inasmuch as men do good they shall in nowise lose their reward.

29. But he that doeth not anything until he is commanded, and receiveth a commandment with doubtful heart, and keepeth it with slothfulness, the same is damned.

30. Who am I that made man, saith the Lord, that will hold him guiltless that obeys not my commandments ?

31. Who am I, saith the Lord, that have promised and have not fulfilled ?

---

f, the Constitutional laws of the U.S.A.   98 : 4—15.   101 : 76—80.
g, vers. 28, 29.

32. I command and a man obeys not, I revoke and they receive not the blessing ;

33. Then they say in their hearts, this is not the work of the Lord, for his promises are not fulfilled. But wo unto such, for their reward lurketh beneath, and not from above.

34. And now I give unto you further directions concerning this land.

35. It is wisdom in me that my servant Martin Harris should be an example unto the church, in ʰlaying his monies before the bishop of the church.

36. And also, this is a ⁱlaw unto every man that cometh unto this land, to receive an inheritance ; and he shall do with his monies according as the law directs.

37. And it is wisdom also, that there should be lands purchased in Independence, for the place of the store-house, and also for the house of the printing.

38. And other directions concerning my servant Martin Harris shall be given him of the Spirit, that he may receive his inheritance as seemeth him good.

39. And let him repent of his sins, for he seeketh the praise of the world.

40. And also let my servant William W. Phelps stand in the office which I have appointed him, and receive his inheritance in the land ;

41. And also he hath need to repent, for I, the Lord, am not well pleased with him, for he seeketh to excel, and he is not sufficiently meek before me.

42. Behold, he who has repented of his sins, the same is forgiven, and I, the Lord, remembereth them no more.

43. By this ye may know if a man repenteth of his sins. Behold, he will ʲconfess them and forsake them.

44. And now, verily, I say, concerning the residue of the elders of my church, the time has not yet come, for many years, for them to receive their inheritance in

this land, except they desire it through the prayer of faith, only as it shall be appointed unto them of the Lord.

45. For, behold, they shall [k]push the people together from the ends of the earth ;

46. Wherefore, assemble yourselves together, and they who are not appointed to stay in this land, let them preach the gospel in the regions round about, and after that let them return to their homes.

47. Let them preach by the way, and bear testimony of the truth in all places, and call upon the rich, the high and the low, and the poor to repent ;

48. And let them build up churches inasmuch as the inhabitants of the earth will repent.

49. And let there be an agent appointed by the voice of the church, unto the church in Ohio, to receive monies to [l]purchase lands in Zion.

50. And I give unto my servant, Sidney Rigdon, a commandment that he shall write a description of the land of Zion, and a statement of the will of God, as it shall be made known by the Spirit unto him ;

51. And an epistle and subscription, to be presented unto all the churches to obtain monies, to be put into the hands of the bishop to [m]purchase lands for an inheritance for the children of God, of himself or the agent, as seemeth him good or as he shall direct.

52. For, behold, verily I say unto you, the Lord willeth that the disciples, and the children of men should open their hearts, even to purchase this whole region of country, as soon as time will permit.

53. Behold, here is wisdom. Let them do this lest they receive [n]none inheritance, save it be by the shedding of blood.

54. And again, inasmuch as there is land obtained, let there be workmen sent forth of all kinds unto this land, to labor for the saints of God.

---

k, 58 : 45. Deut. 33 : 17.   *l*, see *q*, Sec. 42.   *m*, see *q*, Sec. 42.
n, 63 : 27—31.

55. Let all these things be done in order; and let the privileges of the lands be made known from time to time, by the bishop or the agent of the church;

56. And let the work of the [o]gathering be not in haste, nor by flight, but let it be done as it shall be counseled by the elders of the church at the conferences, according to the knowledge which they receive from time to time.

57. And let my servant Sidney Rigdon [p]consecrate and dedicate this land, and the spot of the temple unto the Lord.

58. And let a conference meeting be called, and after that let my servants Sidney Rigdon and Joseph Smith, jun., return, and also Oliver Cowdery with them, to accomplish the residue of the work which I have appointed unto them in their own land, and the residue as shall be ruled by the conferences.

59. And let no man return from this land, except he bear record by the way of that which he knows and most assuredly believes.

60. Let that which has been bestowed upon [q]Ziba Peterson be taken from him; and let him stand as a member in the church, and labor with his own hands, with the brethren, until he is sufficiently chastened for all his sins, for he confesseth them not, and he thinketh to hide them.

61. Let the residue of the elders of this church, who are coming to this land, some of whom are exceedingly blessed even above measure, also hold a conference upon this land.

62. And let my servant Edward Partridge direct the conference which shall be held by them.

63. And let them also return, preaching the gospel by the way, bearing record of the things which are revealed unto them;

64. For, verily, the sound must go forth from this

place into all the world, and unto the uttermost parts of the earth—*r*the gospel must be preached unto every creature, with signs following them that believe.

65. And behold the *s*Son of man cometh. Amen.

SECTION 59.

Revelation given through Joseph the Seer, in Zion, in Jackson County, Missouri, August 7th, 1831.

1. Behold, blessed, saith the Lord, are they who have come up unto this land with an eye single to my glory, according to my commandments;

2. For them that live shall inherit the earth, and them that die shall rest from all their labors, and their works shall follow them, and they shall receive a crown in the *a*mansions of my Father, which I have prepared for them;

3. Yea, blessed are they whose feet stand upon the land of Zion, who have obeyed my gospel, for they shall receive for their reward the good things of the earth; and it shall bring forth in its strength;

4. And they shall also be crowned with blessings from above, yea, and with commandments not a few; and with revelations in their time: they that are faithful and diligent before me.

5. Wherefore I give unto them a commandment, saying thus: *b*Thou shalt love the Lord thy God with all thy heart, with all thy might, mind, and strength; and in the name of Jesus Christ thou shalt serve him.

6. Thou shalt love thy neighbour as thyself. Thou

---

r, see *b*, Sec. 18.   *s*, see *e*, Sec. 1.

a, 76 : 111.   81 : 6.   98 : 18.   100 : 8.   Enos. 1 : 27.   Ether 12 : 32—34.
b, 42 : 29.   Deut. 6 : 5.

shalt not steal; neither commit adultery, nor kill, nor do anything like unto it.

7. Thou shalt thank the Lord thy God in all things.

8. Thou shalt offer a sacrifice unto the Lord thy God in righteousness, even that of a broken heart and a contrite spirit.

9. And that thou mayest more fully keep thyself unspotted from the world, thou shalt ^cgo to the house of prayer and offer up thy sacraments upon my holy day;

10. For verily this is a day appointed unto you to rest from your labors, and to pay thy devotions unto the Most High;

11. Nevertheless thy vows shall be offered up in righteousness on all days and at all times;

12. But remember that on this the ^dLord's day, thou shalt offer thine oblations and thy sacraments unto the Most High, confessing thy sins unto thy brethren, and before the Lord.

13. And on this day thou shalt do none other thing, only let thy food be prepared with singleness of heart that thy fasting may be perfect, or, in other words, that thy joy may be full.

14. Verily, this is fasting and prayer; or in other words, rejoicing and prayer.

15. And inasmuch as ye do these things with thanksgiving, with cheerful hearts and countenances; not with ^emuch laughter, for this is sin, but with a glad heart and a cheerful countenance;

16. Verily I say, that inasmuch as ye do this, the fullness of the earth is yours: the beasts of the field and the fowls of the air, and that which climbeth upon the trees and walketh upon the earth;

17. Yea. and the herb, and the goods things which cometh of the earth, whether for food or for raiment, or for houses, or for barns, or for orchards, or for gardens, or for vineyards;

c, 68 : 29. Alma 1 : 26, 27.   d, 68 : 29.   e, 88 : 69, 121.

18. Yea, all things which come of the earth, in the season thereof, are made for the benefit and the use of man, both to please the eye and to gladden the heart ;

19. Yea, for food and for raiment, for taste and for smell, to strengthen the body and to enliven the soul.

20. And it pleaseth God that he hath given all these things unto man ; for unto this end were they made to be used with judgment, not to excess, neither by extortion :

21. And in nothing doth man offend God, or against none is his wrath kindled, save those *who confess not his hand in all things, and obey not his commandments.

22. Behold, this is according to the law and the prophets : wherefore, trouble me no more concerning this matter,

23. But learn that he who doeth the works of righteousness shall receive his reward, even peace in this world, and eternal life in the world to come.

24. I, the Lord, have spoken it, and the Spirit beareth record. Amen.

SECTION 60.

Revelation, given through Joseph, the Seer, in Jackson County, Missouri, August 8th, 1831.

1. Behold, thus saith the Lord unto the elders of his church, who are to return speedily to the land from whence they came. Behold, it pleaseth me, that you have come up hither ;

2. But with some I am not well pleased, for they will not open their mouths, but hide the talent which I

f, Job 1 : 21. 2 : 10

have given unto them, because of the fear of man. Wo unto such, for mine anger is kindled against them.

3. And it shall come to pass, if they are not more faithful unto me, it shall be taken away, even that which they have ;

4. For I, the Lord, rule in the heavens above, and among the armies of the earth ; and in the day when I shall make up my *jewels, all men shall know what it is that bespeaketh the power of God.

5. But verily, I will speak unto you concerning your journey unto the land from whence you came. Let there be a craft made, or bought, as seemeth you good, it mattereth not unto me, and take your journey speedily for the place which is called St. Louis.

6. And from thence let my servants Sidney Rigdon, and Joseph Smith, jr., and Oliver Cowdery, take their journey for Cincinnati ;

7. And in this place let them lift up their voice and declare my word with loud voices, without wrath or doubting, lifting up holy hands upon them. For I am able to make you holy, and your sins are forgiven you.

8. And let the residue take their journey from St. Louis, two by two, and preach the word, not in haste, among the congregations of the wicked, until they return to the churches from whence they came.

9. And all this for the good of the churches ; for this intent have I sent them.

10. And let my servant Edward Partridge impart of the money which I have given him, a portion unto mine elders who are commanded to return ;

11. And he that is able, let him return it by the way of the agent, and he that is not, of him it is not required.

12. And now I speak of the residue who are to come unto this land.

13. Behold, they have been sent to preach my

a, 101 : 3.

gospel among the congregations of the wicked ; wherefore, I give unto them a commandment thus : Thou shalt not *b*idle away thy time, neither shalt thou *c*bury thy talent that it may not be known.

14. And after thou hast come up unto the land of Zion, and hast proclaimed my word, thou shalt speedily return, proclaiming my word among the congregations of the wicked, not in haste, neither in wrath nor with strife ;

15. And *d*shake off the dust of thy feet against those who receive thee not ; not in their presence, lest thou provoke them ; but in secret, and wash thy feet, as a testimony against them in the day of judgment.

16. Behold, this is sufficient for you, and the will of him who hath sent you.

17. And by the mouth of my servant Joseph Smith, jun., it shall be made known concerning Sidney Rigdon and Oliver Cowdery. The residue hereafter. Even so. Amen.

SECTION 61.

Revelation given through Joseph, the Seer, on the bank of the Missouri river, McIlwair's Bend, August 12th, 1831.

1. Behold, and hearken unto the voice of him who has all power, who is from *a*everlasting to everlasting, even Alpha and Omega, the beginning and the end.

2. Behold, verily thus saith the Lord unto you, O ye elders of my church, who are -assembled upon this

spot, whose sins are now forgiven you, for I, the Lord,
forgive sins, and am merciful unto those who confess
their sins with humble hearts ;

3. But verily I say unto you, that it is not needful
for this whole company of mine elders to be moving
swiftly upon the waters, whilst the inhabitants on either
side are perishing in unbelief ;

4. Nevertheless, I suffered it that ye might bear
record ; behold, there are many dangers upon the
waters, and more especially hereafter ;

5. For I, the Lord, have decreed in mine anger,
many destructions upon the waters; yea, and especially
upon these waters ;

6. Nevertheless, all flesh is in mine hand, and he
that is faithful among you shall not perish by the
waters.

7. Wherefore it is expedient that my servant Sidney
Gilbert, and my servant William W. Phelps, be in haste
upon their errand and mission ;

8. Nevertheless I would not suffer that ye should
part until you are chastened for all your sins, that you
might be one, that you might not perish in wickedness;

9. But now, verily I say, it behoveth me that ye
should part, wherefore let my servants Sidney Gilbert
and William W. Phelps take their former company,
and let them take their journey in haste that they may
fill their mission, and through faith they shall overcome ;

10. And inasmuch as they are faithful they shall
be preserved, and I, the Lord, will be with them.

11. And let the residue take that which is needful
for clothing.

12. Let my servant Sidney Gilbert take that which
is not needful with him, as you shall agree.

13. And now, behold, for your good I gave unto you
a commandment concerning these things ; and I, the
Lord, will reason with you as with men in days of old.

14. Behold, I, the Lord, in the beginning blessed the waters, but in the last days, by the mouth of my servant John, I *b*cursed the waters ;

15. Wherefore, the days will come that no flesh shall be safe upon the waters,

16. And it shall be said in days to come that none is able to go up to the land of Zion upon the waters, but he that is upright in heart.

17. And, as I, the Lord, in the beginning cursed the land, even so in the last days have I blessed it, in its time, for the use of my saints, that they may partake the fatness thereof.

18. And now I give unto you a commandment that what I say unto one I say unto all, that you shall forewarn your brethren concerning *c*these waters, that they come not in journeying upon them, lest their faith fail and they are caught in her snares ;

19. I, the Lord, have decreed, and the destroyer rideth upon the face thereof, and I revoke not the decree ;

20. I, the Lord, was angry with you yesterday, but to-day mine anger is turned away.

21. Wherefore, let those concerning whom I have spoken, that should take their journey in haste ; again I say unto you, let them take their journey in haste,

22. And it mattereth not unto me, after a little, if it so be that they fill their mission, whether they go by water or by land ; let this be as it is made known unto them according to their judgments hereafter.

23. And now, concerning my servants Sidney Rigdon, and Joseph Smith, jun., and Oliver Cowdery, let them come not again upon the waters, save it be upon the canal, while journeying unto their homes, or in other words they shall not come upon the waters to journey, save upon the canal.

24. Behold, I, the Lord, have appointed a way for

---

b, vers. 15, 16, 18, 19.   *c*, the Missouri river.

the journeying of my saints, and behold, this is the
way—that after they leave the canal, they shall journey
by land, inasmuch as they are commanded to journey
and go up unto the land of Zion ;

25. And they shall do like unto the children of
Israel, pitching their tents by the way.

26. And, behold, this commandment you shall give
unto all your brethren ;

27. Nevertheless unto whom it is given power to
command the waters, unto him it is given by the Spirit
to know all his ways ;

28. Wherefore let him do as the Spirit of the living
God commandeth him, whether upon the land or upon
the waters, as it remaineth with me to do hereafter ;

29. And unto you it is given the course for the
saints, or the way for the saints of the camp of the
Lord, to journey.

30. And again, verily I say unto you, my servants
Sidney Rigdon, and Joseph Smith, jun., and Oliver
Cowdery, shall not open their mouths in the congrega-
tions of the wicked, until they arrive at Cincinnati ;

31. And in that place they shall lift up their voices
unto God against that people ; yea unto him whose
anger is kindled against their wickedness ; a people
who are well nigh ripened for destruction ;

32. And from thence let them journey for the congregations of their brethren, for their labors even now,
are wanted more abundantly among them, than among
the congregations of the wicked.

33. And now concerning the residue, let them
journey and declare the word among the congregations
of the wicked, inasmuch as it is given ;

34. And inasmuch as they do this, they shall rid
their garments, and they shall be spotless before me ;

35. And let them journey together, or two by two,
as seemeth them good, only let my servant Reynolds
Cahoon, and my servant Samuel H. Smith, with whom

I am well pleased, be not separated until they return to their homes, and this for a wise purpose in me.

36. And now, verily I say unto you, and what I say unto one I say unto all, be of good cheer little children, for I am in your midst, and I have not forsaken you;

37. And inasmuch as you have humbled yourselves before me, the blessings of the ᵈkingdom are yours.

38. Gird up your loins and be watchful and be sober, looking forth for the ᵉcoming of the Son of Man, for he cometh in an hour you think not.

39. Pray always that you enter not into temptation, that you may abide the day of his coming, whether in life or in death. Even so. Amen.

SECTION 62.

Revelation given through Joseph, the Seer, on the bank of the Missouri river, August 13th, 1831.

1. Behold, and hearken O ye elders of my church, saith the Lord your God, even Jesus Christ, your ᵃadvocate, who knoweth the weakness of man and how to succor them who are tempted;

2. And verily mine eyes are upon those who have not as yet gone up unto the land of Zion; wherefore your mission is not yet full;

3. Nevertheless ye are blessed, for the testimony which ye have borne, is recorded in heaven for the angels to look upon, and they rejoice over you, and your sins are forgiven you.

---

d, see x, Sec. 35.　　e, see e, See. 1.

a, 45: 3—5.

4. And now continue your journey. Assemble yourselves upon the *land of Zion, and hold a meeting and
rejoice together, and offer a sacrament unto the Most
High ;

5. And then you may return to bear record, yea,
even altogether, or two by two, as seemeth you good ;
it mattereth not unto me, only be faithful, and declare
glad tidings unto the inhabitants of the earth, or among
the congregations of the wicked.

6. Behold, I, the Lord, have brought you together
that the promise might be fulfilled, that the faithful
among you should be preserved and rejoice together in
the land of Missouri. I, the Lord, promised the faithful and cannot lie.

7. I, the Lord, am willing, if any among you
desireth to ride upon horses, or upon mules, or in
chariots, he shall receive this blessing, if he receive it
from the hand of the Lord, with a thankful heart in
all things.

8. These things remain with you to do according to
judgment and the directions of the Spirit.

9. Behold, the *kingdom is yours. And behold,
and lo, I am with the faithful always. Even so.
Amen.

SECTION 63.

*Revelation given through Joseph, the Seer, in Kirtland,
about the last of August,* 1831.

1. Hearken, O ye people, and open your hearts and
give ear from afar ; and listen, you that call yourselves
the people of the Lord, and hear the word of the Lord
and his will concerning you :

2. Yea, verily, I say, hear the word of him whose anger is kindled against the wicked and rebellious;

3. Who willeth to take even them whom he will take, and preserveth in life them whom he will preserve;

4. Who buildeth up at his own will and pleasure; and destroyeth when he pleases, and is able to cast the soul down to hell.

5. Behold, I, the Lord, utter my voice, and it shall be obeyed.

6. Wherefore, verily I say, let the wicked take heed, and let the rebellious fear and tremble; and let the unbelieving hold their lips, *for the day of wrath shall come upon them as a whirlwind, and all flesh shall know that I am God.

7. And he that seeketh signs shall see signs, but not unto salvation.

8. Verily, I say unto you, there are those among you who seek signs, and there have been such even from the beginning;

9. But, behold, faith cometh not by signs, but signs follow those that believe.

10. Yea, signs come by faith, not by the will of men, nor as they please, but by the will of God.

11. Yea, signs come by faith, unto mighty works, for without faith no man pleaseth God: and with whom God is angry he is not well pleased; wherefore, unto such he showeth no signs, only in wrath unto their condemnation.

12. Wherefore, I, the Lord, am not pleased with those among you who have sought after signs and wonders for faith, and not for the good of men unto my glory;

13. Nevertheless, I give commandments, and many have turned away from my commandments and have not kept them.

_____

a, see f and g, Sec. 1.

14. There were among you *b*adulterers and adulteresses ; some of whom have turned away from you, and others remain with you, that hereafter shall be revealed.

15. Let such beware and repent speedily, lest judgment shall come upon them as a snare, and their folly shall be made manifest, and their works shall follow them in the eyes of the people.

16. And, verily, I say unto you, as I have said before, *c*he that looketh on a woman to lust after her, or if any shall commit adultery in their hearts, they shall not have the Spirit, but shall deny the faith and shall fear :

17. Wherefore I, the Lord, have *d*said that the fearful, and the unbelieving, and all liars, and whosoever loveth and maketh a lie, and the whoremonger, and the sorcerer, shall have their part in that lake which burneth with fire and brimstone which is the second death.

18. Verily I say, that they shall not have part in the *e*first resurrection.

19. And now, behold, I, the Lord, say unto you, that ye are not justified because these things are among you ;

20. Nevertheless he that endureth in faith and doeth my will, the same shall overcome, and shall receive an *f*inheritance upon the earth when the day of transfiguration shall come ;

21. When the earth shall be transfigured, even according to the pattern which was shown unto mine apostles upon the mount; of which account the fullness ye have not yet received.

22. And now, verily, I say unto you, that as I said that I would make known my will unto you, behold I will make it known unto you, not by the way of com-

---

b, see m, Sec. 42.   *c*, see m, Sec. 42.   *d*, ver. 18.   Rev. 21: 8.
e, ver. 17.   Rev. 20: 6.   *f*, see *b*, Sec. 25.

mandment, for there are many who observe not to keep my commandments ;

23. But unto him that keepeth my commandments, I will give the *g*mysteries of my kingdom, and the same shall be in him a well of living water, springing up unto everlasting life.

24. And now, behold, this is the will of the Lord your God concerning his saints, that they should assemble themselves together unto the *h*land of Zion, not in haste, lest there should be confusion, which bringeth pestilence.

25. Behold, the land of Zion, I, the Lord, holdeth it in mine own hands ;

26. Nevertheless, I, the Lord, rendereth unto Cæsar the things which are Cæsar's:

27. Wherefore, I the Lord, willeth that you should *i*purchase the lands that you may have advantage of the world, that you may have claim on the world, that they may not be stirred up unto anger ;

28. For Satan putteth it into their hearts to anger against you, and to the shedding of blood ;

29. Wherefore the land of Zion shall not be obtained but by *j*purchase or by blood, otherwise there is none inheritance for you.

30. And if by purchase, behold you are blessed ;

31. And if by blood, as you are forbidden to shed blood, lo, your enemies are upon you, and ye shall be scourged from city to city, and from synagogue to synagogue, and but *k*few shall stand to receive an inheritance.

32. I, the Lord, am angry with the wicked ; I am holding my Spirit from the inhabitants of the earth.

33. I have sworn in my wrath, and *l*decreed wars upon the face of the earth, and the wicked shall slay the wicked, and fear shall come upon every man,

---

g, see 2 :, Sec. 42.　　*h*, see *g*, Sec. 42.　　*i*, see *g*, Sec. 42.　　*j*, vers.
30, 31.　58 : 53.　101 : 70—75.　　*k*, 84 : 53.　97 : 26.　112 : 24—26.
l, see *j*, Sec. 1.

34. And the saints also shall hardly escape ; nevertheless, I, the Lord, am with them, and will ^{m}come down in heaven from the presence of my Father, and consume the wicked with ^{n}unquenchable fire.

35. And behold, this is not yet, but by and by ;

36. Wherefore, seeing that I, the Lord, have decreed all these things upon the face of the earth, I will that my saints should be assembled upon the land of Zion ;

37. And that every man should take righteousness in his hands and faithfulness upon his loins, and lift a warning voice unto the inhabitants of the earth ; and declare both by word and by flight, that ^{o}desolation shall come upon the wicked.

38. Wherefore let my disciples in Kirtland arrange their temporal concerns, which dwell upon this farm.

39. Let my servant Titus Billings, who has the care thereof, dispose of the land, that he may be prepared in the coming spring to take his journey up unto the land of Zion, with those that dwell upon the face thereof, excepting those whom I shall reserve unto myself, that shall not go until I shall command them.

40. And let all the monies which can be spared, it mattereth not unto me whether it be little or much, be sent up unto the land of Zion, unto them whom I have ^{p}appointed to receive.

41. Behold, I, the Lord, will give unto my servant Joseph Smith, jun., power that he shall be enabled to discern by the Spirit those who shall go up unto the land of Zion, and those of my disciples who shall tarry.

42. Let my servant Newel K. Whitney retain his store, or in other words, the store yet for a little season.

43. Nevertheless let him impart all the money which he can impart, to be sent up unto the land of Zion.

---

*m, see c, Sec. 1.   n, ver. 54.   19: 6—16. 76: 44—49.   o, see f
and g, Sec. 1.   p, 52 : 6—9.*

44. Behold, these things are in his own hands, let him do according to wisdom.

45. Verily I say, let him be ordained as an agent unto the disciples that shall tarry, and let him be ordained unto this power;

46. And now speedily visit the churches, expounding these things unto them, with my servant Oliver Cowdery. Behold, this is my will, obtaining monies even as I have directed.

47. He that is faithful and endureth shall overcome the world.

48. He that [q]sendeth up treasures unto the land of Zion, shall receive an inheritance in this world, and his works shall follow him, and also a reward in the world to come:

49. Yea, and blessed are the dead that die in the Lord from henceforth, when the Lord shall come, and old things shall pass away, and all things become new, they shall [r]rise from the dead and shall not [s]die after, and shall receive an inheritance before the Lord, in the holy city.

50. And he that liveth when the Lord shall come, and has kept the faith, blessed is he; nevertheless it is appointed to him to die at the age of man;

51. Wherefore children shall grow up until they become old, [t]old men shall die; but they shall not [u]sleep in the dust, but they shall be [v]changed in the twinkling of an eye;

52. Wherefore for this cause preached the apostles unto the world the resurrection of the dead;

53. These things are the things that ye must look for, and speaking after the manner of the Lord, they are now nigh at hand; and in a time to come, even in the day of the [w]coming of the Son of Man.

54. And until that hour there will be foolish virgins

---

q, vers. 40, 43. *r*, see *m*, Sec. 29. *s*, Alma, 11: 45. 12: 18, 20. 88: 116. Rev. 21: 4. *t*, 101: 30. Isa. 65: 20—22. *u*, 88: 116. 101: 31. *v*, 101: 31. *w*, see *e*, Sec. 1.

among the wise, and at that hour cometh an *entire separation of the righteous and the wicked, and in that day will I send mine angels to *pluck out the wicked and cast them into unquenchable fire.

55. And now, behold, verily I say unto you, I the Lord, am not pleased with my servant Sidney Rigdon, he exalted himself in his heart, and received not counsel but grieved the Spirit;

56. Wherefore his writing is not acceptable unto the Lord and he shall make another, and if the Lord receive it not, behold he standeth no longer in the office which I have appointed him.

57. And again, verily I say unto you, those who desire in their hearts, in meekness, to warn sinners to repentance, let them be ordained unto this power;

58. For this is a day of warning, and not a day of many words. For I, the Lord, am not to be mocked in the last days.

59. Behold, I am from above, and my power lieth beneath. I am over all, and in all, and through all, and search all things, and the day cometh that all things shall be subject unto me.

60. Behold, I am Alpha and Omega, even Jesus Christ.

61. Wherefore let all men beware how they take my name in their lips;

62. For, behold, verily I say, that many there be who are under this condemnation, who use the name of the Lord, and use it in vain, having not authority.

63. Wherefore, let the church repent of their sins, and I, the Lord, will own them, otherwise they shall be cut off.

64. Remember that that which cometh from above is sacred, and must be spoken with care, and by constraint of the Spirit, and in this there is no condemnation, and ye *receive the Spirit through prayer; wherefore, without this there remaineth condemnation.

---

65. Let my servants Joseph Smith, jun., and Sidney Rigdon, seek them a home, as they are taught through prayer by the Spirit.

66. These things remain to overcome through patience, that such may receive a more exceeding and eternal weight of glory, otherwise, a greater condemnation. Amen.

SECTION 64.

Revelation given through Joseph, the Seer, in Kirtland, September 11th, 1831.

1. Behold, thus saith the Lord your God unto you, O ye elders of my church, hearken ye and hear, and receive my will concerning you ;

2. For verily I say unto you, I will that ye should overcome the world ; wherefore I will have compassion upon you.

3. There are those among you who have sinned ; but verily I say, for this once, for mine own glory, and for the salvation of souls, I have forgiven you your sins.

4. I will be merciful unto you, for I have ^agiven unto you the kingdom :

5. And the ^bkeys of the mysteries of the kingdom shall not be taken from my servant Joseph Smith, jun., through the means I have appointed, while he liveth, inasmuch as he obeyeth mine ordinances.

6. There are those who have sought occasion against him without cause ;

7. Nevertheless he has sinned, but verily I say unto you, I, the Lord, forgive sins unto those who ^cconfess

---

a, see *z,* Sec. 35.   *b,* see *b,* Sec. 28.   *c,* 42 : 25.   58 : 42, 43.

their sins before me and ask forgiveness, who have not sinned unto death.

8. My disciples, in days of old, sought occasion against one another, and forgave not one another in their hearts, and for this evil they were afflicted, and sorely chastened :

9. Wherefore I say unto you, that ye ought to forgive one another, for he that ^dforgiveth not his brother his trespasses, standeth condemned before the Lord, for there remaineth in him the greater sin.

10. I, the Lord, will forgive whom I will forgive, but of you it is required to ^eforgive all men ;

11. And ye ought to say in your hearts, let God judge between me and thee, and reward thee according to thy deeds.

12. And he that ^frepenteth not of his sins, and confesseth them not, then ye shall bring him before the church, and do with him as the Scripture saith unto you, either by commandment or by revelation.

13. And this ye shall do that God may be glorified, not because ye forgive not, having not compassion, but that ye may be justified in the eyes of the law, that ye may not offend him who is your Lawgiver.

14. Verily I say, for this cause ye shall do these things.

15. Behold, I, the Lord, was angry with him who was my servant Ezra Booth, and also my servant Isaac Morley, for they kept not the law, neither the commandment ;

16. They sought evil in their hearts, and I, the Lord, withheld my Spirit. They condemned for evil that thing in which there was no evil ; nevertheless I have forgiven my servant Isaac Morley.

17. And also my servant Edward Partridge, behold, he hath sinned, and Satan seeketh to destroy his

---

d, vers. 10—14.   98 : 39, 40.   III. Nep. 12 : 23, 24.   13 : 14, 15.
e, 98 : 40.   *f*, 42 : 80—83.

soul ; but when these things are made known unto them, and they repent of the evil, they shall be forgiven.

18. And now, verily I say, that it is expedient in me that my servant Sidney Gilbert, after a few weeks, should return upon his business, and to his agency in the land of Zion ;

19. And that which he hath seen and heard may be made known unto my disciples, that they perish not. And for this cause have I spoken these things.

20. And again, I say unto you, that my servant Isaac Morley may not be tempted above that which he is able to bear, and counsel wrongfully to your hurt, I gave commandment that his farm should be sold.

21. I will not that my servant Frederick G. Williams should sell his farm, for I, the Lord, will to retain a strong hold in the land of Kirtland, for the space of five years, in the which I will not overthrow the wicked, that thereby I may save some ;

22. And after that day, I, the Lord, will not hold any guilty that shall go with an open heart up to the land of Zion ; for I the Lord, require the hearts of the children of men.

23. Behold, now it is called *g*to-day (until the coming of the Son of man), and verily it is a day of sacrifice, and a day for the tithing of my people; for he that is tithed shall not be burned (at his coming) ;

24. For after to-day cometh the *h*burning : this is speaking after the manner of the Lord ; for verily I say, to-morrow all the proud and they that do wickedly shall be as stubble ; and I will burn them up, for I am the Lord of hosts : and I will *i*not spare any that remain in Babylon.

25. Wherefore, if ye believe me, ye will labor while it is called to-day.

---

g, vers. 24, 25.   85 : 3—5, 9.   97 : 12.   119 : 1–.7   Psalm 95 : 7.   Heb 3 : 7, 15.   4 : 7.   *h*, ver. 23.   29 : 21.   45 : 57.   63 : 34, 54.   76 : 105. 88 : 94.   101 : 23—25.   133 : 40, 41, 64.   Psalm 50 : 3   Isa. 24 : 6 .*i* Isa. 66 : 15, 16   *i*, see i, Sec. 1

26. And it is not meet that my servants, Newel K. Whitney and Sidney Gilbert, should sell their store and their possessions here, for this is not wisdom, until the residue of the church, which remaineth in this place, shall go up unto the land of Zion.

27. Behold, it is said in my laws, or forbidden, to get in debt to thine enemies ;

28. But behold it is not said at any time, that the Lord should not take when he please, and pay as seemeth him good :

; 29. Wherefore as ye are agents, and ye are on the Lord's errand ; and whatever ye do according to the will of the Lord, is the Lord's business,

30. And he hath set you to provide for his saints in these last days, that they may obtain an inheritance in the land of Zion :

31. And behold, I, the Lord, declare unto you, and my words are sure and shall not fail, that they shall obtain it ;

32. But all things must come to pass in their time;

33. Wherefore, be not weary in well-doing, for ye are laying the ʲfoundation of a great work. And out of small things proceedeth that which is great.

34. Behold, the Lord requireth the heart and a willing mind ; and the ᵏwilling and obedient shall eat the good of the land of Zion in these last days ;

35. And the rebellious shall be cut off out of the land of Zion, and shall be ˡsent away, and shall not inherit the land :

36. For, verily, I say that the rebellious are ᵐnot of the blood of Ephraim, wherefore they shall be plucked out.

37. Behold, I, the Lord, have made ⁿmy church in these last days like unto a judge sitting on a hill, or in a ᵒhigh place, to judge the nations ;

j, Isa. 60 : 22.   k, Isa. 1 : 19.   l, 41 : 5.   42 : 37.   50 : 8, 9.
66 : 1.   63 : 27—31.   97 : 6, 7.   104 : 4—9.   m, see l.   n, see a,
Sec. 1.   o, see v, Sec. 35.

38. For it shall come to pass that the inhabitants of Zion shall judge all things pertaining to Zion ;

39. And liars and hypocrites shall be proved by them, and they who are not apostles and prophets shall be known.

40. And even the bishop, who is a judge, and his counselors, if they are not faithful in their stewardships, shall be condemned, and others shall be planted in their stead ;

41. For, behold, I say unto you that Zion shall flourish, and the *p*glory of the Lord shall be upon her,

42. And she shall be an *q*ensign unto the people, and there shall come unto her out of every nation under heaven.

43. And the day shall come when the nations of the earth shall *r*tremble because of her, and shall fear because of her terrible ones. The Lord hath spoken it. Amen.

SECTION 65.

Revelation on Prayer, given through Joseph, the Seer, at Hiram, Portage Co., Ohio, in the fore part of October, 1831.

1. Hearken, and lo, a voice as of one from on high, who is mighty and powerful, whose going forth is unto the ends of the earth, yea, whose voice is unto men— *a*Prepare ye the way of the Lord, make his paths straight.

---

p, 124 : 6, 9, 11. See 3*b*, Sec. 45.   *q*, 115 : 5, 6.   See *i*, Soc. 45.
r, 45 : 67, 70, 74.   97 : 18, 24.   105 : 31, 32.   See *e*, Sec. 1.

a, 44 : 4, 5.   45 : 9, 43, 44, 56—58.   58 : 9.   88 : 92.   133 : 7—17.   See *e*, Sec. 1.

2. The *b*keys of the kingdom of God are committed unto man on the earth, and from thence shall the gospel roll forth unto the ends of the earth, as the *c*stone which is cut out of the mountain without hands shall roll forth, until it has filled the whole earth ;

3. Yea, a voice crying—*d*Prepare ye the way of the Lord, prepare ye the supper of the Lamb, make ready for the Bridegroom ;

4. Pray unto the Lord, call upon his holy name, make known *e*his wonderful works among the people ;

5. Call upon the Lord, that his kingdom may go forth upon the earth, that the inhabitants thereof may receive it, and be prepared for the days to come, in the which the Son of man shall come *f*down in heaven, clothed in the brightness of his glory, to meet the kingdom of God which is *g*set up on the earth ;

6. Wherefore may the kingdom of God go forth, that the *h*kingdom of heaven may come, that thou, O God, mayest be glorified in heaven so on earth, that thy enemies may be subdued; for thine is the honour, power and glory, for ever and ever. Amen.

SECTION 66.

Revelation given through Joseph, the Seer, at Orange, Cuyahoga Co., Ohio, October 25th, 1831.

1. Behold, thus saith the Lord unto my servant William E. M'Lellin, Blessed are you, inasmuch as you have turned away from your iniquities, and have re-

b, see *x*, Sec. 35.   *c*, see *m*, Sec. 50.   *d*, see *e*, Sec. 1.
e, see *a*, Sec. 4.   *f*, see *e*, Sec. 1.   *g*, see *m*, Sec. 50.   *h*, 84:
94—102.   88 : 95 - 98.   See *e*, Sec. 1.

ceived my truths, saith the Lord your Redeemer, the Saviour of the world, even of as many as believe on my name.

2. Verily I say unto you, blessed are you for receiving mine *a*everlasting covenant, even the *b*fullness of my gospel, sent forth unto the children of men, that they might have life and be made partakers of the glories which are to be revealed in the last days, as it was written by the prophets and apostles in days of old.

3. Verily I say unto you, my servant William, that you are clean, but not all; repent, therefore of those things which are not pleasing in my sight, saith the Lord, for the Lord will show them unto you.

4. And now, verily, I, the Lord, will show unto you what I will concerning you, or what is my will concerning you;

5. Behold, verily I say unto you, that it is my will that you should proclaim my gospel from land to land, and from city to city; yea, in those regions round about where it has not been proclaimed.

6. Tarry not many days in this place; go not up unto the land of Zion as yet; but inasmuch as you can send, send; otherwise, think not of thy property.

7. Go unto the eastern lands, bear testimony in every place, unto every people, in their synagogues, reasoning with the people.

8. Let my servant Samuel H. Smith go with you, and forsake him not, and give him thine instructions; and he that is faithful shall be made strong in every place, and I, the Lord, will go with you.

9. *c*Lay your hands upon the sick, and they shall recover. Return not till I the Lord shall send you. Be patient in affliction. Ask and ye shall receive. Knock and it shall be opened unto you.

10. Seek not to be cumbered. Forsake all unright-

---

a, see k, Sec. 1.   b, see b, Sec. 18.   c, see z, Sec. 42.

eousness.   Commit not adultery, a temptation with which thou hast been troubled.

11. Keep these sayings, for they are true and faithful, and thou shalt magnify thine office, and push many people to Zion with songs of everlasting joy upon their heads.

12. Continue in these things even unto the end, and you shall have a crown of eternal life at the right hand of my Father, who is full of grace and truth.

13. Verily, thus saith the Lord your God, your Redeemer, even Jesus Christ.   Amen.

SECTION 67.

Revelation given through Joseph, the Seer, at Hiram, Portage Co., Ohio, November, 1831.

1. Behold and hearken, O ye elders of my church, who have assembled yourselves together, whose prayers I have heard, and whose hearts I know, and whose desires have come up before me.

2. Behold and lo, mine eyes are upon you, and the heavens and the earth are in mine hands, and the riches of eternity are mine to give.

3. Ye endeavoured to believe that ye should receive the blessing which was offered unto you; but behold, verily, I say unto you, there were fears in your hearts, and verily this is the reason that ye did not receive.

4. And now I, the Lord, give unto you a testimony of the truth of these commandments which are lying before you;

5. Your eyes have been upon my servant Joseph Smith, jun., and his language you have known, and his imperfections you have known ; and you have sought in your hearts knowledge that you might express beyond his language, this you also know ;

6. Now seek ye out of the book of commandments, even the least that is among them, and appoint him that is the most wise among you ;

7. Or, if there be any among you, that shall make one like unto it, then ye are justified in saying that ye do not know that they are true ;

8. But if ye cannot make one like unto it, ye are under condemnation if ye do not bear record that they are true ;

9. For ye know that there is *no unrighteousness in them, and that which is righteous cometh down from above, from the Father of lights.

10. And again, verily I say unto you, that it is your privilege, and a promise I give unto you that have been ordained unto this ministry, that inasmuch as you strip yourselves from jealousies and fears, and humble yourselves before me, for ye are not sufficiently humble, the vail shall be rent and you shall *see me and know that I AM ; not with the carnal, neither natural mind, but with the spiritual ;

11. For no man has seen God at any time in the flesh, except quickened by the Spirit of God ;

12. Neither can any natural man abide in the presence of God ; neither after the carnal mind ;

13. Ye are not able to abide the presence of God now, neither the ministering of angels ; wherefore continue in patience until ye are perfected.

14. Let not your minds turn back, and when ye are worthy, in mine own due time, ye shall see and know that which was conferred upon you by the hands of my servant Joseph Smith, jun. Amen.

---

a, 50 : 23, 21.　81 : 43—47.　83 : 40, 41, 49, 66, 67.　　*b*, see *o*, Sec. 50.

SECTION 68.

Revelation, given through Joseph, the Seer, at Hiram, Portage Co., Ohio, November, 1831, to Orson Hyde, Luke Johnson, Lyman Johnson, and William E. M'Lellin. The mind and will of the Lord, as made known by the voice of the Spirit, to a conference concerning certain elders, and also certain items as made known in addition to the Covenants and Commandments.

1. My servant, Orson Hyde, was called by his ordinance to proclaim the *a*everlasting gospel, by the Spirit of the living God, from people to people, and from land to land, in the congregations of the wicked, in their synagogues, reasoning with, and expounding all Scriptures unto them.

2. And, behold, and lo, this is an ensample unto all those who were ordained unto this Priesthood, whose mission is appointed unto them to go forth ;

3. And this is the ensample unto them, that they shall speak as they are *b*moved upon by the Holy Ghost,

4. And whatsoever they shall speak when moved upon by the Holy Ghost, shall be ·scripture, shall be the will of the Lord, shall be the mind of the Lord, shall be the word of the Lord, shall be the voice of the Lord, and the power of God unto salvation :

5. Behold this is the promise of the Lord unto you, O ye my servants ;

6. Wherefore be of good cheer, and do not fear, for I the Lord am with you, and will stand by you ; and ye shall bear record of me, even Jesus Christ, that I am the Son of the living God, that I was, that I am, and that I am to come.

---

7. This is the word of the Lord unto you my servant, Orson Hyde, and also unto my servant Luke Johnson, and unto my servant Lyman Johnson, and unto my servant William E. M'Lellin, and unto all the faithful elders of my church.

8. ^cGo ye into all the world, preach the gospel to every creature, acting in the authority which I have given you, ^dbaptizing in the name of the Father, and of the Son, and of the Holy Ghost;

9. And ^ehe that believeth and is baptized shall be saved, and he that believeth ^fnot shall be damned;

10. And he that believeth shall be blest with signs following, even as it is written;

11. And unto you it shall be given to know the signs of the times, and the ^gsigns of the coming of the Son of man;

12. And of as many as the Father shall bear record, to you shall be given power to ^hseal them up unto eternal life. Amen.

13. And now concerning the items in addition to the covenants and commandments, they are these:—

14. There remaineth hereafter, in the due time of the Lord, other bishops to be set apart unto the church, to minister even according to the first;

15. Wherefore they shall be ⁱHigh Priests who are worthy, and they shall be appointed by the ^jFirst Presidency of the Melchisedek priesthood, except they be literal descendants of Aaron,

16. And if they be ^kliteral descendants of Aaron, they have a legal right to the bishopric, if they are the ^lfirstborn among the sons of Aaron;

---

c, see b, Sec. 1.   d, see l, Sec. 5.   e, see q, Sec. 20.   f, 76 : 84, 85, 102—106.   84 : 74, 75.   g, see e, Sec. 1.   h, see d, Sec. 1. i, 20 : 67.   68 : 19.   78 : 15, 19.   81 : 1, 2.   84 : 6—42.   Sec. 102.   Sec. 107. 112 : 30.   132 : 45, 46.   Sec. 124 : 123—145.   j, 68 : 10—23.   81 : 2.   102 : 1, 3, 8—11, 19, 20, 23, 26, 27, 33.   107 : 9, 17, 22, 24, 29, 33, 36, 64—68, 76—84, 91, 92.   112 : 15, 17, 20.   115 : 15.   Sec. 120.   124 : 123—126.   k, 20 : 66, 67.   41 : 9.   42 : 10, 31—34, 71, 73, 82.   46 : 27.   Sec. 51.   57 : 7, 15. 58 : 24.   60 : 10.   64 : 17.   68 : 14—24.   70 : 7—14.   Sec. 72.   84 : 112—114. 85 : 1.   93 : 50.   107 : 15—17, 68—78, 82, 88.   117 : 11.   Sec. 120.   124 : 141. l, 84 : 18, 26, 27, 30.   107 : 13, 16, 70, 76.

17. For the firstborn holds the right of the presidency over this priesthood, and the [m]keys or authority of the same.

18. No man has a legal right to this office to hold the keys of this priesthood, except he be a [n]literal descendant and the firstborn of Aaron;

19. But as a [o]High Priest of the Melchisedek Priesthood has authority to officiate in all the lesser offices, he may officiate in the office of bishop when no literal descendant of Aaron can be found, provided he is called, and set apart and ordained unto this power under the hands of the [p]First Presidency of the Melchisedek Priesthood.

20. And a [q]literal descendant of Aaron, also, must be designated by this [r]Presidency, and found worthy, and [s]anointed, and ordained under the hands of this Presidency, otherwise they are not legally authorized to officiate in their priesthood;

21. But by virtue of the decree concerning their right of the priesthood descending from father to son, they may claim their [t]anointing, if at any time they can prove their lineage, or do ascertain it by revelation from the Lord [u]under the hands of the above named Presidency.

22. And again, no bishop or High Priest who shall be set apart for this ministry, shall be tried or condemned for any crime, save it be before the [v]First Presidency of the church;

23. And inasmuch as he is found guilty before this Presidency, by testimony that cannot be impeached, he shall be condemned;

24. And if he repents he shall be [w]forgiven, according to the covenants and commandments of the church.

25. And again, inasmuch as parents have children

---

m, 15, 16, 18. See *k*. *n*, see *l*. *o*, see *i*. *p*, see *j*. *q*, see *k*. *r*, see *j*. *s*, ver. 21. 124 : 39. *t*, ver. 20. 124 : 39. *u*, see *j*. *v*, how a bishop must be tried, see *j*. *w*, see *d*, Sec. 64.

in Zion, or in any of her Stakes which are organized, that teach them not to understand the ^xdoctrine of repentance, faith in Christ the son of the living God, and of baptism and the gift of the Holy Ghost by the laying on of the hands when ^yeight years old, the sin be upon the heads of the parents ;

26. For this shall be a law unto the inhabitants of Zion, or in any of her Stakes which are organized ;

27. And their children shall be baptized for the remission of their sins when ^zeight years old, and receive the laying on of the hands,

28. And they shall also ^{2a}teach their children to pray and to walk uprightly before the Lord.

29. And the inhabitants of Zion shall, also, observe the ^{2b}Sabbath day to keep it holy.

30. And the inhabitants of Zion, also, shall remember their ^{2c}labors, inasmuch as they are appointed to labor, in all faithfulness ; for the ^{2d}idler shall be had in remembrance before the Lord.

31. Now, I the Lord, am not well pleased with the inhabitants of Zion, for there are idlers among them ; and their children are also growing up in wickedness ; they also seek not earnestly the ^{2e}riches of eternity, but their eyes are full of greediness.

32. These things ought not to be, and must be done away from among them : wherefore let my servant Oliver Cowdery carry these sayings unto the land of Zion.

33. And a commandment I give unto them, that he that observeth not his ^{2f}prayers before the Lord in the season thereof, let him be had in remembrance before the judge of my people.

34. These sayings are true and faithful ; wherefore transgress them not, neither take therefrom.

---

x, see b, Sec. 18.   y, vers. 26, 27.   20 : 71.   z, ver. 25.
2a, ver. 31.   2b, 50 : 9, 10, 12—14.   2c, 42 : 42.   2d, 42 :
42.   2e, see 2a, Sec. 38.   2f, 20 : 47, 51.   Alma 34 : 2L   III. Nep.
18 : 21.

35. Behold, I am Alpha and Omega, and I ^{2g}come quickly. Amen.

SECTION 69.

Revelation given through Joseph, the Seer, at Hiram, Portage Co., Ohio, November, 1831.

1. Hearken unto me, saith the Lord your God, for my servant Oliver Cowdery's sake. It is not wisdom in me that he should be entrusted with the commandments and the moneys which he shall carry unto the land of Zion, except one go with him who will be true and faithful;

2. Wherefore, I the Lord will that my servant, John Whitmer, should go with my servant Oliver Cowdery;

3. And also that he shall continue in writing and making a ^{a}history of all the important things which he shall observe and know concerning my ^{b}church :

4. And also that he receive counsel and assistance from my servant Oliver Cowdery and others.

5. And also my servants who are abroad in the earth, should send forth the accounts of their ^{c}stewardships to the land of Zion ;

6. For the land of Zion shall be a seat and a place to receive and do all these things ;

7. Nevertheless, let my servant, John Whitmer, travel many times from place to place, and from church to church, that he may the more easily obtain knowledge ;

8. Preaching and expounding, writing, copying,

$2g$, see e, Sec. 1.

a, see a, Sec. 21. b, see a, Sec. 1. c, see o, Sec. 42.$^{•}$

selecting, and obtaining all things which shall be for the good of the church, and for the rising generations, that shall grow up on the land of Zion, to possess it from generation to generation, ^dfor ever and ever. Amen.

SECTION 70.

Revelation given through Joseph, the Seer, at Kirtland, Ohio, November, 1831.

1. Behold, and hearken, O ye inhabitants of Zion, and all ye people of my church, who are far off, and hear the word of the Lord which I give unto my servant Joseph Smith, jun., and also unto my servant Martin Harris, and also unto my servant Oliver Cowdery, and also unto my servant John Whitmer, and also unto my servant Sidney Rigdon, and also unto my servant William W. Phelps, by the way of commandment unto them ;

2. For I give unto them a commandment ; wherefore hearken and hear, for thus saith the Lord unto them—

3. I, the Lord, have appointed them, and ordained them to be ^astewards over the revelations and commandments which I have given unto them, and which I shall hereafter give unto them ;

4. And an account of this ^bstewardship will I require of them in the day of judgment :

5. Wherefore I have appointed unto them, and this is their business in the church of God, to manage them and the concerns thereof ; yea, the benefits thereof.

---

d, see *p*, Sec. 38.

a, see *o*, Sec. 42.　　　　*b*, see *o*, Sec. 42.

6. Wherefore a commandment I give unto them, that they shall not give these things unto the church, neither unto the world :

7. Nevertheless, inasmuch as they ^creceive more than is needful for their necessities and their wants, it shall be given into my storehouse,

8. And the benefits shall be consecrated unto the inhabitants of Zion, and unto their generations, inasmuch as they become ^dheirs according to the laws of the kingdom.

9. Behold, this is what the Lord requires of every man in his ^estewardship, even as I, the Lord, have appointed, or shall hereafter appoint unto any man.

10. And, behold ^fnone are exempt from this law who belong to the church of the living God ;

11. Yea, neither the bishop, neither the ^gagent who keepeth the Lord's storehouse, neither he who is appointed in a stewardship over ^htemporal things ; .

12. He who is appointed to administer spiritual things, the same is worthy of his hire, even as those who are appointed to a stewardship, to administer in temporal things ;

13. Yea, even more abundantly, which abundance is multiplied unto them through the ⁱmanifestations of the Spirit ;

14. Nevertheless, in your temporal things you shall be ^jequal, and this not grudgingly, otherwise the abundance of the manifestations of the Spirit shall be withheld.

15. Now this commandment I give unto my servants for their benefit while they remain, for a manifestation of my blessings upon their heads, and for a reward of their diligence and for their security ;

16. For food and for raiment ; for an inheritance ; for houses and for lands, in whatsoever circumstances

---

c, see 2b, Sec. 42.   d, 68 : 25—32.   e, see o, Sec. 42.   f, see Sec. 85.   g, see f, Sec. 57.   h, see 2b, Sec. 42.   i, by revelation. j, see a, Sec. 51.

I, the Lord, shall place them, and whithersoever I, the Lord, shall send them ;

17. For they have been faithful over many things, and have done well inasmuch as they have not sinned.

18. Behold, I, the Lord, am merciful and will bless them, and they shall enter into the joy of these things. Even so. Amen.

SECTION 71.

Revelation given at Hiram, Portage Co., Ohio, December 1st, 1831.

1. Behold, thus saith the Lord unto you my servants, Joseph Smith, jun., and Sidney Rigdon, that the time has verily come, that it is necessary and expedient in me that you should open your mouths in proclaiming my gospel, the things of the kingdom, expounding the ^amysteries thereof out of the scriptures, according to that portion of Spirit and power which shall be given unto you, even as I will.

2. Verily, I say unto you, proclaim unto the world in the regions round about, and in the church also, for the space of a season, even until it shall be made known unto you.

3. Verily this is a mission for a season, which I give unto you,

4. Wherefore, ^blabor ye in my vineyard. Call upon the inhabitants of the earth, and bear record, and prepare the way for the commandments and revelations which are to come.

5. Now, behold this is wisdom ; whoso readeth, let him understand and receive also ;

---

a, see 2 *e*. Sec. 42.   *b*, see *k*, Sec. 24.

6. For unto him that receiveth it shall be given more abundantly, even power ;

7. Wherefore, confound your enemies ; call upon them to ᶜmeet you both in public and in private ; and inasmuch as ye are faithful, their shame shall be made manifest.

8. Wherefore, let them bring forth their strong reasons against the Lord.

9. Verily, thus saith the Lord unto you, there is no weapon that is formed against you shall prosper ;

10. And if any man lift his voice against you, he shall be confounded in mine own due time ;

11. Wherefore, keep my commandments, they are true and faithful. Even so. Amen.

SECTION 72.

Revelation given at Kirtland, Geauga Co., Ohio, December 4th, 1831.

1. Hearken and listen to the voice of the Lord, O ye who have assembled yourselves together, who are the ᵃHigh Priests of my church, to whom the ᵇkingdom and power have been given.

2. For verily thus saith the Lord, it is expedient in me for a ᶜbishop to be appointed unto you, or of you, unto the church in this part of the Lord's vineyard ;

3. And verily in this thing ye have done wisely, for it is required of the Lord, at the hand of ᵈevery steward, to render an account of his stewardship, both in time and in eternity.

---

c, Isa. 41 : 21. 43 : 9.

a, see i, Sec. 68.   b, see x, Sec. 35.   c, see k, Sec. 68.
d, see e. Sec. 42.

4. For he who is faithful and wise in time, is accounted worthy to inherit the ᶜmansions prepared for them of my Father.

5. Verily I say unto you, the elders of the church in this part of my vineyard, shall render an ᶠaccount of their stewardship unto the bishop which shall be appointed of me, in this part of my vineyard.

6. These things shall be had on record, to be handed over unto the bishop in Zion ;

7. And the duty of the bishop shall be made known by the commandments which have been given, and the voice of the conference.

8. And now, verily I say unto you, my servant Newel K. Whitney is the man who shall be appointed and ordained unto this power. This is the will of the Lord your God, your Redeemer. Even so. Amen.

9. The word of the Lord, in addition to the law which has been given, making known the duty of the bishop which has been ordained urto the church in this part of the vineyard, which is verily this :—

10. To keep the Lord's ᵍstorehouse ; to receive the ʰfunds of the church in this part of the vineyard ;

11. To take an ᶦaccount of the elders as before has been commanded ; and to administer to their wants, who shall pay for that which they receive, inasmuch as they have wherewith to pay ;

12. That this also may be consecrated to the good of the church, to the poor and needy ;

13. And he who hath not wherewith to pay, an account shall be taken and handed over to the bishop of Zion, who shall pay the debt out of that which the Lord shall put into his hands ;

14. And the labors of the faithful who ʲlabor in spiritual things, in administering the gospel and the

---

things of the kingdom unto the church, and unto the
world, shall answer the debt unto the bishop in Zion ;

15. Thus it cometh out of the church, for according to the *k*law every man that cometh up to Zion,
must lay all things before the bishop in Zion.

16. And now, verily I say unto you, that as every
elder in this part of the vineyard must give an account
of his stewardship unto the bishop in this part of the
vineyard,

17. A *l*certificate from the judge or bishop in this
part of the vineyard, unto the bishop in Zion, rendereth
every man acceptable, and answereth all things, for an
inheritance, and to be received as a *m*wise steward, and
as a faithful laborer ;

18. Otherwise he shall not be accepted of the
bishop of Zion.

19. And now, verily I say unto you, let every elder
who shall give an account unto the bishop of the
church, in this part of the vineyard, be *n*recommended
by the church or churches, in which he labors, that he
may render himself and his accounts approved in all
things.

20. And again, let my servants who are appointed
as stewards over the *o*literary concerns of my church,
have claim for assistance upon the bishop or bishops,
in all things,

21. That the revelations may be *p*published, and
go forth unto the ends of the earth, that they also
may obtain funds which shall benefit the church in all
things,

22. That they also may render themselves approved
in all things, and be accounted as *q*wise stewards.

23. And now, behold, this shall be an *r*ensample
for all the extensive branches of my church, in what-

k, see n, Sec. 42.   l, vers. 18—26.   52 : 41.   m, see o,
Sec. 42.   n, vers. 17—26.   52 : 41.   o, see Sec. 70.   p, The
Book of Covenants.   q, see o, Sec. 42.   r, an Ensample for all
Stewards.

soever land they shall be established.   And now I make an end of my sayings.   Amen.

24. A few words in addition to the laws of the kingdom, respecting the members of the church ; they that are appointed by the Holy Spirit to go up unto Zion, and they who are privileged to go up unto Zion,

25. Let them carry up unto the bishop a *certificate from three elders of the church, or a certificate from the bishop,

26. Otherwise he who shall go up unto the land of Zion, shall not be accounted as a *wise steward.   This is also an ensample.   Amen.

SECTION 73.

Revelation to Joseph Smith, jun., and Sidney Rigdon, given at Hiram, Portage Co., Ohio, Jan. 10th, 1832. The word of the Lord unto them concerning the Elders of the Church of the living God, established in the last days, making known the will of the Lord unto the Elders, what they shall do until Conference.

1. For verily thus saith the Lord, it is expedient in me, that they should continue preaching the gospel, and in exhortation to the churches in the regions round about, until conference ;

2. And then, behold, it shall be made known unto them, by the *voice of the conference, their several missions.

3. Now, verily, I say unto you my servants, Joseph

---

*, see l.   t, see o, Sec. 42.

a, see Sec. 75.

Smith, jun., and Sidney Rigdon, saith the Lord, it is expedient to *b*translate again,

4. And, inasmuch as it is practicable, to preach in the regions round about until conference; and after that it is expedient to continue the work of *c*translation until it be finished.

5. And let this be a pattern unto the elders until further knowledge, even as it is written.

6. Now I give no more unto you at this time. Gird up your loins and be sober. Even so. Amen.

SECTION 74.

An Explanation of the First Epistle to the Corinthians, Chapter 7, verse 14, given by revelation, through Joseph, the Seer, at Hiram, Portage Co., Ohio, January, 1832.

1. For the unbelieving husband is sanctified by the wife, and the unbelieving wife is sanctified by the husband, else were your children unclean, but now *a*are they holy.

2. Now in the days of the apostles the law of circumcision was had among all the Jews who believed not the gospel of Jesus Christ.

3. And it came to pass that there arose a great contention among the people concerning the law of circumcision, for the unbelieving husband was desirous that his children should be circumcised and become subject to the law of Moses, which law was fulfilled.

4. And it came to pass that the children, being

---

b, the Bible   *c*, until the translation of the Bible is finished.

a, 29: 46—48.   Moro. 8: 8—24.

brought up in subjection to the law of Moses, gave heed to the traditions of their fathers, and believed not the gospel of Christ, wherein they became unholy ;

5. Wherefore, for this cause the apostle wrote unto the church, giving unto them a commandment, not of the Lord, but of himself, that a believer should not be united to an unbeliever, except the law of Moses should be done away among them,

6. That their children might remain without circumcision ; and that the tradition might be done away, which saith that little children are unholy ; for it was had among the Jews,

7. But ᵇlittle children are holy, being ; sanctified through the atonement of Jesus Christ ; and this is what the scriptures mean.

SECTION 75.

Revelation given at Amherst, Loraine Co., Ohio, in Conference, January 25th, 1832.

1. Verily, verily, I say unto you, I who speak even by the voice of my Spirit ; even Alpha and Omega, your Lord and your God ;

2. Hearken, O ye who have given your names to go forth to proclaim my gospel, and to prune my vineyard.

3. Behold, I say unto you, that it is my will that you should go forth and not tarry, neither be ᵃidle, but labor with your mights,

4. Lifting up your voices as with the sound of a trump, proclaiming the truth according to the

---

b, see a.

a, see u, Sec. 42

revelations and commandments which I have given you,

5. And thus if ye are faithful ye shall be *b*laden with many sheaves, and crowned with honor, and glory, and immortality, and eternal life.

6. Therefore, verily I say unto my servant William E. M'Lellin, I *c*revoke the commission which I gave unto him to go unto the eastern countries,

7. And I give unto him a *d*new commission and a new commandment, in the which I, the Lord, chasten him for the murmurings of his heart ;

8. And he sinned, nevertheless I forgive him, and say unto him again, go ye into the south countries,

9. And let my servant Luke Johnson go with him and proclaim the things which I have commanded them,

10. Calling on the name of the Lord for the *e*Comforter, which shall teach them all things that are expedient for them,

11. Praying always that they faint not, and inasmuch as they do this, I will be with them even unto the end.

12. Behold, this is the will of the Lord your God concerning you. Even so. Amen.

13. And again, verily thus saith the Lord, let my servant Orson Hyde, and my servant Samuel H. Smith, take their journey into the eastern countries, and proclaim the things which I have commanded them ; and inasmuch as they are faithful, lo, I will be with them even unto the end.

14. And again, verily I say unto my servant Lyman Johnson, and unto my servant Orson Pratt, they shall also take their journey into the eastern countries ; and behold, and lo, I am with them also, even unto the end.

15. And again, I say unto my servant Asa Dodds,

---

b, 33 : 9.   *c*, see *b*, Sec. 56.   *d*, see *c*.   *e*, see *h*, Sec. 42.

and unto my servant Calves Wilson, that they also
shall take their journey unto the western countries,
and proclaim my gospel, even as I have commanded
them.

16. And he who is faithful shall overcome all things,
and shall be ᶠlifted up at the last day.

17. And again, I say unto my servant Major N.
Ashly, and my servant Burr Riggs, let them take their
journey also into the south country;

18. Yea, let all those take their journey as I have
commanded them, going from house to house, and from
village to village, and from city to city;

19. And in whatsoever house ye enter, and they
receive you, ᵍleave your blessing upon that house;

20. And in whatsoever house ye enter, and they
receive you not, ye shall depart speedily from that
house, and ʰshake off the dust of your feet as a testimony against them;

21. And you shall be filled with joy and gladness;
and know this, that in the day of judgment you shall
be ⁱjudges of that house, and condemn them;

22. And it shall be more tolerable for the heathen
in the day of judgment, than for that house; therefore
gird up your loins and be faithful, and ye shall overcome all things, and be ʲlifted up at the last day. Even
so. Amen.

23. And again, thus saith the Lord unto you, O ye
elders of my church, who have given your names that
you might know his will concerning you;

24. Behold, I say unto you, that it is the ᵏduty of
the church to assist in supporting the families of those,
and also to support the families of those who are called
and must needs be sent unto the world to proclaim the
gospel unto the world;

25. Wherefore, I, the Lord, give unto you this

---

commandment, that ye obtain places for your families, inasmuch as your brethren are willing to open their hearts;

26. And let all such as can obtain places for their families, and support of the church for them, not fail to go into the world, whether to the east or to the west, or to the north, or to the south ;

27. Let them 'ask and they shall receive, knock and it shall be opened unto them, and made known from on high, even by the ᵐComforter, whither they shall go.

28. And again, verily I say unto you, that every man who is obliged to provide for his own family, let him provide, and he shall in no wise lose his crown ; and let him labor in the church.

29. Let every man be diligent in all things. And the ⁿidler shall not have place in the church, except he repents and mends his ways.

30. Wherefore, let my servant Simeon Carter, and my servant Emer Harris, be united in the ministry ;

31. And also my servant Ezra Thayre, and my servant Thomas B. Marsh ;

32. Also my servant Hyrum Smith, and my servant Reynolds Cahoon ;

33. And also my servant Daniel Stanton, and my servant Seymour Brunson ;

34. And also my servant Sylvester Smith, and my servant Gideon Carter ;

35. And also my servant Ruggles Eames, and my servant Stephen Burnett ;

36. And also my servant Micah B. Welton ; and also my servant Eden Smith.   Even so.   Amen.

---

l, see *c,* Sec. 4.   *m,* see *h,* Sec. 42.   *·n,* see *u,* Sec. 42.

SECTION 76.

A Vision, given to Joseph Smith, jun., and Sidney Rigdon, at Hiram, Portage Co., Ohio, February 16th, 1832.

1. Hear O ye heavens, and give ear O earth, and rejoice ye inhabitants thereof, for the Lord is God, and beside him there is no Saviour :

2. Great is his wisdom, marvelous are his ways, and the extent of his doings none can find out ;

3. His purposes fail not, neither are there any who can stay his hand ;

4. From *a*eternity to eternity he is the same, and his years never fail.

5. For thus saith the Lord, I, the Lord, am merciful and gracious unto those who fear me, and delight to honor those who serve me in righteousness and in truth unto the end ;

6. Great shall be their reward and eternal shall be their glory ;

7. And to them will I reveal *b*all mysteries, yea, all the hidden mysteries of my kingdom from days of old, and for ages to come will I make known unto them the good pleasure of my will concerning all things pertaining to my kingdom ;

8. Yea, even the *c*wonders of eternity shall they know, and things to come will I show them, even the things of many generations ;

9. And their wisdom shall be great, and their understanding reach to heaven : and before them the wisdom of the wise shall perish, and the understanding of the prudent shall come to nought ;

10. For by my Spirit will I enlighten them, and

---

a, see *a,* Sec. 39.   *b,* see 24, Sec. 42.   *c,* see *b.*

by my power will I make known unto them the secrets of my will; yea, even those things which [d]eye has not seen, nor ear heard, nor yet entered into the heart of man.

11. We, Joseph Smith, jun., and Sidney Rigdon, being in the Spirit on the sixteenth of February, in the year of our Lord, one thousand eight hundred and thirty-two,

12. By the power of the Spirit our eyes were opened and our understandings were enlightened, so as to see and understand the things of God—

13. Even those things which were from the beginning before the world was, which were ordained of the Father, through his Only Begotten Son, who was in the bosom of the Father, even from the beginning,

14. Of whom we bear record, and the record which we bear is the [e]fullness of the gospel of Jesus Christ, who is the Son, whom we [f]saw and with whom we conversed in the heavenly vision;

15. For while we were doing the work of [g]translation, which the Lord had appointed unto us, we came to the twenty-ninth verse of the fifth chapter of John, which was given unto us as follows.

16. Speaking of the resurrection of the dead, concerning those who shall hear the voice of the Son of Man, and shall come forth;

17. They who have done good in the [h]resurrection of the just, and they who have done evil in the resurrection of the unjust.

18. Now this caused us to marvel, for it was given unto us of the Spirit;

19. And while we meditated upon these things, the Lord touched the eyes of our understandings and they were opened, and the glory of the Lord shone round about;

d, vers. 114—119.   III. Nep. 17: 15—25.   19: 30—36.   26: 14—16.
I. Corinth. 2: 9.   e, see b, Sec. 18.   f, see o, Sec. 50.   g, translating the New Testament.   h, see m, Sec. 29.

20. And we [i]beheld the glory of the Son, on the right hand of the Father, and received of his fullness;

21. And [j]saw the holy angels, and they who are sanctified before his throne, worshiping God, and the Lamb, who worship him for ever and ever.

22. And now, after the many testimonies which have been given of him, this is the [k]testimony last of all, which we give of him, that he lives;

23. For we [l]saw him, even on the right hand of God, and we heard the voice bearing record that he is the Only Begotten of the Father—

24. That by him and through him, and of him [m]the worlds are and were created, and the inhabitants thereof are begotten sons and daughters unto God.

25. And this we saw also, and bear record, that an [n]angel of God who was in authority in the presence of God, who rebelled against the Only Begotten Son, whom the Father loved, and who was in the bosom of the Father—was thrust down from the presence of God and the Son,

26. And was called [o]Perdition, for the heavens wept over him—he was [p]Lucifer, a son of the morning.

27. And we beheld, and lo, he is fallen! is fallen! even a son of the morning.

28. And while we were yet in the Spirit, the Lord commanded us that we should write the vision, for we [q]beheld Satan, that old serpent—even the devil—who rebelled against God, and sought to take the kingdom of our God, and his Christ,

29. Wherefore he maketh war with the saints of God, and encompasses them round about.

30. And we saw a [r]vision of the sufferings of those with whom he made war and overcame, for thus came the voice of the Lord unto us.

---

i, see *o*, Sec. 50.   *j*, ver. 67.   *k*, testimony founded on knowledge.
l, see *o*, Sec. 50.   *m*, 93 : 9, 10.   *n*, see 2*d*, Sec. 29.   *o*, vers.
32, 43.   *p*, Isa. 14 : 12.   *q*, 29 : 36, 37.   *r*, vers. 36, 44—49.

31. Thus saith the Lord, concerning all those who
know my power, and have been made partakers thereof, and suffered themselves, through the power of the
devil, to be overcome, and to deny the truth and defy
my power—

32. They are they who are the sons of *perdition,
of whom I say that it had been better for them never
to have been born,

33. For they are vessels of wrath, doomed to suffer
the wrath of God, with the devil and his angels in
eternity ;

34. Concerning whom I have said there is *no forgiveness in this world nor in the world to come,

35. Having *denied the Holy Spirit after having
received it, and having denied the Only Begotten Son
of the Father—having crucified him unto themselves,
and put him to an open shame.

36. These are they who shall go away into the *lake
of fire and brimstone, with the devil and his angels,

37. And the *only ones on whom the second death
shall have any power ;

38. Yea, verily, the only ones who shall not be redeemed in the due time of the Lord, after the sufferings of his wrath ;

39. For *all the rest shall be brought forth by the
resurrection of the dead, through the triumph and the
glory of the Lamb, who was slain, who was in the bosom
of the Father *before the worlds were made.

40. And this is the gospel, the glad tidings which
the voice out of the heavens bore record unto us,

41. That he came into the world, even Jesus, to be
crucified for the world, and to bear the sins of the world,
and to sanctify the world, and to cleanse it from all
unrighteousness ;

s, 42: 18, 79.   76: 32—34, 38, 43, 44.   84: 41.   132 : 27.   *t*, see *s*.
u, see *s*.   Alma 39 : 6.   III. Nep. 29 : 7.   *v*, 63 : 17.   86 : 44—49.   I. Nep.
15 : 29.   II. Nep. 1 : 13.   2 : 29.   9 : 8—19, 26, 34, 36.   28 : 15, 21, 23.   Jacob
6 : 10.   Alma 12 : 16—18.   III. Nep. 27 : 11, 12.   Moro. 8 : 13, 14, 21.
w, see *v*.   *x*, vers. 41—43, 81—88, 98—112.   *y*, 93 : 7.

42. That through him all might be saved whom the Father had put into his power and made by him,

43. Who glorifies the Father, and saves all the works of his hands, except those sons of [z]perdition, who deny the Son after the Father has revealed him ;

44. Wherefore, he saves all except them : they shall go away into [2a]everlasting punishment, which is endless punishment, which is eternal punishment, to reign with the devil and his angels in eternity, where their [2b]worm dieth not, and the fire is not quenched, which is their torment ;

45. And the end thereof, neither the place thereof, nor their torment, no man knows,

46. Neither was it revealed, neither is, neither will be revealed unto man, except to them who are made partakers thereof :

47. Nevertheless I, the Lord, show it by vision unto many, but straightway shut it up again ;

48. Wherefore the end, the width, the height, the depth, and the misery thereof, they understand not, neither any man except them who are [2c]ordained unto this condemnation.

49. And we heard the voice, saying, Write the vision, for lo! this is the end of the vision of the sufferings of the ungodly !

50. And again, we bear record, for we saw and heard, and this is the testimony of the gospel of Christ, concerning them who come forth in the [2d]resurrection of the just ;

51. They are they who received the testimony of Jesus, and [2e]believed on his name and were baptized after the manner of his burial, being [2f]buried in the water in his name, and this according to the commandment which he has given,

52. That by keeping the commandments they might

---

z, see v.   2a, see v,   2b, see v.   Isa. 66: 24.   2c, sons
of Perdition.   2d, see m, Sec. 29.   2e, see q, Sec. 20.
2f, see l, Sec. 5.

be washed and cleansed from all their sins, and receive the Holy Spirit by the laying on of the hands of him who is ordained and sealed unto this power,

53. And who overcome by faith, and are [2g]sealed by the Holy Spirit of promise, which the Father sheds forth upon all those who are just and true.

54. They are they who are the [2h]church of the first born.

55. They are they into whose hands the Father has given [2i]all things—

56. They are they who are [2j]Priests and Kings, who have received of his fullness, and of his glory,

57. And are Priests of the Most High, after the order of Melchisedek, which was after the order of Enoch, which was after the order of the Only Begotten Son ;

58. Wherefore, as it is written, [2k]they are Gods, even the sons of God—

59. Wherefore [2l]all things are theirs, whether life or death, or things present, or things to come, all are theirs and they are Christ's and Christ is God's ·

60. And they shall overcome all things ;

61. Wherefore let no man glory in man, but rather let him glory in God, who shall subdue all enemies under his feet—

62. These shall dwell in the [2m]presence of God and his Christ for ever and ever.

63. These are they whom he shall [2n]bring with him, when he shall come in the clouds of heaven, to reign on the earth over his people.

64. These are they who shall have part in the [2o]first resurrection.

65. These are they who shall come forth in the resurrection of the just.

2g, see d, Sec. 1.   2h, see a, Sec. 1.   2i, see d, Sec. 50.   2j, ver. 57.
78 : 15, 18.   128: 23.   132 : 19, 20, 37.   2k, 132 : 17—20, 37.   2l, see d,
Sec. 50.   2m, vers. 94—96.   2n, see e, Sec. 1.   2o, see m, Sec. 20.

66. These are they who are come unto [2p]Mount Zion, and unto the city of the living God, the heavenly place, the holiest of all.·

67. These are they who have come to an innumerable company of angels, to the general assembly and church of Enoch, and of the first born.

68. These are they whose names are written in heaven, where God and Christ are the judge of all.

69. These are they who are just men made perfect through Jesus the mediator of the [2q]new covenant, who wrought out this perfect atonement through the shedding of his own blood.

70. These are they whose [2r]bodies are celestial, whose glory is that of the sun, even the glory of God, the highest of all, whose glory the [2s]sun of the firmament is written of as being typical.

71. And again, we saw the [2t]terrestrial world, and behold and lo, these are they who are of the terrestrial, whose glory differs from that of the [2u]church of the first born, who have received the fullness of the Father, even as that of the [2v]moon differs from the sun in the firmament.

72. Behold, these are they who [2w]died without law,

73. And also they who are the spirits of men [2x]kept in prison, whom the Son visited, and preached the gospel unto them, that they might be judged according to men in the flesh,

74. Who received not the testimony of Jesus in the flesh, but afterwards received it.

75. These are they who are honorable men of the earth, who were blinded by the craftiness of men.

76. These are they who receive of his glory, but not of his fullness.

2*p*, Heb. 12 : 22—24.   2*q*, see *k*, Sec. 1.   2*r*, 79 : 7, 14. 88 : 2, 4, 20, 22, 25, 28. 105 : 4, 5. 131 : 1.   2*s*, Matt. 13 : 43. I. Corin:h. 15 : 40 —42.   2*t*, see 88 : 99, 100. 128 : 22. I. Cor. 15 : 40.   2*u*, see *a*, Sec. 1.   2*v*, I. Cor. 15 : 41.   2*w*, 45 : 54. 88 : 99.   2*x*, 88 : 99, 100. 128 : 22.

77. These are they who receive of the presence of the Son, but not of the fullness of the Father ;

78. Wherefore they are bodies terrestrial, and not bodies celestial, and differ in glory as the moon differs from the sun.

79. These are they who are ²ʸnot valiant in the testimony of Jesus ; wherefore they obtain ²ᶻnot the crown over the kingdom of our God.

80. And now this is the end of the vision which we saw of the terrestrial, that the Lord commanded us to write while we were yet in the Spirit.

81. And again, we saw the glory of the telestial, which glory is that of the lesser, even as the glory of the ³ᵃstars differs from that of the glory of the moon in the firmament.

82. These are they who received not the gospel of Christ, neither the testimony of Jesus.

83. These are they who deny not the Holy Spirit.

84. These are they who are ³ᵇthrust down to hell.

85. These are they who shall not be redeemed from the devil, until the ³ᶜlast resurrection, until the Lord, even Christ the Lamb shall have finished his work.

86. These are they who receive not of his fullness in the eternal world, but of the Holy Spirit through the ministration of the terrestrial ;

87. And the terrestrial through the ministration of the celestial ;

88. And also the telestial receive it of the ³ᵈadministering of angels who are appointed to minister for them, or who are appointed to be ministering spirits for them, for they ³ᵉshall be heirs of salvation.

89. And thus we saw in the heavenly vision, the glory of the telestial, which surpasses all understanding,

---

2y, receive a reward according to their works.   2z, they cannot
become kings.   3a, vers. 88—90, 98—106, 109—112.   88: 31, 32.
1. Cor. 15: 41.   3b, see v.   3c, 43: 18.   88: 100, 101.
3d, Heb. 1: 14.   3e, Heb. 1: 14.

90. And no man knows it except him to whom God has revealed it.

91. And thus we saw the glory of the terrestrial, which excels in all things the glory of the telestial, even in glory, and in power, and in might, and in dominion.

92. And thus we saw the glory of the celestial, which excels in all things—where God, even the Father, reigns upon his throne for ever and ever ;

93. Before whose throne all things bow in humble reverence and give him glory for ever and ever.

94. They who dwell in [3f]his presence are the church of the first born, and they see as they are seen, and know as they are known, having received of his fullness and of his grace ;

95. And he makes them [3g]equal in power, and in might, and in dominion.

96. And the glory of the celestial is one, even as the glory of the [3h]sun is one.

97. And the glory of the terrestrial is one, even as the glory of the [3i]moon is one.

98. And the glory of the telestial is one, even as the glory of the stars is one, for as one [3j]star differs from another star in glory, even so differs one from another in glory in the telestial world;

99. For these are they who are of Paul, and of Apollos, and of Cephas.

100. These are they who say they are some of one and some of another—some of Christ and some of John, and some of Moses, and some of Elias, and some of Esaias, and some of Isaiah, and some of Enoch ;

101. But received not the gospel, neither the testimony of Jesus, neither the prophets, neither the [3k]everlasting covenant.

102. Last of all, these all are they who will not be

3f, ver. 62. See a, Sec. 1.   3g, 29 : 12, 13.   35 : 2. 38 : 24—27.
50 : 43, 44.   78 : 5—7.   84 : 35—39.   132 : 20.   3h, 1. Cor. 15 :
40, 41.   3i, 1. Cor. 15 : 40, 41.   3j, 1. Cor. 15 : 41.   3k, see k, Sec. 1.

gathered with the saints, to be caught up unto [3l]the church of the first born, and received into the cloud.

103. These are [3m]they who are liars, and sorcerers, and adulterers, and whoremongers, and whosoever loves and makes a lie.

104. These are they who suffer the [3n]wrath of God on the earth.

105. These are they who suffer the [3o]vengeance of eternal fire.

106. These are they who are [3p]cast down to hell and suffer the wrath of Almighty God, until the fullness of times when Christ shall have subdued all enemies under his feet, and shall have perfected his work,

107. When he shall [3q]deliver up the kingdom, and present it unto the Father spotless, saying—I have overcome and have [3r]trodden the wine-press alone, even the wine-press of the fierceness of the wrath of Almighty God.

108. Then shall [3s]he be crowned with the crown of his glory, to sit on the throne of his power to reign for ever and ever.

109. But behold, and lo, we saw the glory and the [3t]inhabitants of the telestial world, that they were as innumerable as the stars in the firmament of heaven, or as the sand upon the sea shore,

110. And heard the voice of the Lord, saying—these all shall [3u]bow the knee, and every tongue shall confess to him who sits upon the throne for ever and ever ;

111. For they shall be judged according to their works, and every man shall receive according to his own works, his own dominion, in the [3v]mansions which are prepared,

112. And they shall be [3w]servants of the Most

[3l], see a, Sec. 1.   [3m], 63 : 17, 18.   Rev. 21 : 8.   22 : 15.   [3n], Jude 1 : 14—16.   [3o], Jude 1 : 7.   [3p], see v.   [3q], I. Cor. 15 : 24—28.   [3r], 133 : 46—51.   [3s], Rev. 19 : 16.   22 : 3—5.   [3t], 132 : 25.   [3u], Rom. 14 : 10—12.   Philip. 2 : 9—11.   [3v], telestial mansions.   [3w], servants of God, but not Gods nor sons of God.   132 : 16, 17.

High, but where God and Christ dwell they cannot come, worlds without end.

113. This is the end of the vision which we saw, which we were commanded to write while we were yet in the Spirit.

114. But great and marvelous are the works of the Lord, and the mysteries of his kingdom which he showed unto us, which surpasses all understanding in glory, and in might, and in dominion,

115. Which he commanded us we should not write while we were yet in the Spirit, and are not [3x]lawful for man to utter;

116. Neither is man capable to make them known, for they are [3y]only to be seen and understood by the power of the Holy Spirit, which God bestows on those who love him, and purify themselves before him;

117. To [3z]whom he grants this privilege of seeing and knowing for themselves;

118. That through the power and manifestation of the Spirit, while in the flesh, they may be able to bear his presence in the world of glory.

119. And to God and the Lamb be glory, and honor, and dominion for ever and ever. Amen.

SECTION 77.

Key to John's Revelation, given through Joseph, the Seer, at Hiram, Portage Co., Ohio, about the 1st of March, 1832.

1. Q.—What is the [a]sea of glass spoken of by John, 4th chapter, and 6th verse of the Revelations?

3x, III. Nep. 28 : 12—14.   3y, I. Cor. 2 : 9—15.   3z, vers. 5—10.
See o, Sec. 50.

a, 130 : 6—9.

A.—It is the earth, in its sanctified, immortal, and eternal state.

2. Q.—What are we to understand by the four [b]beasts, spoken of in the same verse?

A.—They are figurative expressions, used by the Revelator John, in describing heaven, the [c]Paradise of God, the happiness of man, and of [d]beasts, and of creeping things, and of the fowls of the air ; that, which is spiritual, being in the [e]likeness of that which is temporal ; and that which is [f]temporal, is in the likeness of that which is spiritual ; the [g]spirit of man in the likeness of his person, as also the [h]spirit of the beast, and every other creature which God has created.

3. Q.—Are the four beasts limited to individual beasts, or do they represent classes or orders?

A.—They are limited to four individual beasts, which were shown to John, to represent the glory of the [i]classes of beings, in their destined order or sphere of creation, in the enjoyment of their eternal felicity.

4. Q.—What are we to understand by the eyes, and wings, which the beasts had?

A.—Their eyes are a [j]representation of light, and knowledge ; that is, they are full of knowledge ; and their wings are a [k]representation of power, to move, to act, &c.

5. Q.—What are we to understand by the four and twenty elders, spoken of by John?

A.—We are to understand that these elders whom

---

b, every living creature to be made immortal, to be endowed with knowledge and language.   c, a place for the departed spirits of all flesh. d, a condition of happiness.   e, the spirit of every living thing, being in the likeness of its temporal body.   f, the likeness consists in the resemblance of form.   g, the spirit of man, in the image or form of the body.   h, the spirits of beasts, fowls, fish, creeping things, &c., resembling their temporal bodies.   i, the eternal glory, power, knowledge and happiness of every class of animated beings, represented by four individual or figurative beasts.   j, that they are full of light and knowledge, is manifest from the wisdom of their language.   k, their actions and movements, like that of man, are by the power of their wills, and, like all intelligence, they are independent in their respective spheres. For the last ten letters of reference, see Sec. 29 : 22—25. Also 1st and 2nd chapters of Gen., Inspired Translation. Pearl of Great Price, pp. 4—6. pp. 34—36.

John saw, were elders who had been faithful in the work of the ministry and were dead; who [l]belonged to the seven churches,—and were then in the [m]Paradise of God.

6. Q.—What are we to understand by the book which John saw, which was sealed on the back with. [n]seven seals?

A.—We are to understand that it contains the revealed will, mysteries, and works of God; the hidden things of his economy concerning this earth during the [o]seven thousand years of its continuance, or its temporal existence.

7. Q.—What are we to understand by the [p]seven seals with which it was sealed?

A.—We are to understand that the [q]first seal contains the things of the first thousand years, and the [r]second also of the second thousand years, and so on until the seventh.

8. Q.—What are we to understand by the [s]four angels, spoken of in the 7th chap. and 1st verse of Revelations?

A.—We are to understand that they are four angels sent forth from God, to whom is given power over the four parts of the earth, to save life and to destroy; these are they who have the [t]everlasting gospel to commit to every nation, kindred, tongue, and people; having power to shut up the heavens, to [u]seal up unto life, or to cast down to the [v]regions of darkness.

9. Q.—What are we to understand by the angel

---

l, Rev. 1 : 20.　Chapters 2 and 3.　　*m*, ver. 2.　Luke 23 : 43. 　*n*. Cor. 12 : 4.　Rev. 2 : 7.　*n*. Nep. 9 : 13.　Alma 40 : 12, 14.　*iv*. Nep. 1 : 14.　Moro. 10 : 34.　　*n*, Rev. 5 : 1.　　*o*, one of the secret Records kept in heaven : no man in heaven or on earth, or even angel, found worthy to open it, or look thereon.　　*p*, the hidden mysteries of God's economy, concerning this earth, during its temporal existence of seven thousand years. *q*, the secrets of the first thousand years.　　*r*, the secrets of the second thousand years, &c.　　*s*, four heavenly messengers who commit the gospel preparatory to the Second Coming of Christ　　*t*, see *b*, Sec. 18. *u*, see *d*, Sec. 1.　　*v*, see *d*, Sec. 1.

ascending from the east, Revelations 7th chap. and 2nd verse ?

A.—We are to understand that the angel ascending from the east, is he to whom is given the ^wseal of the living God, over the twelve tribes of Israel ; wherefore he crieth unto the four angels having the ^xeverlasting gospel, saying, hurt not the earth, neither the sea, nor the trees, till we have ^ysealed the servants of our God in their foreheads ; and if you will receive it, this is ^zElias which was to come to gather together the tribes of Israel and restore all things.

10. Q.—What time are the things spoken of in ^{2a}this chapter to be accomplished ?

A.—They are to be accomplished in the sixth thousandth year, or the opening of the ^{2b}sixth seal.

11. Q.—What are we to understand by ^{2c}sealing the one hundred and forty-four thousand, out of all the tribes of Israel ; twelve thousand out of every tribe ?

A.—We are to understand that those who are sealed are ^{2d}High Priests, ordained unto the holy order of God, to administer the ^{2e}everlasting gospel; for they are they who are ordained out of every nation, kindred, tongue, and people, by ^{2f}the angels to whom is given power over the nations of the earth, to bring as many as will come to the ^{2g}church of the first born.

12. Q.—What are we to understand by the ^{2h}sounding of the trumpets, mentioned in the 8th chapter of Revelations ?

A.—We are to understand that as God made the world in six days, and on the ²ⁱseventh day he finished his work, and sanctified it, and also formed man out of

---

w, see d, Sec. 1.   x, see b, Sec. 18.   y, see d, Sec. 1.
z, see g, Sec. 27.   2a, Rev. 8.   2b, His hidden purposes, relating to the sixth thousandth years, before they close.   2c, ver. 9.   2d, these 144,000 High Priests are messengers sent forth to prepare the way for the coming of the Lord.   2e, see b, Sec. 18.   2f, ordained by angels who are in possession of the High Priesthood.   2g, see a, Sec. 1. 2h, 88 : 94—107.   2i, God finished the work of creation on the seventh day. See pp. 6 and 35, Pearl of Great Price.

the [2j]dust of the earth ; even so, in the [2k]beginning of
the seventh thousand years will the Lord God sanctify
the earth, and complete the salvation of man, and judge
all things, and shall redeem all things, except that which
he hath not put into his power, when he shall have
[2l]sealed all things, unto the end of all things ; and the
sounding of the [2m]trumpets of the seven angels, are the
preparing, and finishing of his work, in the [2n]beginning
of the seventh thousand years ;—the preparing of the
way before the [2o]time of his coming.

13. Q.—When are the things to be accomplished,
which are written in the 9th chapter of Revelations ?

A.—They are to be accomplished [2p]after the opening
of the seventh seal, before the coming of Christ.

14. Q.—What are we to understand by the little
book which was eaten by John, as mentioned in the
10th chapter of Revelations ?

A.—We are to understand that it was a [2q]mission,
and an ordinance, for him to gather the tribes of Israel ;
behold, this is [2r]Elias ; who, as it is written, must come
and restore all things.

15. Q.—What is to be understood by the [2s]two witnesses, in the eleventh chapter of Revelations ?

A.—They are two prophets that are to be raised up
to the Jewish nation in the last days, at the time of the
restoration, and to prophesy to the Jews, after they are
gathered, and build the city of Jerusalem, in the land
of their fathers.

2j, Pearl of Great Price, pp. 6 and 35.   II. Nep. 2 : 15.   29 : 7.   Jacob
4 : 9.   Mos. 2 : 25.   4 : 21.   7 : 27.   28 : 17.   Alma 1c : 28, 34, 36.   22 : 10—13.
42 : 2.   Mor. 6 : 15.   9 : 11, 12, 17.   Ether 3 : 15, 16.   Moro. 10 : 3.
2k, in the morning of the seventh great day of rest, the bodies of the saints
will be resurrected.   See m, Sec. 29.   2l, see d, Sec. 1.   2m, 88 :
94—107.   2n, a period which is nigh, even at the doors.   2o, see e,
Sec. 1.   2p, the opening of the seventh seal, and the sounding of the
trumpets of the fifth and sixth angel, are events of the morning of the
seventh thousand years, before the coming of Christ.   2q, see Sec. 7.
Rev. 10 : 8—11.   2r, see g, Sec. 27.   2s, II. Nep. 8 : 18—20.

SECTION 78.

Revelation given at Hiram, Portage County, Ohio, between the 1st and 20th of March, 1832. The order given of the Lord to Enoch, (Joseph Smith, jr.,) for the purpose of establishing the poor.

1. The Lord spake unto Enoch, (Joseph Smith, jr.,) saying, Hearken unto me, saith the Lord your God, who are ordained unto the ªhigh priesthood of my church, who have assembled yourselves together;

2. And listen to the counsel of him who has ordained you from on high, who shall speak in your ears the words of wisdom, that salvation may be unto you in that thing which you have presented before me, saith the Lord God;

3. For verily I say unto you, the time has come, and is now at hand; and behold, and lo, it must needs be that there be an ᵇorganization of my people, in regulating and establishing the affairs of the storehouse for the poor of my people, both in this place and in the land of Zion,

4. Or in other words, the city of Enoch, (Joseph) for a permanent and ᶜeverlasting establishment and order unto my church, to advance the cause, which ye have espoused to the salvation of man, and to the glory of your Father who is in heaven,

5. That you may be ᵈequal in the bands of heavenly things; yea, and earthly things also, for the obtaining of heavenly things;

6. For if ye are not ᵉequal in earthly things, ye cannot be equal in obtaining heavenly things;

7. For if you will that I give unto you a place in

the celestial world, you must prepare yourselves by doing the things which I have commanded you and required of you.

8. And now, verily thus saith the Lord, it is expedient that all things be done unto my glory, by you who are joined together in this order;

9. Or in other words, let my servant Ahashdah (Newel K. Whitney) and my servant Gazelam, or Enoch, (Joseph Smith, jr.,) and my servant Pelagoram, (Sidney Rigdon,) sit in council with the saints which are ꞙin Zion;

10. Otherwise Satan seeketh to turn their hearts away from the truth, that they become blinded and understand not the things which are prepared for them;

11. Wherefore a commandment I give unto you, to prepare and ᵍorganize yourselves by a bond or everlasting covenant that cannot be broken.

12. And he who breaketh it shall lose his office and standing in the church, and shall be delivered over to the ʰbuffetings of Satan until the day of redemption.

13. Behold, this is the preparation wherewith I prepare you, and the foundation, and the ensample which I give unto you, whereby you may accomplish the commandments which are given you,

14. That through my providence, notwithstanding the ⁱtribulation which shall descend upon you, that the church may stand ʲindependent above all other creatures beneath the celestial world,

15. That you may come up unto the crown prepared for you, and be made rulers over ᵏmany kingdoms, saith the Lord God, the Holy One of Zion, who hath established the foundations of ˡAdam-ondi-Ahman;

16. Who hath appointed ᵐMichael your prince, and

ꞙ, see q, Sec. 42.   ᵍ, ver. 3.   ʰ, 82 : 21.   104 : 9, 10.
ⁱ, 58 : 3, 4.   See k, Sec. 63.   ʲ, see Sec. 44.   ᵏ, 132 : 19, 53.
ˡ, 107 : 53.   Sec. 116. 117 : 8, 11.   ᵐ, 107 : 54, 55.

established his feet, and set him upon high, and given unto him the keys of salvation "under the counsel and direction of the Holy One, who is without beginning of days or end of life.

17. Verily, verily I say unto you, ye are little children, and ye have not as yet understood how great blessings the Father hath in his own hands and prepared for you ;

18. And ye cannot bear all things now, nevertheless be of good cheer, for I will lead you along : the °kingdom is yours and the blessings thereof are yours ; and the ᵖriches of eternity are yours ;

19. And he who receiveth all things with thankfulness shall be made glorious ; and the things of this earth shall be added unto him, even an ᵠhundred fold, yea, more ;

20. Wherefore, do the things which I have commanded you, saith your Redeemer, even the Son ʳAhman, who prepareth all things before he taketh you ;

21. For ye are the ˢchurch of the first born, and he will take you ᵗup in a cloud, and appoint every man his portion.

22. And he that is a faithful and ᵘwise steward shall inherit all things. Amen.

SECTION 79.

Revelation through Joseph, the Seer, given at Hiram, Portage County, Ohio, between the 1st and 20th of March, 1832.

1. Verily I say unto you, that it is my will that

n, ver. 15.   107 : 54, 55.   *o*, see *x*, Sec. 35.   *p*, see 2*a*, Sec. 33.
q, 132 : 55.   *r*, in the pure language, signifies God.   *s*, see *a*, Sec. 1.
t, 76 : 102.   88 : 96.   *u*, 51 : 19.   84 : 38.   101 : 61.   .124 : 14.

my servant Jared Carter should go again into the
eastern countries, from place to place, and from city to
city, in the power of the ordination wherewith he has
been ordained, proclaiming glad tidings of great joy,
even the *a*everlasting gospel ;

2. And I will send upon him the *b*Comforter, which
shall teach him the truth and the way whither he
shall go ;

3. And inasmuch as he is faithful, I will crown him
again with *c*sheaves ;

4. Wherefore, let your heart be glad, my servant
Jared Carter, and fear not, saith your Lord, even Jesus
Christ. Amen.

SECTION 80.

Revelation through Joseph, the Seer, given at Hiram,
Portage Co., Ohio, between the 1st and 20th of
March, 1832.

1. Verily, thus saith the Lord, unto you my servant
Stephen Burnett, go ye, go ye into the world and
preach the gospel to every creature that cometh under
the sound of your voice ;

2. And inasmuch as you desire a companion, I will
give unto you my servant *a*Eden Smith ;

3. Wherefore go ye and preach my gospel, whether
to the north or to the south, to the east or to the west,
it mattereth not, for ye cannot go amiss ;

4. Therefore, declare the things which ye have
heard and verily believe, and *b*know to be true.

5. Behold, this is the will of him who hath called you, your Redeemer, even Jesus Christ Amen.

SECTION 81.

Revelation through Joseph, the Seer, given at Hiram, Portage Co., Ohio, between the 1st and 20th of March, 1832.

1. Verily, verily I say unto you my servant Frederick G. Williams, listen to the voice of him who speaketh, to the word of the Lord your God, and hearken to the calling wherewith you are called, even to be a ^aHigh Priest in my church, and a counselor unto my servant Joseph Smith, jun.,

2. Unto whom I have given the ^bkeys of the kingdom, which belongeth always unto the ^cPresidency of the High Priesthood :

3. Therefore, verily, I acknowledge him and will bless him, and also thee, inasmuch as thou art faithful in counsel, in the office which I have appointed unto you, in prayer always vocally and in thy heart, in public and in private, also in thy ministry in proclaiming the gospel in the land of the living, and among thy brethren :

4. And in doing these things thou wilt do the greatest good unto thy fellow beings, and will promote the glory of him who is your Lord ;

5. Wherefore, be faithful, stand in the office which I have appointed unto you, succor the weak, lift up the hands which hang down, and strengthen the feeble knees ;

· 6. And if thou art faithful unto the end, thou shalt

---

a, see *i*, Sec. 68.   *b*, see *x*, Sec. 35.   *c*, see *j*, Sec. 68.

have a crown of immortality and eternal life in the ᵈmansions which I have prepared in the house of my Father.

7. Behold, and lo, these are the words of Alpha and Omega, even Jesus Christ. Amen.

SECTION 82.

Revelation given in Jackson County, Missouri, April 26th, 1832, showing the order given to Enoch, and the Church in his day.

1. Verily, verily I say unto you, my servants, that inasmuch as you have forgiven one another your trespasses, even so I, the Lord, forgive you ;

2. Nevertheless there are those among you who have sinned exceedingly ; yea, even all of you have sinned, but verily I say unto you, beware from henceforth, and refrain from sin, lest sore judgments fall upon your heads;

3. For unto whom ᵃmuch is given much is required; and he who sins against the greater light shall receive the greater condemnation.

4. Ye call upon my name for revelations, and I give them unto you ; and inasmuch as ye keep not my sayings, which I give unto you, ye become transgressors, and justice and judgment are the penalty which is affixed unto my law ;

5. Therefore, what I say unto one I say unto all, Watch, for the adversary ᵇspreadeth his dominions and darkness reigneth ;

---

d, see a, Sec. 59.

---

a, Luke 12 : 48.   b, 38 : 11, 12.

6. And the anger of God kindleth against the inhabitants of the earth ; and none doeth good, for all have gone out of the way.

7. And now, verily I say unto you, I, the Lord, will not lay any sin to your charge ; go your ways and sin no more; but unto that soul who sinneth shall the ^cformer sins return, saith the Lord your God.

8. And again, I say unto you, I give unto you a new commandment, that you may understand my will concerning you,

9. Or, in other words, I give unto you directions how you may act before me, that it may turn to you for your salvation.

10. I, the Lord, am bound when ye do what I say, but when ye do not what I say, ye have no promise.

11. Therefore, verily I say unto you, that it is expedient for my servant Alam, and Ahashdah, (Newel K. Whitney,) Mahalaleel, and Pelagoram, (Sidney Rigdon,) and my servant Gazelam, (Joseph Smith,) and Horah, and Olihah, (Oliver Cowdery,) and Shalemanasseh, and Mahemson, (Martin Harris,) to be bound together by a ^dbond and covenant that cannot be broken by transgression, (except judgment shall immediately follow,) in your several stewardships,

12. To manage the affairs of the poor, and all things pertaining to the bishopric both in the land of Zion and in the land of Shinehah, (Kirtland,)

13. For I have consecrated the land of Shinehah, (Kirtland,) in mine own due time for the benefit of the saints of the Most High, and for a ^eStake to Zion ;

14. For Zion must increase in beauty, and in holiness ; her borders must be enlarged ; her Stakes must be strengthened ; yea, verily I say unto you, Zion must arise and put on her ^fbeautiful garments :

15. Therefore I give unto you this commandment, that ye bind yourselves by this covenant, and it shall be done according to the laws of the Lord.

16. Behold, here is wisdom also in me for your good.

17. And you are to be ^gequal, or in other words, you are to have equal claims on the properties, for the benefit of managing the concerns of your stewardships, every man according to his wants and his needs, inasmuch as his wants are just;

18. And all this for the benefit of the ^hchurch of the living God, that every man may ⁱimprove upon his talent, that every man may gain other talents, yea, even an hundred fold, to be cast into the Lord's storehouse, to become the ^jcommon property of the whole church,

19. Every man seeking the ^kinterest of his neighbor, and doing all things with an eye single to the glory of God.

20. This order I have appointed to be an ^leverlasting order unto you, and unto your successors, inasmuch as you sin not;

21. And the soul that sins against this covenant, and hardeneth his heart against it, shall be dealt with according to the laws of my church, and shall be delivered over to the ^mbuffetings of Satan until the day of redemption.

22. And now, verily I say unto you, and this is wisdom, make unto yourselves friends with the ⁿmammon of unrighteousness, and they will not destroy you.

23. Leave judgment alone with me, for it is mine and I will repay. Peace be with you; my blessings continue with you,

24. For even yet the ^okingdom is yours, and shall be for ever, if you fall not from your steadfastness. Even so. Amen.

---

g, see *a*, Sec. 51.   *h*, see *a*, Sec. 1.   *i*, Matt. 25 : 14– 30.
j, see *n*, Sec. 42.   *k*, see *a*, Sec. 51.   *l*, 78 : 11—13.   82 : 11, 17—22.
m, see *h*, Sec. 78.   *n*, Luke 16 : 9.   *o*, see *z*, Sec. 35.

SECTION 83.

Revelation given through Joseph, the Seer, at Independence, Jackson County, Missouri, April 30th, 1832.

1. Verily, thus saith the Lord, in addition to the laws of the church concerning women and children, those who belong to the church, who have lost their husbands or fathers.

2. Women have ^aclaim on their husbands for their maintenance, until their husbands are taken, and if they are not found transgressors they shall have fellowship in the church;

3. And if they are not faithful, they shall not have fellowship in the church; yet they may remain upon their inheritances according to the laws of the land.

4. All children have ^bclaim upon their parents for their maintenance until they are of age.

5. And after that they have ^cclaim upon the church, or in other words upon the Lord's storehouse, if their parents have not wherewith to give them inheritances.

6. And the storehouse shall be kept by the ^dconsecrations of the church, and widows and orphans shall be provided for, as also the poor. Amen.

SECTION 84.

A Revelation, given through Joseph, the Prophet, at Kirtland, Geauga County, Ohio, the 22nd and 23rd of September, 1832.

1. A revelation of Jesus Christ unto his servant

---

a, I. Tim. 5.   I. Pet. 3.   *b*, 29 : 47, 48.   68 : 25—31.   *c*, see *a*,
Sec. 51.   *d*, see n, Sec. 42.

Joseph Smith, jun., and six elders, as they united their hearts and lifted their voices on high.

2. Yea, the word of the Lord concerning his church, established in the last days for the restoration of his people, as he has spoken by the mouth of his prophets, and for the *a*gathering of his saints to stand upon Mount Zion, which shall be the city of *b*New Jerusalem,

3. Which city shall be built, *c*beginning at the temple lot, which is appointed by the finger of the Lord, in the western boundaries of the state of Missouri, and dedicated by the hand of Joseph Smith, jun., and others with whom the Lord was well pleased.

4. Verily this is the word of the Lord, that the city New Jerusalem shall be built by the gathering of the saints beginning at this place, even the place of the temple, which temple shall be *e*reared in this generation ;

5. For verily, this generation shall not *f*all pass away until an house shall be built unto the Lord, and a *g*cloud shall rest upon it, which cloud shall be even the glory of the Lord, which shall fill the house.

6. And the *h*sons of Moses, according to the Holy Priesthood which he received under the hand of his father-in-law, *i*Jethro ;

7. And Jethro received it under the hand of Caleb ;

8. And Caleb received it under the hand of Elihu ;

9. And Elihu under the hand of Jeremy ;

10. And Jeremy under the hand of Gad ;

11. And Gad under the hand of Esaias ;

12. And Esaias received it under the hand of God.

13. Esaias also lived in the days of Abraham, and was blessed of him—

14. Which Abraham received the *j*Priesthood from

a, see *j*, Sec. 10.   *b*, see *d*, Sec. 28.   *c*, 57 : 1—3.
e, 124 : 49—54.   *f*, a generation does not all pass away in one hundred years.   *h*, vers. 31, 34.   *i*, Exo-
g. vers. 31, 32.   dus 18.   *j* Gen. 14 : 18—20.

Melchisedek, who received it through the lineage of his fathers, even till Noah ;

15. And from Noah till Enoch, through the *k*lineage of their fathers ;

16. And from Enoch *l*to Abel, who was slain by the conspiracy of his brother, who received the *m*Priesthood by the commandments of God, by the hand of his father Adam, who was the first man—

17. Which *n*Priesthood continueth in the church of God in all generations, and is without beginning of days or end of years.

18. And the Lord confirmed a priesthood also upon *o*Aaron and his seed, throughout all their generations—which priesthood also continueth and *p*abideth forever with the Priesthood, which is *q*after the holiest order of God.

19. And this *r*greater Priesthood administereth the gospel and holdeth the key of the mysteries of the kingdom even the key of the knowledge of God ;

20. Therefore, in the ordinances thereof, the *s*power of godliness is manifest ;

21. And without the ordinances thereof, and the authority of the Priesthood, the power of godliness is *t*not manifest unto men in the flesh ;

22. For without this no man can *u*see the face of God, even the Father, and live.

23. Now this Moses plainly taught to the children of Israel in the wilderness, and sought diligently to sanctify his people that they might *v*behold the face of God ;

24. But they hardened their hearts and could not endure his presence, therefore the Lord in his wrath (for his anger was kindled against them) swore that they

---

k, through Lamech and Methuselah.   *l*, through six successive generations, to Abel, or Seth.   *m*, 107 : 40—57.   *n*, 107 : 1. See *i*, Sec. 68.   *o*, vers. 26—28, 30.   *p*, Exodus 40 : 15.   Num. 25 : 13. *q*, see *i*, Sec. 68.   *r*, see *i*, Sec. 68.   *s*, vers. 21—30.   107 : 8—12, 18, 19. 113 : 8.   123 : 11.   *t*, Luke 3 : 16. John 10 : 41.   *u*, see *o*, Sec. 50.   *v*, see *o*, Sec. 50.

should not "enter into his rest while in the wilderness, which rest is the fullness of his glory.

25. Therefore he took Moses out of their midst, and the *Holy Priesthood also ;

26. And the ʸlesser priesthood continued, which priesthood holdeth the ᶻkey of the ministering of angels and the preparatory gospel ;

27. Which gospel is the gospel of repentance and of baptism, and the remission of sins, and the law of carnal commandments, which the Lord in his wrath, caused to continue with the ²ᵃhouse of Aaron among the children of Israel until John, whom God raised up, being filled with the Holy Ghost from his mother's womb ;

28. For he was baptized while he was yet in his childhood, and was ordained by the angel of God at the time he was eight days old unto this power, to overthrow the kingdom of the Jews, and to make ²ᵇstraight the way of the Lord before the face of his people, to prepare them for the coming of the Lord, in whose hand is given ²ᶜall power.

29. And again, the offices of elder and bishop are necessary ²ᵈappendages belonging unto the ²ᵉHigh Priesthood.

30. And again, the offices of teacher and deacon are necessary ᵢ²ᶠappendages belonging to the lesser priesthood, which priesthood was confirmed upon Aaron and his sons.

31. Therefore, as I said ²ᵍconcerning the sons of Moses—for the sons of Moses, and also the sons of Aaron shall offer an acceptable offering and sacrifice in the house of the Lord, which house shall be built unto the Lord in ²ʰthis generation, upon the ²ⁱconsecrated spot as I have appointed ;

w, Heb. 3 : 11, 18, 19.   4 : 1—11.   x, see i, Sec. 68.   y, The
Aaronic.   z, 107 : 13—15, 20.   Exod. 33 : 1—4.   2a, Ezek. 20 : 25.
2b, Matt. 3 : 3.   2c, 93 : 17.   2d, 107 : 7, 11, 22—26, 36, 37.
2e, see i, Sec. 68.   2f, 107 : 85—88.   2g, vers. 6, 32.   2h, see f.
2i, ver. 3.   57 : 1—3.

32. And the sons of Moses and of Aaron shall be [2j]filled with the glory of the Lord, upon Mount Zion in the Lord's house, whose sons are ye ; and also many whom I have called and sent forth to build up my church ;

33. For whoso is faithful unto the obtaining these two Priesthoods of which I have spoken, and the magnifying their calling, are sanctified by the Spirit unto the [2k]renewing of their bodies ;

34. They become the sons of Moses and of Aaron and the seed of Abraham, and the church and [2l]kingdom, and the [2m]elect of God ;

35. And also all they who receive this [2n]Priesthood receiveth me, saith the Lord ;

36. For he that receiveth my servants receiveth me ;

37. And he that receiveth me [2o]receiveth my Father ;

38. And he that receiveth my Father, [2p]receiveth my Father's kingdom ; therefore [2q]all that my Father hath shall be given unto him ;

39. And this is according to the oath and covenant which belongeth to the Priesthood.

40. Therefore, all those who receive the Priesthood, receive this [2r]oath and covenant of my Father, which he cannot break, neither can it be moved ;

41. But whoso breaketh this covenant, after he hath received it, and altogether turneth therefrom, shall [2s]not have forgiveness of sins in this world nor in the world to come.

42. And all those who come not unto this [2t]Priesthood which ye have received, which I now confirm upon you who are present this day, by mine own voice out of the heavens, and even I have given the [2u]heavenly hosts and mine angels charge concerning you.

2j, ver. 5.   2k, Gal. 3: 27—29.   2l, see x, Sec. 35.
2m, ver. 99.   29: 7.   2n, vers. 88—90.   112: 20.   2o, John 13:
20.   2p, see x, Sec. 35.   2q, see d, Sec. 50.   2r, vers.
40, 48.   2s, 41: 1.   76: 29—37.   2t, see i, Sec. 68.   2u, ver. 88.

43. And I now give unto you a commandment to beware concerning yourselves, to give diligent heed to the words of eternal life :

44. For you shall live by every word that proceedeth forth from the mouth of God.

45. For the word of the Lord is truth, and [2v]whatsoever is truth is light, and [2w]whatsover is light is Spirit, even the Spirit of Jesus Christ ;

46. And the Spirit giveth light to [2x]every man that cometh into the world ; and the Spirit enlighteneth every man [2y]through the world, that hearkeneth to the voice of the Spirit ;

47. And every one that hearkeneth to the voice of the Spirit, cometh unto God, even the Father ;

48. And the Father teacheth him of the [2z]covenant which he has renewed and confirmed upon you, which is confirmed upon you for your sakes, and not for your sakes only, but for the sake of the whole world ;

49. And the whole world lieth in sin, and groaneth under darkness and under the bondage of sin ;

50. And by this you may know they are under the bondage of sin, because they come not unto me.

51. For whoso cometh not unto me is under the bondage of sin ;

52. And whoso receiveth not my voice is not acquainted with my voice, and is not of me ;

53. And by this you may know the righteous from the wicked, and that the whole world groaneth under sin and darkness even now.

54. And your minds in times past have been darkened because of unbelief, and because you have treated lightly the things you have received,

55. Which vanity and unbelief hath brought the [3a]whole church under condemnation.

---

2 v, 88 : 6—13, 41, 49, 50, 66, 67.   2 w, see 2 v.   2 x, 93 : 2.
2 y, 93 : 28.   2 z, see k, Sec. 1.   3 a, see a, Sec. 1.

56. And this condemnation resteth upon the children of Zion, even all :

57. And they shall remain under this condemnation until they repent and remember the [3b]new covenant, even the Book of Mormon and the former commandments which I have given them, not only to say, but to do according to that which I have written,

58. That they may bring forth fruit meet for their Father's kingdom, otherwise there remaineth a scourge and a judgment to be poured out upon the [3c]children of Zion :

59. For shall the children of the kingdom pollute my holy land? Verily, I say unto you, Nay.

60. Verily, verily, I say unto you who now hear my words, which are my voice, blessed are ye inasmuch as you receive these things ;

61. For I will forgive you of your sins with this commandment, that you remain steadfast in your minds in [3d]solemnity and the spirit of prayer, in bearing testimony to all the world of those things which are communicated unto you.

62. Therefore [3e]go ye into all the world, and whatsoever place ye cannot go into ye shall send, that the testimony may go from you into all the world unto every creature.

63. And as I said unto mine apostles, even so I say unto you, for you are [3f]mine apostles, even God's High Priests ; ye are they whom my Father hath given me—ye are my friends ;

64. Therefore, as I said unto mine apostles I say unto you again, that [3g]every soul who believeth on your words, and is baptized by water for the remission of sins, shall receive the Holy Ghost ;

65. And these [3h]signs shall follow them that believe.

3b, see k, Sec. 1.   3c, upon those gathered in Missouri.   3d, 43:
34. 88: 121.   3e, see b, Sec. 1.   3f, 20: 2, 3. 27: 12. 95: 4.
3g, Mark 16: 15—18. Acts 2: 37—39.   3h, Mark 16: 17, 18.

66. In my name they shall do many wonderful works;

67. In my name they shall cast out devils;

68. In my name they shall heal the sick;

69. In my name they shall open the eyes of the blind, and unstop the ears of the deaf;

70. And the tongue of the dumb shall speak;

71. And if any man shall administer poison unto them it shall not hurt them;

72. And the poison of a serpent shall not have power to harm them.

73. But a commandment I give unto them, that they shall [3i]not boast themselves of these things, neither speak them before the world, for these things are given unto you for your profit and for salvation.

74. Verily, verily, I say unto you [3j]they who believe not on your words, and are not baptized in water, in my name, for the remission of their sins, that they may receive the Holy Ghost, shall be damned, and shall not come into my Father's kingdom, where my Father and I am.

75. And this revelation unto you, and commandment, is in force [3k]from this very hour upon all the world, and the gospel is unto all who have not received it.

76. But, verily, I say unto all those to whom the [3l]kingdom has been given, from you it must be preached unto them, that they shall repent of their former evil works, for they are to be upbraided for their evil hearts of unbelief; and your brethren in Zion for their [3m]rebellion against you at the time I sent you.

77. And again I say unto you, my friends, (for from henceforth I shall call you friends,) it is expedient that I give unto you this commandment, that ye become

---

3 i, Luke 8 : 54—56.   9 : 36.   3 j, Mark 16 : 16.   3 k, ver. 74.
3 l, see x, Sec. 35.   3 m, in April, 1832.

even as my friends in days when I was with them traveling to preach the gospel in my power,

78. For I suffered them not to have purse or scrip, neither two coats ;

79. Behold I send you out to [3n]prove the world, and the laborer is worthy of his hire.

80. And any man that shall go and preach Jhis gospel of the kingdom, and fail not to continue faithful in all things shall [3o]not be weary in mind, neither darkened, neither in body, limb, nor joint : and an hair of his head shall not fall to the ground unnoticed. And they shall not go hungry, neither athirst.

81. Therefore, [3p]take no thought for the morrow, for what ye shall eat, or what ye shall drink, or wherewithal ye shall be clothed ;

82. For consider the lilies of the field, how they grow, they toil not, neither do they spin ; and the kingdoms of the world, in all their glory, are not arrayed like one of these ;

83. For your Father who art in heaven, knoweth that you have need of all these things.

84. Therefore, let the morrow take thought for the things of itself.

85. Neither take ye thought beforehand [3q]what ye shall say, but [3r]treasure up in your minds continually the words of life, and it shall be given you in the very hour that portion that shall be meted unto every man.

86. Therefore let no man among you, (for this commandment is unto all the faithful who are called of God in the church unto the ministry,) from this hour [3s]take purse or scrip, that goeth forth to proclaim this gospel of the kingdom.

87. Behold, I send you out to reprove the world of all their [3t]unrighteous deeds, and to teach them of a judgment which is to come.

3n, vers. 86—97.   3o, 89: 18—21.   3p, III. Nep. 13: 25—34.
3q, Matt. 10: 19, 20.   3r, 11: 22.   3s, see j, Sec. 24.
3t, ver. 117.

88. And whoso receiveth you, there I will be also, for I will go before your face : I will be on your right hand and on your left, and my Spirit shall be in your hearts, and mine angels round about you, to bear you up.

89. Whoso receiveth you receiveth me, and the same [3u]will feed you, and clothe you, and give you money.

90. And he who feeds you, or clothes you, or gives you money, shall in no wise lose his reward :

91. And he that doeth not these things is not my disciple ; by this you may know my disciples.

92. He that receiveth you not, go away from him alone by yourselves, and [3v]cleanse your feet even with water, pure water, whether in heat or in cold, and bear testimony of it unto your Father which is in heaven, and return not again unto that man.

93. And in whatsoever village or city ye enter, do likewise.

94. Nevertheless, search diligently and spare not ; and [3w]wo unto that house, or that village or city that rejecteth you, or your words, or your testimony concerning me.

95. Wo, I say again, unto that house, or that village or city that rejecteth you, or your words, or your testimony of me ;

96. For I the Almighty, have laid my hands upon the nations, to [3x]scourge them for their wickedness :

97. And plagues shall go forth, and they shall not be taken from the earth until I have completed my work which shall be cut short in righteousness,

98. Until all shall [3y]know me, who remain, even from the least unto the greatest, and shall be filled with the knowledge of the Lord, and shall [3z]see eye to eye,

---

3*u*, Matt. 10: 40—42.   3*v*, see *d*, Sec. 60.   3*w*, see *f* and *g*, Sec. 1.
3*x*, see *f* and *g*, Sec. 1.   3*y*, Jer. 31: 33, 34.   3*z*, Isa. 52: 8.

and shall lift up their voice, and with the voice together
sing this new song, saying—

99. The Lord hath brought [4a]again Zion
The Lord hath [4b]redeemed his people, Israel,
According to the election of grace,
Which was brought to pass by the faith
And [4c]covenant of their fathers.

100. The Lord hath redeemed his people,
And [4d]Satan is bound and time is no longer :
The Lord hath gathered [4e]all things in one :
The Lord hath brought down [4f]Zion from above.
The Lord hath brought up [4g]Zion from beneath.

101. The earth hath travailed and brought forth
her strength :
And truth is established in her bowels :
And the heavens have smiled upon her :
And she is clothed [4h]with the glory of her God :
For he stands in the midst of his people :

102. Glory, and honor, and power, and might,
Be ascribed to our God ; for he is full of mercy,
Justice, grace and truth, and peace,
For ever and ever, Amen.

103. And again, verily, verily, I say unto you, it is
expedient that every man who goes forth to proclaim
mine everlasting gospel, that inasmuch as they have
families, and receive monies by gift, that they should
send it unto them or make use of it for their benefit, as
the Lord shall direct them, for thus it seemeth me good.

104. And let all those who have not families, who
receive monies, send it up unto the Bishop in Zion, or
unto the Bishop in Ohio, that it may be consecrated
for the bringing forth of the revelations and the printing thereof, and for establishing Zion.

105. And if any man shall give unto any of you a

4a, Isa. 52 : 8.   4b, Rom. 11 : 25—28.   4c, Rom. 11 : 27, 28.
4d, see 2f, Sec. 45.   4e, see j, Sec. 10.   4f, 45 : 11—14.   The
Zion of Enoch.   Pearl of Great Price, p. 22.   4g, Zion to be taken up in
a cloud.   4h, Isa. 11 : 9.

coat, or a suit, take the old and cast it unto the poor, and go your way rejoicing.

106. And if any man among you be strong in the Spirit, let him take with him he that is weak, that he may be edified in all meekness, that he may become strong also.

107. Therefore, take with you those who are ordained unto the [i]lesser priesthood, and send them before you to make appointments, and to prepare the way, and to fill appointments that you yourselves are not able to fill.

108. Behold, this is the way that mine apostles, in ancient days, built up my church unto me.

109. Therefore, let every man stand in his own office, and labor in his own calling; and let not the head say unto the feet, it hath [j]no need of the feet, for without the feet how shall the body be able to stand?

110. Also the body hath need of every member, that all may be edified together, that the system may be kept perfect.

111. And behold the [k]High Priests should travel, and also the elders, and also the lesser priests; but the deacons and teachers should be appointed to watch over the church, to be standing ministers unto the church.

112. And the bishop, Newel K. Whitney, also, should travel round about and among all the churches, searching after the poor to administer to their wants by humbling the rich and the proud;

113. He should also employ an agent to take charge and to do his secular business as he shall direct;

114. Nevertheless, let the bishop go unto the city of New York, also to the city of Albany, and also to the city of Boston, and warn the people of those cities with the sound of the gospel, with a loud voice, of

---

4i, the Aaronic.   4j, I. Cor. 12: 21.   4k, see i, Sec. 58.

the [l]desolation and utter abolishment which await
them if they do reject these things ;

115. For if they do reject these things the hour of
their judgment is nigh, and their house shall be left
unto them desolate.

116. Let him trust in me and he shall not be confounded ; and an hair of his head shall not fall to the
ground unnoticed.

117. And verily I say unto you, the rest of my servants, go ye forth as your circumstances shall permit, in
your several callings unto the great and notable cities
and villages, reproving the world in righteousness of all
their [m]unrighteous and ungodly deeds, setting forth
clearly and understandingly the [n]desolation of abomination in the last days ;

118. For, with you saith the Lord Almighty, I will
[o]rend their kingdoms : I will not only [p]shake the
earth, but the [q]starry heavens shall tremble ;

119. For I, the Lord, have put forth my hand to
[r]exert the powers of heaven ; ye cannot see it now,
yet a little while and ye shall see it, and know that I
am, and that I will [s]come and reign with my people.

120. I am Alpha and Omega, the beginning and the
end. Amen.

SECTION 85.

*Revelation given through Joseph, the Seer, in Kirtland,
Ohio, November 27th, 1832, concerning the Saints in
Zion, Jackson Co., Missouri.*

1. It is the duty of the Lord's clerk, whom he has

4 l, see f and g, Sec. 1.   4 m, ver. 87.   4 n, see f and g, Sec. 1.
4 o, Dan. 2 : 34, 35, 44, 45.   4 p, see e, Sec. 21.   4 q, see e, Sec. 21.
4 r, see e, Sec. 21.   4 s, see e, Sec. 1.

appointed, to keep a *a*history, and a General Church
Record of all things that transpire in Zion, and of all
those who consecrate properties, and receive inheritances legally from the bishop ;

2. And also their manner of life, their faith, and
works ; and also of all the apostates who apostatize
after receiving their inheritances.

3. It is contrary to the will and commandment of
God, that those who receive not their inheritance by
*b*consecration, agreeably to his law, which he has given,
that he may tithe his people, to prepare them against
the day of *c*vengeance and burning, should have their
names enrolled with the people of God ;

4. Neither is their *d*genealogy to be kept, or to be
had where it may be found on any of the records or
history of the church ;

5. Their names shall not be found, neither the
names of the fathers, nor the names of the children
written in the *e*book of the law of God, saith the Lord
of Hosts.

6. Yea, thus saith the *f*still small voice, which
whispereth through and pierceth all things, and often
times it maketh my bones to quake while it maketh
manifest, saying :

7. And it shall come to pass that I, the Lord God,
will *g*send one mighty and strong, holding the sceptre of
power in his hand, clothed with *h*light for a covering,
whose mouth shall utter words, eternal words ; while
his bowels shall be a fountain of truth, to set in order
the house of God, and to arrange by *i*lot the inheritances of the saints, whose names are found, and the
names of their fathers, and of their children, enrolled
in the *j*book of the law of God :

8. While that man, who was called of God and ap-

a, see *a*, Sec. 21.   *b*, see *n*, Sec. 42.   *c*, see *f* and *g*, Sec. 1.
d, Ezra 2 : 62, 63.   *e*, vers. 1, 9.   *f*, I. Kings 19 : 11—13.
g, A future messenger promised.   *h*, brilliant and glorious in appearance.   *i*, Joshua, chap. 14—19.   *j*, vers. 1, 5, 9, 11.

pointed, that putteth forth his hand to *steady the ark
of God, shall fall by the shaft of death, like as a tree
that is smitten by the vivid shaft of lightning ;

9. And all they who are not found written in
the ˡbook of remembrance, shall find none inheritance
in that day, but they shall be cut asunder, and their
portion shall be appointed them among unbelievers,
where are ᵐwailing and gnashing of teeth.

10. These things I say not of myself ; therefore, as
the Lord speaketh, he will also fulfill.

11. And they who are of the ⁿHigh Priesthood,
whose names are not found written in the book of the
law, or that are found to have apostatized, or to have
been cut off from the church ; as well as the lesser
priesthood, or the members, in that day, shall ᵒnot find
an inheritance among the saints of the Most High ;

12. Therefore it shall be done unto them as unto
the children of the priest, as will be found recorded in
the second chapter and sixty-first and second verses of
Ezra.

SECTION 86.

*Revelation given through Joseph, the Prophet, at Kirt-
land, Geauga Co., Ohio, Dec. 6th, 1832, explaining
the Parable of the Wheat and the Tares.*

1. Verily, thus saith the Lord unto you my servants, concerning the parable of the wheat and of the
tares.

2. Behold, verily I say, that the field was the world,
and the apostles were the sowers of the seed ;

k, ɪ. Chron. 13 : 9—12.   *l*, see *j*.   *m*, see *e*, Sec. 19.
n, see *i*, Sec. 58.   *o*, see *e*, Sec. 19.

3. And after they have fallen asleep, the *a*great persecutor of the church, the apostate, the whore, even *b*Eabylon, that maketh all nations to drink of her cup, in whose hearts the enemy, even Satan, sitteth to reign, behold he soweth the tares, wherefore the tares choke the wheat and *c*drive the church into the wilderness.

4. But behold, in the last days, even now while the Lord is beginning to bring forth the word, and the blade is springing up and is yet tender.

5. Behold, verily I say unto you, the angels are *d*crying unto the Lord day and night, who are ready and waiting to be sent forth to reap down the fields;

6. But the Lord saith unto them, pluck not up the tares while the blade is yet tender, (for verily your faith is weak,) lest you destroy the wheat also.

7. Therefore let the wheat and the tares grow together until the harvest is fully ripe, then ye shall first gather out the wheat from among the tares, and after the gathering of the wheat, behold and lo! the tares are bound in bundles, and the field remaineth to be burned.

8. Therefore, thus saith the Lord unto you, with whom the Priesthood hath continued through the *e*lineage of your fathers,

9. For ye are lawful heirs, according to the flesh, and have been hid from the world *f*with Christ in God;

10. Therefore your life and the Priesthood hath remained and must needs remain through you and your lineage, *g*until the restoration of all things spoken by the mouths of all the holy prophets since the world began.

11. Therefore, blessed are ye if ye continue in my

---

a, Rev. 17 chap.   *b*, Rev. 14, 17, 18 chap.   *c*, Rev. 12 : 14.
d, Matt. 13 : 39—42.   *e*, being of the seed of Abraham.   *f*, spirits
hid with Christ, reserved for the last dispensation.   *g*, Acts 3 : 21.

goodness, a light unto the Gentiles, and through this Priesthood, a *saviour unto my people Israel. The Lord hath said it. Amen.

SECTION 87.

Revelation and Prophecy, given through Joseph, the Seer, on War. Given December 25th, 1832.

1. Verily, thus saith the Lord, concerning the wars that will shortly come to pass, beginning at the rebellion of South Carolina, which will eventually terminate in the death and misery of many souls.

2. The days will come that war will be poured out upon all nations, *beginning at that place;

3. For behold, the Southern States shall be divided against the Northern States, and the Southern States will call on other nations, even the nation of Great Britain, as it is called, and they shall also call upon other nations, in order to defend themselves against other nations; and thus *war shall be poured out upon all nations.

4. And it shall come to pass, after many days, *slaves shall rise up against their masters, who shall be marshalled and disciplined for war:

5. And it shall come to pass also, that the *remnants who are left of the land will marshal themselves, and shall become exceeding angry, and shall vex the Gentiles with a sore vexation;

6. And thus, with the sword, and by bloodshed, the inhabitants of the earth shall mourn; and with

---

h, Obadiah 1 : 21. Rom. 11 : 25—31.

a, 130 : 12, 13. *b*, 45 : 69. *c*, fulfilled, in part, in the last American war. *d*, remnants of Joseph.

famine, and plague, and earthquakes, and the thunder of heaven, and the fierce and vivid lightning also, shall the inhabitants of the earth be made to feel the wrath, and indignation and chastening hand of an Almighty God, until the *consumption decreed, hath made a full end of all nations;

7. That the cry of the saints, and of the *blood of the saints, shall cease to come up into the ears of the Lord of Sabaoth, from the earth, to be avenged of their enemies.

8. Wherefore, stand ye in *holy places, and be not moved, until the *day of the Lord come; for behold it cometh quickly, saith the Lord. Amen.

SECTION 88.

Revelation given through Joseph, the Seer, at Kirtland, Geauga Co., Ohio, December 27th, 1832.

1. Verily, thus saith the Lord unto you who have assembled yourselves together to receive his will concerning you.

2. Behold, this is pleasing unto your Lord, and the angels rejoice over you; the alms of your prayers have come up into the ears of the Lord of Sabaoth, and are recorded in the book of the names of the sanctified: even them of the celestial world.

3. Wherefore, I now send upon you another *Comforter, even upon you my friends, that it may abide in your hearts, even the Holy Spirit of promise; which

---

e, see *f* and *g*, Sec. 1.   *f*, 58 : 53.   63 : 28—31.   I. Nep. 14 : 13.
22 : 14.   II. Nep. 5 : 16.   28 : 10.   Mor. 8 : 27, 40, 41.   Ether 8 : 22—24.
Rev. 18 : 24. 19 : 2.   *g*, the Stakes of Zion intended to be holy places.
45 : 32. 101 : 64.   *h*, see *e*, Sec. 1.

a, vers. 4, 5.

other Comforter is the same that I promised unto my disciples, as is recorded in the testimony of John.

4. This Comforter is the promise which I give unto you of eternal life; even the glory of the celestial kingdom:

5. Which glory is that of the ᵇchurch of the first born; even of God the holiest of all, through Jesus Christ his Son:

6. He that ascended up on high, as also he ᶜdescended below all things; in that he comprehended all things, that he might be in all and through all things, ᵈthe light of truth;

7. Which truth shineth. This is the light of Christ. As also he is ᵉin the sun, and the light of the sun, and the power thereof by which it was made.

8. As also he is in the ᶠmoon, and is the light of the moon, and the power thereof by which it was made.

9. As also the ᵍlight of the stars, and the power thereof by which they were made.

10. And the earth also, and the power thereof; even the earth upon which you stand.

11. And the light which now shineth, which giveth you light, is through him who enlighteneth your eyes, which is the ʰsame light that quickeneth your understandings;

12. Which light proceedeth forth from the presence of God to fill the ⁱimmensity of space.

13. The light which is in all things; which giveth ʲlife to all things: which is the ᵏlaw by which all things are governed: even the power of God who sitteth upon his throne, who is in the bosom of eternity, who is in the midst of all things.

---

b, see *a*, Sec. 1.   *c*, 122 : 8. Eph. 4 : 9, 10.   *d*, vers. 7—13,
40, 41, 49, 50, 66, 67.   14 : 9.   84 : 44—48.   93 : 2, 8—17, 20, 23—39.
e, see *d.*   *f*, see *d.*   *g*, see *d.*   *h*, see *d.*   *i*, the light
of all worlds as transmitted through space.   *j*, the great principle of
life.   *k*, the law and power by which all things are governed.

14. Now, verily I say unto you, that through the redemption which is made for you is brought to pass the ʰresurrection from the dead.

15. And the spirit and the body is the soul of man.

16. And the resurrection from the dead is the redemption of the soul ;

17. And the redemption of the soul is through him who quickeneth all things, in whose bosom it is decreed that the poor and the meek of the earth ᵐshall inherit it.

18. Therefore it must needs be sanctified from all unrighteousness, that it may be prepared for the celestial glory ;

19. For after it hath filled the measure of its creation, it shall be crowned with glory, even with the ⁿpresence of God the Father;

20. That bodies who are of the celestial kingdom may ᵒpossess it for ever and ever ; for, for this intent was it made and created, and for this intent are they sanctified.

21. And they who are not sanctified through the law which I have given unto you, even the law of Christ, must inherit ᵖanother kingdom, even that of a terrestrial kingdom, or that of a telestial kingdom.

22. For he who is not able to abide the law of a ᑫcelestial kingdom, cannot abide a celestial glory ;

23. And he who cannot abide the law of a ʳterrestrial kingdom, cannot abide a terrestrial glory :

24. He who cannot abide the law of a ˢtelestial kingdom, cannot abide a telestial glory ; therefore he is not meet for a kingdom of glory. Therefore he must abide a kingdom which is not a kingdom of glory.

---

l, vers. 15—17, 20, 27—29.   See *m*, Sec. 29.   Also II. Nep. 2: 8.   9: 4, 6—19, 22.   Mos. 13: 35.   15: 8, 9, 20—27.   16: 7—11.   Alma 5: 15.   7: 12. 11: 41—45.   12: 12—18, 24, 25.   22: 14.   33: 22.   40 chap.   41: 2—5.   42: 23.   Hela. 14: 15—17, 25.   III. Nep. 23: 9—13.   26: 5.   Mor. 6: 21.   7: 6. 9: 13.   Moro. 7: 41.   10: 34.   *m*, see *p*, Sec. 38.   *n*, 101: 65. 130: 7, 9.   *o*, see *p*, Sec. 38.   *p*, 43: 18, 33.   76: 102, 111, 112. *q*, vers. 38, 39.   *r*, vers. 38, 39.   *s*, vers. 38, 39.

25. And again, verily I say unto you, the earth abideth the law of a celestial kingdom, for it filleth the measure of its creation, and transgresseth not the law.

26. Wherefore it shall be sanctified ; yea, notwithstanding ⁴it shall die, it shall be quickened again, and shall abide the power by which it is quickened, and ᵘthe righteous shall inherit it :

27. For notwithstanding they die, they also shall rise again a ᵛspiritual body :

28. They who are of a celestial spirit shall receive the same body which was a natural body ; even ye shall receive your bodies, and your glory shall be that glory by which your bodies are quickened.

29. Ye who are ʷquickened by a portion of the celestial glory shall then receive of the same, even a fullness ;

30. And they who are ˣquickened by a portion of the terrestrial glory, shall then receive of the same, even a fullness :

31. And also they who are ʸquickened by a portion of the telestial glory shall then receive of the same, even a fullness ;

32. And they who remain shall also be quickened ; nevertheless they shall return again to their own place, to enjoy that which they are willing to receive, because they were not willing to enjoy that which they might have received.

33. For what doth it profit a man if a gift is bestowed upon him, and he receiveth not the gift ? Behold he rejoices not in that which is given unto him, neither rejoices in him who is the giver of the gift.

34. And again, verily I say unto you, that which is governed by law is also preserved by law, and ᶻperfected and sanctified by the same.

---

t, 101 : 25. 43 : 32.   *u,* see *p,* Sec. 33.   *v,* see *m,* Sec. 29.
w, 76 : 50—70, 94—96.   *x,* 76 : 71—80.   *y,* 76 : 81—90, 98—112.
z, perfected, according to the law obeyed.

35. That which breaketh a law, and abideth not by law, but seeketh to become a law unto itself, and willeth to abide in sin, and altogether abideth in sin, cannot be sanctified by law, neither by mercy, justice, nor judgment. Therefore they must ^{2a}remain filthy still.

36. All ^{2b}kingdoms have a law given :

37. And there are many kingdoms; for there is ^{2c}no space in the which there is no kingdom ; and there is no kingdom in which there is no space, either a greater or a lesser kingdom.

38. And unto ^{2d}every kingdom is given a law ; and unto every law there are certain bounds also and conditions.

39. All beings who abide not in those conditions are not justified ;

40. For intelligence cleaveth unto intelligence ; wisdom receiveth wisdom ; truth embraceth truth ; virtue loveth virtue ; light cleaveth unto light ; mercy hath compassion on mercy, and claimeth her own ; justice continueth its course, and claimeth its own ; judgment goeth before the face of him who sitteth upon the throne, and governeth and executeth all things ;

41. He ^{2e}comprehendeth all things, and all things are before him, and all things are round about him : and he is above all things, and in all things, and is through all things, and is round about all things ; and all things are by him, and of him, even God, for ever and ever.

42. And again, verily I say unto you, he hath given a ^{2f}law unto all things by which they move in their times and their seasons ;

43. And their courses are fixed ; even the courses

2a, I. Nep. 15 : 33—35.   II. Nep. 9 : 16.   Alma 7 : 21.   Mor. 9 : 14.
2b, laws of the universe.   2c, infinity of kingdoms.   2d, laws
adapted to every kingdom.   2e, 93 : 30, 35, 36.   2f, laws of
planetary motion.

of the heavens and the earth, which comprehend the earth and all the planets ;

44. And they give light to each other in their times and in their seasons, in their minutes, in their hours, in their days, in their weeks, in their months, in their years : all these are [2g]one year with God, but not with man.

45. The earth rolls upon her wings, and the sun giveth his light by day, and the moon giveth her light by night, and the stars also giveth their light, as they roll upon their wings in their glory, in the midst of the power of God.

46. Unto what shall I liken these kingdoms, that ye may understand ?

47. Behold, all these are kingdoms, and any man who hath seen any or the least of these, hath seen God moving in his majesty and power.

48. I say unto you, he hath seen him ; nevertheless, he who came unto his own was not comprehended.

49. The light [2h]shineth in darkness, and the darkness comprehendeth it not ; nevertheless, the day shall come when [2i]you shall comprehend even God ; being quickened in him and by him.

50. Then shall ye know that ye [2j]have seen me, that I am, and that I am the true light that is in you, and that you are in me, otherwise ye could not abound.

51. Behold, I will liken these kingdoms unto a man having a field, and he [2k]sent forth his servants into the field to dig in the field ;

52. And he said unto the first, go ye and labor in the field, and in the first hour I will come unto you, and ye shall behold the joy of my countenance ;

53. And he said unto the second, go ye also into the

2g, Celestial time.   2h, see h, Sec. 6.   2i, vers. 66—68.   93 :
28.   101 : 32—34.   2j, every spirit of man, in his pre-existent state,
saw God.   2k, each planetary kingdom is visited by its Creator in its
time and season.

field, and in the second hour I will visit you with the joy of my countenance;

54. And also unto the third saying, I will visit you;

55. And unto the fourth, and so on unto the twelfth.

56. And the lord of the field went unto the first in the first hour, and tarried with him all that hour, and he was made glad with the light of the countenance of his lord;

57. And then he withdrew from the first that he might visit the second also, and the third, and the fourth, and so on unto the twelfth;

58. And thus they all received the light of the countenance of their lord; every man in his hour, and in his time, and in his season;

59. Beginning at the first, and so on unto the last, and from the last unto the first, and from the first unto the last;

60. Every man in his own order, until his hour was finished, even according as his lord had commanded him, that his lord might be glorified in him, and he in him, that they all might be glorified.

61. Therefore, unto this parable will I liken ²ˡall these kingdoms, and the inhabitants thereof; every kingdom in its hour, and in its time, and in its season; even according to the decree which God hath made.

62. And again, verily I say unto you, my friends, I leave these sayings with you, to ponder in your hearts with this commandment which I give unto you, that ye shall call upon me while I am near;

63. Draw near unto me and I will draw near unto you : seek me diligently and ye shall find me ; ²ᵐask and ye shall receive; knock and it shall be opened unto you;

---

2 *l*, the inhabitants of each planet blessed with the presence and visits of their Creator.   2 *m*, see *c*, Sec. 4.

64. Whatsoever ye ask the Father in my name it shall be given unto you, that is expedient for you;

65. And if ye ask anything that is not expedient for you, it shall turn unto your condemnation.

66. Behold, that which you hear is as the [2n]voice of one crying in the wilderness—in the wilderness, because you cannot see him—my voice, because my voice is Spirit; my Spirit is truth; truth abideth and hath no end; and if it be in you it shall abound.

67. And if your eye be single to my glory, your whole bodies shall be filled with light, and there shall be no [2o]darkness in you, and that body which is filled with light comprehendeth all things.

68. Therefore sanctify yourselves that your minds become single to God, and the days will come that you shall [2p]see him; for he will unvail his face unto you, and it shall be in his own time, and in his own way, and according to his own will.

69. Remember the great and last promise which I have made unto you; cast away your idle thoughts and your [2q]excess of laughter far from you;

70. Tarry ye, tarry ye in this place, and call a [2r]solemn assembly, even of those who are the first laborers in this last kingdom;

71. And let those whom they have warned in their traveling, call on the Lord, and ponder the warning in their hearts which they have received for a little season.

72. Behold, and lo! I will take care oi your flocks, and will raise up elders and send unto them.

73. Behold, I will hasten my work in its time;

74. And I give unto you, who are the first laborers in this last kingdom, a commandment that you assemble yourselves together, and organize yourselves, and pre-

---

2n, 5: 14. He who beholds God is no longer in the wilderness.
2o, ver. 49.   2p, see o, Sec. 50.   2q, ver. 121. 59: 15.
2r, vers. 74—82, 117. 95: 7. 108: 4. 109: 6, 10.

pare yourselves, and sanctify yourselves ; yea, purify your hearts, and [2e]cleanse your hands and your feet before me, that I may make you clean ;

75. That I may testify unto your Father, and your God, and my God, that you are clean from the blood of this wicked generation : that I may fulfill this promise, this great and last promise, which I have made unto you, when I will.

76. Also, I give unto you a commandment, that ye shall continue in [2t]prayer and fasting from this time forth.

77. And I give unto you a commandment, that you shall teach one another the doctrine of the kingdom ;

78. Teach ye diligently and my grace shall attend you, that you may be instructed more perfectly in theory, in principle, in doctrine, in the law of the gospel, in [2u]all things that pertain unto the kingdom of God, that are expedient for you to understand ;

79. Of things both in heaven and in the earth, and under the earth ; things which have been, things which are, things which must shortly come to pass ; things which are at home, things which are abroad ; the wars and the perplexities of the nations, and the judgments which are on the land, and a knowledge also of countries and of kingdoms,

80. That ye may be prepared in all things when I shall send you again to magnify the calling whereunto I have called you, and the mission with which I have commissioned you.

81. Behold, I sent you out to testify and warn the people, and it becometh every man who hath been warned, to warn his neighbor.

82. Therefore, they are left without excuse, and their sins are upon their own heads.

2s, vers. 138—141.　2t, see c, Sec. 4.　Mos. 27: 22, 23.　6: 6.　8: 26.　10: 7.　17: 3, 9.　28: 6.　30: 2.　Hela. 3: 35.　III. Nep. 13: 16—18. 27: 1.　IV. Nep. 1: 12.　Moro. 6: 5.　2u, 11: 22.　90: 15.

83. He that seeketh me early shall find me, and shall not be forsaken.

84. Therefore, tarry ye, and labor diligently, that you may be perfected in your ministry to go forth among the Gentiles for the last time, as many as the mouth of the Lord shall name, to [2v]bind up the law and seal up the testimony, and to prepare the saints for the hour of judgment which is to come ;

85. That their souls may escape the wrath of God, the [2w]desolation of abomination which awaits the wicked, both in this world and in the world to come. Verily, I say unto you, let those who are not the first elders continue in the vineyard until the mouth of the Lord shall call them, for their time is not yet come ; their garments are not clean from the blood of this generation.

86. Abide ye in the liberty wherewith ye are made free ; entangle not yourselves in sin, but let your hands be clean, until the Lord come ;

87. For not many days hence and the earth shall tremble and [2x]reel to and fro as a drunken man, and the sun shall [2y]hide his face, and shall refuse to give light, and the moon shall be bathed in blood, and the stars shall become exceeding angry, and shall cast themselves down as a fig that falleth from off a fig tree.

88. And after your testimony cometh wrath and indignation upon the people ;

89. For after your testimony cometh the [2z]testimony of earthquakes, that shall cause groanings in the midst of her, and men shall fall upon the ground, and shall not be able to stand.

90. And also cometh the testimony of the voice of thunderings, and the voice of lightnings, and the voice of tempests, and the voice of the waves of the sea, heaving themselves beyond their bounds.

---

2 v, see d, Sec. 1.   2 w, 84 : 114, 117.   2 x, see x, Sec. 45.
2 y, see n, Sec. 29.   2 z, see x, Sec. 45.

91. And all things shall be in commotion; and surely, men's hearts shall fail them; for fear shall come upon all people;

92. And angels shall fly through the midst of heaven, crying with a [3a]loud voice, sounding the trump of God, saying, Prepare ye, prepare ye, O inhabitants of the earth; for the judgment of our God is come: behold, and lo! the Bridegroom cometh, go ye out to meet him.

93. And immediately there shall appear a [3b]great sign in heaven, and all people shall see it together.

94. And another angel shall sound his trump, saying, That [3c]great church, the mother of abominations, that made all nations drink of the wine of the wrath of her fornication, that persecuteth the saints of God, that shed their blood; her who sitteth upon many waters, and upon the islands of the sea; behold, she is the tares of the earth, she is bound in bundles, her bands are made strong, no man can loose them; therefore, she is ready to be burned. And he shall sound his trump both long and loud, and all nations shall hear it.

95. And there shall be [3d]silence in heaven for the space of half an hour, and immediately after shall the curtain of heaven be unfolded, as a scroll is unfolded after it is rolled up, and the [3e]face of the Lord shall be unvailed;

96. And the [3f]saints that are upon the earth, who are alive, shall be quickened, and be caught up to meet him.

97. And they who have [3g]slept in their graves shall come forth; for their graves shall be opened, and they also shall be caught up to meet him in the midst of the pillar of heaven:

---

3 a, 43 : 18, 25.   Sec. 13.   20: 6.   Sec. 27.   128 : 19—21.   133 : 17.
Testimony of three witnesses.   3 b, Luke 21 : 25—27.   3 c, 29 : 21.
3 d, 38 : 12. Rev. 8 : 1.   3 e, see e, Sec. 1.   3 f, 84 : 100.   76 : 102.
3 g, see l, Sec. 29.

98. They are Christ's, the first fruits : they who shall descend with him first, and they who are on the earth and in their graves, who are first caught up to meet him : and all this by the voice of the sounding of the trump of the angel of God.

99. And after this another angel shall sound, which is the second trump ; and then cometh the redemption of those who are Christ's at his coming ; who have received their [3h]part in that prison which is prepared for them, that they might receive the gospel, and be judged according to men in the flesh.

100. And again, another trump shall sound, which is the third trump ; and then cometh the [3i]spirits of men who are to be judged, and are found under condemnation :

101. And these are the rest of the dead,.and they live not again until the thousand years are ended, neither again, until the end of the earth.

102. And another trump shall sound, which is the fourth trump, saying, There are found among those who are to remain until that great and last day, even the end, who shall remain [3j]filthy still.

103. And another trump shall sound, which is the fifth trump, which is the fifth angel who committeth the everlasting gospel,—flying through the midst of heaven, unto all nations, kindreds, tongues, and people ;

104. And this shall be the sound of his trump, saying to all people, both in heaven and in earth, and that are under the earth ; for every ear shall hear it, and [3k]every knee shall bow, and every tongue shall confess, while they hear the sound of the trump, saying, Fear God, and give glory to him who sitteth upon the throne, for ever and ever : for the hour of his judgment is come.

105. And again, another angel shall sound his

---

3 h, see 2 x, Sec. 76.   3 i, 76 : 81—85, 102—107.   Mat. 25 : 31—46.
3 j, The Sons of Perdition.   3 k, Isa. 45 : 23.   Rom. 14 : 11,   Phil. 2 :
10, 11.

trump, which is the sixth angel, saying, [3l]She is fallen who made all nations drink of the wine of the wrath of her fornication : she is fallen ! is fallen !

106. And again, another angel shall sound his trump, which is the seventh angel, saying, It is finished ! it is finished ! the Lamb of God hath overcome and [3m]trodden the wine-press alone ; even the wine-press of the fierceness of the wrath of Almighty God ;

107. And then shall the angels be crowned with the glory of his might, and the saints shall be filled with his glory, and [3n]receive their inheritance and be made [3o]equal with him.

108. And then shall the first angel again sound his trump in the ears of all living, and reveal the secret acts of men, and the mighty works of God in the first thousandth year.

109. And then shall the second angel sound his trump, and reveal the secret acts of men, and the thoughts and intents of their hearts, and the mighty works of God in the second thousandth year :

110. And so on, until the seventh angel shall sound his trump : and he shall stand forth upon the land and upon the sea, and swear in the name of him who sitteth upon the throne, that there shall be time no longer ; and Satan shall be [3p]bound, that old serpent, who is called the devil, and shall not be loosed for the space of a thousand years.

111. And then he shall be loosed for a little season, that he may gather together his armies :

112. And [3q]Michael, the seventh angel, even the archangel, shall gather together his armies, even the hosts of heaven.

113. And the devil shall gather together his armies ; even the hosts of hell, and shall come up to battle against Michael and his armies :

---

3 *l*, ver. 94, see *i*, Sec. 1.   3 *m*, 133 : 46—51. Joel 3 : 9—17. Rev.
14 : 14—20.   3 *n*, see *b*, Sec. 25.   3 *o*, see 3 *g*, Sec. 76.   3 *p*, see
2 *t*, Sec. 45.   3 *q*, see *k*, Sec. 27.

114. And then cometh the battle of the great God ; and the devil and his armies shall be cast away into their own place, that they shall not have power over the saints any more at all ;

115. For Michael shall fight their battles, and shall overcome him who seeketh the throne of him who sitteth upon the throne, even the Lamb.

116. This is the glory of God, and the sanctified ; and they shall not any more see death.

117. Therefore, verily I say unto you, my friends, call your sole.... assembly, as I have commanded you ;

118. And as all have not faith, seek ye diligently and teach one another words of wisdom ; yea, seek ye out of the ³ʳbest books words of wisdom : seek learning even by study, and also by faith.

119. Organize yourselves, prepare every needful thing, and ³ˢestablish a house, even a house of prayer, a house of fasting, a house of faith, a house of learning, a house of glory, a house of order, a house of God ;

120. That your incomings may be in the name of the Lord ; that your outgoings may be in the name of the Lord ; that all your salutations may be in the name of the Lord, with uplifted hands unto the Most High.

121. Therefore, cease from all your light speeches ; from all ³ᵗlaughter ; from all your lustful desires ; from all your pride and light-mindedness, and from all your wicked doings.

122. Appoint among yourselves a teacher, and let not all be spokesmen at once ; but let one speak at a time, and let all listen unto his sayings, that when all have spoken, that all may be edified of all, and that every man may have an equal privilege.

123. See that ye love one another ; cease to be covetous, learn to impart one to another as the gospel requires ;

124. Cease to be idle ; cease to be unclean ; cease to find fault one with another ; cease to sleep longer than is needful ; retire to thy bed early, that ye may not be weary ; arise early, that your bodies and your minds may be invigorated ;

125. And above all things, clothe yourselves with the bonds of charity, as with a mantle, which is the bond of perfectness and peace;

126. Pray always, that ye may not faint until I come : behold, and lo, I will [3]"come quickly, and receive you unto myself.   Amen.

127. And again, the order of the house prepared for the presidency of the school of the prophets, established for their instruction in all things that are expedient for them, even for all the officers of the church, or in other words, those who are called to the ministry in the church, beginning at the High Priests, even down to the deacons :

128. And this shall be the order of the house of the presidency of the school : He that is appointed to be president, or teacher, shall be found standing in his place, in the house which shall be prepared for him.

129. Therefore he shall be first in the house of God, in a place that the congregation in the house may hear his words carefully and distinctly, not with loud speech.

130. And when he cometh into the house of God, (for he should be first in the house ; behold, this is beautiful, that he may be an example).

131. Let him offer himself in prayer upon his knees before God, in token or remembrance of the [3]"everlasting covenant,

132. And when any shall come in after him, let the teacher arise, and, with uplifted hands to heaven ; yea, even directly, salute his brother or brethren with these words :

---

3 u, see e, Sec. 1.   3 v, see k, Sec. 1.

133. Art thou a brother or brethren? I salute you in the name of the Lord Jesus Christ, in token or remembrance of the ³ʷeverlasting covenant, in which covenant I receive you to fellowship, in a determination that is fixed, immovable, and unchangeable, to be your friend and brother through the grace of God, in the bonds of love, to walk in all the commandments of God blameless, in thanksgiving, for ever and ever. Amen.

134. And he that is found unworthy of this salutation, shall not have place among you : for ye shall not suffer that mine house shall be polluted by him.

135. And he that cometh in and is faithful before me, and is a brother, or if they be brethren, they shall salute the president or teacher with uplifted hands to heaven, with this same prayer and covenant, or by saying Amen, in token of the same.

136. Behold, verily, I say unto you, this is a sample unto you for a salutation to one another in the house of God, in the ³ˣschool of the prophets.

137. And ye are called to do this by prayer and thanksgiving as the Spirit shall give utterance in all your doings in the house of the Lord, in the school of the prophets, that it may become a sanctuary, a tabernacle of the Holy Spirit to your edification.

138. And ye shall not receive any among you into this school save he is clean from the blood of this generation:

139. And he shall be received by the ordinance of the ³ʸwashing of feet, for unto this end was the ordinance of the washing of feet instituted.

140. And again, the ordinance of washing feet is to be administered by the President, or Presiding elder of the church.

141. It is to be commenced with prayer, and after

---

³ʷ, see k, Sec. 1.   ³ˣ, vers. 137—141.   90 : 7, 13.   95 : 10, 17.
97 : 5, 6.   ³ʸ, vers. 74, 75, 140, 141.

partaking of bread and wine, he is to gird himself according to the pattern given in the thirteenth chapter of John's testimony concerning me.   Amen.

SECTION 89.

Revelation given through Joseph, the Seer, at Kirtland, Geauga County, Ohio, February 27th, 1833.

1. A Word of Wisdom, for the benefit of the Council of High Priests, assembled in Kirtland, and church; and also the saints in Zion.

2. To be sent greeting—not by commandment or constraint, but by revelation and the word of wisdom, showing forth the order and will of God in the temporal salvation of all saints in the last days.

3. Given for a principle with *a*promise, adapted to the capacity of the weak and the weakest of all saints, who are or can be called saints.

4. Behold, verily, thus saith the Lord unto you, in consequence of evils and designs which do and will exist in the hearts of conspiring men in the last days, I have warned you, and forewarn you, by giving unto you this word of wisdom by revelation,

5. That inasmuch as any man drinketh wine or strong drink among you, behold it is not good, neither meet in the sight of your Father, only in assembling yourselves together to offer up your sacraments before him.

6. And, behold, this should be wine, yea, *b*pure wine of the grape of the vine, of your own make.

7. And, again, *c*strong drinks are not for the belly, but for the washing of your bodies.

---

a, vers. 18—21.   *b,* 27: 1—14.   *c,* 27: 3, 4.

8. And again, tobacco is not for the body, neither for the belly, and is not good for man, but is an herb for bruises and all sick cattle, to be used with judgment and skill.

9. And again, hot drinks are not for the body or belly.

10. And again, verily I say unto you, ^dall wholesome herbs God hath ordained for the constitution, nature, and use of man.

11. Every herb in the season thereof, and every fruit in the season thereof; all these to be used with prudence and thanksgiving.

12. Yea, flesh also of beasts and of the fowls of the air, I, the Lord, have ordained for the use of man with thanksgiving; nevertheless they are to be used sparingly;

13. And it is pleasing unto me that they should not be used ^eonly in times of winter, or of cold, or famine.

14. All grain is ordained for the use of man and of beasts, to be the staff of life, not only for man but for the beasts of the field, and the fowls of heaven, and all wild animals that run or creep on the earth;

15. And these hath God made for the use of man only in ^ftimes of famine and excess of hunger.

16. All grain is good for the food of man, as also the fruit of the vine, that which yieldeth fruit, whether in the ground or above the ground.

17. Nevertheless, wheat for man, and corn for the ox, and oats for the horse, and rye for the fowls and for swine, and for all beasts of the field, and barley for all useful animals, and for mild drinks, as also other grain.

18. And all saints who remember to keep and do these sayings, walking in obedience to the command-

ments, shall *receive health in their navel, and marrow
to their bones,

19. And shall *find wisdom and great treasures of
knowledge, even hidden treasures;

20. And shall run and not be weary, and shall walk
and not faint;

21. And I, the Lord, give unto them a promise,
that the destroying angel *shall pass by them, as the
children of Israel, and not slay them. Amen.

SECTION 90.

*Revelation to Joseph Smith, jun., given in Kirtland,
Geauga County, Ohio, March 8th, 1833.*

1. Thus saith the Lord, verily, verily I say unto
you my son, thy sins are forgiven thee, according to
thy petition, for thy prayers and the prayers of thy
brethren, have come up into my ears;

2. Therefore thou art blessed from henceforth
that bear the keys of the kingdom given unto you;
which *kingdom is coming forth for the last time.

3. Verily, I say unto you, the keys of this kingdom
shall never be taken from you, while thou art in the
world, neither in the world to come;

4. Nevertheless, through you shall the oracles be
given to another; yea, *even unto the church.

5. And all they who receive the oracles of God, let
them beware how they hold them, lest they are accounted
as a light thing, and are brought under condemnation
thereby; and stumble and fall, when the storms de-

---

g, Prov. 3 : 8. h, 76 : 5—10. i, Exod. 12 : 23, 29.

a, see x, Sec. 35. b, 124 : 91—96.

scend, and the winds blow, and the rains descend, and beat upon their house.

6. And again, verily I say unto thy brethren, Sidney Rigdon and Frederick G. Williams, their sins are forgiven them also, and they are accounted as equal with thee in holding the keys of this last kingdom;

7. As also through your administration the keys of the ᶜschool of the prophets, which I have commanded to be organized,

8. That thereby they may be perfected in their ministry for the salvation of Zion, and of the nations of Israel, and of the Gentiles, as many as will believe,

9. That through your administration they may receive the word, and through their administration, the word may go forth unto the ends of the earth, ᵈunto the Gentiles first, and then, behold, and lo, ᵉthey shall turn unto the Jews;

10. And then cometh the day when the arm of the Lord shall be ᶠrevealed in power in convincing the nations, the heathen nations, the house of Joseph, of the gospel of their salvation.

11. For it shall come to pass in that day, that every man shall hear the fullness of the gospel in his own tongue, and in his own language, through those who are ordained unto this power, by the administration of the ᵍComforter, shed forth upon them, for the revelation of Jesus Christ.

12. And now, verily I say unto you, I give unto you a commandment, that you continue in the ministry and Presidency,

13. And when you have finished the ʰtranslation of the prophets, you shall from thenceforth preside over the affairs of the church and the school;

14. And from time to time, as shall be manifest by

---

c, see 3 a, Sec. 88.   d, see o, Sec. 18.   e, see o, Sec. 18.   f, 42 : 58—60. 43 : 22—27. 58 : 63, 64. 88 : 84, 87—92. 133 : 37—60, 68—74. See e, Sec. 58. g, see h, Sec. 42. h, the Prophets of the Old Testament.

the Comforter, receive revelations to unfold the mysteries of the kingdom,

15. And set in order the churches, and study and learn, and become acquainted with 'all good books, and with languages, tongues, and people.

16. And this shall be your business and mission in all your lives, to preside in council, and set in order all the affairs of this church and kingdom.

17. Be not ashamed, neither confounded; but be admonished in all your high-mindedness and pride, for it bringeth a snare upon your souls.

18. Set in order your houses; keep slothfulness and uncleanness far from you.

19. Now, verily I say unto you, let there be a place provided as soon as it is possible, for the family of thy counselor and scribe, even Frederick G. Williams:

20. And let mine aged servant Joseph Smith, sen., continue with his family upon the place where he now lives, and let it not be sold until the mouth of the Lord shall name.

21. And let my counselor, even Sidney Rigdon, remain where he now resides, until the mouth of the Lord shall name.

22. And let the bishop search diligently to obtain an agent, and let it be a man who has got riches in store —a man of God, and of strong faith;

23. That thereby he may be enabled to discharge every debt; that the storehouse of the Lord may not be brought into disrepute before the eyes of the people.

24. Search diligently, pray always, and be believing, and all things shall work together for your good, if ye walk uprightly and remember the covenant wherewith ye have covenanted one with another.

25. Let your families be small, especially mine aged servant Joseph Smith, sen., as pertaining to those who do not belong to your families;

i, see *c*, Sec. 55.

26. That those things that are provided for you, to bring to pass my work, are not taken from you and given to those that are not worthy,

27. And thereby you are hindered in accomplishing those things which I have commanded you.

28. And again, verily I say unto you, it is my will that my handmaid, Vienna Jaques, should receive money to bear her expenses, and go up unto the land of Zion;

29. And the residue of the money may be consecrated unto me, and she be rewarded in mine own due time.

30. Verily I say unto you, that it is meet in mine eyes that she should go up unto the land of Zion, and receive an inheritance from the hand of the bishop,

31. That she may settle down in peace inasmuch as she is faithful, and not be idle in her days from thenceforth.

32. And behold, verily I say unto you, that ye shall write this commandment, and say unto your brethren in Zion, in love greeting, that I have called you also to preside over Zion in mine own due time:

33. Therefore, let them cease wearying me concerning this matter.

34. Behold, I say unto you that your brethren in Zion begin to repent, and the angels rejoice over them;

35. Nevertheless, I am not well pleased with many things, and I am not well pleased with my servant William E. M'Lellin, neither with my servant Sidney Gilbert; and the bishop also, and others have many things to repent of;

36. But verily I say unto you, that I, the Lord, will contend with Zion, and plead with her strong ones, and *j*chasten her until she overcomes and is clean before me:

37. For she shall not be removed out of her place. I the Lord, have spoken it. Amen.

---

j, 97 : 28.

SECTION 91.

Revelation given through Joseph, the Seer, at Kirtland, Geauga County, Ohio, March 9th, 1833.

1. Verily, thus saith the Lord unto you concerning the Apocrypha, there are many things contained therein that are true, and it is mostly translated correctly ;

2. There are many things contained therein that are not true, which are interpolations by the hands of men.

3. Verily, I say unto you, that it is not needful that the Apocrypha should be translated.

4. Therefore, whoso readeth it, let him understand, for the Spirit manifesteth truth ;

5. And whoso is enlightened by the Spirit, shall obtain benefit therefrom ;

6. And whoso receiveth not by the Spirit, cannot be benefited, therefore it is not needful that it should be translated. Amen.

SECTION 92.

Revelation given to Enoch (Joseph Smith, jr.,) on the order of the church for the benefit of the poor. Given to the Saints in Kirtland, March 15th, 1833.

1. Verily, thus saith the Lord, I give unto the *a*united order, organized agreeable to the commandment previously given, a revelation and commandment con-

a, 78 : 3—7, 11—15.   82 : 11, 15—21.   85 : 1—5, 9—12.

cerning my servant Shederlaomach, (Frederick G. Williams,) that ye shall receive him into the order. What I say unto one, I say unto all.

2. And again, I say unto you, my servant Shederlaomach, (Frederick G. Williams,) you shall be a lively member in this order, and inasmuch as you are faithful in keeping all former commandments, you shall be blessed for ever. Amen.

SECTION 93.

Revelation given through Joseph, the Seer, at Kirtland, Geauga County, Ohio, May 6th, 1833.

1. Verily, thus saith the Lord, it shall come to pass that every soul who forsaketh their sins and cometh unto me, and calleth on my name, and obeyeth my voice, and keepeth my commandments, shall *a*see my face and know that I am,

2. And that I am the true light that *b*lighteth every man that cometh into the world ;

3. And that I am *c*in the Father, and the Father *d*in me, and the Father and I are one :

4. The Father because he gave me of his fullness, and the Son because I was in the world and made flesh my tabernacle, and dwelt among the sons of men.

5. I was in the world and received of my Father, and the *e*works of him were plainly manifest ;

6. And John saw and bore record of the fullness of my glory, and the fullness of John's record is hereafter to be revealed :

---

a, see o, Sec. 50.   *b*, 84 : 45—48.   *c*, 50 : 43. Sec. v, on Faith.
d, 50 : 43. Sec. v, on Faith.   *e*, John 5 : 36.   10 : 25.   12 : 47—50.
14 : 10—12.

7. And he bore record, saying, I saw his glory that he ˢwas in the beginning before the world was;

8. Therefore in the beginning the Word was, for he was the Word, even the messenger of salvation,

9. The light and the Redeemer of the world; the Spirit of truth, who came into the world, because the world was made by him, and in him was the life of men and the light of men.

10. The worlds were made by him: men were made by him: all things were made by him, and through him, and of him.

11. And I, John, bear record that I beheld his glory, as the glory of the Only Begotten of the Father, full of grace and truth, even the Spirit of truth, which came and dwelt in the flesh, and dwelt among us.

12. And I, John, saw that he received not of the ᵍfullness at the first, but received grace for grace:

13. And he received not of the fullness at first, but continued from grace to grace, until he received a fullness;

14. And thus he was called the Son of God, because he received not of the fullness at the first.

15. And I, John, bear record, and lo, the heavens were opened, and the Holy Ghost descended upon him in the form of a dove, and sat upon him, and there came a voice out of heaven saying, This is my beloved Son.

16. And I, John, bear record that he received a fullness of the glory of the Father;

17. And he received ʰall power, both in heaven and on earth, and the glory of the Father was with him, for he dwelt in him.

18. And it shall come to pass, that if you are faithful you shall receive the fullness of the record of John.

ƒ, vers. 8—10, 21.   76:13, 24.   John 1:1—3, 10.   ᵍ, vers. 13—
17, 26.   Luke 2:52.   II. Nep. 9:20.   Alma 7:13.   13:7.   18:32. 26:35.
Hela. 9:41.   III. Nep. 27:26.   Mor. 8:17.   Moro. 7:22.   ʰ, Mat. 28:18.

19. I give unto you these sayings that ye may understand and know how to worship, and know what you worship, that you may come unto the Father in my name, and in due time receive of his fullness,

20. For if you keep my commandments you shall receive of his *fullness, and be glorified in me as I am in the Father; therefore, I say unto you, you shall receive grace for grace.

21. And now, verily I say unto you, I was in the beginning with the Father, and am the *first-born;

22. And all those who are begotten through me are partakers of the glory of the same, and are the *church of the first-born.

23. Ye were also in the beginning with the Father; that which is *Spirit, even the Spirit of truth,

24. And truth is knowledge of things as they are, and as they were, and as they are to come;

25. And whatsoever is more or less than this, is the spirit of that wicked one who was a liar from the beginning.

26. The Spirit of truth is of God. I *am the Spirit of truth, and John bore record of me, saying—He received a fullness of truth, yea, even of all truth,

27. And no man receiveth a fullness unless he keepeth his commandments.

28. He that keepeth his commandments receiveth truth and light, until he is glorified in truth and *knoweth all things.

29. Man was also in the *beginning with God. Intelligence, or the light of truth, was not created or made, neither indeed can be.

30. All truth is independent in that sphere in which God has placed it, to act for itself, as all intelligence also, otherwise there is no existence.

i, vers. 26—28.   *j*, Colos. 1: 16—18.   *k*, see *a*, Sec. 1.   *l*, vers. 24—38.   *m*, vers. 9, 11, 23.   *n*, 88: 49, 67. See *g*.   *o*, vers. 23, 24, 32—38. Pearl of Great Price, pp. 6, 35. Job, 38: 7.   Eccles. 12: 7. Heb. 12: 9. Mos. 7: 27. Alma 18: 34. Ether 3: 15.

31. Behold, here is the agency of man, and here is the condemnation of man, because that which was from the beginning is plainly manifest unto them, and they receive not the light.

32. And every man whose spirit receiveth not the light is under condemnation,

33. For *p*man is spirit. The elements are *q*eternal, and spirit and element, inseparably connected, receiveth a fullness of joy ;

34. And when separated, man cannot receive a fullness of joy.

35. The elements are the *r*tabernacle of God ; yea, man is the tabernacle of God, *s*even temples ; and whatsoever temple is defiled, God shall destroy that temple.

36. The glory of God is intelligence, or, in other words, light and truth ;

37. Light and truth forsaketh that evil one.

38. Every spirit of man was *t*innocent in the beginning, and God having redeemed man from the fall, men became again in their *u*infant state, innocent before God.

39. And that wicked one cometh and taketh away light and truth, through disobedience, from the children of men, and because of the tradition of their fathers.

40. But I have commanded you to bring up your children in light and truth ;

41. But verily I say unto you, my servant Frederick G. Williams, you have continued under this condemnation ;

42. You have not taught your children light and truth, according to the commandments, and that wicked one hath power, as yet, over you, and this is the cause of your affliction.

---

p, ver. 23, 77 : 2.   *q*, vers. 29—32. 132 : 20.   *r*, 88 : 12, 41, 45, *s*, l. Cor. 3 : 16, 17. 6 : 19. ll. Cor. 6 : 16.   *t*, 29 : 46, 47. Mos. 3 : 16—19. 15 : 25. Moro. 8 : 8, 12, 22.   *u*, see *t*.

43. And now a commandment I give unto you, if you will be delivered, you shall set in order your own house, for there are many things that are not right in your house.

44. Verily, I say unto my servant Sidney Rigdon, that in some things he hath not kept the commandments concerning his children ; therefore, firstly set in order thy house.

45. Verily, I say unto my servant Joseph Smith, jun., or, in other words, I will call you friends, for you are my friends, and ye shall have an inheritance with me.

46. I called you servants for the world's sake, and ye are their servants for my sake ;

47. And now, verily, I say unto Joseph Smith, jun., you have not kept the commandments, and must needs stand rebuked before the Lord.

48. Your family must needs repent and forsake some things, and give more earnest heed unto your sayings, or be removed out of their place.

49. What I say unto one I say unto all; *pray always lest that wicked one have power in you, and remove you out of your place.

50. My servant Newel K. Whitney, also a bishop of my church, hath need to be chastened and set in order his family, and see that they are more diligent and concerned at home, and pray always, or they shall be removed out of their place.

51. Now, I say unto you, my friends, let my servant Sidney Rigdon go his journey, and make haste, and also proclaim the acceptable year of the Lord, and the gospel of salvation, as I shall give him utterance, and by your prayer of faith with one consent, I will uphold him.

52. And let my servant Joseph Smith, jun., and Frederick G. Williams, make haste also, and it shall

be given them even according to the prayer of faith, and inasmuch as you keep my sayings, you shall not be confounded in this world, nor in the world to come.

53. And verily, I say unto you, that it is my will that you should hasten to *translate my scriptures, and to obtain a knowledge of history, and of countries, and of kingdoms, of laws of God and man, and all this for the salvation of Zion. Amen.

SECTION 94.

Revelation given through Joseph, the Seer, at Kirtland, Geauga County, Ohio, May 6th, 1833.

1. And again, verily I say unto you, my friends, a commandment I give unto you, that ye shall commence a work of laying out and preparing a beginning and foundation of the city of the Stake of Zion, here in the land of Kirtland, beginning at my house;

2. And behold it must be done according to the pattern which I have given unto you.

3. And let the first lot on the south, be consecrated unto me for the building of an house for the Presidency, for the work of the Presidency, in obtaining revelations; and for the work of the ministry of the Presidency, in all things pertaining to the church and kingdom.

4. Verily I say unto you, that it shall be built fifty-five by sixty-five feet in the width thereof and in the length thereof, in the inner court;

5. And there shall be a lower court and a higher court, according to the pattern which shall be given unto you hereafter;

6. And it shall be dedicated unto the Lord from

w, the scriptures given by revelation.

the foundation thereof, according to the order of the Priesthood, according to the pattern which shall be given unto you hereafter :

7. And it shall be wholly dedicated unto the Lord for the work of the Presidency.

8. And ye shall not suffer any unclean thing to come in unto it ; and my glory shall be there, and my presence shall be there ;

9. But if there shall come into it any unclean thing, my glory shall not be there ; and my presence shall not come into it.

10. And again, verily I say unto you, the second lot on the south shall be dedicated unto me for the building of an house unto me, for the work of the printing of the translation of my scriptures, and all things whatsoever I shall command you ;

11. And it shall be fifty-five by sixty-five feet in the width thereof and the length thereof, in the inner court ; and there shall be a lower and a higher court ;

12. And this house shall be wholly dedicated unto the Lord from the foundation thereof, for the work of the printing, in all things whatsoever I shall command you, to be holy, undefiled, according to the pattern in all things, as it shall be given unto you.

13. And on the third lot shall my servant Hyrum Smith receive his inheritance.

14. And on the first and second lots on the north shall my servants Reynolds Cahoon and Jared Carter receive an inheritance,

15. That they may do the work which I have appointed unto them, to be a committee to build mine houses, according to the commandment, which I, the Lord God, have given unto you.

16. These two houses are not to be built until I give unto you a commandment concerning them.

17. And now I give unto you no more at this time. Amen.

SECTION 95.

Revelation given through Joseph, the Seer, at Kirtland,
Geauga County, Ohio, June 1st, 1833.

1. Verily, thus saith the Lord unto you, whom I love, and whom I love I also chasten, that their sins may be forgiven, for with the chastisement I prepare a way for their deliverance in all things out of temptation, and I have loved you.

2. Wherefore ye must needs be chastened and stand rebuked before my face,

3. For ye have sinned against me a very grievous sin, in that ye have not considered the great commandment in all things, that I have given unto you concerning the *building of mine house,

4. For the preparation wherewith I design to prepare mine apostles to *prune my vineyard for the last time, that I may bring to pass my *strange act, that I may pour out my Spirit upon *all flesh.

5. But behold, verily I say unto you, that there are many who have been ordained among you, whom I have called, but *few of them are chosen;

6. They who are not chosen have sinned a very grievous sin, in that they are walking in darkness at noon-day;

7. And for this cause I gave unto you a commandment that you should call your *solemn assembly, that your fastings and your mourning might come up into the ears of the Lord of Sabaoth, which is by interpretation, the Creator of the first day, the beginning and the end.

8. Yea, verily I say unto you, I gave unto you a commandment, that you should build an house, in the

---

a, 88: 119.   b, see k, Sec. 24.   c, 101: 95. Isa. 28: 21.
d, Joel, 2: 23. Acts, 2: 17.   e, 105: 35, 36. 121: 34—40.   f, see
2 r, Sec. 88.

which house I design to ⁹endow those whom I have chosen with power from on high ;

9. For this is the ʰpromise of the Father unto you; therefore I commanded you to tarry, even as mine apostles at Jerusalem ;

10. Nevertheless my servants sinned a very grievous sin, and contentions arose in the ⁱschool of the prophets, which was very grievous unto me, saith your Lord ; therefore I sent them forth to be chastened.

11. Verily I say unto you, it is my will that you should build an house. If you keep my commandments, you shall have power to build it ;

12. If you keep not my commandments, the love of the Father shall not continue with you, therefore you shall walk in darkness.

13. Now here is wisdom, and the mind of the Lord ; let the house be built, not after the manner of the world, for I give not unto you that ye shall live after the manner of the world ;

14. Therefore let it be built after the manner which I shall show unto ʲthree of you, whom ye shall appoint and ordain unto this power.

15. And the size thereof shall be fifty and five feet in width, and let it be sixty-five feet in length, in the inner court thereof ;

16. And let the lower part of the inner court be dedicated unto me for your sacrament offering, and for your preaching, and your fasting, and your praying, and the offering up your most holy desires unto me, saith your Lord.

17. And let the higher part of the inner court be dedicated unto me, for the ᵏschool of mine apostles, saith Son Ahman ; or, in other ·words, Alphus ; or, in other words, Omegus ; even Jesus Christ your Lord. Amen.

---

g, see *x*, Sec. 38.   *h*, see *x*, Sec. 38.   *i*, see 3 *x*, Sec. 88.
j, Hyrum Smith, Reynolds Cahoon, and Jared Carter.   See 94 : 13—15.
k, see 3 *x*, Sec. 88.

SECTION 96.

Revelation to Enoch (Joseph Smith, jr.,) showing the order of the city or Stake of Zion, Shinehah, (Kirtland,) given at Kirtland, Geauga County, Ohio, June 4th, 1833.

1. Behold, I say unto you, Here is wisdom, whereby ye may know how to act concerning this matter, for it is expedient in me that this Stake that I have set for the strength of Zion should be made strong ;

2. Therefore let my servant Ahashdah (Newel K. Whitney) take charge of the place which is named among you, upon which I design to build mine holy house ;

3. And again, let it be divided in lots according to wisdom, for the benefit of those who seek inheritances, as it shall be determined in council among you.

4. Therefore, take heed that ye see to this matter, and that portion that is necessary to benefit "mine order, for the purpose of bringing forth my word to the children of men ;

5. For behold, verily I say unto you, this is the most expedient in me, that my word should go forth unto the children of men, for the purpose of subduing the hearts of the children of men for your good. Even so. Amen.

6. And again, verily I say unto you, it is wisdom and expedient in me, that my servant Zombre (John Johnson) whose offering I have accepted, and whose prayers I have heard, unto whom I give a promise of eternal life inasmuch as he keepeth my commandments from henceforth,

7. For he is a descendant of Seth, (Joseph,) and a

___

a, see a, Sec. 92.

partaker of the blessings of the promise made unto his fathers.

8. Verily I say unto you, it is expedient in me that he should become a member of the order, that he may assist in bringing forth my word unto the children of men;

9. Therefore ye shall ordain him unto this blessing, and he shall seek diligently to take away incumbrances that are upon the house named among you, that he may dwell therein. Even so. Amen.

SECTION 97.

Revelation given through Joseph, the Seer, at Kirtland, Geauga County, Ohio, August 2nd, 1833.

1. Verily I say unto you my friends, I speak unto you with my voice, even the voice of my Spirit, that I may show unto you my will concerning your brethren in the land of Zion, many of whom are truly humble and are seeking diligently to learn wisdom and to find truth.

2. Verily, verily I say unto you, blessed are such, for they shall obtain, for I, the Lord, show mercy unto all the meek, and upon all whomsoever I will, that I may be justified when I shall bring them into judgment.

3. Behold, I say unto you, concerning the *a*school in Zion, I, the Lord, am well pleased that there should be a school in Zion, and also with my servant Parley P. Pratt, for he abideth in me ;

4. And inasmuch as he continueth to abide in me ;

---

a, vers. 4—6. See *x*, Sec. 88.

he shall continue to preside over the school in the land of Zion, until I shall give unto him other commandments ;

5. And I will bless him with a multiplicity of blessings, in expounding all scriptures and mysteries to the edification of the school, and of the church in Zion ;

6. And to the residue of the school, I, the Lord, am willing to show mercy, nevertheless there are those that must needs be chastened, and their works shall be made known.

7. The axe is laid at the root of the trees, and every tree that bringeth *b*not forth good fruit, shall be hewn down and cast into the fire : I, the Lord, have spoken it.

8. Verily I say unto you, all among them who know their hearts are honest, and are broken, and their spirits contrite, and are willing to observe their covenants by sacrifice; yea, every sacrifice which I, the Lord, shall command, they are all accepted of me,

9. For I, the Lord, will cause them to bring forth as a very fruitful tree which is planted in a goodly land, by a pure stream, that yieldeth much precious fruit.

10. Verily, I say unto you, that it is my will that an *c*house should be built unto me in the land of Zion, like unto the pattern which I have given you ;

11. Yea, let it be built speedily, by the *d*tithing of my people :

12. Behold, this is the tithing and the sacrifice which I, the Lord, require at their hands, that there may be an house built unto me for the salvation of Zion,

13. For a place of thanksgiving for all saints, and for a place of instruction for all those who are called

---

b, Mat. 3 : 10.   *c*, 124 : 49—54.   *d*, ver. 12.   See *n*, Sec. 42.

to the work of the ministry in all their several callings and offices,

14. That they may be perfected in the understanding of their ministry—in theory, in principle, and in doctrine—in all things pertaining to the kingdom of God on the earth, the keys of which kingdom have been conferred upon you.

15. And inasmuch as my people build an house unto me in the name of the Lord, and do not suffer any unclean thing to come into it that it be not defiled, *e*my glory shall rest upon it ;

16. Yea, and *f*my presence shall be there, for I will come into it, and all the pure in heart that shall come into it shall *g*see God ;

17. But if it be defiled I will not come into it, and my glory shall not be there, for I will not come into unholy temples.

18. And, now, behold, if Zion do these things she shall prosper, and spread herself and become very glorious, very great, and very terrible,

19. And the nations of the earth shall honor her, and shall say, Surely Zion is the city of our God, and surely Zion cannot fall, neither be moved out of her place, for God is there, and the hand of the Lord is there,

20. And he hath sworn by the power of his might, to be her salvation and her high tower ;

21. Therefore, verily, thus saith the Lord, let Zion rejoice, for this is Zion—*h*THE PURE IN HEART ; therefore, let Zion rejoice, while all the wicked shall mourn ;

22. For behold, and lo, *i*vengeance cometh speedily upon the ungodly as the whirlwind, and who shall escape it ;

23. The Lord's *j*scourge shall pass over by night and

e, 84 : 5, 31, 32.   *f*, ver. 17.   *g*, see *o*, Sec. 50.   *h*, Pearl of Great Price, p. 18.   *i*, see *f* and *g*, Sec. 1.   *j*, Isa. 28 : 15.

by day, and the report thereof shall vex all people ; yet
it shall not be stayed until the Lord come ;

24. For the indignation of the Lord is kindled
against their abominations and all their wicked works;

25. Nevertheless Zion shall escape if she observe to
do all things whatsoever I have commanded her,

26. But if she observe not to do whatsoever I have
commanded her, I will visit her ᵏaccording to all her
works, with sore affliction, with pestilence, with plague,
with sword, with vengeance, with devouring fire ;

27. Nevertheless, let it be read this once in their
ears, that I, the Lord, have accepted of their offering,
and if she sin no more, none of these things shall come
upon her,

28. And I will bless her with blessings, and multiply a multiplicity of blessings upon her, and upon her
generations for ever and ever, saith the Lord your God.
Amen.

SECTION 98.

*Revelation given through Joseph, the Seer, at Kirtland,
Geauga County, Ohio, August 6th, 1833.*

1. Verily I say unto you my friends, fear not, let
your hearts be comforted ; yea, rejoice evermore, and
in everything give thanks,

2. Waiting patiently on the Lord, for your prayers
have entered into the ears of the Lord of Sabaoth, and
are recorded with this seal and testament ; the Lord
hath sworn and decreed that they shall be granted ;

3. Therefore he giveth this promise unto you, with
an immutable covenant that they shall be fulfilled, and

---

k, 90 : 36, 37.

all things wherewith you have been afflicted, shall work together for your good, and to my name's glory, saith the Lord.

4. And now, verily I say unto you concerning the laws of the land, it is my will that my people should observe to do all things whatsoever I command them;

5. And that law of the land which is constitutional, supporting that principle of freedom in maintaining rights and privileges, belongs to all mankind, and is justifiable before me;

6. Therefore, I, the Lord, justify you, and your brethren of my church, in befriending that law which is the *constitutional law of the land;

7. And as pertaining to law of man, whatsoever is more or less than these, cometh of evil.

8. I, the Lord God, make you free, therefore ye are free indeed; and the law also maketh you free;

9. Nevertheless, when the *wicked rule the people mourn;

10. Wherefore, honest men, and wise men should be sought for diligently, and good men and wise men ye should observe to uphold; otherwise whatsoever is less than these cometh of evil.

11. And I give unto you a commandment, that ye shall forsake all evil and cleave unto all good, that ye shall live by every word which proceedeth forth out of the mouth of God;

12. For he will give unto the faithful line upon line, precept upon precept; and I will try you and prove you herewith;

13. And whoso *layeth down his life in my cause, for my name's sake, shall find it again, even life eternal:

14. Therefore be not afraid of your enemies, for I have decreed in my heart, saith the Lord, that I will prove you in all things, whether you will abide in my

---

covenant, [d]even unto death, that you may be found worthy;

15. For if ye will not abide in my covenant, ye are not worthy of me;

16. Therefore renounce war and proclaim peace, and seek diligently to turn the [e]hearts of their children to their fathers, and the hearts of the fathers to the children;

17. And again, the [f]hearts of the Jews unto the prophets, and the prophets unto the Jews, lest I come and smite the whole earth with a curse, and all flesh be consumed before me.

18. Let not your hearts be troubled, for in my Father's house are [g]many mansions, and I have prepared a place for you, and where my Father and I am, there ye shall be also.

19. Behold, I, the Lord, am not well pleased with many who are in the church at Kirtland,

20. For they do not forsake their sins, and their wicked ways, the pride of their hearts, and their covetousness, and all their detestable things, and observe the words of wisdom and eternal life which I have given unto them.

21. Verily I say unto you, that I, the Lord, will chasten them, and will do whatsoever I list, if they do not repent and observe all things whatsoever I have said unto them.

22. And again I say unto you, if ye observe to do whatsoever I command you, I, the Lord, will turn away all wrath and indignation from you, and the [h]gates of hell shall not prevail against you.

23. Now I speak unto you concerning your families; if men will smite you, or your families, once, and ye bear it patiently and revile not against them, neither seek revenge, ye shall be rewarded;

---

d, see *c*. *e*, see *a*, Sec. 2. *f*, Rom. 11: 26—31. *g*, see *a*, Sec. 59. *h*, see *l*, Sec. 10.

24. But if ye bear it not patiently, it shall be accounted unto you as being meted out a just measure unto you.

25. And again, if your enemy shall smite you the second time, and you revile not against your enemy, and bear it patiently, your reward shall be an hundred fold.

26. And again, if he shall smite you the third time, and ye bear it patiently, your reward shall be doubled unto you four fold ;

27. And these three testimonies shall stand against your enemy if he repent not, and shall not be blotted out.

28. And now verily I say unto you, if that enemy shall escape my vengeance, that he be not brought into judgment before me, then ye shall see to it that ye warn him in my name, that he come no more upon you, neither upon your family, even your children's children unto the third and fourth generation ;

29. And then if he shall come upon you, or your children, or your children's children unto the third and fourth generation ; I have delivered thine enemy into thine hands,

30. And then if thou wilt spare him, thou shalt be rewarded for thy righteousness ; and also thy children and thy children's children unto the third and fourth generation ;

31. Nevertheless thine enemy is in thine hands, and if thou reward him according to his works, thou art justified, if he has sought thy life, and thy life is endangered by him, thine enemy is in thine hands and thou art justified.

32. Behold, this is the law I gave unto my servant Nephi, and thy fathers Joseph, and Jacob, and Isaac, and Abraham, and all mine ancient prophets and apostles.

33. And again, this is the 'law that I gave unto

---

‡, Alma 48 : 10—25.

mine ancients, that they should not go out unto battle against any nation, kindred, tongue, or people, save I, the Lord, commanded them.

34. And if any nation, tongue, or people, should proclaim war against them, they should first lift a ⅉstandard of peace unto that people, nation, or tongue ;

35. And if that people did not accept the offering of peace neither the second nor the third time, they should bring these testimonies before the Lord ;

36. Then I, the Lord, would give unto them a commandment, and justify them in going out to battle against that nation, tongue, or people,

37. And I, the Lord, would fight their battles, and their children's battles, and their children's children's, until they had avenged themselves on all their enemies, to the third and fourth generation.

38. Behold, this is an ensample unto all people, saith the Lord your God, for justification before me.

39. And again, verily I say unto you, if after thine enemy has come upon thee the first time, he repent and come unto thee praying thy forgiveness, thou shalt forgive him, and shall hold it no more as a testimony against thine enemy,

40. And so on unto the second and third time ; and as oft as thine enemy repenteth of the trespass wherewith he has trespassed against thee, thou shalt forgive him, until seventy times seven :

41. And if he trespass against thee and repent not the first time, nevertheless thou shalt forgive him ;

42. And if he trespass against thee the second time, and repent not, nevertheless thou shalt forgive him ;

43. And if he trespass against thee the third time, and repent not, thou shalt also forgive him ;

44. But if he trespass against thee the fourth time, thou shalt not forgive him, but shalt bring these testimonies before the Lord, and they shall not be blotted

out until he repent and reward thee four fold in all
things wherewith he has trespassed against thee ;

45. And if he do this, thou shalt forgive him with
all thine heart, and if he do not this, I, the Lord, will
avenge thee of thine enemy an hundred fold ;

46. And upon his children, and upon his children's
children of all them that hate me, unto the third and
fourth generation ;

47. But if the children shall repent, or the children's children, and turn to the Lord their God, with
all their hearts, and with all their might, mind, and
strength, and restore four fold for all their trespasses,
wherewith they have trespassed, or wherewith their
fathers have trespassed, or their father's fathers, then
thine indignation shall be turned away,

48. And vengeance shall no more come upon them,
saith the Lord thy God, and their trespasses shall never
be brought any more as a testimony before the Lord
against them. Amen.

SECTION 99.

*Revelation given through Joseph, the Seer, at Kirtland,
Geauga County, Ohio, August, 1833.*

1. Behold, thus saith the Lord unto my servant
John Murdock, thou art called to go into the eastern
countries from house to house, from village to village,
and from city to city, to proclaim mine *a*everlasting
gospel unto the inhabitants thereof, in the midst of
persecution and wickedness ;

2. And whoso receiveth you receiveth me, and you

a, see b, Sec. 18.

shall have power to declare my word in the demonstration of my Holy Spirit;

3. And whoso receiveth you as a little child, ᵇreceiveth my kingdom, and blessed are they, for they shall obtain mercy;

4. And whoso rejecteth you shall be ᶜrejected of my Father and his house; and you shall cleanse ᵈyour feet in the secret places by the way for a testimony against them.

5. And behold, and lo, I ᵉcome quickly to judgment, to convince all of their ungodly deeds which they have committed against me, as it is written of me in the volume of the book.

6. And now, verily I say unto you, that it is not expedient that you should go until your children are provided for, and kindly sent up unto the bishop in Zion;

7. And after a few years, if thou desirest of me, thou mayest go up also unto the goodly land, to possess thine inheritance:

8. Otherwise thou shalt continue proclaiming my gospel until thou be taken. Amen.

SECTION 100.

Revelation given in Perrysburg, N. Y., to Joseph Smith, jun., and Sidney Rigdon, October 12th, 1833.

1. Verily, thus saith the Lord unto you, my friends Sidney, and Joseph, your families are well; they are in mine hands, and I will do with them as seemeth me good; for in me there is all power;

2. Therefore, follow me, and listen to the counsel which I shall give unto you.

3. Behold, and lo, I have much people in this place, in the regions round about, and an effectual door shall be opened in the regions round about in this eastern land.

4. Therefore, I, the Lord, have suffered you to come unto this place ; for thus it was expedient in me for the salvation of souls ;

5. Therefore, verily, I say unto you, lift up your voices unto this people, speak the thoughts that I shall put into your hearts, and you shall not be confounded before men ;

6. For it shall be given you in the very hour, yea, in the very moment, *what ye shall say.

7. But a commandment I give unto you, that ye shall declare whatsoever things ye declare in my name, in solemnity of heart, in the spirit of meekness, in all things.

8. And I give unto you this promise, that inasmuch as ye do this, the Holy Ghost shall be shed forth in bearing record unto all things whatsoever ye shall say.

9. And it is expedient in me that you, my servant Sidney, should be a *spokesman unto this people ; yea, verily, I will ordain you unto this calling, even to be a spokesman unto my servant Joseph ;

10. And I will give unto him power to be mighty in testimony ;

11. And I will give unto thee power to be mighty in expounding all scriptures, that thou mayest be a spokesman unto him, and he shall be a *revelator unto thee, that thou mayest know the certainty of all things pertaining to the things of my kingdom on the earth.

12. Therefore, continue your journey and let your

hearts rejoice; for behold, and lo, I am with you even
unto the end.

13. And now I give unto you a word concerning
Zion. Zion shall be ^dredeemed, although she is chastened for a little season.

14. Thy brethren, my servants Orson Hyde, and
John Gould, are in my hands, and inasmuch as they
keep my commandments, they shall be saved.

15. Therefore let your hearts be comforted, for all
things shall work together for good to them that walk
uprightly, and to the sanctification of the church;

16. For I will raise up unto myself a pure people,
that will serve me in righteousness;

17. And all that call on the name of the Lord, and
keep his commandments, shall be saved. Even so.
Amen.

SECTION 101.

*Revelation given to Joseph, the Seer, at Kirtland,
Geauga County, Ohio, December 16th, 1833.*

1. Verily I say unto you, concerning your brethren
who have been afflicted, and persecuted, and ^acast out
from the land of their inheritance,

2. I, the Lord, have suffered the affliction to come
upon them, wherewith they have been afflicted, in consequence of ^btheir transgressions;

3. Yet I will own them, and they shall be mine in
that day when I shall come to make up ^cmy jewels.

4. Therefore, they must needs be chastened and

---

d, 101: 18, 43, 74, 75.   103: 1, 11, 13, 15.   105: 1, 2, 9, 13, 16, 34.   109:
51.   136: 18.

a, ver. 76.   64: 30—36.   84: 54—59.   103: 2, 11.   104: 51.   109: 47.
121: 23.   b, vers. 8—9.   c, 60: 4.   Mal. 3: 17.

tried, even as Abraham, who was commanded to offer up his only son ;

5. For all those who will not endure chastening, but deny me, cannot be sanctified.

6. Behold, I say unto you, there were jarrings, and contentions, and envyings, and strifes, and lustful and covetous desires among them ; therefore by these things they ᵈpolluted their inheritances.

7. They were slow to hearken unto the voice of the Lord their God, therefore the Lord their God is slow to hearken unto their prayers, to answer them in the day of their trouble.

8. In the day of their peace they esteemed lightly my counsel; but, in the ᶠday of their trouble, of necessity they feel after me.

9. Verily I say unto you, notwithstanding their sins, my bowels are filled with compassion towards them : I will not utterly cast them off ; and in the day of wrath I will ᵍremember mercy.

10. I have sworn, and the decree hath gone forth by a former commandment which I have given unto you, that I would let ʰfall the sword of mine indignation in the behalf of my people ; and even as I have said, it shall come to pass.

11. Mine indignation is ⁱsoon to be poured out without measure upon all nations, and this will I do when the cup of their iniquity is full.

12. And in that day all who are found upon the watch tower, or in other words, all mine Israel shall be saved.

13. And they that have been scattered shall be ʲgathered ;

14. And all they who have mourned shall be ᵏcomforted ;

d, 84 : 55—59.   e, vers. 39—42.   f, vers. 39—42, 44—54.
g, vers. 10—19.   103 : 11—20.   h, see f and g, Sec. 1.   i, see f
and g, Sec. 1.   j, the saints shall again be gathered to Zion.   vers. 17—19.
29 : 7.   38 : 31.   39 : 22.   42 : 36.   45 : 43.   84 : 2, 4.   133, 4, 7.   103 : 11—13.
k, 56 : 18—20.

15. And all they who have given their lives for my name shall be *l*crowned.

16. Therefore, let your hearts be comforted concerning Zion; for all flesh is in mine hands: be still and know that I am God.

17. Zion shall not be *m*moved out of her place, notwithstanding her children are scattered;

18. They that remain, and are pure in heart, shall return, and come to their inheritances, they and their children, with *n*songs of everlasting joy, to build up the waste places of Zion;

19. And all these things that the prophets might be fulfilled.

20. And, behold, there is none other place appointed than that which I have appointed; neither shall there be any other place appointed than that which I have appointed, for the work of the gathering of my saints,

21. Until the day cometh when there is found no more room for them; and then I have other places which I will appoint unto them, and they shall be called *o*Stakes, for the curtains, or the strength of Zion.

22. Behold, it is my will, that all they who call on my name, and worship me according to mine everlasting gospel, should *p*gather together, and stand in holy places,

23. And prepare for the revelation which is to come, when the vail of the covering of my temple, in my tabernacle, which hideth the earth, shall be taken off, and all flesh shall *q*see me together.

24. And every corruptible thing, both of man, or of the beasts of the field, or of the fowls of the heavens, or of the fish of the sea, that dwell upon all the face of the earth, shall be *r*consumed;

---

l, Rev. 20 : 4.   *m,* vers. 20—22.   *n,* 45 : 71.   Isa. 35 : 10.
o, see *d,* Sec. 88.   *p,* see *j,* Sec. 10.   *q,* 38: 8.   93 : 1.   See *s,*
Sec 1.   *r,* 29: 24.

25. And also that of element shall *melt with fervent heat; and all things shall become new, that my knowledge and *glory may dwell upon all the earth.

26. And in that day the enmity of man, and the *enmity of beasts, yea, the enmity of all flesh, shall cease from before my face.

27. And in that day *whatsoever any man shall ask, it shall be given unto him.

28. And in that day Satan shall not have power *to tempt any man.

29. And there shall be no sorrow because there is no death.

30. In that day an infant shall not die *until he is old, and his life shall be as the *age of a tree,

31. And when he dies he shall not sleep, (that is to say in the earth,) but shall be changed in the twinkling of an eye, and shall be *caught up, and his rest shall be glorious.

32. Yea, verily I say unto you, in that day when the Lord *²ashall come, he shall reveal ²ball things—

33. Things which have passed, and hidden things which no man knew—things of the earth, by which it was made, and the purposes and the end thereof—

34. Things most precious—things that are above, and things that are beneath—things that are in the earth, and upon the earth, and in heaven.

35. And all they who suffer persecution for my name, and endure in faith, though they are called to lay down their lives for my sake, yet shall they partake of all this glory.

36. Wherefore, fear not even ²ᶜunto death; for in this world your joy is not full, but in me your joy is full.

---

s, 29 : 23, 24.   43 : 32.   133 : 41, 49.   *t*, 76 : 7—9.   88 : 19.   93 : 1.
u, 77 : 2.   *v*, see *c*, Sec. 4.   *w*, see 2*t*, Sec. 45.   *x*, see *t*,
Sec. 63.   *y*, Isa. 65 : 22.   *z*, The resurrection, during the
Millennium, a continued work, old people, as they fall asleep, being raised.
2*a*, see *c*, Sec. 1.   2*b*, vers. 33—35.   88 : 108, 109.   121 : 26—33.   Isa.
51 : 9.   2*c*, ver. 37.   See *c*, Sec. 98.

37. Therefore, care not for the body, neither the life of the body; but care for the soul, and for the [2d]life of the soul;

38. And seek the [2e]face of the Lord always, that in patience ye may possess your souls, and ye shall have eternal life.

39. When men are called unto mine everlasting gospel, and covenant with an everlasting covenant, they are accounted as the [2f]salt of the earth, and the savor of men;

40. They are called to be the savor of men. Therefore, if that salt of the earth lose its savor, behold, it is thenceforth good for nothing, only to be cast out, and trodden under the [2g]feet of men.

41. Behold, here is wisdom concerning the children of Zion, even many, but not all; they were found transgressors, therefore they must needs be chastened.

42. He that exalteth himself shall be [2h]abased, and he that abaseth himself shall be [2i]exalted.

43. And now, I will show unto you a parable, that you may know my will concerning the redemption of Zion.

44. A certain nobleman had a spot of land, very choice; and he said unto his servants, Go ye unto my vineyard, even upon this very choice piece of land, and plant twelve olive trees,

45. And set watchmen round about them, and build a tower, that one may overlook the land round about, to be a watchman upon the tower, that mine olive trees may not be broken down, when the enemy shall come to spoil, and take unto themselves the fruit of my vineyard.

46. Now, the servants of the nobleman went and did as their lord commanded them; and planted the olive trees, and built a hedge round about, and set watchmen, and began to build a tower.

2d, Luke 12: 15—21.   2e, see o, Sec. 50.   2f, 103: 10.
2g, vers. 41, 42.   2h, Matt. 23: 12.   2i, Matt. 23: 12.

47. And while they were yet laying the foundation thereof, they began to say among themselves, And what need hath my lord of this tower?

48. And consulted for a long time, saying among themselves, What need hath my lord of this tower, seeing this is a time of peace?

49. Might not this money be given to the exchangers? for there is no need of these things!

50. And while they were at variance one with another they became very slothful, and they hearkened not unto the commandments of their lord,

51. And the enemy [2j]came by night, and broke down the hedge, and the servants of the nobleman arose and were affrighted, and fled; and the enemy destroyed their works, and broke down the olive trees.

52. Now behold, the nobleman, the lord of the vineyard, called upon his servants, and said unto them, Why! what is the cause of this great evil?

53. Ought ye not to have done even as I commanded you? and after ye had planted the vineyard, and built the hedge round about, and set watchmen upon the walls thereof, built the tower also, and set a [2k]watchman upon the tower, and watched for my vineyard, and not have fallen asleep, lest the enemy should come upon you?

54. And behold, the watchman upon the tower would have seen the [2l]enemy while he was yet afar off, and then ye could have made ready and kept the enemy from breaking down the hedge thereof, and saved my vineyard from the hands of the destroyer.

55. And the lord of the vineyard said unto one of his servants, Go and gather together the residue of my servants, and take [2m]all the strength of mine house, which are my warriors, my young men, and they that are of middle age also among all my servants, who are

the strength of mine house, save those only whom I have appointed to tarry ;

56. And go ye straightway unto the land of my vineyard, and [2n]redeem my vineyard, for it is mine, I have bought it with money.

57. Therefore, get ye straightway unto my land ; break down the walls of mine enemies ; throw down their tower, and scatter their watchmen :

58. And inasmuch as they gather together against you, [2o]avenge me of mine enemies, that by and by I may [2p]come with the residue of mine house, and possess the land.

59. And the servant said unto his lord, When shall these things be ?

60. And he said unto his servant, When I will, go ye straightway, and do all things [2q]whatsoever I have commanded you;

61. And this shall be my seal and blessing upon you—a faithful and [2r]wise steward in the midst of mine house, a ruler in my kingdom.

62. And his servant went straightway, and did all things whatsoever his lord commanded him, and [2s]after many days all things were fulfilled.

63. Again, verily I say unto you, I will show unto you [2t]wisdom in me concerning all the churches, inasmuch as they are willing to be guided in a right and proper way for their salvation,

64. That the work of the gathering together of my saints may [2u]continue, that I may build them up unto my name upon [2v]holy places; for the time of [2w]harvest is come, and my word must needs be fulfilled.

65. Therefore, I must gather together my people, according to the parable of the wheat and the tares,

2 n, referring to the lands purchased by the saints in Jackson Co., Missouri.   2 o, the principle of self-defence justified.   2 p, see e, Sec. 1.   2 q, 95 : 16—19.   2 r, see u, Sec. 78.   2 s, 58 : 44. 105 : 15.   136 : 18.   Complete fulfillment, at the coming of Christ with the residue of his house.   2 t, vers. 64—74.   2 u, see j, Sec. 10. 2 v, see g, Sec. 87.   2 w, see b, Sec. 4.

that the wheat may be secured in the garners to possess eternal life, and be [2x]crowned with celestial glory when I shall [2y]come in the kingdom of my Father, to reward every man according as his work shall be,

66. While the tares shall be bound in [2z]bundles, and their bands made strong, that they may be burned with unquenchable fire.

67. Therefore, a commandment I give unto all the churches, that they shall continue to [3a]gather together unto the places which I have appointed ;

68. Nevertheless, as I have said unto you in a former commandment, let not your gathering be in [3b]haste, nor by flight ; but let all things be prepared before you :

69. And in order that all things be prepared before you, observe the commandments which I have given concerning these things,

70. Which saith, or teacheth, to [3c]purchase all the lands by money, which can be purchased for money, in the region round about the land which I have appointed to be the land of Zion, for the beginning of the gathering of my saints ;

71. All the land which can be purchased in Jackson county, and the counties round about, and leave the residue in mine hand.

72. Now, verily I say unto you, let all the churches gather together [3d]all their monies ; let these things be done in their time, be not in haste, and observe to have all things prepared before you.

73. And let honorable men be appointed, even [3e]wise men, and send them to purchase these lands ;

74. And every church in the eastern countries when they are built up, if they will hearken unto this counsel, they may buy lands and gather together upon them, and in this way they may establish Zion.

2x, 29 : 11—13. 63 : 49. 76 : 50—70, 94, 95. 88 : 28, 29. 2y, see e, Sec. 1. 2z, see l, Sec. 38. 3a, see j, Sec. 10. 3b, see j, Sec. 10. 3c, see j, Sec. 63. 3d, see j, Sec. 63. 3e, 105 : 28—30.

75. There is even now already in store a sufficient, yea, even abundance, to redeem Zion, and establish her waste places, no more to be thrown down, were the churches, who call themselves after my name, willing to hearken to my voice.

76. And again I say unto you, those who have been scattered by their enemies, it is my will that they should continue to *ʃ*importune for redress, and redemption, by the hands of those who are placed as rulers, and are in authority over you,

77. According to the laws and constitution of the people which I have suffered to be established, and should be maintained for the rights and protection of all flesh, according to just and holy principles,

78. That every man may act in doctrine and principle pertaining to futurity, according to the moral agency which I have given unto them, that every man may be accountable for his own sins in the day of judgment.

79. Therefore, it is not right that any man should be in *ᵍ*bondage one to another.

80. And for this purpose have I established the constitution of this land, by the hands of *ʰ*wise men whom I raised up unto this very purpose, and redeemed the land by the shedding of blood.

81. Now, unto what shall I liken the children of Zion? I will liken them unto the *ⁱ*parable of the woman and the unjust judge (for men ought always to pray and not to faint) which saith,

82. There was in a city a judge which feared not God, neither regarded man.

83. And there was a widow in that city, and she came unto him, saying, Avenge me of mine adversary.

84. And he would not for a while, but afterward he said within himself, Though I fear not God, nor regard man, yet because this widow troubleth me I will avenge her, lest, by her continual coming, she weary me.

3*f*, vers. 77—95.   3*g*, 104 : 16—18, 83, 84.   3*h*, the Lord
raised up the framers of the American Constitution.   3*i*, Luke 18 : 1—8.

85. Thus will I liken the children of Zion.

86. Let them importune at the feet of the Judge ;

87. And if he heed them not, let them importune at the feet of the Governor ;

88. And if the Governor heed them not, let them importune at the feet of the President ;

89. And if the President heed them not, then will the Lord arise and come forth out of his [3j]hiding place, and in his fury vex the nation,

90. And in his hot displeasure, and in his fierce anger, in his time, will cut off those wicked, unfaithful, and unjust stewards, and appoint them their portion among hypocrites, and unbelievers ;

91. Even in outer darkness, where there is [3k]weeping, and wailing, and gnashing of teeth.

92. Pray ye, therefore, that their ears may be opened unto your cries, that I may be merciful unto them, that these things may not come upon them.

93. What I have said unto you, must needs be, that all men may be left without excuse ;

94. That wise men and rulers may hear and know that which they have [3l]never considered ;

95. That I may proceed to bring to pass [3m]my act, my strange act, and perform my work, my strange work, that men may discern between the righteous and the wicked, saith your God.

96. And again, I say unto you, it is contrary to my commandment, and my will, that my servant Sidney Gilbert should sell my storehouse, which I have appointed unto my people, into the hands of mine enemies.

97. Let not that which I have appointed be polluted by mine enemies, by the consent of those who call themselves after my name ;

98. For this is a very sore and grievous sin against me, and against my people, in consequence of those

---

3j, 101 : 89.   121 : 1, 4.   123 : 6.   3 k, see e, Sec. 19.   3 l, III. Nep.
20 : 45.   21 : 8.   3 m, see c, Sec. 95.

things which I have decreed and are soon to befall the nations.

99. Therefore, it is my will that my people should claim, and hold claim upon that which I have appointed unto them, though they should not be permitted to dwell thereon ;

100. Nevertheless, I do not say they shall not dwell thereon ; for inasmuch as they bring forth fruit and works meet for my kingdom, they shall dwell thereon;

101. They shall build, and [3n]another shall not inherit it ; they shall plant vineyards, and they shall eat the fruit thereof. Even so. Amen.

SECTION 102.

Minutes of the Organization of the High Council of the Church of Christ of Latter-day Saints. Kirtland, February 17, 1834.

1. This day a general council of twenty-four High Priests assembled at the house of Joseph Smith, jun., by revelation, and proceeded to organize the High Council of the Church of Christ, which was to consist of twelve High Priests, and one or three Presidents, as the case might require.

2. The High Council was appointed by revelation for the purpose of settling important difficulties which might arise in the church, which could not be settled by the church or the bishop's council to the satisfaction of the parties.

3. Joseph Smith, jun., Sidney Rigdon, and Frederick G. Williams, were acknowledged Presidents by the voice of the council ; and Joseph Smith, sen., John Smith, Joseph Coe, John Johnson, Martin Harris, John S. Carter, Jared Carter, Oliver Cowdery, Samuel H.

[3n], Isa. 65 : 20—22.

Smith, Orson Hyde, Sylvester Smith, and Luke Johnson, High Priests, were chosen to be a standing Council for the church, by the unanimous voice of the Council.

4. The above-named counselors were then asked whether they accepted their appointments, and whether they would act in that office according to the law of heaven : to which they all answered that they accepted their appointments, and would fill their offices according to the grace of God bestowed upon them.

5. The number composing the council, who voted in the name and for the church, in appointing the above-named counselors were forty-three, as follows :— Nine High Priests, seventeen elders, four priests, and thirteen members.

6. Voted : that the High Council cannot have power to act without seven of the above-named counselors, or their regularly-appointed successors are present.

7. These seven shall have power to appoint other High Priests, whom they may consider worthy and capable to act in the place of absent counselors.

8. Voted : that whenever any vacancy shall occur by the death, removal from office for transgression, or removal from the bounds of this church government, of any one of the above-named counselors, it shall be filled by the nomination of the President or Presidents, and sanctioned by the voice of a general council of High Priests, convened for that purpose, to act in the name of the church.

9. The President of the church, who is also the President of the council, is appointed by revelation, and acknowledged in his administration, by the voice of the church ;

10. And it is according to the dignity of his office that he should preside over the Council of the church ; and it is his privilege to be assisted by two other Presidents, appointed after the same manner that he himself was appointed ;

11. And in case of the absence of one or both of

those who are appointed to assist him, he has power to preside over the Council without an assistant : and in case that he himself is absent, the other Presidents have power to preside in his stead, both, or either of them.

12. Whenever an High Council of the church of Christ is regularly organized, according to the foregoing pattern, it shall be the duty of the twelve counselors to cast lots by numbers, and thereby ascertain, who of the twelve shall speak first, commencing with number one, and so in succession to number twelve.

13. Whenever this Council convenes to act upon any case, the twelve counselors shall consider whether it is a difficult one or not ; if it is not, two only of the counselors shall speak upon it, according to the form above written.

14. But if it is thought to be difficult, four shall be appointed ; and if more difficult, six ; but in no case shall more than six be appointed to speak.

15. The accused, in all cases, has a right to one half of the Council, to prevent insult or injustice ;

16. And the counselors appointed to speak before the Council, are to present the case after the evidence is examined, in its true light before the Council, and every man is to speak according to equity and justice.

17. Those counselors who draw even numbers, that is 2, 4, 6, 8, 10, and 12, are the individuals who are to stand up in behalf of the accused, and prevent insult or injustice.

18. In all cases the accuser and the accused shall have a privilege of speaking for themselves before the Council after the evidences are heard, and the counselors who are appointed to speak on the case, have finished their remarks.

19. After the evidences are heard, the counselors, accuser and accused have spoken, the President shall give a decision according to the understanding which he shall have of the case, and call upon the twelve counselors to sanction the same by their vote.

20. But should the remaining counselors, who have not spoken, or any one of them, after hearing the evidences and pleadings impartially, discover an error in the decision of the President, they can manifest it, and the case shall have a re-hearing ;

21. And if, after a careful re-hearing, any additional light is shown upon the case, the decision shall be altered accordingly ;

22. But in case no additional light is given, the first decision shall stand, the majority of the Council having power to determine the same.

23. In cases of difficulty, respecting doctrine or principle, (if there is not a sufficiency written to make the case clear to the minds of the Council,) the President may inquire and obtain the mind of the Lord by revelation.

24. The High Priests, when abroad, have power to call and organize a council after the manner of the foregoing to settle difficulties when the parties, or either of them shall request it :

25. And the said council of High Priests shall have power to appoint one of their own number, to preside over such council for the time being.

26. It shall be the duty of said council to transmit immediately, a copy of their proceedings, with a full statement of the testimony accompanying their decision, to the High Council of the seat of the First Presidency of the church.

27. Should the parties, or either of them be dissatisfied with the decision of said council, they may appeal to the High Council of the seat of the First Presidency of the church, and have a re-hearing, which case shall there be conducted, according to the former pattern written, as though no such decision had been made.

28. This council of High Priests abroad, is only to be called on the most difficult cases of church matters ; and no common or ordinary case is to be sufficient to call such council.

29. The traveling or located High Priests abroad, have power to say whether it is necessary to call such a council or not.

30. There is a distinction between the High Council of traveling High Priests abroad, and the traveling High Council composed of the Twelve apostles, in their decisions.

31. From the decision of the former there can be an appeal, but from the decision of the latter there cannot.

32. The latter can only be called in question by the general authorities of the church in case of transgression.

33. Resolved, that the President or Presidents of the seat of the First Presidency of the church, shall have power to determine whether any such case, as may be appealed, is justly entitled to a re-hearing, after examining the appeal and the evidences and statements accompanying it.

34. The twelve counselors then proceeded to cast lots or ballot, to ascertain who should speak first, and the following was the result, namely :—

1 OLIVER COWDERY,
2 JOSEPH COE,
3 SAMUEL H. SMITH,
4 LUKE JOHNSON,
5 JOHN S. CARTER,
6 SYLVESTER SMITH,
7 JOHN JOHNSON,
8 ORSON HYDE,
9 JARED CARTER,
10 JOSEPH SMITH, Sen.,
11 JOHN SMITH,
12 MARTIN HARRIS.

After prayer the conference adjourned.

OLIVER COWDERY, } Clerks.
ORSON HYDE,

SECTION 103.

Revelation given through Joseph, the Seer, at Kirtland,
Geauga County, Ohio, February 24th, 1834.

1. Verily I say unto you, my friends, behold I will
give unto you a revelation and commandment, that you
may know how to act in the discharge of your duties
concerning the salvation and *a*redemption of your
brethren, who have been scattered on the land of
Zion ;

2. Being driven and smitten by the hands of mine
enemies, on whom I will pour out my wrath without
measure in mine own time ;

3. For I have suffered them thus far, that they
might fill up the measure of their iniquities, that their
cup might be full ;

4. And that those who call themselves after my
name might be chastened for a *b*little season with a
sore and grievous chastisement, because they did not
hearken altogether unto the precepts and commandments which I gave unto them.

5. But verily I say unto you, that I have decreed
a decree which my people shall realize, inasmuch as
they hearken from this very hour, unto the counsel
which I, the Lord their God, shall give unto them.

6. Behold they shall, for I have decreed it, *c*begin
to prevail against mine enemies from this very hour,

7. And by hearkening to observe all the words
which I, the Lord their God, shall speak unto them,
they shall never cease to prevail until the *d*kingdoms
of the world are subdued under my feet, and the earth
is given unto the saints, to *e*possess it for ever and
ever.

---

a, vers. 11—40.   *b*, 84 : 58.   95 : 1, 2.   97 : 6, 7, 26—28.   101 : 1,
2, 4, 5, 41.   105 : 6.   *c*, vers. 7, 11—14.   *d*, Dan. 2 : 34, 35, 44,
45.   *e*, 88 : 20.   56 : 19, 20.

8. But inasmuch as they keep not my commandments, and hearken not to observe all my words, the *kingdoms of the world shall prevail against them,

9. For they were set to be a light unto the world, and to be the saviours of men ;

10. And inasmuch as they are not the saviours of men, they are *as salt that has lost its savor, and is thenceforth good for nothing but to be cast out and trodden under foot of men.

11. But verily I say unto you, I have decreed that your brethren which have been scattered shall *retu to the land of their inheritances, and build up tno waste places of Zion ;

12. For after much tribulation, as I have said unto you in a *former commandment, cometh the blessing.

13. Behold, this is the blessing which I have promised after your tribulations, and the tribulations of your brethren ; your redemption, and the redemption of your brethren, even their *restoration to the land of Zion, to be established no more to be thrown down ;

14. Nevertheless, if they pollute their inheritances, they shall be thrown down, for I will not spare them if they pollute their inheritances.

15. Behold, I say unto you, the redemption of Zion must needs come by *power ;

16. Therefore, I will *raise up unto my people a man, who shall lead them like as Moses led the children of Israel,

17. For ye are the children of Israel, and of the seed of Abraham, and ye must needs be led out of *bondage by power, and with a stretched out arm :

18. And as your fathers were *led at the first, even so shall the redemption of Zion be.

---

f, Dan. 7 : 21, 22. *g*, 101 : 39—41. *h*, 101 : 17—19. Isa.
35 : 10. *i*, 58 : 3—5. *j*, see *h*. *k*, vers. 16—20, 23—23.
l, the one referred to, in this prophecy, is not yet revealed. *m*, an indication that the saints will be in bondage. *n*. 101 : 55. 103 : 15,
17—20. 105 : 30. 133 : 67. 136 : 18, 22.

19. Therefore let not your hearts faint, for I say not unto you as I said unto your fathers, mine angel shall go up before you, but °not my presence;

20. But I say unto you, mine angels shall go before you, and ᵖalso my presence, and in ᵠtime ye shall possess the goodly land.

21. Verily, verily I say unto you, that my servant Baurak Ale (Joseph Smith, jr.) is the man to whom I likened the servant to whom the Lord of the vineyard spake in the parable which I have given unto you.

22. Therefore let my servant Baurak Ale (Joseph Smith, jr.) say unto the ʳstrength of my house, my young men and the middle aged, gather yourselves together unto the land of Zion, upon the land which I have bought with moneys that has been consecrated unto me;

23. And let all the churches send up wise men with their moneys, and ˢpurchase lands even as I have commanded them;

24. And inasmuch as mine enemies come against you to drive you from my goodly land, which I have consecrated to be the land of Zion; even from your ᵗown lands after these testimonies, which ye have brought before me, against them, ye shall ᵘcurse them;

25. And whomsoever ye curse, I will ᵛcurse, and ye shall avenge me of mine enemies;

26. And my presence shall be with you even in avenging me of mine enemies, unto the ʷthird and fourth generation of them that hate me.

27. Let no man be afraid to lay down his life for my sake, for whoso layeth down ˣhis life for my sake shall find it again;

28. And whoso is ʸnot willing to lay down his life for my sake, is not my disciple.

---

o, 84: 23—28. Exod. 33: 1—4.   p, vers. 22—27.   q, see h.
r, 101: 55.   s, see q, Sec. 42.   t, see q, Sec. 42.   u, 24:
15—17. 124: 93. 132: 45—48.   v, see u.   w, 97: 22. 98: 45.
101: 58. 103: 2, 7, 25, 26. 105: 15, 30.   133: 51.   x, see c, Sec. 98.
y, see c, Sec. 98.

29. It is my will that my servant Sidney Rigdon shall lift up his voice in the congregations in the eastern countries, in preparing the churches to keep the commandments which I have given unto them, concerning the restoration and *redemption of Zion.

30. It is my will that my servant Parley P. Pratt, and my servant Lyman Wight should not return to the land of their brethren, until they have obtained companies to go up unto the land of Zion, by tens, or by twenties, or by fifties, or by an hundred, until they have obtained to the number of five hundred of the ²ᵃstrength of my house.

31. Behold this is my will; ask and you shall receive, but men do not always do my will;

32. Therefore, if you cannot obtain five hundred, seek diligently, that peradventure you may obtain three hundred;

33. And if ye cannot obtain three hundred, seek diligently, that peradventure ye may obtain one hundred.

34. But verily I say unto you, a commandment I give unto you, that ye shall not go up unto the land of Zion, until you have obtained one hundred of the strength of my house, to go up with you unto the land of Zion.

35. Therefore as I said unto you, ask and ye shall receive; pray earnestly that peradventure my servant Baurak Ale (Joseph Smith, jr.) may go with you, and preside in the midst of my people, and organize my kingdom upon the consecrated land, and ²ᵇestablish the children of Zion upon the laws and commandments which have been, and which shall be given unto you.

36. All victory and glory is brought to pass unto you through your diligence, faithfulness, and prayers of faith.

37. Let my servant Parley P. Pratt journey with my servant Joseph Smith, jr.

---

z, see h.　　　　2a, ver. 22.　101 : 55.　　　2b, Sec. 42.

38. Let my servant Lyman Wight journey with my servant Sidney Rigdon.

39. Let my servant Hyrum Smith journey with my servant Frederick G. Williams.

40. Let my servant Orson Hyde journey with my servant Orson Pratt, whithersoever my servant Joseph Smith, jr., shall counsel them, in obtaining the fulfillment of these commandments which I have given unto you, and leave the residue in my hands. Even so. Amen.

SECTION 104.

Revelation given April 23rd, 1834, to Enoch, (Joseph Smith, jun.,) concerning the order of the church for the benefit of the poor.

1. Verily I say unto you, my friends, I give unto you counsel, and a commandment, concerning all the properties which belong to the order which I commanded to be organized and established, to be an ªunited order, and an everlasting order for the benefit of my church, and for the salvation of men until I come,

2. With promise immutable and unchangeable, that inasmuch as those whom I commanded were faithful they should be blessed with a multiplicity of blessings;

3. But inasmuch as they were not faithful they were nigh unto cursing.

4. Therefore, inasmuch as some of my servants have not kept the commandment but have broken the covenant by covetousness, and with feigned words, I ᵇhave cursed them with a very sore and grievous curse ;

---

5. For I, the Lord, have decreed in my heart, that inasmuch as any man belonging to the order, shall be found a transgressor, or, in other words, shall break the covenant with which ye are bound, he shall be ᶜcursed in his life, and shall be trodden down by whom I will,

6. For I, the Lord, am not to be mocked in these things ;

7. And all this that the innocent among you may not be condemned with the unjust, and that the guilty among you may not escape, because I, the Lord, have promised unto you a ᵈcrown of glory at my right hand.

8. Therefore, inasmuch as you are found transgressors, ye cannot escape my ᵉwrath in your lives ;

9. Inasmuch as ye are cut off by transgressions, ye cannot escape the ᶠbuffetings of Satan, until the day of redemption.

10. And I now give unto you power from this very hour, that if any man among you, of the order, is found a transgressor, and repenteth not of the evil, that ye shall deliver him over unto the ᵍbuffetings of Satan, and he shall not have power to bring evil upon you.

11. It is wisdom in me : therefore, a commandment I give unto you, that ye shall organize yourselves and appoint ʰevery man his stewardship,

12. That every man may give an account unto me of his stewardship which is appointed unto him ;

13. For it is expedient that I, the Lord, should make every man accountable, ᶦas stewards over earthly blessings, which I have made and prepared for my creatures.

14. I, the Lord, stretched out the heavens, and built the earth as a very handy work, and all things therein are mine:

---

c, see b.   d, 76 : 50—70.   88 : 2—5.   e, ver. 5.   82 : 21.   f, see h,
Sec. 78.   g, see h, Sec. 78.   h, see o, Sec. 42.   i, see o, Sec. 42.

15. And it is my purpose to provide for my saints, for all things are mine ;

16. But it must needs be done in mine own way ; and behold this is the way that I, the Lord, have decreed to provide for my saints, that the poor shall be exalted, in that the rich are made low ;

17. For the earth is full, and there is enough and to spare ; yea, I prepared all things, and have given unto the children of men to be agents unto themselves.

18. Therefore, if any man shall take of the abundance which I have made, and impart not his portion, according to the ʲlaw of my gospel, unto the poor and the needy, he shall, with the wicked, lift up his eyes in hell, being in torment.

19. And now, verily I say unto you, concerning the properties of the order.

20. Let my servant Pelagoram (Sidney Rigdon) have appointed unto him the place where he now resides, and the lot of Tahhanes (the tannery) for his stewardship, for his support while he is laboring in my vineyard, even as I will when I shall command him ;

21. And let all things be done according to the counsel of the order, and united consent or voice of the order, which dwell in the land of Shinehah. (Kirtland.)

22. And this stewardship and blessing, I, the Lord, confer upon my servant Pelagoram, (Sidney Rigdon,) for a blessing upon him, and his seed after him ;

23. And I will multiply blessings upon him, inasmuch as he shall be humble before me.

24. And again, let my servant Mahemson (Martin Harris) have appointed unto him, for his stewardship, the lot of land which my servant Zombre (John Johnson) obtained in exchange for his former inheritance, for him and his seed after him ;

---

j, see n, Sec. 12.

25. And inasmuch as he is faithful, I will multiply blessings upon him, and his seed after him.

26. And let my servant Mahemson (Martin Harris) devote his moneys for the proclaiming of my words, according as my servant Gazelam (Joseph Smith, jr.) shall direct.

27. And again, let my servant Shederlaomach (Frederick G. Williams) have the place upon which he now dwells.

28. And let my servant Olihah (Oliver Cowdery) have the lot which is set off joining the house, which is to be for the Laneshine-house, (printing office,) which is lot number one, and also the lot upon which his father resides.

29. And let my servants Shederlaomach (Frederick G. Williams) and Olihah (Oliver Cowdery) have the Laneshine-house, (printing office,) and all things that pertain unto it;

30. And this shall be their stewardship which shall be appointed unto them:

31. And inasmuch as they are faithful, behold I will bless, and multiply blessings upon them,

32. And this is the beginning of the stewardship which I have appointed them, for them and their seed after them;

33. And, inasmuch as they are faithful, I will multiply blessings upon them, and their seed after them, even a multiplicity of blessings.

34. And again, let my servant Zombre (John Johnson) have the house in which he lives, and the inheritance—all, save the ground which has been reserved for the [k]building of my houses, which pertains to that inheritance, and those lots which have been named for my servant Olihah. (Oliver Cowdery.)

35. And, inasmuch as he is faithful, I will multiply blessings upon him.

36. And it is my will that he should sell the lots that are laid off for the building up of the city of my saints, inasmuch as it shall be made known to him by the voice of the Spirit, and according to the counsel of the order, and by the voice of the order.

37. And this is the beginning of the stewardship which I have appointed unto him, for a blessing unto him, and his seed after him ;

38. And, inasmuch as he is faithful, I will multiply a multiplicity of blessings upon him.

39. And again, let my servant Ahashdah (Newel K. Whitney) have appointed unto him the houses and lot where he now resides, and the lot and building on which the Ozondah (mercantile establishment) stands, and also the lot which is on the corner south of the Ozondah (mercantile establishment), and also the lot on which the Shule (ashery) is situated.

40. And all this I have appointed unto my servant Ahashdah, (Newel K. Whitney,) for his stewardship, for a blessing upon him and his seed after him, for the benefit of the Ozondah (mercantile establishment) of my order which I have established for my Stake in the land of Shinehah ; (Kirtland ;)

41. Yea, verily, this is the stewardship which I have appointed unto my servant Ahashdah, (N. K. Whitney,) even this whole Ozondah, (mercantile establishment,) him and his agent, and his seed after him ;

42. And, inasmuch as he is faithful in keeping my commandments which I have given unto him, I will multiply blessings upon him, and his seed after him, even a multiplicity of blessings.

43. And again, let my servant Gazelam (Joseph Smith, jr.) have appointed unto him the lot which is laid off for the building of my house, which is forty rods long, and twelve wide, and also the inheritance upon which his father resides ;

44. And this is the beginning of the stewardship which I have appointed unto him, for a blessing upon him, and upon his father;

45. For, behold, I have reserved an inheritance for his father, for his support; therefore he shall be reckoned in the house of my servant Gazelam, (Joseph Smith, jr.,)

46. And I will multiply blessings upon the house of my servant Gazelam, (Joseph Smith, jr.,) inasmuch as he is faithful, even a multiplicity of blessings.

47. And now, a commandment I give unto you concerning Zion, that you shall no longer be bound as an *m*United Order to your brethren of Zion, only on this wise.

48. After you are organized, you shall be called the United Order of the *n*Stake of Zion, the city of Shinehah. (Kirtland.) And your brethren, after they are organized, shall be called the United Order of the *o*City of Zion;

49. And they shall be organized in their own names, and in their own name; and they shall do their business in their own name, and in their own names;

50. And you shall do your business in your own name, and in your own names.

51. And this I have commanded to be done for your salvation, and also for their salvation, in consequence of their being *p*driven out, and that which is to come.

52. The covenants being broken through transgression, by covetousness and feigned words;

53. Therefore, you are dissolved as an *q*United Order with your brethren, that you are not bound only up to this hour unto them, only on this wise, as I said, by loan as shall be agreed by this order in council, as your cir-

---

m, see *l*, Sec. 82. *n*, 94 : 1. In Ohio. *o*, in the western part of Missouri. *p*, see *a*, Sec. 101. *q*, dissolution between the United Order of Kirtland, and the United Order of the City of Zion.

cumstances will admit and the voice of the council
direct.

54. And again, a commandment I give unto you
concerning your stewardship which I have appointed
unto you.

55. Behold, all these properties are mine, or else
your faith is vain, and ye are found hypocrites, and
the covenants which ye have made unto me are
broken;

56. And if the properties are mine, then ye are
stewards, otherwise ye are no stewards.

57. But, verily I say unto you, I have appointed
unto you to be stewards over mine house, even stewards
indeed;

58. And for this purpose I have commanded you to
organize yourselves, even to Shinelah (print) my words,
the fullness of my ʳscriptures, the revelations which I
have given unto you, and which I shall, hereafter, from
time to time give unto you,

59. For the purpose of building up my church and
kingdom on the earth, and to prepare my people for the
time when I shall ˢdwell with them, which is nigh at
hand.

60. And ye shall prepare for yourselves a treasury,
and consecrate it unto my name;

61. And ye shall appoint one among you to keep
the treasury, and he shall be ordained unto this blessing;

62. And there shall be a seal upon the treasury,
and all the sacred things shall be delivered into the
treasury, and no man among you shall call it his own,
or any part of it, for it shall belong to you all with one
accord;

63. And I give it unto you from this very hour:
and now see to it, that ye go to and make use of the
stewardship which I have appointed unto you, exclusive

of the sacred things, for the purpose of Shinelane (printing) these sacred things as I have said ;

64. And the avails of the sacred things shall be had in the treasury, and a seal shall be upon it, and it shall not be used or taken out of the treasury by any one, neither shall the seal be loosed which shall be placed upon it, only by the voice of the order, or by commandment.

65. And thus shall ye preserve the avails of the sacred things in the treasury, for sacred and holy purposes :

66. And this shall be called the sacred treasury of the Lord ; and a seal shall be kept upon it that it may be holy and consecrated unto the Lord.

67. And again, there shall be another treasury prepared, and a treasurer appointed to keep the treasury, and a seal shall be placed upon it ;

68. And all moneys that you receive in your stewardships, by improving upon the properties which I have appointed unto you, in houses, or in lands, or in cattle, or in all things save it be the holy and sacred writings, which I have reserved unto myself for holy and sacred purposes, shall be cast into the treasury as fast as you receive moneys, by hundreds, or by fifties, or by twenties, or by tens, or by fives ;

69. Or in other words, if any man among you obtain five talents, (dollars,) let him cast them into the treasury ; or if he obtain ten, or twenty, or fifty, or an hundred, let him do likewise ;

70. And let not any man among you say that it is his own, for it shall not be called his, nor any part of it ;

71. And there shall not any part of it be used, or taken out of the treasury, only by the voice and common consent of the order.

72. And this shall be the voice and common consent of the order ; that any man among you, say unto the

treasurer, I have need of this to help me in my stewardship ;

73. If it be five talents, (dollars,) or, if it be ten
talents, (dollars,) or twenty, or fifty, or an hundred,
the treasurer shall give unto him the sum which he
requires, to help him in his stewardship,

74. Until he be found a transgressor, and it is manifest before the council of the order plainly, that he is
an unfaithful and an ‘unwise steward ;

75. But so long as he is in full fellowship, and is
faithful, and wise in his stewardship, this shall be his
token unto the treasurer, that the treasurer shall not
withhold.

76. But in case of transgression, the treasurer shall
be subject unto the council and voice of the order.

77. And in case the treasurer is found an unfaithful,
and an unwise steward, he shall be subject to the council and voice of the order, and shall be removed out of
his place, and another shall be appointed in his stead.

78. And again, verily I say unto you, concerning
your debts, behold it is my will that you should pay all
your debts ;

79. And it is my will that you should humble yourselves before me, and obtain this blessing by your
diligence and humility, and the prayer of faith ;

80. And inasmuch as you are diligent and humble,
and exercise the prayer of faith, behold, I will soften
the hearts of those to whom you are in debt, until I
shall send means unto you for your deliverance.

81. Therefore write speedily unto Cainhannoch,
(New York,) and write according to that which shall
be dictated by my Spirit, and I will soften the hearts of
those to whom you are in debt, that it shall be taken
away out of their minds to bring affliction upon you.

82. And inasmuch as ye are humble and faithful,

‘, Luke 16: 1—12.

and call upon my name, behold, I will give you the victory.

83. I give unto you a promise, that you shall be delivered this once out of your bondage ;

84. Inasmuch as you obtain a chance to loan money by hundreds, or thousands, even until you shall loan enough to deliver yourselves from bondage, it is your privilege ;

85. And pledge the properties which I have put into your hands, this once, by giving your names by common consent or otherwise, as it shall seem good unto you.

86. I give unto you this privilege, this once, and behold, if you proceed to do the things which I have laid before you, according to my commandments, all these things are mine, and ye are my stewards, and the master will not suffer his house to be broken up. Even so. Amen.

SECTION 105.

Revelation given through Joseph, the Seer, on Fishing River, Missouri, June 22nd, 1834.

1. Verily I say unto you who have assembled yourselves together that you may learn my will concerning the ^aredemption of mine afflicted people.

2. Behold, I say unto you, were it not for the transgressions of my people, speaking concerning the church and not individuals, they might have been redeemed even now ;

3. But behold, they have not learned to be obedient to the things which I required at their hands, but are

---

a, see *h,* Sec. 103.

full of all manner of evil, and do not impart of their substance, as becometh saints, to the poor and afflicted among them,

4. And are not united according to the [b]union required by the law of the celestial kingdom;

5. And Zion cannot be built up unless it is by the principles of the law of the celestial kingdom, otherwise I cannot receive her unto myself;

6. And my people must needs be chastened until they learn obedience, if it must needs be, by the things which they suffer.

7. I speak not concerning those who are appointed to lead my people, who are the first elders of my church, for they are not all under this condemnation;

8. But I speak concerning my churches abroad—there are many who will say, Where is their God? Behold, he will deliver them in time of trouble, otherwise we will not go up unto Zion, and will keep our moneys.

9. Therefore, in consequence of the transgression of my people, it is expedient in me that mine elders should [c]wait for a little season for the redemption of Zion,

10. That they themselves may be prepared, and that my people may be taught more perfectly, and have experience, and know more perfectly concerning their duty, and the things which I require at their hands.

11. And this cannot be brought to pass until mine elders are [d]endowed with power from on high;

12. For behold, I have prepared a great endowment and blessing to be poured out upon them, inasmuch as they are faithful and continue in humility before me;

13. Therefore it is expedient in me that mine elders

b, see a, Sec. 51. 33: 27. 104: 1. 105: 4, 5.   c, vers. 10—19.
d, see x, Sec. 38.

should wait for a little season, for the redemption of Zion ;

14. For behold, I do not require at their hands to *fight the battles of Zion ; for, as I said in a former commandment, even so will I fulfill. I will fight your battles.

15. Behold, the *f*destroyer I have sent forth to destroy and lay waste mine enemies : and not many years hence they shall not be left to pollute mine heritage, and to blaspheme my name upon the lands which I have consecrated for the gathering together of my saints.

16. Behold, I have commanded my servant Baurak Ale (Joseph Smith, jr.) to say unto the *g*strength of my house, even my warriors, my young men, and middle-aged, to gather together for the redemption of my people, and throw down the towers of mine enemies, and scatter their watchmen ;

17. But the strength of mine house have not hearkened unto my words ;

18. But inasmuch as there are those who have hearkened unto my words, I have prepared a blessing and an *h*endowment for them, if they continue faithful.

19. I have heard their prayers, and will accept their offering ; and it is expedient in me, that they should be brought thus far for a trial of their faith.

20. And now, verily I say unto you, a commandment I give unto you, that as many as have come up hither, that can stay in the region round about, let them stay ;

21. And those that cannot stay, who have families in the east, let them tarry for a little season, inasmuch as my servant Joseph shall appoint unto them ;

22. For I will counsel him concerning this matter,

---

e, 98 : 37.   *f*, see *f* and *g*, Sec. 1.   *g*, 101 : 55. 103 : 22, 30.
h, see *z*, Sec. 38.

and all things whatsoever he shall appoint unto them shall be fulfilled.

23. And let all my people who dwell in the regions round about be very faithful, and prayerful, and humble before me, and reveal not the things which I have revealed unto them, until it is wisdom in me that they should be revealed.

24. Talk not of judgment, neither boast of faith, nor of mighty works, but carefully gather together, as much in one region as can be consistently with the feelings of the people;

25. And behold, I will give unto you favor and grace in their eyes, that you may rest in peace and safety, while you are saying unto the people, Execute judgment and justice for us according to law, and 'redress us of our wrongs.

26. Now, behold, I say unto you, my friends, in this way you may find favor in the eyes of the people, until the army of Israel becomes ʲvery great;

27. And I will soften the hearts of the people, as I did the heart of Pharaoh, from time to time, until my servant Baurak Ale, (Joseph Smith, jr.,) and Baneemy, (mine elders,) whom I have appointed, shall have time to gather up the strength of my house,

28. And to have sent wise men, to fulfill that which I have commanded concerning the ᵏpurchasing of all the lands in Jackson county that can be purchased, and in the adjoining counties round about;

29. For it is my will that these lands should be purchased, and after they are purchased that my saints should possess them according to the laws of ˡconsecration which I have given;

30. And after these lands are ᵐpurchased, I will hold the armies of Israel guiltless in taking possession of their own lands, which they have previously purchased with their moneys, and of throwing down the

towers of mine enemies that may be upon them, and scattering their watchmen, and avenging me of mine enemies unto the third and fourth generation of them that hate me.

31. But firstly, let my army become *n*very great, and let it be sanctified before me, that it may become *o*fair as the sun, and clear as the moon, and that her banners may be terrible unto all nations;

32. That the kingdoms of this world may be constrained to acknowledge, that the *p*kingdom of Zion is in very deed the kingdom of our God and his Christ; therefore, let us become subject unto her laws.

33. Verily I say unto you, it is expedient in me that the first elders of my church should receive their *q*endowment from on high in my house, which I have commanded to be built unto my name in the land of Kirtland;

34. And let those commandments which I have given concerning Zion and her *r*law be executed, and fulfilled, after her redemption.

35. There has been a day of calling, but the time has come for a day of *s*choosing, and let those be chosen that are worthy;

36. And it shall be manifest unto my servant, by the voice of the Spirit, those that are chosen, and they shall be sanctified;

37. And inasmuch as they follow the counsel which they receive, they shall have power *t*after many days to accomplish all things pertaining to Zion.

38. And again I say unto you, sue for peace, not only the people that have smitten you, but also to all people;

39. And lift up an ensign of peace, and make a proclamation for peace unto the ends of the earth;

40. And make proposals for peace unto those who

---

n, ver. 26.   o, 5 : 14.   p, Isa. 60 : 1—5, 11, 12.   q, see x,
Sec. 38.   r, Sec. 42.   s, see e, Sec. 95.   t, see 2 s,
Sec. 101.

have smitten you, according to the voice of the Spirit
which is in you, and all things shall work together for
your good ;

41. Therefore be faithful, and behold, and lo, I am
with you even unto the end. Even so. Amen.

SECTION 106.

*Revelation given through Joseph, the Seer, at Kirtland,
Ohio, November 25th, 1834.*

1. It is my will that my servant Warren A. Cowdery
should be appointed and ordained a presiding High
Priest over my church, in the land of Freedom and the
regions round about ;

2. And should preach my *a*everlasting gospel, and
lift up his voice and warn the people, not only in his
own place, but in the adjoining countries,

3. And devote his whole time in this high and holy
calling which I now give unto him, seeking diligently
the kingdom of heaven and its righteousness, and all
things necessary shall be added thereunto, for the laborer
is worthy of his hire.

4. And again, verily I say unto you, the *b*coming
of the Lord draweth nigh, and it overtaketh the world
as a thief in the night :

5. Therefore, gird up your loins that you may be
the *c*children of the light, and that day shall not overtake you as a thief.

6. And again, verily I say unto you, there was joy
in heaven when my servant Warren bowed to my
sceptre, and separated himself from the crafts of men :

---

a, see *b*, Sec. 18.   *b*, see *e*, Sec. 1.   *c*, see *e*, Sec. 1.

7. Therefore, blessed is my servant Warren, for I will have mercy on him ; and notwithstanding the vanity of his heart, I will lift him up, inasmuch as he will humble himself before me ;

8. And I will give him grace and assurance wherewith he may stand, and if he continue to be a faithful witness and a light unto the church, I have prepared a crown for him in the ᵈmansions of my Father. Even so. Amen.

SECTION 107.

A Revelation through Joseph, the Prophet, given at Kirtland, Ohio, on Priesthood ; the fore part, or the first fifty-eight verses, being given March 28th, 1835 ; the other items were revealed at sundry times.

1. There are, in the church, ᵃtwo Priesthoods, namely, the Melchisedek, and Aaronic, including the Levitical priesthood.

2. Why the first is called the Melchisedek Priesthood, is because Melchisedek was such a great High Priest.

3. Before his day it was called *the Holy Priesthood, after the order of the Son of God ;*

4. But out of respect or reverence to the name of the Supreme Being, to avoid the too frequent repetition of his name, they, the church, in ancient days, called that Priesthood after Melchisedek, or the Melchisedek Priesthood.

---

d, see *a,* Sec. 59.

a, 84 : 6—41.

5. All other authorities or offices in the church are *b*appendages to this Priesthood ;

6. But there are two divisions or grand heads—one is the Melchisedek Priesthood, and the other is the Aaronic, or Levitical priesthood.

7. The office of an *c*elder comes under the Priesthood of Melchisedek.

8. The Melchisedek Priesthood holds the right of Presidency, and has power and authority *d*over all the offices in the church in all ages of the world, to administer in spiritual things.

9. The Presidency of the High Priesthood, after the order of Melchisedek, have a right to officiate in all the offices in the church.

10. High Priests after the order of the Melchisedek Priesthood, have a right to officiate in their own standing, under the direction of the Presidency, in administering spiritual things; and also in the office of an elder, priest, (of the Levitical order,) teacher, deacon, and member.

11. An elder has a right to officiate in his stead when the High Priest is not present.

12. The High Priest and elder are to administer in spiritual things, agreeable to the covenants and commandments of the church ; and they have a right to officiate in all these offices of the church when there are no higher authorities present.

13. The second priesthood is called the priesthood of *e*Aaron, because it was conferred upon Aaron and his seed, throughout all their generations.

14. Why it is called the lesser priesthood, is because it is an *f*appendage to the greater or the Melchisedek Priesthood, and has power in administering outward ordinances.

15. The bishopric is the presidency of this priesthood and holds the keys or authority of the same.

b, vers. 6—20.   84 : 18—30.   c, vers. 11, 12, 89.   d, vers. 64, 65.   e, 84 : 27.   f, ver. 5.

16. No man has a legal right to this office, to hold the keys of this priesthood, except he be a literal descendant of Aaron.

17. But as a High Priest of the Melchisedek Priesthood has authority to officiate in all the lesser offices, he may officiate in the office of bishop when no literal descendant of Aaron can be found, provided he is called and set apart and ordained unto this power by the hands of the *g*Presidency of the Melchisedek Priesthood.

18. The power and authority of the Higher or Melchisedek Priesthood, is to hold the keys of all the spiritual blessings of the church—

19. To have the privilege of receiving the *h*mysteries of the kingdom of heaven—to have the *i*heavens opened unto them—to commune with the *j*general assembly and church of the first born, and to enjoy the communion and *k*presence of God the Father, and Jesus the Mediator of the new covenant.

20. The power and authority of the lesser, or Aaronic priesthood, is to hold the keys of the *l*ministering of angels, and to administer in outward ordinances, the letter of the gospel—the *m*baptism of repentance for the remission of sins, agreeable to the covenants and commandments.

21. Of necessity there are presidents, or presiding offices growing out of, or appointed of or from among those who are ordained to the several offices in these two priesthoods.

22. Of the Melchisedek Priesthood, *n*three Presiding High Priests, chosen by the body, appointed and ordained to that office, and upheld by the confidence, faith, and prayer of the church, form a quorum of the Presidency of the church.

23. The Twelve traveling counselors are called to be

g, 68 : 15, 19—24.   *h*, 84 : 19—24.   *i*, 84 : 19—24.   *j*, Heb.
12 : 22—24.   *k*, 84 : 22—24.   *l*, 84 : 26.   *m*, 84 : 27.
n, see *j*, Sec. 68.

the Twelve apostles, or special witnesses of the name of Christ in all the world; thus differing from other officers in the church in the duties of their calling.

24. And they form a quorum, °equal in authority and power to the three Presidents previously mentioned.

25. The seventy are also called to preach the gospel, and to be especial witnesses unto the Gentiles and in all the world. Thus differing from other officers in the church in the duties of their calling ;

26. And they form a quorum ?equal in authority to that of the Twelve special witnesses or apostles just named.

27. And every decision made by either of these quorums, must be by the unanimous voice of the same ; that is, every member in each quorum must be agreed to its decisions, in order to make their decisions of the same power or validity one with the other.

28. (A majority may form a quorum, when circumstances render it impossible to be otherwise.)

29. Unless this is the case, their decisions are not entitled to the same blessings which the decisions of a quorum of three Presidents were anciently, who were ordained after the order of Melchisedek, and were righteous and holy men.

30. The decisions of these quorums, or either of them, are to be made in all righteousness, in holiness, and lowliness of heart, meekness and long-suffering, and in faith, and virtue, and knowledge, temperance, patience, godliness, brotherly kindness and charity ;

31. Because the promise is, if these things abound in them, they shall not be unfruitful in the knowledge of the Lord.

32. And in case that any decision of these quorums is made in ?unrighteousness, it may be brought before

---

o, vers. 36, 37.   p, ver. 23.   q, an Appeal may be had before a general assembly of councils.

a general assembly of the several quorums, which constitute the spiritual authorities of the church, otherwise there can be no appeal from their decision.

33. The Twelve are a traveling presiding High Council, to officiate in the name of the Lord, under the direction of the Presidency of the church, agreeable to the institution of heaven ; to build up the church, and regulate all the affairs of the same in all nations ; *first unto the Gentiles, and *secondly unto the Jews.

34. The *seventy are to act in the name of the Lord, under the direction of the Twelve or the traveling High Council, in building up the church and regulating all the affairs of the same in all nations—first unto the Gentiles and then to the Jews ;

35. The Twelve being sent out, holding the keys, to open the door by the proclamation of the gospel of Jesus Christ—and first unto the Gentiles and then unto the Jews.

36. The standing High Councils, at the Stakes of Zion, form a quorum *equal in authority, in the affairs of the church, in all their decisions, to the quorum of the Presidency, or to the traveling High Council.

37. The High Council in Zion, form a quorum *equal in authority, in the affairs of the church, in all their decisions, to the Councils of the Twelve at the Stakes of Zion.

38. It is the duty of the traveling High Council to call upon the *seventy, when they need assistance, to fill the several calls for preaching and administering the gospel, instead of any others.

39. It is the duty of the Twelve, in all large branches of the church, to ordain *evangelical ministers, as they shall be designated unto them by revelation.

40. The order of this Priesthood was confirmed to

r, see *o*, Sec. 18.   *s*, see *o*, Sec. 18.   *t*, vers. 25, 26, 35, 38, 90, 93—98.   *u*, ver. 37.   *v*, ver. 36.   *w*, ver. 34. *x*, Patriarchs.

be handed down from father to son, and rightly belongs to the literal descendants of the chosen seed, to whom the promises were made.

41. This order was instituted in the days of Adam, and came down by lineage in the following manner :—

42. From Adam to Seth, who was ordained by Adam at the age of 69 years, and was blessed by him three years previous to his (Adam's) death, and received the promise of God by his father, that his posterity should be the chosen of the Lord, and that they should be preserved unto the end of the earth,

43. Because he (Seth) was a perfect man, and his likeness was the express likeness of his father's, insomuch that he seemed to be like unto his father in all things, and could be distinguished from him only by his age.

44. Enos was ordained at the age of 134 years and four months, by the hand of Adam.

45. God called upon Cainan in the wilderness, in the fortieth year of his age, and he met Adam in journeying to the place Shedolamak. He was 87 years old when he received his ordination.

46. Mahalaleel was 496 years and seven days old when he was ordained by the hand of Adam, who also blessed him.

47. Jared was 200 years old when he was ordained under the hand of Adam, who also blessed him.

48. Enoch was 25 years old when he was ordained under the hand of Adam, and he was 65 and Adam blessed him.

49. And he saw the Lord, and he walked with him, and was before his face continually ; and he walked with God 365 years, making him 430 years old when he was translated.

50. Methuselah was 100 years old when he was ordained under the hand of Adam.

51. Lamech was 32 years old when he was ordained under the hand of Seth.

52. Noah was 10 years old when he was ordained under the hand of Methuselah.

53. Three years previous to the death of Adam, he called Seth, Enos, Cainan, Mahalaleel, Jared, Enoch, and Methuselah, who were all *y*High Priests, with the residue of his posterity who were righteous, into the valley of *z*Adam-ondi-Ahman, and there bestowed upon them his last blessing.

54. And the Lord [2a]appeared unto them, and the rose up and blessed Adam, and called him [2b]Michael, the Prince, the Archangel.

55. And the Lord administered comfort unto Adam, and said unto him, I have set thee to be at the head— a multitude of nations shall come of thee, and thou art a [2c]prince over them for ever.

56. And Adam stood up in the midst of the congregation, and notwithstanding he was bowed down with age, being full of the Holy Ghost, predicted whatsoever should befall his posterity unto the [2d]latest generation.

57. These things were all written in the book of Enoch, and are to be testified of in due time.

58. It is the duty of the Twelve, also, to ordain and set in order all the other officers of the church, agreeable to the revelation which says :

59. To the church of Christ in the land of Zion, in addition to the church laws respecting church business—

60. Verily, I say unto you, says the Lord of hosts, there must needs be [2e]presiding elders to preside over those who are of the office of an elder ;

61. And also priests to preside over those who are of the office of a priest ;

---

y, Pearl of Great Price, pp. 13, 14.   *z*, see *l*, Sec. 78.   2*a*, Pearl of Great Price, p. 18.   2*b*, 78 : 16.   2*c*, 78 : 16. Dan. 12 : 1. 2*d*, Pearl of Great Price, p. 14.   2*e*, vers. 89, 90.

62. And also teachers to preside over those who are of the office of a teacher ; in like manner, and also the deacons ;

63. Wherefore, from deacon to teacher, and from teacher to priest, and from priest to elder, severally as they are appointed, according to the covenants and commandments of the church.

64. Then comes the [2f]High Priesthood, which is the greatest of all ;

65. Wherefore it must needs be that one be appointed of the High Priesthood to preside over the Priesthood, and he shall be called President of the High Priesthood of the church ;

66. Or, in other words, the Presiding High Priest over the High Priesthood of the church.

67. From the same comes the administering of ordinances and blessings upon the church, by the laying on of the hands.

68. Wherefore the office of a bishop is not equal unto it ; for the [2g]office of a bishop is in administering all temporal things ;

69. Nevertheless a bishop must be chosen from the High Priesthood, unless he is a [2h]literal descendant of Aaron ;

70. For unless he is a literal descendant of Aaron he cannot hold the keys of that priesthood.

71. Nevertheless, a High Priest that is after the order of Melchisedek, may be set apart unto the ministering of temporal things, having a knowledge of them by the Spirit of truth,

72. And also to be a judge in Israel, to do the business of the church, to sit in judgment upon transgressors upon testimony as it shall be laid before him according to the laws, by the assistance of his counselors, whom he has chosen, or will choose among the elders of the church.

2f, the Melchisedek.   2g, see k, Sec. 68.   2h, see k, Sec. 68.

73. This is the duty of a bishop who is not a literal descendant of Aaron, but has been ordained to the High Priesthood after the order of Melchisedek.

74. Thus shall he be a judge, even a common judge among the inhabitants of Zion, or in a Stake of Zion, or in any branch of the church where he shall be set apart unto this ministry, until the borders of Zion are enlarged, and it becomes necessary to have other bishops or judges in Zion, or elsewhere ;

75. And inasmuch as there are other bishops appointed they shall act in the same office.

76. But a literal descendant of Aaron has a legal right to the presidency of this priesthood, to the keys of this ministry, to act in the office of bishop independently, without counselors, except in a case where a President of the High Priesthood, after the order of Melchisedek, is tried, to sit as a judge in Israel.

77. And the decision of either of these councils, agreeable to the commandment which says,

78. Again, verily, I say unto you, the most important business of the church, and the most difficult cases of the church, inasmuch as there is not satisfaction upon the decision of the bishop or judges, it shall be handed over and carried up unto the Council of the church, before the Presidency of the High Priesthood ;

79. And the Presidency of the Council of the High Priesthood shall have power to call other High Priests, even twelve, to assist as counselors; and thus the Presidency of the High Priesthood and its counselors shall have power to decide upon testimony according to the laws of the church.

80. And after this decision it shall be had in remembrance no more before the Lord ; for this is the highest Council of the church of God, and a final decision upon controversies in spiritual matters.

81. There is not any person belonging to the church who is exempt from this Council of the church.

82. And inasmuch as a President of the High Priesthood shall transgress, he shall be had in remembrance before the common council of the church, who shall be assisted by twelve counselors of the High Priesthood ;

83. And their decision upon his head shall be an end of controversy concerning him.

84. Thus, none shall be exempted from the justice and the laws of God, that all things may be done in order and in solemnity before him, according to truth and righteousness.

85. And again, verily I say unto you, the duty of a president over the office of a deacon is to preside over twelve deacons, to sit in council with them, and to teach them their duty—edifying one another, as it is given according to the covenants.

86. And also the duty of the president over the office of the teachers is to preside over twenty-four of the teachers, and to sit in council with them, teaching them the duties of their office, as given in the covenants.

87. Also the duty of the president over the priesthood of Aaron is to preside over forty-eight priests, and sit in council with them, to teach them the duties of their office, as is given in the covenants.

88. This president is to be a bishop ; for this is one of the duties of this priesthood.

89. Again, the duty of the president over the office of elders is to preside over ninety-six elders, and to sit in council with them, and to teach them according to the covenants.

90. This presidency is a distinct one from that of the seventy, and is designed for those who do not travel into all the world.

91. And again, the duty of the President of the

office of the High Priesthood is to preside over the whole church, and to be like unto Moses.

92. Behold, here is wisdom ; yea, to be a [2i]seer, a revelator, a translator, and a prophet, having all the gifts of God which he bestows upon the head of the church.

93. And it is according to the vision, showing the order of the [2j]seventy, that they should have seven presidents to preside over them, chosen out of the number of the seventy;

94. And the seventh president of these presidents is to preside over the six ;

95. And these seven presidents are to choose other seventy besides the first seventy, to whom they belong, and are to preside over them ;

96. And also other seventy, until seven times seventy, if the labor in the vineyard of necessity requires it.

97. And these seventy are to be traveling ministers unto the Gentiles first, and also unto the Jews ;

98. Whereas other officers of the church, who belong not unto the Twelve, neither to the seventy, are not under the responsibility to travel among all nations, but are to travel as their circumstances shall allow, notwithstanding they may hold as high and responsible offices in the church.

99. Wherefore now let every man learn his duty, and to act in the office in which he is appointed, in all diligence.

100. He that is slothful shall not be counted worthy to stand, and he that learns not his duty and shows himself not approved, shall not be counted worthy to stand.   Even so.   Amen.

2i, 21 : 1.   124 : 94, 125.   2j, Joseph Young is the senior president of the seven presidents.

SECTION 108.

A Revelation through Joseph Smith, jr., concerning Lyman Sherman, given at Kirtland, Geauga County, Ohio, December 26th, 1835.

1. Verily thus saith the Lord unto you, my servant Lyman, your sins are forgiven you, because you have obeyed my voice in coming up hither this morning to receive counsel of him whom I have appointed.

2. Therefore, let your soul be at rest concerning your spiritual standing, and resist no more my voice ;

3. And arise up and be more careful henceforth, in observing your vows which you have made, and do make, and you shall be blessed with exceeding great blessings.

4. Wait patiently until the *a*solemn assembly shall be called of my servants, then you shall be remembered with the first of mine elders, and receive right by ordination with the rest of mine elders, whom I have chosen.

5. Behold, this is the promise of the Father unto you if you continue faithful ;

6. And it shall be fulfilled upon you in that day that you shall have right to preach my gospel wheresoever I shall send you, from henceforth from that time.

7. Therefore, strengthen your brethren in all your conversation, in all your prayers, and in all your exhortations, and in all your doings ;

8. And behold ! and lo ! I am with you to bless you, and deliver you for ever.   Amen.

---

a, see 2r, Sec. 88.

SECTION 109.

The following Prayer was given by revelation to Joseph, the Seer, and was repeated in the Kirtland Temple at the time of its dedication, March 27th, 1836.

1. Thanks be to thy name, O Lord God of Israel, who keepest covenant and showest mercy unto thy servants who walk uprightly before thee, with all their hearts ;

2. Thou who hast *a*commanded thy servants to build a house to thy name in this place.   (Kirtland.)

3. And now thou beholdest, O Lord, that thy servants have done according to thy commandment,

4. And now we ask thee, Holy Father, in the name of Jesus Christ, the Son of thy bosom, in whose name alone, salvation can be administered to the children of men, we ask thee, O Lord, to accept of this house, the workmanship of the hands of us, thy servants, which thou didst command us to build ;

5. For thou knowest that we have done this work through great tribulation ; and out of our poverty we have given of our substance, to build a house to thy name, that the Son of man might have a place to manifest himself to his people.

6. And as thou hast said in a *b*revelation, given to us, calling us thy friends, saying, " Call your solemn assembly, as I have commanded you ;

7. And as all have not faith, seek ye diligently, and teach one another words of wisdom ; yea, seek ye out of the best books, words of wisdom, seek learning even by study, and also by faith.

8. Organize yourselves ; prepare every needful

---

a, see 3*s*, Sec. 88.   *b*, 88 : 117—120.

thing, and establish a house, even a house of prayer, a house of fasting, a house of faith, a house of learning, a house of glory, a house of order, a house of God,

9. That your incomings may be in the name of the Lord, that your outgoings may be in the name of the Lord, that all your salutations may be in the name of the Lord, with uplifted hands unto the Most High."

10. And now, Holy Father, we ask thee to assist us, thy people, with thy grace, in calling our ᶜsolemn assembly, that it may be done to thy honor, and to thy divine acceptance,

11. And in a manner that we may be found worthy, in thy sight, to secure a fulfillment of the promises which thou hast made unto us, thy people, in the revelations given unto us ;

12. That thy glory may rest down upon thy people, and upon this thy house, which we now dedicate to thee, that it may be sanctified and consecrated to be holy, and that thy holy presence may be continually in this house,

13. And that all people who shall enter upon the threshold of the Lord's house, may feel thy power, and feel constrained to acknowledge that thou hast sanctified it, and that it is thy house, a place of thy holiness.

14. And do thou grant, Holy Father, that all those who shall worship in this house, may be taught words of wisdom out of the ᵈbest books, and that they may seek learning even by study, and also by faith, as thou hast said ;

15. And that they may grow up in thee, and receive a fullness of the Holy Ghost, and be organized according to thy laws, and be prepared to obtain every needful thing ;

16. And that this house may be a house of prayer, a house of fasting, a house of faith, a house of glory and of God, even thy house ;

---

17. That all the incomings of thy people, into this house, may be in the name of the Lord ;

18. That all the outgoings from this house may be in the name of the Lord ;

19. And that all their salutations may be in the name of the Lord, with holy hands, uplifted to the Most High ;

20. And that no *unclean thing shall be permitted to come into thy house to pollute it ;

21. And when thy people transgress, any of them, they may speedily repent, and return unto thee, and find favor in thy sight, and be restored to the blessings which thou hast ordained to be poured out upon those who shall reverence thee in thy house.

22. And we ask thee, Holy Father, that thy servants may go forth from this house, armed with thy power, and that thy name may be upon them, and thy glory be round about them, and thine *angels have charge over them ;

23. And from this place they may bear exceedingly great and glorious tidings, in truth, unto the *ends of the earth, that they may know that this is thy work, and that thou hast put forth thy hand, to fulfill that which thou hast spoken by the mouths of the prophets, concerning the last days.

24. We ask thee, Holy Father, to establish the people that shall worship, and honorably hold a name and standing in this thy house, to all generations, and for eternity,

25. That no weapon *formed against them shall prosper ; that he who diggeth a pit for them shall fall into the same himself ;

26. That no combination of wickedness shall have power to rise up and prevail over thy people upon whom thy name shall be put in this house ;

---

e, 97 : 15—17.   *f*, 84 : 88.   *g*, see *b*, Sec. 1.   *h*, Isa.
54 : 17.

27. And if any people shall ᶦrise against this people, that thine anger be kindled against them,

28. And if they shall smite this people, thou wilt smite them, thou wilt fight for thy people as thou didst in the day of battle, that they may be delivered from the hands of all their enemies.

29. We ask thee, Holy Father, to confound, and astonish, and bring to ʲshame and confusion, all those who have spread lying reports, abroad, over the world, against thy servant, or servants, if they will not repent, when the ᵏeverlasting gospel shall be proclaimed in their ears,

30. And that all their works may be brought to naught, and be swept away by the ˡhail, and by the judgments which thou wilt send upon them in thine anger, that there may be an ᵐend to lyings and slanders against thy people ;

31. For thou knowest, O Lord, that thy servants have been innocent before thee in bearing record of thy name, for which they have suffered these things ;

32. Therefore we plead before thee a full and complete deliverance from under this yoke ;

33. Break it off, O Lord ; break it off from the necks of thy servants, by thy power, that we may rise up in the midst of this generation and do thy work.

34. O Jehovah, have mercy upon this people, and as all men sin, forgive the transgressions of thy people, and let them be blotted out forever.

35. Let the ⁿanointing of thy ministers be sealed upon them with power from on high ;

36. Let it be fulfilled upon them, as upon those on the day of Pentecost, let the ᵒgift of tongues be poured out upon thy people, even cloven tongues as of fire, and the interpretation thereof,

---

ᶦ, 98 : 34—33.   ʲ, Isa. 28 : 15—19.   Jer. 16 : 19.   ᵏ, see b,
Sec. 18.   ˡ, see j.   m, III. Nep. 21 : 11, 19—21.   29 : 4, 9.   Chap.
30.   Mor. 8 : 21, 41.   n, 124 : 39.   o, Acts 2 : 2—12.

37. And let thy house be filled, as with a rushing mighty wind, with thy glory.

38. Put upon thy servants the testimony of the covenant, that when they go out and proclaim thy word, they may *p*seal up the law, and prepare the hearts of thy saints for all those judgments thou art about to send, in thy wrath, upon the inhabitants of the earth, because of their transgressions, that thy people may not faint in the day of trouble.

39. And whatsoever city thy servants shall enter, and the people of that city receive their testimony, let thy peace and thy salvation be upon that city, that they may *q*gather out of that city the righteous, that they may come forth to Zion, or to her Stakes, the places of thine appointment, with songs of everlasting joy ;

40. And until this be accomplished, let not thy judgments fall upon that city.

41. And whatsoever city thy servants shall enter, and the people of that city receive not the testimony of thy servants, and thy servants warn them to save themselves from this untoward generation, let it be upon *r*that city according to that which thou hast spoken by the mouths of thy prophets ;

42. But deliver thou, O Jehovah, we beseech thee, thy servants from their hands, and cleanse them from their blood.

43. O Lord, we delight not in the destruction of our fellow men ! their souls are precious before thee ;

44. But thy word must be fulfilled ; help thy servants to say, with thy grace assisting them, thy will be done, O Lord, and not ours.

45. We know that thou hast spoken by the mouth of thy prophets terrible things concerning the wicked, in the last days—that thou wilt pour out thy judgments, without measure ;

---

p, see *d,* Sec. 1.   *q,* see *j,* Sec. 10.   *r,* see *f* and *g,* Sec. 1.

46. Therefore, O Lord, deliver thy people from the calamity of the wicked; enable thy servants to ᵉseal up the law, and bind up the testimony, that they may be prepared against the day of burning.

47. We ask thee, Holy Father, to remember those who have been driven (by the inhabitants of Jackson County, Missouri) from the lands of their inheritance, and break off, O Lord, this yoke of affliction that has been put upon them.

48. Thou knowest, O Lord, that they have been greatly oppressed and afflicted by wicked men, and our hearts flow out with sorrow, because of their grievous burdens.

49. O Lord, how long wilt thou suffer this people to bear this affliction, and the cries of their innocent ones to ascend up in thine ears, and their blood come up in testimony before thee, and not make a display of thy testimony in their behalf?

50. Have mercy, O Lord, upon that wicked mob, who have driven thy people, that they may cease to spoil, that they may repent of their sins, if repentance is to be found;

51. But if they will not, make bare thine arm, O Lord, and ᶠredeem that which thou didst appoint a Zion unto thy people!

52. And if it cannot be otherwise, that the cause of thy people may not fail before thee, ᵘmay thine anger be kindled, and thine indignation fall upon them, that they may be wasted away, both root and branch, from under heaven;

53. But inasmuch as they will repent, thou art gracious and merciful, and wilt turn away thy wrath, when thou lookest upon the face of thine anointed.

54. Have mercy, O Lord, upon all the nations of the earth, have mercy upon the rulers of our land, may those principles which were so honorably and nobly

defended, viz., the ᵛConstitution of our land, by our fathers, be established for ever;

55. Remember the kings, the princes, the nobles, and the great ones of the earth, and all people, and the churches, all the poor, the needy, and afflicted ones of the earth,

56. That their hearts may be softened, when thy servants shall go out from thy house, O Jehovah, to bear testimony of thy name, that their prejudices may give way before the truth, and thy people may obtain favor in the sight of all,

57. That all the ends of the earth may know that we thy servants have ʷheard thy voice, and that thou hast sent us,

58. That from among all these, thy servants the sons of Jacob may gather out the righteous to build a ˣholy city to thy name, as thou hast commanded them.

59. We ask thee to appoint unto Zion other ʸStakes, besides this one which thou hast appointed, that the gathering of thy people may roll on in great power and majesty, that thy work may be cut short in righteousness.

60. Now these words, O Lord, we have spoken before thee, concerning the revelations and commandments which thou hast given unto us, who are identified with the Gentiles;

61. But thou knowest that thou hast a great love for the children of Jacob, who have been scattered upon the mountains, for a long time, in a cloudy and dark day;

62. We therefore ask thee to have mercy upon the children of Jacob, that Jerusalem, from ᶻthis hour, may begin to be redeemed,

63. And the yoke of bondage may begin to be broken off from the house of David,

---

64. And the children of Judah may begin to return to the lands which thou didst give to Abraham, their father;

65. And cause that the [2a]remnants of Jacob, who have been cursed and smitten, because of their transgression, be converted from their wild and savage condition, to the fullness of the everlasting gospel,

66. That they may lay down their weapons of bloodshed, and cease their rebellions;

67. And may all the scattered remnants of Israel, who have been driven to the ends of the earth, come to a knowledge of the truth, believe in the Messiah, and be redeemed from oppression, and rejoice before thee.

68. O Lord, remember thy servant, Joseph Smith, junior, and all his afflictions and persecutions, how he has covenanted with Jehovah, and vowed to thee, O mighty God of Jacob, and the commandments which thou hast given unto him, and that he hath sincerely striven to do thy will.

69. Have mercy, O Lord, upon his wife and children, that they may be exalted in thy presence, and preserved by thy fostering hand;

70. Have mercy upon all their immediate connexions, that their prejudices may be broken up, and swept away as with a flood, that they may be converted and redeemed with Israel, and know that thou art God.

71. Remember, O Lord, the presidents, even all the presidents of thy church, that thy right hand may exalt them, with all their families, and their immediate connexions, that their names may be perpetuated, and had in everlasting remembrance, from generation to generation.

72. Remember all thy church, O Lord, with all their families, and all their immediate connexions, with

all their sick and afflicted ones, with all the poor and meek of the earth, that the [2b]kingdom which thou hast set up without hands, may become a great mountain, and fill the whole earth ;

73. That thy [2c]church may come forth out of the wilderness of darkness, and shine forth [2d]fair as the moon, clear as the sun, and terrible as an army with banners,

74. And be adorned as a bride for that day when thou shalt [2e]unvail the heavens, and cause the [2f]mountains to flow down at thy presence, and the valleys to be exalted, the rough places made smooth ; that thy glory may fill the earth,

75. That when the trump shall sound [2g]for the dead we shall be caught up in the cloud to meet thee, that we may ever be with the Lord,

76. That our garments may be pure, that we may be clothed upon with robes of righteousness, with palms in our hands, and crowns of glory upon our heads, and reap eternal joy for all our sufferings.

77. O Lord God Almighty, hear us in these our petitions, and answer us from heaven, thy holy habitation, where thou sittest enthroned, with glory, honor, power, majesty, might, dominion, truth, justice, judgment, mercy, and an infinity of fullness, from everlasting to everlasting.

78. O hear, O hear, O hear us, O Lord, and answer these petitions, and accept the dedication of this house unto thee, the work of our hands, which we have built unto thy name !

79. And also this church, to put upon it thy name ; and help us by the power of thy Spirit, that we may mingle our voices with those bright, shining seraphs around thy throne, with acclamations of praise, singing, Hosanna to God and the Lamb ;

2b, see x, Sec. 35.　　　2c, see a, Sec. 1.　　　2d, see i, Sec. 5.
2e, see d, Sec. 1.　　2f, 133 : 44.　　2g, see m, Sec. 29.

80. And let these thine [2h]anointed ones be clothed
with salvation, and thy saints shout aloud for joy.
Amen, and Amen.

SECTION 110.

*Visions manifested to Joseph, the Seer, and Oliver Cow-
dery in the Kirtland Temple, April 3rd, 1836.*

1. The [a]vail was taken from our minds, and the eyes
of our understanding were opened.

2. We [b]saw the Lord standing upon the breast work
of the pulpit, before us, and under his feet was a paved
work of pure gold in color like amber.

3. His eyes were as a flame of fire, the hair of his
head was white like the pure snow, his countenance
shone above the brightness of the sun, and his voice
was as the sound of the rushing of great waters, even
the voice of Jehovah, saying—

4. I am the first and the last, I am he who liveth,
I am he who was slain, I am your [c]advocate with the
Father.

5. Behold, your sins are forgiven you, you are clean
before me, therefore lift up your heads and rejoice,

6. Let the hearts of your brethren rejoice, and let
the hearts of all my people rejoice, who have, with
their might, built this house to my name,

7. For behold, I have accepted this house, and my
name shall be here, and I will manifest myself to my
people in mercy in this house,

---

8. Yea, I will ^dappear unto my servants, and speak
unto them with mine own voice, if my people will keep
my commandments, and do not pollute this holy
house,

9. Yea the hearts of thousands and tens of thousands shall greatly rejoice in consequence of the blessings which shall be poured out, and the ^eendowment
with which my servants have been endowed in this
house ;

10. And the fame of this house shall spread to
foreign lands, and this is the beginning of the blessing
which shall be poured out upon the heads of my people.
Even so. Amen.

11. After this vision closed, the heavens were again
opened unto us, and Moses appeared before us, and committed unto us the ^fkeys of the gathering of Israel
from the four parts of the earth, and the leading of
the ^gten tribes from the land of the north.

12. After this, ^hElias appeared, and committed the
dispensation of the gospel of Abraham, saying, that in
us, and ⁱour seed, all generations after us should be
blessed.

13. After this vision had closed, another great and
glorious vision burst upon us, for ^jElijah the prophet,
who was taken to heaven without tasting death, stood
before us, and said—

14. Behold, the time has fully come, which was
spoken of by the mouth of Malachi, testifying that he
(Elijah) should be sent before the great and dreadful
day of the Lord come,

15. To turn the hearts of the ^kfathers to the children, and the children to the fathers, lest the whole
earth be smitten with a curse.

16. Therefore the keys of this dispensation are com-

d, see o, Sec. 50.   e, see x, Sec. 38.   f, 45 : 43. 133: 13.
g, Keys given to this kingdom, through the Prophet, to lead the ten tribes.
h, see g, Sec. 27.   i, 124 : 57, 58.   j, see a, Sec. 2.   k, see c,
Sec. 2.

mitted into your hands, and by this ye may know that
the great and dreadful day of the Lord is 'near, even
at the doors.

SECTION 111.

*Revelation given through Joseph, the Seer, August
6th, 1836.*

1. I, the Lord your God, am not displeased with
your coming this journey, notwithstanding your follies ;

2. I have much treasure in this city for you, for
the benefit of Zion ; and many people in this city whom
I will gather out in due time for the benefit of Zion,
through your instrumentality !

3. Therefore it is expedient that you should form
acquaintance with men in this city, as you shall be
led, and as it shall be given you ;

4. And it shall come to pass in due time, that I
will give this city into your hands, that you shall
have power over it, insomuch that they shall not discover your secret parts ; and its wealth pertaining to
gold and silver shall be yours.

5. Concern not yourselves about your debts, for I
will give you power to pay them.

6. Concern not yourselves about Zion, for I will
deal mercifully with her.

7. Tarry in this place, and in the regions round
about ;

8. And the place where it is my will that you
should tarry, for the main, shall be signalized unto you
by the peace and power of my Spirit, that shall flow
unto you.

---

l, see e, Sec. 1.

9. This place you may obtain by hire, &c. And inquire diligently concerning the more ancient inhabitants and founders of this city ;

10. For there are more treasures than one for you in this city ;

11. Therefore be ye as wise as serpents and yet without sin, and I will order all things for your good, as fast as ye are able to receive them. Amen.

SECTION 112.

The word of the Lord, given through Joseph, the Prophet, unto Thomas B. Marsh, at Kirtland, July 23rd, 1837, concerning the Twelve Apostles of the Lamb.

1. Verily, thus saith the Lord unto you my servant Thomas, I have heard thy prayers, and thine alms have come up as a memorial before me, in behalf of those thy brethren who were chosen to bear testimony of my name, and to ªsend it abroad among all nations, kindreds, tongues, and people, and ordained through the instrumentality of my servants.

2. Verily I say unto you, there have been some few things in thine heart and with thee with which I, the Lord, was not well pleased ;

3. Nevertheless, inasmuch as thou hast abased thyself thou shalt be exalted; therefore all thy sins are forgiven thee.

4. Let thy heart be of good cheer before my face, and thou shalt bear record of my name, not only unto the Gentiles, but also unto the Jews; and thou shalt send forth my word unto the ends of the earth.

---

a, see g, Sec. 18.

5. Contend thou, therefore, morning by morning, and day after day let thy warning voice go forth, and when the night cometh, let not the inhabitants of the earth slumber because of thy speech.

6. Let thy habitation be known in Zion, and remove not thy house, for I, the Lord, have a great work for thee to do, in publishing my name among the children of men ;

7. Therefore, gird up thy loins for the work. Let thy feet be shod also, for thou art chosen, and thy path lieth among the mountains, and among many nations ;

8. And by thy word many high ones shall be brought low, and by thy word many low ones shall be exalted.

9. Thy voice shall be a rebuke unto the transgressor, and at thy rebuke let the tongue of the slanderer cease its perverseness.

10. Be thou humble, and the Lord thy God shall lead thee by the hand, and give thee answer to thy prayers.

11. I know thy heart, and have heard thy prayers concerning thy brethren. Be not partial towards them in love above many others, but let thy love be for them as for thyself ; and let thy love abound unto all men, and unto all who love my name.

⊦ 12. And pray for thy brethren of the Twelve. Admonish them sharply for my name's sake, and let them be admonished for all their sins, and be ye faithful before me unto my name.

13. And after their temptations, and much tribulation, behold, I, the Lord, will feel after them, and if they harden not their hearts, and stiffen not their necks against me, they shall be converted, and I will heal them.

14. Now, I say unto you, and what I say unto you, I say unto all the ᵇTwelve, Arise and gird up your

---

b, John 21 : 15—17.

loins, take up your cross, follow me, and feed my sheep.

15. Exalt not yourselves; rebel not against my servant Joseph, for verily I say unto you, I am with him, and my hand shall be over him; and the ᶜkeys which I have given unto him, and also to youward, shall not be taken from him till I come.

16. Verily I say unto you, my servant Thomas, Thou art the man whom I have chosen to hold the keys of my kingdom (as pertaining to the Twelve) abroad among all nations,

17. That thou mayest be my servant to unlock the door of the kingdom in all places where my servant Joseph, and my servant Sidney, and my servant Hyrum, cannot come;

18. For on them have I laid the burden of all the churches for a little season;

19. Wherefore, whithersoever they shall send you, go ye, and I will be with you; and in whatsoever place ye shall proclaim my name, an effectual door shall be opened unto you, that they may receive my word; ᵢ

20. Whosoever receiveth my word receiveth me, and whosoever receiveth me, receiveth those (the First Presidency) whom I have sent, whom I have made counselors for my name's sake unto you.

21. And again, I say unto you, That whosoever ye shall send in my name, by the voice of your brethren, the Twelve, duly recommended and authorized by you, shall have ᵈpower to open the door of my kingdom unto any nation whithersoever ye shall send them,

22. Inasmuch as they shall humble themselves before me, and abide in my word, and hearken to the voice of my Spirit.

23. Verily, verily I say unto you, ᵉDarkness covereth the earth, and gross darkness the minds of the people, and ᶠall flesh has become corrupt before my face.

c, see b, Sec. 28.   d, 107 : 34, 35, 38, 95—98.   e, Isa. 60 : 2.
f, 88 : 10—12.

24. Behold, *g*vengeance cometh speedily upon the inhabitants of the earth, a day of wrath, a day of burning, a day of desolation, of weeping, of mourning, and of lamentation, and as a whirlwind it shall come upon all the face of the earth, saith the Lord.

25. And upon my house *h*shall it begin, and from my house shall it go forth, saith the Lord.

26. First among those among you, saith the Lord, who have professed to know my name and have not known me, and have blasphemed against me in the midst of my house, saith the Lord.

27. Therefore, see to it that ye trouble not yourselves concerning the affairs of my church in this place, saith the Lord ;

28. But purify your hearts before me, and then *i*go ye into all the world, and preach my gospel unto every creature who has not received it,

29. And *j*he that believeth and is baptized shall be saved, and he that believeth not, and is not baptized, shall be damned.

30. For unto you, (the Twelve,) and those (the First Presidency) who are appointed with you, to be your counselors and your leaders, is the power of this Priesthood given, for the last days and for the last time, in the which is the *k*dispensation of the fullness of times.

31. Which power you hold in connection with all those who have received a dispensation at any time from the beginning of the creation ;

32. For verily I say unto you, the *l*keys of the dispensation which ye have received, have come down from the fathers ; and last of all, being sent down from heaven unto you.

33. Verily I say unto you, Behold how great is your calling. Cleanse your hearts and your garments,

---

g, see *f* and *g*, Sec. 1.   *h*, I. Pet. 4 : 17, 18.   *i*, see *q*, Sec. 18.
j, see *q*, Sec. 20.   *k*, see *n*, Sec. 27.   *l*, see *b*, Sec. 28.

lest the blood of this generation be required at your hands.

34. Be faithful until I come, for I ^{m}come quickly, and my reward is with me to recompense every man according as his work shall be. I am Alpha and Omega. Amen.

SECTION 113.

Answers by revelation to certain Questions on Scripture, given through Joseph, the Seer, March, 1838.

1. Who is the Stem of Jesse spoken of in the 1st, 2nd, 3rd, 4th, and 5th verses of the 11th chapter of Isaiah?

2. Verily thus saith the Lord, it is Christ.

3. What is the rod spoken of in the first verse of the 11th chapter of Isaiah that should come of the Stem of Jesse?

4. Behold thus saith the Lord, it is a servant in the hands of Christ, who is partly a descendant of Jesse as well as of Ephraim, or of the house of Joseph, on whom there is laid much power.

5. What is the root of Jesse spoken of in the 10th verse of the 11th chapter?

6. Behold thus saith the Lord, it is a descendant of Jesse, as well as of Joseph, unto whom rightly belongs the Priesthood, and the keys of the Kingdom, for an ^{a}ensign, and for the gathering of my people in the last days.

7. Questions by Elias Higbee, as follows—"What is meant by the command in Isaiah, 52nd chapter, 1st

---

m, see e, Sec. 1.

a, see i, Sec. 45.

verse, which saith, put on thy strength O Zion? And what people had Isaiah reference to?"

8. He had reference to those whom God should call in the last days, who should hold the power of Priesthood to bring again Zion, and the redemption of Israel; and to put on her strength is to put on the authority of the Priesthood, which she (Zion) has a right to by lineage; also to return to that power which she had lost.

9. "What are we to understand by Zion's loosing herself from the bands of her neck, 2nd verse?"

10. We are to understand that the scattered remnants are exhorted to return to the Lord from whence they have fallen, which if they do, the promise of the Lord is that he will speak to them, or give them revelation. See the 6th, 7th, and 8th verses. The bands of her neck are the curses of God upon her, or the remnants of Israel in their scattered condition among the Gentiles.

SECTION 114.

Revelation, given through Joseph, the Seer, at Far West, Caldwell County, Missouri, April 17th, 1838.

1. Verily thus saith the Lord, it is wisdom in my servant David W. Patten, that he settle up all his business as soon as he possibly can, and make a disposition of his merchandise, that he may perform a mission unto me next spring, in company with others, even Twelve, including himself, to testify of my name, and bear glad tidings unto all the world;

2. For verily thus saith the Lord, that inasmuch as there are those among you who ᵃdeny my name, others

---

a, 118 : 1. 6.

shall be planted in their stead, and receive their bishopric. Amen.

SECTION 115.

*Revelation, given through Joseph, the Seer, at Far West,
Missouri, April 26th, 1838, making known the will
of God concerning the building up of this place, and
of the Lord's House, &c.*

1. Verily thus saith the Lord unto you, my servant
Joseph Smith, jr., and also my servant Sidney Rigdon,
and also my servant Hyrum Smith, and your counselors who are and shall be appointed hereafter ;

2. And also unto you my servant Edward Partridge,
and his counselors ;

3. And also unto my faithful servants, who are of
the High Council of my church in Zion (for thus it
shall be called,) and unto all the elders and people of
my church of Jesus Christ of Latter-day Saints, scattered abroad in all the world ;

4. For thus shall *a*my church be called in the last
days, even the Church of Jesus Christ of Latter-day
Saints.

5. Verily I say unto you all, Arise and shine forth,
that thy light may be a *b*standard for the nations,

6. And that the gathering together upon the land
of Zion, and upon her Stakes, may be for a *c*defence,
and for a refuge from the storm, and from wrath when
it shall be *d*poured out without mixture upon the whole
earth.

7. Let the city, Far West, be a holy and consecrated

---

a, see a, Sec. 1.   b, see i, Sec. 45.   c, 45 : 62—71.   d, see f
and g, Sec. 1.

land unto me, and it shall be called most holy, for the ground upon which thou standest is holy ;

8. Therefore I command you to build an house unto me, for the gathering together of my saints, that they may worship me ;

9. And let there be a beginning of this work, and a foundation, and a preparatory work, this following summer ;

10. And let the beginning be made on the 4th day of July next, and from that time forth let my people labor diligently to build an house unto my name,

11. And in one year from this day let them 're-commence laying the foundation of my house :

12. Thus let them from that time forth labor diligently until it shall be finished, from the corner stone thereof unto the top thereof, until there shall not any thing remain that is not finished.

13. Verily I say unto you, let not my servant Joseph, neither my servant Sidney, neither my servant Hyrum, get in debt any more for the building of an house unto my name ;

14. But let an house be built unto my name according to the ƒpattern which I will show unto them.

15. And if my people build it not according to the pattern which I shall show unto their Presidency, I will not accept it at their hands ;

16. But if my people do build it according to the pattern which I shall show unto their Presidency, even my servant Joseph and his counselors, then I will accept it at the hands of my people.

17. And again, verily I say unto you, it is my will that the city of Far West should be built up speedily by the gathering of my saints,

18. And also that other places should be appointed

---

e, Before the year expired the saints were driven out of Missouri. But the Twelve laid the corner stone very early in the morning of the 26th of April, 1839, before the mob were awake. 124 : 49—54.   ƒ, see *e.*

for Stakes in the regions round about, as they shall be manifest unto my servant Joseph, from time to time ;

19. For behold, I will be with him, and I will sanctify him before the people, for unto him have I given the *⁹keys of this kingdom and ministry. Even so. Amen.

SECTION 116.

Revelation to Joseph, the Seer, given near Wight's Ferry, at a place called Spring Hill, Davis County, Missouri, May 19th, 1838, wherein Spring Hill is named by the Lord,

1. *ᵃ*ADAM-ONDI-AHMAN, because, said he, it is the place where Adam shall come to visit his people, or the *ᵇ*Ancient of days shall sit, as spoken of by Daniel the prophet.

SECTION 117.

Revelation, given through Joseph, the Seer, concerning William Marks, Newel K. Whitney, Oliver Granger, and others.   Far West, Missouri, July 8th, 1838.

1. Verily thus saith the Lord unto my servant William Marks, and also unto my servant N. K. Whitney, let them settle up their business speedily and

---

g, see *b,* Sec. 28.

a, see *l,* Sec. 78.   *b,* Dan. 7 : 9—14 .

journey from the land of Kirtland, before I, the Lord, send again the snows upon the earth;

2. Let them awake, and arise, and come forth, and not tarry, for I, the Lord, command it;

3. Therefore if they tarry it shall not be well with them

4. Let them repent of all their sins, and of all their covetous desires, before me, saith the Lord, for what is property unto me, saith the Lord?

5. Let the properties of Kirtland be turned out for debts, saith the Lord. Let them go, saith the Lord, and whatsoever remaineth, let it remain in your hands, saith the Lord;

6. For have I not the fowls of heaven, and also the fish of the sea, and the beasts of the mountains? Have I not made the earth? Do I not hold the destinies of all the armies of the nations of the earth?

7. Therefore will I not make *solitary places to bud and to blossom, and to bring forth in abundance, saith the Lord.

8. Is there not room enough upon the *mountains of Adam-ondi-Ahman, and upon the plains of Olaha Shinehah, or the land where Adam dwelt, that you should covet that which is but the drop, and neglect the more weighty matters?

9. Therefore come up hither unto the land of my people, even Zion.

10. Let my servant William Marks be faithful over a few things, and he shall be a ruler over many. Let him preside in the midst of my people in the city Far West, and let him be blessed with the blessings of my people.

11. Let my servant N. K. Whitney be ashamed of the Nicholatine band and of all their secret abominations, and of all his littleness of soul before me, saith

a, Great American Desert and extensive prairies, then unsettled
b, the great Rocky Mountains, the valleys of which were then unsettled.

the Lord, and come up to the land of cAdam-ondi-Ahman, and be a bishop unto my people, saith the Lord, not in name but in deed, saith the Lord.

12. And again, I say unto you, I remember my servant Oliver Granger, behold, verily I say unto him, that his name shall be had in sacred remembrance from generation to generation, for ever and ever, saith the Lord.

13. Therefore let him contend earnestly for the redemption of the First Presidency of my church, saith the Lord, and when he falls he shall rise again, for his sacrifice shall be more sacred unto me, than his increase, saith the Lord:

14. Therefore let him come up hither speedily, unto the land of Zion, and in the due time he shall be made a merchant unto my name, saith the Lord, for the benefit of my people;

15. Therefore let no man despise my servant Oliver Granger, but let the blessings of my people be on him for ever and ever.

16. And again, verily I say unto you, let all my servants in the land of Kirtland remember the Lord their God, and mine house also, to keep and preserve it holy, and to overthrow the money changers in mine own due time, saith the Lord. Even so. Amen.

SECTION 118.

Revelation, given through Joseph, the Seer, at Far West, Missouri, July 8th, 1838, in answer to the question, " Show us thy will, O Lord, concerning the Twelve ? "

1. Verily, thus saith the Lord, let a conference be held immediately, let the Twelve be organized, and let

c, see l, Sec. 78. .

men be appointed to ^asupply the place of those who are fallen.

2. Let my servant Thomas remain for a season in the land of Zion, to publish my word.

3. Let the residue continue to preach from that hour, and if they will do this in all lowliness of heart, in meekness and humility, and long-suffering, I, the Lord, give unto them a promise that I will provide for their families, and an effectual door shall be opened for them, from henceforth ;

4. And next spring let them depart to go over the great waters, and there promulgate my gospel, the fullness thereof, and bear record of my name.

5. Let them take leave of my saints in the city Far West, on the 26th day of April next, on the building spot of my house, saith the Lord.

6. Let my servant John Taylor, and also my servant John E. Page, and also my servant Wilford Woodruff, and also my servant Willard Richards, be appointed ^bto fill the places of those who have fallen, and be officially notified of their appointment.

SECTION 119.

Revelation given through Joseph, the Prophet, at Far West, Missouri, July 8th, 1838, in answer to the question, O Lord, show unto thy servants how much thou requirest of the properties of the people for a tithing?

1. Verily, thus saith the Lord, I require ^aall their surplus property to be put into the hands of the bishop of my church of Zion,

2. For the building of mine house, and for the laying of the foundation of Zion and for the Priesthood, and for the debts of the Presidency of my church ;

3. And this shall be the *b*beginning of the tithing of my people ;

4. And after that, those who have thus been tithed, shall pay *c*one-tenth of all their interest annually ; and this shall be a *d*standing law unto them for ever, for my holy Priesthood, saith the Lord.

5. Verily I say unto you, it shall come to pass, that all those who gather unto the land of Zion shall be tithed of their *e*surplus properties, and shall observe this law, or they shall not be found worthy to abide among you.

6. And I say unto you, if my people observe not this law, to keep it holy, and by this law sanctify the land of Zion unto me, that my statutes and my judgments may be kept thereon, that it may be most holy, behold, verily I say unto you, it shall not be a land of Zion unto you ;

7. And this shall be an ensample unto *f*all the Stakes of Zion. Even so. Amen.

SECTION 120.

Revelation given through Joseph, the Seer, at Far West, Missouri, July 18th, 1838, making known the disposition of property tithings, as named in the revelation given on the 8th inst.

1. Verily, thus saith the Lord, the time is now

---

b, see *n*, Sec. 42.   *c*, 64 : 23.   97 : 11, 12.   Lev. 27 : 30, 32.   Num. 18 : 26.   Deut. 12 : 17.   14 : 23, 28.   II. Chron. 31 : 5, 6, 12.   Neh. 12 : 44.   13 : 5, 12.   10 : 37, 38.   Matt. 23 : 23.   Deut. 14 : 22.   26 : 12.   Luke 11 : 42.   18 : 12.   Gen. 14 : 20.   Lev. 27 : 31.   Num. 18 : 24, 26, 28.   Deut. 12 : 6, 11.   26 : 12.   Amos 4 : 4.   Mal. 3 : 8, 10.   Heb. 7 : 5, 6, 8, 9.   *d*, tithing, a standing law for ever.   *e*, see *n*, Sec. 42.   *f*, a law not only for Zion, but for all her Stakes.

come, that it shall be disposed of by a Council, composed of the First Presidency of my church, and of the bishop and his council, and by my High Council ; and by mine own voice unto them, saith the Lord. Even so. Amen.

SECTION 121.

A Prayer and Prophecies, written by Joseph, the Seer, while in Liberty jail, Clay County, Missouri, March 20th, 1839.

1. O God ! where art thou ? And where is the pavilion that covereth thy *a*hiding place ?

2. How long shall thy hand be stayed, and thine eye, yea thy pure eye, behold from the eternal heavens, the wrongs of thy people, and of thy servants, and thine ear be penetrated with their cries ?

3. Yea, O Lord, how long shall they suffer these wrongs and unlawful oppressions, before thine heart shall be softened towards them, and thy bowels be moved with compassion towards them ?

4. O Lord God Almighty, Maker of the heaven, earth, and seas, and of all things that in them are and who controlleth and subjecteth the devil, and the dark and benighted dominion of Shayole ! Stretch forth thy hand ; let thine eye pierce ; let thy pavilion be taken up ; let thy *b*hiding place no longer be covered ; let thine ear be inclined ; let thine heart be softened, and thy bowels moved with compassion towards us ;

5. Let thine anger be kindled against our enemies ; and in the fury of thine heart, with thy *c*sword avenge us of our wrongs ;

---

6. Remember thy suffering saints, O our God ! and thy servants will rejoice in thy name forever.

7. My son, peace be unto thy soul ; thine adversity and thine afflictions shall be but a small moment ;

8. And then, if thou endure it well, God shall exalt thee on high ; thou shalt triumph over all thy foes ;

9. Thy friends do stand by thee, and they shall hail thee again, with warm hearts and friendly hands ;

10. Thou art not yet as Job ; thy friends do not contend against thee, neither charge thee with transgression, as they did Job ;

11. And they who do charge thee with transgression, their hope shall be blasted, and their prospects shall melt away as the hoar frost melteth before the burning rays of the rising sun ;

12. And also that God hath set to his hand and seal, to change the times and seasons, and to blind their minds, that they may not understand ^dhis marvelous workings ; that he may prove them also, and take them in their own craftiness ;

13. Also because their hearts are corrupted, and the things which they are willing to bring upon others, and love to have others suffer, may come upon themselves, to the very uttermost ;

14. That they may be disappointed also, and their hopes may be cut off ;

15. And not many years hence, that they and their posterity shall be ^eswept from under heaven, saith God, that not one of them is left to stand by the wall :

16. ^fCursed are all those that shall lift up the heel against mine anointed, saith the Lord, and cry they have sinned when they have not sinned before me, saith the Lord, but have done that which was meet in mine eyes, and which I commanded them ;

17. But those who cry transgression, do it because

---

d, see a, Sec. 4.   e, Terrible judgments pronounced upon apostates.
f, apostates cursed.

they are the servants of sin, and are the children of disobedience themselves ;

18. And those who ^gswear falsely against my servants, that they might bring them into bondage, and death :

19. Wo unto them; because they have offended my little ones, they shall be severed from the ordinances of mine house ;

20. Their basket shall not be full, their houses and their barns shall perish, and they themselves shall be despised by those that flattered them ;

21. They shall not have ^hright to the Priesthood, nor their posterity after them, from generation to generation ;

22. It had been better for them that a millstone had been hanged about their necks, and they drowned in the depth of the sea.

23. Wo unto all those that ⁱdiscomfort my people, and drive, and murder, and testify against them, saith the Lord of Hosts ; a generation of vipers shall not escape the damnation of hell.

24. Behold, mine eyes see and know all their works, and I have in reserve a ^jswift judgment in the season thereof, for them all ;

25. For there is a time appointed for every man, according as his works shall be.

26. God shall give unto you (the saints) ^kknowledge by his Holy Spirit, yea by the unspeakable gift of the Holy Ghost, that has not been revealed since the world was until now ;

27. Which our forefathers have waited with anxious expectation to be revealed in the last times, which their minds were pointed to, by the angels, as ^lheld in reserve for the fullness of their glory :

---

g, the doom of false-swearers among apostates.   *h*, they and their posterity cursed in regard to the rights of the Priesthood.   *i*, the doom of mobs who murder and drive the saints.   *j*, war, scourges, pestilences, cyclones, tempests, whirlwinds and other swift judgments will waste them away.   *k*, see 2*b*, Sec. 101.   *l*, see 2*b*, Sec. 101.

28. A time to come in the which nothing shall be withheld, whether there be one God or ᵐmany Gods, they shall be manifest;

29. All thrones and dominions, principalities and powers, shall be revealed and set forth upon ⁿall who have endured valiantly for the gospel of Jesus Christ;

30. And also if there be bounds set to the heavens, or to the seas; or to the dry land, or to the sun, moon, or stars;

31. All the times of their revolutions; all the appointed days, months, and years, and all the days of their days, months, and years, and all their glories, laws, and set times, shall be revealed, in the days of the °dispensation of the fullness of times,

32. According to that which was ordained in the midst of the Council of the Eternal God of all other Gods, before this world was, that should be ᵖreserved unto the finishing and the end thereof, when every man shall enter into his eternal presence, and into his immortal rest.

33. How long can rolling waters remain impure? What power shall stay the heavens? As well might man stretch forth his puny arm to stop the Missouri river in its decreed course, or to turn it up stream, as to hinder the Almighty from ᵠpouring down knowledge from heaven, upon the heads of the Latter-day Saints.

34. Behold, there are many called, but ʳfew are chosen. And why are they not chosen?

35. Because their hearts are set so much upon the things of this world, and aspire to the honors of men, that they do not learn this one lesson—

36. That the rights of the Priesthood are inseparably connected with the powers of heaven, and that the powers of heaven ˢcannot be controlled nor handled only upon the principles of righteousness.

---

m, 76 : 58. 132 : 20.   n, see 2b, Sec. 101.   o, see n.
Sec. 27.   p, see 2b, Sec. 101.   q, see 2b, Sec. 101.   r, see s,
Sec. 95.   s, 107 : 30—32.

37. That they may be conferred upon us, it is true ; but when we undertake to cover our sins, or to gratify our pride, our vain ambition, or to exercise control, or dominion, or compulsion, upon the souls of the children of men, in any degree of unrighteousness, behold, the heavens withdraw themselves ; the Spirit of the Lord is grieved ; and when it is withdrawn, Amen to the Priesthood, or the authority of that man.

38. Behold ! ere he is aware, he is left unto himself, to kick against the pricks ; to persecute the saints, and to fight against God.

39. We have learned, by sad experience, that it is the nature and disposition of almost all men, as soon as they get a little authority, as they suppose, they will immediately begin to exercise ᵗunrighteous dominion.

40. Hence many are called, but ᵘfew are chosen.

41. No power or influence can or ought to be maintained by virtue of the Priesthood, only by persuasion, by long suffering, by gentleness, and meekness, and by love unfeigned ;

42. By kindness, and pure knowledge, which shall greatly enlarge the soul without hypocrisy, and without guile,

43. Reproving betimes with sharpness, when moved upon by the Holy Ghost, and then showing forth afterwards an increase of love toward him whom thou hast reproved, lest he esteem thee to be his enemy ;

44. That he may know that thy faithfulness is stronger than the cords of death ;

45. Let thy bowels also be full of charity towards all men, and to the household of faith, and let virtue garnish thy thoughts unceasingly, then shall thy confidence wax strong in the presence of God, and the doctrine of the Priesthood shall distil upon thy soul as the dews from heaven.

46. The Holy Ghost shall be thy constant com-

panion, and thy sceptre an unchanging sceptre of righteousness and truth, and thy dominion shall be an everlasting dominion, and without compulsory means it shall flow unto thee for ever and ever.

SECTION 122.

The word of the Lord to Joseph, the Prophet, while in Liberty jail, Clay County, Missouri, March, 1839.

1. The ends of the earth shall enquire after thy name, and fools shall have thee in derision, and hell shall rage against thee,

2. While the pure in heart, and the wise, and the noble, and the virtuous, shall seek counsel, and authority, and blessings constantly from under thy hand,

3. And thy people shall never be turned against thee by the testimony of traitors ;

4. And although their influence shall cast thee into trouble, and into bars and walls, thou shalt be had in honor, and but for a small moment and thy voice shall be more terrible in the midst of thine enemies, than the fierce lion, because of thy righteousness ; and thy God shall stand by thee for ever and ever.

5. If thou art called to pass through tribulation ; if thou art in perils among false brethren ; if thou art in perils among robbers ; if thou art in perils by land or by sea ;

6. If thou art accused with all manner of false accusations ; if thine enemies fall upon thee ; if they tear thee from the society of thy father and mother and brethren and sisters ; and if with a drawn sword thine enemies tear thee from the bosom of thy wife, and of

thine offspring, and thine elder son, although but six
years of age, shall cling to thy garments, and shall say,
My father, my father, why can't you stay with us?   O,
my father, what are the men going to do with you? and
if then he shall be thrust from thee by the sword, and
thou be dragged to prison, and thine enemies prowl
around thee like wolves for the blood of the lamb;

7. And if thou shouldst be cast into the pit, or
into the hands of murderers, and the sentence of death
passed upon thee; if thou be cast into the deep; if the
billowing surge conspire against thee; if fierce winds
become thine enemy; if the heavens gather blackness,
and all the elements combine to hedge up the way;
and above all, if the very jaws of hell shall gape open
the mouth wide after thee, know thou, my son, that
all these things shall give thee experience, and shall be
for thy good.

8. The Son of Man hath ᵃdescended below them
all; art thou greater than he?

9. Therefore, hold on thy way, and the Priesthood
shall remain with thee, for their bounds are set, they
cannot pass. Thy days are known, and thy years
shall not be numbered less; therefore, fear not what
man can do, for God shall be with you for ever and
ever.

SECTION 123.

*Duty of the Saints in relation to their persecutors, as
set forth by Joseph, the Prophet, while in Liberty
jail, Clay County, Missouri, March, 1839.*

1. And again, we would suggest for your considera-
tion the propriety of all the saints gathering up a

ᵃ, see c, Sec. 88.

knowledge of all the facts, and sufferings and abuses put upon them by the people of this State ;

2. And also of all the property and amount of damages which they have sustained, both of character and personal injuries, as well as real property ;

3. And also the names of all persons that have had a hand in their oppressions, as far as they can get hold of them and find them out ;

4. And perhaps a committee can be appointed to find out these things, and to take statements, and affidavits, and also to gather up the libelous publications that are afloat,

5. And all that are in the magazines, and in the encyclopedias, and all the libelous histories that are published, and are writing, and by whom, and present the whole concatenation of diabolical rascality, and nefarious and murderous impositions that have been practised upon this people,

6. That we may not only publish to all the world, but present them to the heads of government in all their dark and hellish hue, as the last effort which is enjoined on us by our Heavenly Father, before we can fully and completely claim that promise which shall call him forth from his ⁿhiding place, and also that the whole nation may be left without excuse before he can send forth the power of his mighty arm.

7. It is an imperious duty that we owe to God, to angels, with whom we shall be brought to stand, and also to ourselves, to our wives and children, who have been made to bow down with grief, sorrow, and care, under the most damning hand of murder, tyranny, and oppression, supported, and urged on, and upheld by the influence of that spirit which hath so strongly riveted the creeds of the fathers, who have inherited lies, upon the hearts of the children, and filled the world with confusion, and has been growing stronger

---

a, see 3 j, Sec. 101.

and stronger, and is now the very main-spring of all corruption, and the whole earth groans under the weight of its iniquity.

8. It is an iron yoke, it is a strong band; they are the very hand-cuffs, and chains, and shackles, and fetters of hell.

9. Therefore it is an imperious duty that we owe, not only to our own wives and children, but to the widows and fatherless, whose husbands and fathers have been murdered under its iron hand;

10. Which dark and blackening deeds are enough to make hell itself shudder, and to stand aghast and pale, and the hands of the very devil to tremble and palsy.

11. And also it is an imperious duty that we owe to all the rising generation, and to all the pure in heart;

12. (For there are many yet on the earth among all sects, parties, and denominations, who are blinded by the subtle craftiness of men, whereby they lie in wait to deceive, and who are only kept from the truth because they know not where to find it;)

13. Therefore, that we should waste and wear out our lives in bringing to light all the hidden things of darkness, wherein we know them; and they are truly manifest from heaven.

14. These should then *b*be attended to with great earnestness.

15. Let no man count them as small things; for there is much which lieth in futurity, pertaining to the saints, which depends upon these things.

16. You know, brethren, that a very large ship is benefited very much by a very small helm in the time of a storm, by being kept workways with the wind and the waves.

17. Therefore, dearly beloved brethren, let us cheer-

---

b, Elder A. M. Musser is appointed to gather up these libelous reports.

fully do all things that lie in our power, and then may
we stand still with the utmost assurance, to see the
salvation of God, and for his arm to be revealed.

SECTION 124.

*Revelation given to Joseph Smith, at Nauvoo, Hancock
County, Illinois, January 19th, 1841.*

1. Verily, thus saith the Lord unto you, my servant
Joseph Smith, I am well pleased with your offering and
acknowledgments, which you have made, for unto this
end have I raised you up, that I might show forth my
wisdom through the *a*weak things of the earth.

2. Your prayers are acceptable before me, and in
answer to them I say unto you, that you are now called
immediately to make a *b*solemn proclamation of my
gospel, and of this *c*Stake which I have planted to be
a corner stone of Zion, which shall be polished with
that refinement which is after the similitude of a
palace.

3. This proclamation shall be made to all the kings
of the world—to the four corners thereof—to the
honorable President elect, and the high minded Gover-
nors of the nation in which you live, and to all the
nations of the earth scattered abroad.

4. Let it be written in the spirit of meekness and
by the power of the Holy Ghost, which shall be in you
at the time of the writing of the same ;

5. For it shall be *d*given you by the Holy Ghost to
know my will concerning those kings and authorities,
even what shall befall them in a time to come.

---

a, see j, Sec. 1.   b, see b, Sec. 18.   c, see g, Sec. 87.
d, the spirit of prophecy more fully to be made manifest.

6. For, behold! I am about to call upon them to give heed to the light and glory of Zion, for the set time has come to favor her.

7. Call ye, therefore, upon them with loud proclamation, and with your testimony, fearing them not, for they are as grass, and all their glory as the flower thereof which soon falleth, that they may be left also without excuse,

8. And that I may visit them in the day of visitation, when I shall *unvail the face of my covering, to appoint the portion of the oppressor among hypocrites, where there is gnashing of teeth, if they reject my servants and my testimony which I have revealed unto them.

9. And again, I will visit and soften their hearts, many of them for your good, that ye may find grace in their eyes, that they may ʃcome to the light of truth, and the Gentiles to the exaltation or lifting up of Zion.

10. For the day of my visitation cometh speedily, in an hour when ye think not of, and where shall be the safety of my people, and refuge for those who shall be left of them?

11. Awake! O, kings of the earth! Come ye, O, come ye, with your gold and your silver, to the help of my people, to the house of the daughters of Zion.

12. And again, verily I say unto you, Let my servant Robert B. Thompson help you to write this proclamation, for I am well pleased with him, and that he should be with you;

13. Let him, therefore, hearken to your counsel, and I will bless him with a multiplicity of blessings; let him be faithful and true in all things from henceforth, and he shall be great in mine eyes;

14. But let him remember that his ᵍstewardship will I require at his hands.

---

e, see e, Sec. 1.   f, Isa. 60: 3, 10, 11, 12.   g, see u,
Sec. 78.

15. And again, verily I say unto you, Blessed is my servant Hyrum Smith, for I, the Lord, love him because of the integrity of his heart, and because he loveth that which is right before me, saith the Lord.

16. Again, let my servant John C. Bennett, help you in your labor in sending my word to the kings of the people of the earth, and stand by you, even you my servant Joseph Smith, in the hour of affliction, and his reward shall not fail if he receive counsel ;

17. And for his love he shall be great, for he shall be mine if he do this, saith the Lord. I have seen the work which he hath done, which I accept, if he continue, and will crown him with blessings and great glory.

18. And again, I say unto you, that it is my will that my servant Lyman Wight should continue in preaching for Zion, in the spirit of meekness, confessing me before the world, and I will bear him up as on eagle's wings, and he shall beget glory and honor to himself, and unto my name.

19. That when he shall finish his work, that I may receive him unto myself, even as I did my servant David Patten, who is with me at this time, and also my servant Edward Partridge, and also my aged servant Joseph Smith, sen., who sitteth with Abraham at his right hand, and blessed and holy is he, for he is mine.

20. And again, verily I say unto you, my servant George Miller is without guile ; he may be trusted because of the integrity of his heart; and for the love which he has to my testimony I, the Lord, love him ;

21. I therefore say unto you, I seal upon his head the office of a bishopric, like unto my servant Edward Partridge, that he may receive the consecrations of mine house, that he may administer blessings upon the heads of the poor of my people, saith the Lord. Let no man despise my servant George, for he shall honor me.

22. Let my servant George, and my servant Lyman, and my servant John Snider, and others, build a ʰhouse unto my name, such an one as my servant Joseph shall show unto them ; upon the place which he shall show unto them also.

23. And it shall be for a house for boarding, a house that strangers may come from afar to lodge therein : therefore let it be a good house, worthy of all acceptation, that the weary traveler may find health and safety while he shall contemplate the word of the Lord ; and the corner stone I have appointed for Zion.

24. This house shall be a healthy habitation if it be built unto my name, and if the governor which shall be appointed unto it shall not suffer any pollution to come upon it. It shall be holy, or the Lord your God will not dwell therein.

25. And again, verily I say unto you, Let ⁱall my saints come from afar ;

26. And send ye swift messengers, yea, chosen messengers, and say unto them ; come ye, with all your gold, and your silver, and your precious stones, and with all your antiquities; and with all who have knowledge of antiquities, that will come, may come, and bring the box tree, and the fir tree, and the pine tree, together with all the precious trees of the earth ;

27. And with iron, with copper, and with brass, and with zinc, and with all your precious things of the earth, and build a house to my name, for the ʲMost High to dwell therein ;

28. For there is not a place found on earth that he may come and restore again that which was lost unto you, or which he hath taken away, even the fullness of the Priesthood ;

29. For a ᵏbaptismal font there is not upon the

---

earth, that they, my saints, may be 'baptized for those who are dead ;

30. For this ordinance belongeth to my house, and cannot be acceptable to me, only in the days of your poverty, wherein ye are not able to build a house unto me.

31. But I command you, all ye my saints, to build a house unto me ; and I grant unto you a sufficient time to build a house unto me, and during this time your *m*baptisms shall be acceptable unto me.

32. But behold, at the end of this appointment, your *n*baptisms for your dead shall not be acceptable unto me ; and if you do not these things at the end of the appointment, ye shall be *o*rejected as a church, with your dead, saith the Lord your God.

33. For verily I say unto you, that after you have had sufficient time to build a house to me, wherein the ordinance of *p*baptizing for the dead belongeth, and for which the same was instituted from before the foundation of the world, *q*your baptisms for your dead cannot be acceptable unto me,

34. For therein are the keys of the holy Priesthood, ordained that you may receive honor and glory.

35. And *r*after this time, your baptisms for the dead, by those who are scattered abroad, are not acceptable unto me, saith the Lord ;

36. For it is ordained that in Zion, and in her Stakes, and in Jerusalem, those places which I have appointed for refuge, shall be the *s*places for your baptisms for your dead.

37. And again, verily I say unto you, How shall your *t*washings be acceptable unto me, except ye perform them in a house which you have built to my name ?

---

l, see *k*.　　*m*, see *k*.　　*n*, an ordinance of the Lord's house.
o, the saints to be rejected if they refuse to build the Lord's house.
p, see *k*.　　*q*, see *k*.　　*r*, that is, after the date of this revelation.
s, an ordinance of the house of the Lord, built in the places named
t, ver. 39.　88 : 138　141.

38. For, for this cause I *u*commanded Moses that he should build a tabernacle, that they should bear it with them in the wilderness, and to build a house in the land of promise, that those ordinances might be revealed which had been hid from before the world was;

39. Therefore, verily I say unto you, that your *v*anointings, and your washings, and your baptisms for the dead, and your solemn assemblies, and your memorials for your sacrifices, by the sons of Levi, and for your oracles in your most holy places, wherein you receive conversations, and your statutes and judgments, for the beginning of the revelations and foundation of Zion, and for the glory, honor, and endowment of all her municipals, are ordained by the ordinance of my holy house which my people are *w*always commanded to build unto my holy name.

40. And verily I say unto you, Let this house be built unto my name, that I *x*may reveal mine ordinances therein, unto my people;

41. For I deign to reveal unto my church, things which have been kept hid from before the foundation of the world, things that pertain to the *y*dispensation of the fullness of times;

42. And I will show unto my servant Joseph all things pertaining to this house, and the Priesthood thereof; and the place whereon it shall be built;

43. And ye shall build it on the place where you have contemplated building it, for that is the spot which I have chosen for you to build it;

44. If ye labor with all your might, I will consecrate that spot that it shall be made holy;

45. And if my people will hearken unto my voice, and unto the voice of my servants whom I have ap-

---

u, Exod. 25 : 1—9. i. Chron. chapters 28, 29.   *v*, enumeration of things belonging to the house of God.   88 : 74, 139—141.   *w*, a standing commandment.   *x*, revelation of ordinances to be given in the house of God.   *y*, see *n*, Sec. 27.

pointed to lead my people, behold, verily I say unto you, they shall not be moved out of their place.

46. But if they will not hearken to my voice, nor unto the voice of these men whom I have appointed, they shall not be blest, because they pollute mine holy grounds, and mine holy ordinances, and charters, and my holy words which I give unto them.

47. And it shall come to pass, That if you build a house unto my name, and do not do the things that I say, I will not perform the oath which I make unto you, neither fulfill the promises which ye expect at my hands, saith the Lord;

48. For instead of blessings, ye, by your own works, bring cursings, wrath, indignation, and judgments upon your own heads, by your follies, and by all your abominations, which you practise before me, saith the Lord.

49. Verily, verily I say unto you, That when I give a commandment to any of the sons of men, to do a work unto my name, and those sons of men go with all their might, and with all they have, to perform that work, and cease not their diligence, and their enemies come upon them, and hinder them from performing that work; behold, it behoveth me to require that work no more at the hands of those sons of men, but to accept of their offerings;

50. And the iniquity and transgression of my holy laws and commandments, I will visit upon the heads of those who hindered my work, unto the third and fourth generation, so long as they repent not, and hate me, saith the Lord God.

51. Therefore for this cause ᶻhave I accepted the offerings of those whom I commanded to build up a city and a house unto my name, in Jackson county, Missouri, and were hindered by their enemies, saith the Lord your God:

52. And I will ²ᵃanswer judgment, wrath, and in-

---

z, vers. 49, 50, 52, 53. of Zion.　　　2a, judgments decreed against the enemies dignation, wailing, and anguish, and gnashing of teeth upon their heads, unto the third and fourth generation, so long as they repent not and hate me, saith the Lord your God.

53. And this I make an example unto you, for your consolation concerning all those who have been commanded to do a work, and have been [2b]hindered by the hands of their enemies, and by oppression, saith the Lord your God ;

54. For I am the Lord your God, and will save all those of your brethren who have been pure in heart, and have been slain in the land of Missouri, saith the Lord.

55. And again, verily I say unto you, I command you again to build a house to my name, even in this place, that you may [2c]prove yourselves unto me that ye are faithful in all things whatsoever I command you, that I may bless you, and crown you with honor, immortality, and eternal life.

56. And now I say unto you, as pertaining to my boarding house which I have commanded you to build for the boarding of strangers, let it be built unto my name, and let my name be named upon it, and let my servant Joseph, and his house have place therein, from generation to generation ;

57. For this [2d]anointing have I put upon his head, that his blessing shall also be put upon the head of his posterity after him,

58. And as I said unto Abraham concerning the kindreds of the earth, even so I say unto my servant Joseph, in thee and in [2e]thy seed shall the kindred of the earth be blessed.

59. Therefore, let my servant Joseph and his seed after him have place in that house, from generation to generation, for ever and ever, saith the Lord,

---

2b, see z.   2c, vers. 25—43   2d, ver. 58.   110 : 12.
2c, ver. 57.   110 : 12.

60. And let the name of that house be called Nauvoo house, and let it be a delightful habitation for man, and a resting place for the ²/weary traveler, that he may contemplate the glory of Zion, and the glory of this the corner-stone thereof;

61. That he may receive also the counsel from those whom I have set to be as plants of renown, and as watchmen upon her walls.

62. Behold, verily I say unto you, let my servant George Miller, and my servant Lyman Wight, and my servant John Snider, and my servant Peter Haws, organize themselves, and appoint one of them to be a president over their quorum for the purpose of building that house.

63. And they shall form a constitution whereby they may receive stock for the building of that house.

64. And they shall not receive less than fifty dollars for a share of stock in that house, and they shall be permitted to receive fifteen thousand dollars from any one man for stock in that house;

65. But they shall not be permitted to receive over fifteen thousand dollars stock from any one man;

66. And they shall not be permitted to receive under fifty dollars for a share of stock from any one man in that house;

67. And they shall not be permitted to receive any man as a stockholder in this house, except the same shall pay his stock into their hands at the time he receives stock;

68. And in proportion to the amount of stock he pays into their hands, he shall receive stock in that house; but if he pays nothing into their hands, he shall not receive any stock in that house.

69. And if any pay stock into their hands, it shall be for stock in that house, for himself, and for his generation after him, from generation to generation, so long

as he and his heirs shall hold that stock, and do not sell or convey the stock away out of their hands by their own free will and act, if you will do my will, saith the Lord your God.

70. And again, verily I say unto you, if my servant George Miller, and my servant Lyman Wight, and my servant John Snider, and my servant Peter Haws, receive any stock into their hands, in moneys or in properties, wherein they receive the real value of moneys, they shall not appropriate any portion of that stock to any other purpose, only in that house ;

71. And if they do appropriate any portion of that stock any where else, only in that house, without the consent of the stockholder, and do not repay fourfold for the stock which they appropriate any where else, only in that house, they shall be accursed, and shall be moved out of their place, saith the Lord God, for I, the Lord, am God, and cannot be mocked in any of these things.

72. Verily I say unto you, Let my servant Joseph pay stock into their hands for the building of that house, as seemeth him good ; but my servant Joseph cannot pay over fifteen thousand dollars stock in that house, nor under fifty dollars ; neither can any other man, saith the Lord.

73. And there are others also who wish to know my will concerning them, for they have asked it at my hands.

74. Therefore I say unto you concerning my servant Vinson Knight, if he will do my will, let him put stock into that house for himself, and for his generation after him, from generation to generation,

75. And let him lift up his voice long and loud, in the midst of the people, to plead the cause of the poor and the needy, and let him not fail, neither let his heart faint, and I will accept of his offerings, for they shall not be unto me as the offerings of Cain, for he shall be mine, saith the Lord.

76. Let his family rejoice, and turn away their hearts from affliction, for I have chosen him and anointed him, and he shall be honored in the midst of his house, for I will forgive all his sins, saith the Lord. Amen.

77. Verily I say unto you, let my servant Hyrum· put stock into that house as seemeth him good, for himself and his generation after him, from generation to generation.

78. Let my servant Isaac Galland put stock into that house, for I, the Lord, love him for the work he hath done, and will forgive all his sins ; therefore, let him be remembered for an interest in that house from generation to generation.

79. Let my servant Isaac Galland be appointed among you, and be ordained by my servant William Marks, and be blessed of him, to go with my servant Hyrum, to accomplish the work that my servant Joseph shall point out to them, and they shall be greatly blessed.

80. Let my servant William Marks pay stock into that house, as it seemeth him good, for himself and his generation, from generation to generation.

81. Let my servant Henry G. Sherwood pay stock into that house, as it seemeth him good for himself and his seed after him, from generation to generation.

82. Let my servant William Law pay stock into that house, for himself and his seed after him, from generation to generation.

83. If he will do my will, let him not take his family unto the eastern lands, even unto Kirtland ; nevertheless, I, the Lord, will build up Kirtland, but I, the Lord, have a scourge prepared for the inhabitants thereof.

84. And with my servant Almon Babbitt, there are many things with which I am not well pleased ; behold, he aspireth to establish his counsel instead of the counsel which I have ordained, even the Presidency of my

church, and he setteth up a golden calf for the worship
of my people.

85. Let no man go from this place who has come
here essaying to keep my commandments.

86. If they [2g]live here let them live unto me ; and
if they die, let them die unto me ; for they shall rest
from all their labors here, and shall continue their
works.

87. Therefore let my servant William put his trust
in me, and cease to fear concerning his family, because
of the sickness of the land. If ye love me, keep my
commandments, and the sickness of the land shall re-
dound to your glory.

88. Let my servant William go and proclaim [2h]my
everlasting gospel with a loud voice, and with great joy,
as he shall be moved upon by my Spirit, unto the inhabitants of Warsaw, and also unto the inhabitants of
Carthage, and also unto the inhabitants of Burlington,
and also unto the inhabitants of Madison, and await
patiently and diligently for further instructions at my
general conference, saith the Lord.

89. If he will do my will, let him from henceforth
hearken to the counsel of my servant Joseph, and with
his interest support the cause of the poor, and [2i]publish
the new translation of my holy word unto the inhabitants of the earth ;

90. And if he will do this, I will bless him with a
multiplicity of blessings, that he shall not be forsaken,
nor his seed be found begging bread.

91. And again, verily I say unto you, Let my servant William be appointed, ordained, and anointed, as
a counselor unto my servant Joseph, in the room of my
servant Hyrum, that my servant Hyrum may take the
office of Priesthood and [2j]Patriarch, which was appointed unto him by his father, by blessing and also by
right,

2g, vers. 85, 87, 108—110.   2h, see b, Sec. 18. .   2i, inspired
translation of the scriptures.   2j, vers. 92, 96, 124.   107 : 39.   translation

92. That from henceforth he shall hold the [2k]keys of the patriarchal blessings upon the heads of all my people,

93. That [2l]whoever he blesses shall be blessed, and whoever he [2m]curses shall be cursed; that whatsoever he shall bind on earth shall be bound in heaven; and whatsoever he shall loose on earth shall be loosed in heaven;

94. And from this time forth I [2n]appoint unto him that he may be a prophet, and a seer, and a revelator unto my church, as well as my servant Joseph,

95. That he may act in concert also with my servant Joseph, and that he shall receive counsel from my servant Joseph, who shall show unto him the [2o]keys whereby he may ask and receive, and be crowned with the same blessing, and glory, and honor, and Priesthood, and gifts of the Priesthood, that once were put upon him that was my servant Oliver Cowdery;

96. That my servant Hyrum may bear record of the things which I shall show unto him, that his name may be had in honorable remembrance from generation to generation, for ever and ever.

97. Let my servant William Law also receive [2p]the keys by which he may ask and receive blessings; let him be humble before me, and be without guile, and he shall receive of my Spirit, even the [2q]Comforter, which shall manifest unto him the truth of all things, and shall give him in the very hour, what he shall say.

98. And these signs shall follow him; he shall heal the sick, he shall cast out devils, and shall be delivered from those who would administer unto him deadly poison;

99. And he shall be led in paths where the poisonous serpent cannot lay hold upon his heel, and he shall

2k, the Presiding Patriarch.   2l, see d, Sec. 1.   2m, see d, Sec. 1.   2n, ver. 95.   2o, the order of God for receiving revelations.   2p, the order, ordained of God.   2q, see h, Sec. 42.

mount up in the imagination of his thoughts as upon
eagles' wings ;

100. And what if I will that he should raise the
dead, let him not withhold his voice.

101. Therefore, let my servant William cry aloud
and spare not, with joy and rejoicing, and with hosan-
nas to him that sitteth upon the throne for ever and
ever, saith the Lord your God.

102. Behold, I say unto you, I have a mission in
store for my servant William, and my servant Hyrum,
and for them alone ; and let my servant Joseph tarry
at home, for he is needed : the remainder I will show
unto you hereafter. Even so. Amen.

103. And again, verily I say unto you, if my servant Sidney will serve me and be counselor unto my
servant Joseph, let him arise and come up and stand
in the office of his calling, and humble himself before
me ;

104. And if he will offer unto me an acceptable
offering, and acknowledgments, and remain with my
people, behold, I, the Lord your God, will heal him
that he shall be healed ; and he shall lift up his voice
again on the mountains, and be a [2r]spokesman before
my face.

105. Let him come and locate his family in the
neighbourhood in which my servant Joseph resides,

106. And in all his journeyings let him lift up his
voice as with the sound of a trump, and warn the inhabitants of the earth to flee the wrath to come ;

107. Let him assist my servant Joseph ; and also let
my servant William Law assist my servant Joseph, in
making a [2s]solemn proclamation unto the kings of the
earth, even as I have before said unto you.

108. If my servant Sidney will do my will, let him
not remove his family unto the eastern lands, but let
him change their habitation, even as I have said.

109. Behold, it is not my will that he shall seek to find safety and refuge out of the city which I have appointed unto you, even the city of Nauvoo.

110. Verily I say unto you, even now, if he will hearken to my voice, it shall be well with him. Even so. Amen.

111. And again, verily I say unto you, Let my servant Amos Davies pay stock into the hands of those whom I have appointed to build a house for boarding, even the Nauvoo House;

112. This let him do if he will have an interest, and let him hearken unto the counsel of my servant Joseph, and labor with his own hands that he may obtain the confidence of men;

113. And when he shall prove himself faithful in all things that shall be entrusted unto his care, yea, even a few things, he shall be made ruler over many;

114. Let him therefore abase himself that he may be exalted. Even so. Amen.

115. And again, verily I say unto you, if my servant Robert D. Foster will obey my voice, let him build a house for my servant Joseph, according to the contract which he has made with him, as the door shall be open to him from time to time;

116. And let him repent of all his folly, and clothe himself with charity, and cease to do evil, and lay aside all his hard speeches,

117. And pay stock also into the hands of the quorum of the Nauvoo House, for himself and for his generation after him, from generation to generation,

118. And hearken unto the counsel of my servants Joseph and Hyrum and William Law, and unto the authorities which I have called to lay the foundation of Zion, and it shall be well with him for ever and ever. Even so. Amen.

119. And again, verily I say unto you, Let no man

pay stock to the quorum of the Nauvoo House, unless he shall be a believer in the Book of Mormon, and the revelations I have given unto you, saith the Lord your God;

120. For that which is more or less than this cometh of evil, and shall be attended with cursings and not blessings, saith the Lord your God. Even so. Amen.

121. And again, verily I say unto you, Let the quorum of the Nauvoo House have a just recompense of wages for all their labors which they do in building the Nauvoo House, and let their wages be as shall be agreed among themselves, as pertaining to the price thereof;

122. And let every man who pays stock bear his proportion of their wages, if it must needs be, for their support, saith the Lord; otherwise, their labors shall be accounted unto them for stock in that house. Even so. Amen.

123. Verily I say unto you, I now give unto you [2t] the officers belonging to my Priesthood, that ye may hold the keys thereof, even the Priesthood which is after the order of Melchisedek, which is after the order of my Only Begotten Son.

124. First, I give unto you Hyrum Smith, to be a [2u] Patriarch unto you, to hold the sealing blessings of my church, even the Holy Spirit of promise, whereby ye are sealed up unto the day of redemption, that ye may not fall, notwithstanding the hour of temptation that may come upon you.

125. I give unto you my servant Joseph, to be a presiding elder over all my church, to [2v] be a translator, a revelator, a seer, and prophet.

126. I give unto him for counselors my servant Sidney Rigdon, and my servant William Law, that

these may const ute a quorum and [2w]First Presidency,
to receive the o les for the whole church.

127. I give unto you my servant Brigham Young, to
be a President over the [2x]Twelve traveling Council,

128. Which Twelve hold the keys to open up the
authority of my kingdom upon the four corners of the
earth, and after that to send my word to every creature ;

129. They are—Heber C. Kimball, Parley P. Pratt,
Orson Pratt, Orson Hyde, William Smith, John Taylor,
John E. Page, Wilford Woodruff, Willard Richards,
George A. Smith ;

130. David Patten I have [2y]taken unto myself;
behold, his Priesthood no man taketh from him ; but,
verily I say unto you, another may be appointed unto
the same calling.

131. And again, I say unto you, I give unto you a
[2z]High Council, for the corner stone of Zion ;

132. Viz., Samuel Bent, H. G. Sherwood, George
W. Harris, Charles C. Rich, Thomas Grover, Newel
Knight, David Dort, Dunbar Wilson ; (Seymour Brunson I have taken unto myself, no man taketh his
Priesthood, but another may be appointed unto the
same Priesthood in his stead and verily I say unto you,
let my servant Aaron Johnson be ordained unto this
calling in his stead;) David Fullmer, Alpheus Cutler,
William Huntington.

133. And again, I give unto you Don C. Smith, to
be a president over a [3a]quorum of High Priests ;

134. Which ordinance is instituted for the purpose
of qualifying those who shall be appointed standing
presidents or servants over different Stakes scattered
abroad,

135. And they may travel also if they choose, but
rather be ordained for standing presidents, this is the
office of their calling, saith the Lord your God.

[2w], see j, Sec. 68.   [2x], see p, Sec. 18.   [2y], David Patten
was killed by a Missouri mob.   [2z], for Nauvoo.   [3a], vers. 134—136.

136. I give unto him Amasa Lyman, and Noah Packard, for counselors, that they may preside over the quorum of High Priests of my church, saith the Lord.

137. And again, I say unto you, I give unto you John A. Hicks, Samuel Williams, and Jesse Baker, which Priesthood is to preside over the ^{3b}quorum of elders, which quorum is instituted for standing ministers, nevertheless they may travel, yet they are ordained to be standing ministers to my church, saith the Lord.

138. And again, I give unto you Joseph Young, Josiah Butterfield, Daniel Miles, Henry Herriman, Zera Pulsipher, Levi Hancock, James Foster, to ^{3c}preside over the quorum of seventies,

139. Which quorum is instituted for traveling elders to bear record of my name in all the world, wherever the traveling High Council, my apostles, shall send them to prepare a way before my face.

140. The difference between this quorum and the quorum of elders is, that one is to travel continually, and the other is to preside over the churches from time to time; the one has the responsibility of presiding from time to time, and the other has no responsibility of presiding, saith the Lord your God.

141. And again, I say unto you I give unto you Vinson Knight, Samuel H. Smith, and Shadrach Roundy, if he will receive it, to ^{3d}preside over the bishopric; a knowledge of said bishopric is given unto you in the Book of Doctrine and Covenants.

142. And again, I say unto you, Samuel Rolfe and his counselors for priests, and the president of the teachers and his counselors, and also the president of the deacons and his counselors, and also the ^{3e}president of the stake and his counselors;

143. The above offices I have given unto you, and

3b, 107: 60, 89.   3c, 107: 93—98.   3d, Presiding Bishop.
3e, 107: 10.

the keys thereof, for helps and for governments, for the work of the ministry, and the perfecting of my saints ;

144. And a commandment I give unto you that you should fill all these offices and ³⁄approve of those names which I have mentioned, or else disapprove of them at my general conference,

145. And that ye should prepare rooms for all these offices in my house when you build it unto my name, saith the Lord your God. Even so. Amen.

SECTION 125.

Revelation given through Joseph, the Seer, at Nauvoo, Hancock County, Illinois, March, 1841, concerning the Saints in the Territory of Iowa.

1. "What is the will of the Lord, concerning the saints in the Territory of Iowa?"

2. Verily, thus saith the Lord, I say unto you, if those who call themselves by my name, and are essaying to be my saints, if they will do my will and keep my commandments concerning them ; let them gather themselves together, unto the places which I shall appoint unto them by my servant Joseph, and build up cities unto my name, that they may be prepared for that which is in store for a time to come.

3. Let them build up a city unto my name upon the land opposite to the city of Nauvoo, and let the name of Zarahemla be named upon it.

4. And let all those who come from the east, and the west, and the north, and the south, that have de-

---

3 f, see 2 v, Sec. 20.

sires to dwell therein, take up their inheritance in the
same, as well as in the city of Nashville, or in the city
of Nauvoo, and in all the *Stakes which I have appointed, saith the Lord.

SECTION 126.

*Revelation, given through Joseph, the Seer, in the house
of Elder Brigham Young, Nauvoo, Illinois, July
9th, 1841.*

1. Dear and well-beloved brother Brigham Young,
verily thus saith the Lord unto you, my servant Brigham, it is no more required at your hand to leave your
family as in times past, for your offering is acceptable
to me ;

2. I have seen your labor and toil in journeyings for
my name.

3. I therefore command you to *send my word
abroad, and take special care of your family from this
time, henceforth, and for ever.   Amen.

SECTION 127.

*Address to the Saints in Nauvoo, dated Nauvoo,
September 1st, 1842.*

1. Forasmuch as the Lord has revealed unto me
that my enemies, both in Missouri and this State, were

---

a, see *g,* Sec. 87.

a, 107 : 38. See *q,* Sec. 18.

again in the pursuit of me; and inasmuch as they pursue me without a cause, and have not the least shadow or coloring of justice or right on their side, in the getting up of their prosecutions against me; and inasmuch as their pretensions are all founded in falsehood of the blackest die, I have thought it expedient and wisdom in me to leave the place for a short season, for my own safety, and the safety of this people. I would say to all those with whom I have business, that I have left my affairs with agents and clerks, who will transact all business in a prompt and proper manner, and will see that all my debts are canceled in due time, by turning out property, or otherwise, as the case may require, or as the circumstances may admit of. When I learn that the storm is fully blown over, then I will return to you again.

2. And as for the perils which I am called to pass through, they seem but a small thing to me, as the envy and wrath of man have been my common lot all the days of my life; and for what cause it seems mysterious, unless I was ordained from before the foundation of the world for some good end, or bad, as you may choose to call it. Judge ye for yourselves. God knoweth all these things, whether it be good or bad. But nevertheless, deep water is what I am wont to swim in. It all has become a second nature to me, and I feel like Paul, to glory in tribulation, for to this day has the God of my fathers delivered me out of them all, and will deliver me from henceforth; for behold, and lo, I shall triumph over all my enemies, for the Lord God hath spoken it.

3. Let all the saints rejoice, therefore, and be exceedingly glad, for Israel's God is their God, and he will meet out a just recompense of reward upon the heads of all their oppressors.

4. And again, verily thus saith the Lord, Let the work of ᵃmy temple, and all the works which I have

---

a, 124: 25—48, 55.

appointed unto you, be continued on and not cease; and let your diligence, and your perseverance, and patience, and your works be redoubled, and you shall in nowise lose your reward, saith the Lord of hosts. And if they persecute you, so persecuted they the prophets and righteous men that were before you. For all this there is a reward in heaven.

5. And again, I give unto you a word in relation to the baptism for your dead.

6. Verily, thus saith the Lord unto you concerning your dead: When any of you are *b*baptized for your dead, let there be a *c*Recorder, and let him be eye witness of your baptisms; let him hear with his ears, that he may testify of a truth, saith the Lord;

7. That in all your recordings it may be recorded in heaven; whatsoever you *d*bind on earth, may be bound in heaven; whatsoever you loose on earth, may be loosed in heaven;

8. For I am about to restore many things to the earth, pertaining to the Priesthood, saith the Lord of hosts.

9. And again, let all the *e*records be had in order, that they may be put in the archives of my Holy Temple, to be held in remembrance from generation to generation, saith the Lord of hosts.

10. I will say to all the saints, that I desired, with exceedingly great desire, to have addressed them from the stand, on the subject of baptism for the dead, on the following sabbath. But inasmuch as it is out of my power to do so, I will write the word of the Lord from time to time, on that subject, and send it to you by mail, as well as many other things.

11. I now close my letter for the present, for the want of more time; for the enemy is on the alert, and as the Saviour said, the prince of this world cometh, but he hath nothing in me.

---

b, see k, Sec. 124.   e, 128: 8, 4, 7.   d, see d, Sec. 1.
c, 128: 4, 7—10.

12. Behold, my prayer to God is, that you all may be saved. And I subscribe myself your servant in the Lord, Prophet and Seer of the Church of Jesus Christ of Latter-day Saints.

JOSEPH SMITH.

SECTION 128.

Address to the Church of Jesus Christ of Latter-day Saints, dated Nauvoo, September 6th, 1842.

1. As I stated to you in my letter before I left my place, that I would write to you from time to time, and give you information in relation to many subjects, I now resume the subject of the baptism for the dead, as that subject seems to occupy my mind, and press itself upon my feelings the strongest, since I have been pursued by my enemies.

2. I wrote a few words of revelation to you concerning a recorder. I have had a few additional views in relation to this matter, which I now certify. That is, it was declared in my former letter that there should be a recorder, who should be eye witness, and also to hear with his ears, that he might make a record of a truth before the Lord.

3. Now, in relation to this matter, it would be very difficult for one recorder to be present at all times, and to do all the business. To obviate this difficulty, there can be a ªrecorder appointed in each ward of the city, who is well qualified for taking accurate minutes ; and let him be very particular and precise in taking the whole proceedings, certifying in his record that he saw with his eyes, and heard with his ears, giving the date,

---

and names, &c., and the history of the whole transaction ; naming also, some three individuals that are present, if there be any present, who can at any time when called upon, certify to the same, that in the *b*mouth of two or three witnesses, every word may be established.

4. Then let there be a general recorder, to whom these other records can be handed, being attended with certificates over their own signatures, certifying that the record they have made is true. Then the general church recorder, can enter the record on the general church book, with the certificates and all the attending witnesses, with his own statement that he verily believes the above statement and records to be true, from his knowledge of the general character and appointment of those men by the church. And when this is done on the general church book, the record shall be just as holy, and shall answer the ordinance just the same as if he had seen with his eyes, and heard with his ears, and made a record of the same on the general church book.

5. You may think this order of things to be very particular, but let me tell you, that it is only to answer the will of God, by conforming to the ordinance and preparation that the Lord ordained and prepared *c*before the foundation of the world, for the salvation of the dead who should die without a knowledge of the gospel.

6. And further I want you to remember that John the Revelator was contemplating this very subject in relation to the dead, when he declared, as you will find recorded in Revelations xx. 12—"And I saw the dead, small and great, stand before God ; and the *d*books were opened ; and another book was opened, which was the book of life ; and the dead were judged out of those things which were written in the books, according to their works."

---

b, records and witnesses necessary when the dead are judged.   *c*, plan laid before the foundation of the world.   *d*, Rev. 20 : 12.

7. You will discover in this quotation, that the books were opened; and another book was opened, which was the book of life; but the dead were judged out of those things which were written in the books, according to their works; consequently the books spoken of must be the books which contained the record of their works; and refer to the *records which are kept on the earth. And the book which was the book of life, is the record which is kept in heaven; the principle agreeing precisely with the doctrine which is commanded you in the revelation contained in the letter which I wrote to you previously to my leaving my place —that in all your recordings it may be *recorded in heaven.

8. Now the nature of this ordinance consists in the power of the Priesthood, by the revelation of Jesus Christ, wherein it is granted, that *whatsoever you bind on earth, shall be bound in heaven, and whatsoever you loose on earth, shall be loosed in heaven. Or, in other words, taking a different view of the translation, whatsoever you *record on earth, shall be recorded in heaven; and whatsoever you *do not record on earth, shall not be recorded in heaven; for out of the books shall your dead be judged, according to their own works, whether they themselves have attended to the ordinances in their own *propria persona*, or by the means of their own agents, according to the ordinance which God has prepared for their salvation from before the foundation of the world, according to the *records which they have kept concerning their dead.

9. It may seem to some to be a very bold doctrine that we talk of—a power which records or binds on earth, and binds in heaven. Nevertheless in all ages of the world, whenever the Lord has given a dispensa-

---

e, ordinances for the dead recorded on earth.   *f,* also recorded in heaven.   *g,* see *d,* Sec. 1.   *h,* ver. 3.   *i,* a record. necessary as well as the ordinance.   *j,* these records essential in the great judgment.

tion of the Priesthood to any man by actual revelation, or any set of men, this power has always been given. Hence, whatsoever those men did in authority, in the name of the Lord, and did it truly and faithfully, and kept a proper and *k*faithful record of the same, it became a law on earth and in heaven, and could not be annulled, according to the decrees of the great Jehovah. This is a faithful saying ! Who can hear it ?

10. And again, for the *l*precedent, Matthew xvi. 18, 19, "And I also say unto thee, that thou art Peter: and upon this rock I will build my church ; and the gates of hell shall not prevail against it; and I will give unto thee the keys of the kingdom of heaven, and whatsoever thou shalt bind on earth, shall be bound in heaven; and whatsoever thou shalt loose on earth, shall be loosed in heaven."

11. Now the great and grand secret of the whole matter, and the *summum bonum* of the whole subject that is lying before us, consists in obtaining the powers of the Holy Priesthood. For him to whom these keys are given, there is no difficulty in obtaining a knowledge of facts in relation to the salvation of the children of men, both as well for the dead as for the living.

12. Herein is glory and honor, and immortality and eternal life. The ordinance of baptism by water, to be immersed therein in order to *m*answer to the likeness of the dead, that one principle might accord with the other. To be immersed in the water and come forth out of the water is in the likeness of the resurrection of the dead in coming forth out of their graves ; hence this ordinance was instituted to form a relationship with the ordinance of baptism for the dead, being in likeness of the dead.

13. Consequently the *n*baptismal font was instituted

---

k, these records will be a law on earth and in heaven, in behalf of the dead.   *l*, 14.   21 : 1.   85 : 1—5, 9—12.   88 : 2.   127 : 6, 9.   Matt. 16 : 18, 19.   *m*, baptism for the dead being a symbol of the burial and the resurrection.   *n*, symbol of the grave.

as a simile of the grave, and was commanded to be in a place underneath where the living are wont to assemble, to show forth the living and the dead; and that all things may have their likeness, and that they may accord one with another; that which is earthly conforming to that which is heavenly, as Paul hath declared, 1 Corinthians xv. 46, 47, and 48.

14. "Howbeit that was not first which is spiritual, but that which is natural, and afterwards that which is spiritual. The first man is of the earth, earthy; the second man is the Lord, from heaven. As is the earthy, such are they also that are earthy; and as is the heavenly, such are they also that are heavenly." And as are the [o]records on the earth in relation to your dead, which are truly made out, so also are the records in heaven. This, therefore, is the sealing and binding power, and, in one sense of the word, the [p]keys of the kingdom which consist in the key of knowledge.

15. And now, my dearly beloved brethren and sisters, let me assure you that these are principles in relation to the dead, and the living, that cannot be lightly passed over, as pertaining to our salvation. For their salvation is necessary, and essential to our salvation, as Paul says concerning the fathers "that they without us cannot be made perfect;" neither can [q]we without our dead be made perfect.

16. And now, in relation to the baptism for the dead, I will give you another quotation of Paul, 1 Corinthians xv. 29, "Else what shall they do which are baptized for the dead, if the dead rise not at all; why are they then baptized for the dead?"

17. And again, in connection with this quotation, I will give you a quotation from one of the prophets, who had his eye fixed on the restoration of the Priesthood, the glories to be revealed in the last days, and in an

---

o, records on earth and in heaven must agree. *p*, see *d*, Sec. 1.
q, 2: 2. 110: 15. Heb. 11: 40.

especial manner this most glorious of all subjects belonging to the everlasting gospel, viz., the baptism for
the dead ; for Malachi says, last chapter, verses 5th
and 6th, " Behold, I will send you 'Elijah the prophet,
before the coming of the great and dreadful day of
the Lord ; and he shall turn the 'heart of the fathers
to the children, and the heart of the children to
their fathers, lest I come and smite the earth with a
curse."

18. I might have rendered a plainer translation to
this, but it is sufficiently plain to suit my purpose as it
stands.   It is sufficient to know, in this case, that the
earth will be smitten with a curse, unless there is a
welding link of some kind or other, between the fathers
and the children, upon some subject or other, and behold what is that subject?   It is the 'baptism for the
dead.   For we without them cannot be made perfect ;
neither can they without us be made perfect.   Neither
can they nor we, be made perfect, without those who
have died in the gospel also ; for it is necessary in the
ushering in of the dispensation of the fullness of times ;
which "dispensation is now beginning to usher in, that
a whole and complete and perfect union, and welding
together of dispensations, and keys, and powers, and
glories should take place, and be revealed from the days
of Adam even to the present time ; and not only this,
but those things which never have been revealed from
the foundation of the world, but have been kept hid
from the wise and prudent, shall be revealed unto ᵛbabes
and sucklings in this the dispensation of the fullness of
times.

19. Now, what do we hear in the gospel which we
have received ?   " A voice of gladness !   A voice of
mercy from heaven ; and a voice of ᵂtruth out of the

r, see a, Sec. 2.   s, see c, Sec. 2.   t, baptism for the dead, the
connecting link between the fathers who are dead, and the living children.
u, see n, Sec. 27.   27 : 8—13.   84 : 6—19, 25—34, 64—72.   86 : 8—11.   87 :
8—11, 88 : 108—110.   90 : 2, 7.   110 : 11—16.   112 : 15, 32.   115 : 19.   124 :
28, 40, 41.   v, Matt. 11 : 25.   Luke 10 : 21.   w, 1 : 29, 30.   20 :
8—10.   27 : 5.

earth ; glad tidings for the dead ; a voice of gladness
for the living and the dead ; glad tidings of great joy;
how beautiful upon the mountains are the feet of those
that bring glad tidings of good things ; and that say
unto Zion, behold ! thy God reigneth.   As the dews of
Carmel, so shall the knowledge of God descend upon
them."

20. And again, what do we hear ?   Glad tidings
from Cumorah !   Moroni, an angel from heaven, declaring the fulfillment of the prophets—*the book to be
revealed.   A voice of the Lord in the wilderness of
Fayette, Seneca county, declaring the *three witnesses
to bear record of the book.   The voice of *Michael on
the banks of the Susquehanna, detecting the devil when
he appeared as an angel of light.   The voice of *ᵃPeter,
James, and John in the wilderness between Harmony,
Susquehanna county, and Colesville, Broome county,
on the Susquehanna river, declaring themselves as
possessing the keys of the kingdom, and of the dispensation of the fullness of times.

21. And again, the voice of God in the chamber of
old father Whitmer, in Fayette, Seneca county, and at
sundry times, and in divers places through all the
travels and tribulations of this Church of Jesus Christ
of Latter-day Saints.   And the voice of *ᵇMichael, the
archangel; the voice of Gabriel, and of Raphael, and
of divers angels, from Michael or Adam, down to the
present time, all declaring their dispensation, their
rights, their keys, their honors, their majesty and glory,
and the power of their Priesthood; giving line upon
line, precept upon precept ; here a little, and there a
little—giving us consolation by holding forth that which
is to come, confirming our hope.

22. Brethren, shall we not go on in so great a cause?
Go forward and not backward.   Courage, brethren ;
and on, on to the victory !   Let your hearts rejoice,

---

x, see f, Sec. 27.   y, Sec. 17.   z, see k, Sec. 27.   2a, see d,
Sec. 5.   2b, see k, Sec. 27.

and be exceedingly glad. Let the earth break forth into singing. Let the [2c]dead speak forth anthems of eternal praise to the King Immanuel, who hath ordained before the world was, that which would enable us to redeem them out of their [2d]prison; for the prisoners shall go free.

23. Let the mountains shout for joy, and all ye valleys cry aloud ; and all ye seas and dry lands tell the wonders of your eternal king. And ye rivers, and brooks, and rills flow down with gladness. Let the woods, and all the trees of the field praise the Lord ; and ye solid rocks weep for joy. And let the sun, moon, and the morning stars sing together, and let all the sons of God shout for joy. And let the eternal creations declare his name for ever and ever. And again I say, how glorious is the voice-we hear from heaven, proclaiming in our ears, glory, and salvation, and honor, and immortality, and eternal life ; kingdoms, principalities, and powers.

24. Behold the great day of the Lord is at hand, and who can abide the day of his coming, and who can stand when he appeareth ; for he is like a refiner's fire, and like fuller's soap ; and he shall sit as a refiner and purifier of silver, and he shall purify the sons of Levi, and purge them as gold and silver, that they may offer unto the Lord an offering in righteousness. Let us therefore, as a church and a people, and as Latter-day Saints offer unto the Lord an offering in righteousness, and let us present in his [2e]holy temple, when it is finished, a [2f]book containing the records of our dead, which shall be worthy of all acceptation.

25. Brethren, I have many things to say to you on the subject; but shall now close for the present, and continue the subject another time. I am, as ever, your humble servant and never deviating friend,

JOSEPH SMITH.

2c, vers. 1—18. See Sec. 127.   2d, 76 : 73, 74. Isa. 24 : 17—23.
42 : 7. 49 : 9. 61 : 1. L. Pet. 3 : 19. 4 : 6. Zech. 9 : 11, 12.   2e, 84 :
31. Mal. 3 : 1—3.   2f, Sections 127, 128.

SECTION 129.

Three Grand Keys by which Good or Bad Angels or Spirits may be known.   Revealed to Joseph, the Prophet, at Nauvoo, Illinois, February 9th, 1843.

1. There are two kinds of beings in heaven—viz., angels who are resurrected personages, having *a*bodies of flesh and bones.

2. For instance, Jesus said, "Handle me and see, for a spirit hath not flesh and bones, as ye see me have."

3. 2nd. The *b*spirits of just men made perfect— they who are not resurrected, but inherit the same glory.

4. When a messenger comes, saying he has a message from God, offer him your hand, and request him to shake hands with you.

5. If he be an angel, he will do so, and you will feel his hand.

6. If he be the spirit of a just man made perfect, he will come in his glory; for that is the only way he can appear.

7. Ask him to shake hands with you, but he will not move, because it is contrary to the order of heaven for a just man to deceive ; but he will still deliver his message.

8. If it be the Devil as an angel of light, when you ask him to shake hands, he will offer you his hand, and you will not feel anything : you may therefore detect him.

9. These are *c*three grand keys whereby you may know whether any administration is from God.

---

a, Matt. 27 : 52, 53.   Luke 24 : 36—40.   Rev. 19 : 10.   22 : 8, 9.   Hela. 14 : 25.   III. Nep. 23 : 9—13.   *b*, Heb. 12 : 23.   *c*, vers. 1—8.

SECTION 130.

Important Items of Instruction, given by Joseph, the Prophet, April 2nd, 1843.

1. When the Saviour shall appear, we shall see him as he is. We shall see that he is a man like ourselves ;

2. And that same sociality which exists among us here will exist among us there, only it will be coupled with eternal glory, which glory we do not now enjoy.

3. (John xiv. 23.) The appearing of the Father and the Son, in that verse, is a *personal* appearance ; and the idea that the Father and the Son dwell in a man's heart, is an old sectarian notion, and is false.

4. In answer to the question, "Is not the reckoning of God's time, angel's time, prophet's time, and man's time according to the planet on which they reside ? "

5. I answer, yes. But there are no angels who minister to this earth but those who do belong or have belonged to it.

6. The angels do not reside on a planet like this earth ·

7. But they reside in the presence of God, on a globe like a *ᵃsea of glass and fire, where all things for their glory are manifest—past, present, and future, and are continually before the Lord.

8. The place where God resides is a great *ᵇUrim and Thummim.

9. This earth, in its sanctified and immortal state, will be made like unto crystal and will be a *ᶜUrim and Thummim to the inhabitants who dwell thereon, whereby all things pertaining to an inferior kingdom, or all kingdoms of a lower order, will be manifest to those who dwell on it ; and this earth will be Christ's.

---

a, vers. 8, 9.   77 : 1.   *b*, vers. 9—11. See *d*, Sec. 17.   *c*, see *b*.

10. Then the [d]white stone mentioned in Revelations ii. 17, will become a [e]Urim and Thummim to each individual who receives one, whereby things pertaining to a higher order of kingdoms, even all kingdoms, will be made known;

11. And a [f]white stone is given to each of those who come into the celestial kingdom, whereon is a new name written, which no man knoweth save he that receiveth it. The new name is the [g]key word.

12. I prophesy, in the name of the Lord God, that the commencement of the difficulties which will cause much bloodshed previous to the coming of the Son of Man will be [h]in South Carolina.

13. It may probably arise through the slave question. This a voice declared to me, while I was praying earnestly on the subject, December 25th, 1832.

14. I was once praying very earnestly to know the time of the coming of the Son of Man, when I heard a voice repeat the following :—

15. "Joseph, my son, if thou livest until thou art [i]eighty-five years old, thou shalt see the face of the Son of Man : therefore let this suffice, and trouble me no more on this matter."

16. I was left thus, without being able to decide whether this coming referred to the [j]beginning of the millennium or to some previous appearing, or whether I should die and thus see his face.

17. I believe the coming of the Son of Man will not be any [k]sooner than that time.

18. Whatever principles of intelligence we attain

---

d, Exod. 39. Lev. 8 : 6—8. Num. 27 : 21. Deut. 33 : 8.   *e*, see *d*.
f, see *d*.   *g*, Rev. 2 : 17.   *h*, ver. 13.   See Sec. 87.
i, near the end of the year A.D. 1890.   45 : 42—44.   49 : 6, 7.   See
prophecy of Joseph, uttered 14th March, 1835.   (Published in Mil. Star,
No. 13, Vol. 15.) "Even 56 years should wind up the scene." Whether
this had reference to the coming of Christ or to the fulfillment of the
"times of the Gentiles" is unknown.   *j*, The beginning of the
seventh Millennium will be before the seven angels sound their trumpets,
preparatory to the coming of Christ.   See 77 : 12.   *k*, Joseph's
opinion.

unto in this life, it will rise 'with us in the resurrection ;

19. And if a person gains more knowledge and intelligence in this life through his diligence and obedience than another, he will have so much the advantage in the world to come.

20. There is a ᵐlaw, irrevocably decreed in heaven before the foundations of this world, upon which all blessings are predicated ;

21. And when we obtain any blessing from God, it is by obedience to that law upon which it is predicated.

22. The Father has a body of flesh and bones as tangible as man's ; the Son also : but the Holy Ghost has not a body of flesh and bones, but is a ⁿpersonage of Spirit. Were it not so, the Holy Ghost could not dwell in us.

23. A man may receive the Holy Ghost, and it may descend upon him and not tarry with him.

SECTION 131.

Remarks of Joseph, the Prophet, at Ramus, Illinois, May 16th and 17th, 1843.

1. In the celestial glory there are ᵃthree heavens or degrees ;

2. And in order to obtain the highest, a man must enter in to this ᵇOrder of the Priesthood ; (meaning the new and everlasting covenant of marriage ;)

---

l, knowledge gained by obedience in this life, will be retained in the resurrection.   *m*, Ancient law and decrees, through which blessings are granted.   *n*, Lecture 5 : 2, 3.

a, II. Cor. 12 : 1—4.   *b*, 132.

3. And if he does not, he cannot obtain it.

4. He may enter into the other, but that is the end of his kingdom : he cannot have an increase.

5. (May 17th, 1843.) The more sure word of prophecy (mentioned by Peter) means a man's ^cknowing that he is sealed up unto eternal life, by revelation and the spirit of prophecy, through the power of the Holy Priesthood.

6. It is impossible for a man to be saved in ignorance.

7. There is no such thing as ^dimmaterial matter. All spirit is ^ematter, but it is more fine or pure, and can only be discerned by purer eyes.

8. We cannot see it; but when our bodies are purified, we shall see that it is all matter.

SECTION 132.

Revelation on the Eternity of the Marriage Covenant, including Plurality of Wives. Given through Joseph, the Seer, in Nauvoo, Hancock County, Illinois, July 12th, 1843.

1. Verily, thus saith the Lord unto you, my servant Joseph, that inasmuch as you have inquired of my hand, to know and understand wherein I, the Lord, justified my servants Abraham, Isaac and Jacob; as also Moses, David and Solomon, my servants, as touching the principle and doctrine of their having ^amany wives and concubines:

c, 68: 12. 76: 53. 124: 124. II. Pet. 1: 19.   d, see pamphlet on "Absurdities of Immaterialism."   e, see pamphlet on "Absurdities of Immaterialism."

a, vers. 3, 34, 37—40, 61—63. Gen. 16. 21: 3, 18—21. 25: 6. Chapters 29, 30. 33: 5—7. 37: 2. Exod. 21: 7—11. 22: 16. Lev. 18: 18.

2. Behold! and lo, I am the Lord thy God, and will answer thee as touching this matter:

3. Therefore, prepare thy heart to receive and obey the instructions which I am about to give unto you; for all those who have this law revealed unto them [b]must obey the same;

4. For behold! I reveal unto you a [c]new and an everlasting covenant; and if ye abide not that [d]covenant, then are ye damned; for no one can [e]reject this covenant, and be permitted to enter into my glory;

5. For all who will have a blessing at my hands, shall [f]abide the law which was appointed for that blessing, and the conditions thereof, as were [g]instituted from before the foundation of the world:

6. And as pertaining to the [h]new and everlasting covenant, it was instituted for the fullness of my glory; and he that receiveth a fullness thereof, [i]must and shall abide the law, or he shall be damned, saith the Lord God.

7. And verily I say unto you, that the [j]conditions of this law are these:—All covenants, contracts, bonds, obligations, oaths, vows, performances, connections, associations, or expectations, that are not made, and entered into, and [k]sealed, by the Holy Spirit of promise, of him who is anointed, both as well for time and for all eternity, and that too most holy, by revelation and commandment through the medium of mine anointed, whom I have appointed on the earth to hold this power, (and I have appointed unto my servant Joseph to hold this power in the last days, and there is

Num. 12: 1.   Deut. 17: 14—18.   21: 10—17.   22: 28, 29.   25: 5—10. Judges 1: 16.   4: 11.   8: 29—32.   See also chapters 6 and 7.   10: 4. 12: 8, 9, 13, 14.   I. Sam. 1: 1, 2.   25: 42, 43.   27: 3.   30: 5, 8.   II. Sam. 2: 1—4.   3: 2—5, 14—16.   5: 13, 23.   12: 8.   15: 16.   16: 21, 22. 19: 5.   20: 3.   I. Kings 1: 1—4.   11: 1—10.   15: 5.   I. Chron. 2: 18, 19, 46, 48.   3: 1—9.   4: 5.   7: 4, 14.   8: 8, 9.   14: 3.   28: 5.   II. Chron. 11: 21.   13: 21.   24: 2, 3.   Isaiah 4: 1.   Hosea 1: 2, 3, 6, 8.   3: 1—3. Matt. 19: 3—9.   Mark 10: 11, 12.   Luke 20: 27—36.   I. Cor. 11: 11.   I. Tim. 3: 2, 12.   Rev. 21: 12   b, vers. 4, 5, 13—18, 27.   c, vers. 3, 5, 13—18, 27.   31: 2, 3, 4.   d, vers. 6, 13—18, 27.   e, 131: 1—4. f, 88: 38, 39.   g, vers. 11, 28, 63.   h, see c.   i, see d. j, 88: 38, 39.   k, vers. 19, 46, 47.

never but one on the earth at a time, on whom this power and the keys of this Priesthood are conferred,) are of no efficacy, virtue or force, in and after the resurrection from the dead ; for all contracts that are not made unto this end, have an end when men are dead.

8. Behold ! mine house is a house of order, saith the Lord God, and not a house of confusion.

9. Will I accept of an offering, saith the Lord, that is not made in my name !

10. Or, will I receive at your hands that which I have not appointed !

11. And will I appoint unto you, saith the Lord, except it be by *law, even as I and my Father *ordained unto you, before the world was !

12. I am the Lord thy God, and I give unto you this commandment, that no man shall come unto the Father but by me, or by my word, which is my law, saith the Lord ;

13. And everything that is in the world, whether it be ordained of men, by thrones, or principalities, or powers, or things of name, whatsoever they may be, that are not by me, or by my word, saith the Lord, shall be thrown down, and shall *not remain after men are dead, neither in nor after the resurrection, saith the Lord your God ;

14. For whatsoever things *remain, are by me ; and whatsoever things are not by me, shall be shaken and destroyed.

15. Therefore, if a man marry him a wife in the world, and he marry her not by me, nor by my word ; and he covenant with her so long as he is in the world, and she with him, their *covenant and marriage are not of force when they are dead, and when they are out of the world ; therefore, they are not bound by any law when they are out of the world ;

l, vers. 5, 63.　　　　*m*, 49 : 15.　See *l*.　　　　*n*, vers. 14—18.
o, vers. 15—27.　　*p*, vers. 16, 17.

16. Therefore, when they are *out of the world, they neither marry, nor are given in marriage; but are appointed angels in heaven, which angels are ministering servants, to minister for those who are worthy of a far more, and an exceeding, and an eternal weight of glory;

17. For these angels did not abide my law, therefore they cannot be enlarged, but remain separately and singly, without exaltation, in their saved condition, to all eternity, and from henceforth are not Gods, but are angels of God, for ever and ever.

18. And again, verily I say unto you, if a man marry a wife, and make a covenant with her for time and for all eternity, if that *covenant is not by me, or by my word, which is my law, and is not sealed by the Holy Spirit of promise, through him whom I have anointed and appointed unto this power—then it is not valid, neither of force when they are out of the world, because they are not joined by me, saith the Lord, neither by my word; when they are out of the world, it cannot be received there, because the angels and the Gods are appointed there, by whom they cannot pass; they cannot, therefore, inherit my glory, for my house is a house of order, saith the Lord God.

19. And again, verily I say unto you, if a man marry a wife by my word, which is my law, and by the *new and everlasting covenant, and it is *sealed unto them by the Holy Spirit of promise, by him who is anointed, unto whom I have appointed this power, and the keys of this Priesthood; and it shall be said unto them, ye shall come forth in the first resurrection; and if it be after the first resurrection, in the next resurrection; and shall inherit thrones, kingdoms, principalities, and powers, dominions, all heights and depths —then shall it be written in the Lamb's Book of Life, that he shall commit no murder whereby to shed innocent blood, and if ye abide in my covenant, and

---

q, all ordinances must be properly attended to in this world, or they will be invalid and of no effect in the world to come.   *r*, vers. 7, 46, 47.
s, see *d*.   *t*, vers. 7, 46, 47.

commit no murder whereby to shed innocent blood, it shall be done unto them in all things whatsoever my servant hath put upon them, in time, and through all eternity, and shall be of full force when they are out of the world ; and they shall *pass by the angels, and the Gods, which are set there, to their exaltation and glory in all things, as hath been sealed upon their heads, which glory shall be a fullness and a continuation of the seeds for ever and ever.

20. Then shall they be *Gods, because they have no end ; therefore shall they be from everlasting to everlasting, because they continue ; then shall they be above all, because *all things are subject unto them. Then shall they be Gods, because they have all power, and the angels are subject unto them.

21. Verily, verily I say unto you, except ye *abide my law, ye cannot attain to this glory ;

22. For *strait is the gate, and narrow the way that leadeth unto the exaltation and continuation of *the lives, and few there be that find it, because ye receive me not in the world, neither do ye know me.

23. But if ye receive me in the world, then shall ye know me, and shall receive ²*your exaltation, that where I am, ye shall be also.

24. This is eternal lives, to know the only wise and true God, and Jesus Christ, whom he hath sent. I am he. Receive ye, therefore, my law.

25. Broad is the gate, and ²*wide the way that leadeth to the deaths, and many there are that go in thereat ; because they receive me not, neither do they abide in my law.

26. Verily, verily I say unto you, if a man ²*marry a wife according to my word, and they are ²*sealed

u, vers. 16—18, 20.   v, 17—19, 37.   John 10 : 34, 35.   Rev. 14 : 1.
22 : 4.   w, 50 : 26—28.   x, 131 : 1—4.   y, III. Nep. 9 : 41.
31 : 9, 17, 18.   33 : 9.   Alma 37 : 44, 45.   Hela. 3 : 29, 30.   III. Nep. 14 : 13,
14.   z, continuation of posterity in the eternal world.   vers. 30, 31.
Numbers 16 : 22.   Heb. 12 : 9.   2a, John 14 : 2, 3.   2b, III. Nep.
14 : 13.   Matt. 7 : 13.   2c, ver. 19.   2d, vers. 7, 19, 20.

by the Holy Spirit of promise, according to mine appointment, and he or she shall commit any sin or transgression of the [2e]new and everlasting covenant whatever, and all manner of blasphemies, and if they commit no murder, wherein they shed innocent blood— yet [2f]they shall come forth in the first resurrection, and enter into their exaltation; but they shall be [2g]destroyed in the flesh, and shall be delivered unto the [2h]buffetings of Satan unto the day of redemption, saith the Lord God.

27. The blasphemy against the Holy Ghost, which shall not be forgiven in the world, nor out of the world, is in that ye [2i]commit murder, wherein ye shed innocent blood, and assent unto my death, after ye have received my [2j]new and everlasting covenant, saith the Lord God; and he that abideth not this law, can in no wise enter into my glory, but shall be damned, saith the Lord.

28. I am the Lord thy God, and will give unto thee the law of my Holy Priesthood, as was ordained by me, and my Father, before the world was.

29. Abraham received all things, whatsoever he received, by revelation and commandment, by my word, saith the Lord, and [2k]hath entered into his exaltation, and sitteth upon his throne.

30. Abraham received promises concerning his seed, and of the fruit of his loins,—from whose loins [2l]ye are, namely, my servant Joseph,—which were to continue so long as they were in the world; and as touching Abraham and his seed, [2m]out of the world they should continue; both in the world and out of the world should they continue as innumerable as the stars; or, if ye were to count the sand upon the sea shore, ye could not number them.

2e, see c.   2f, vers. 19, 23.   2g, vers. 41—43, 54, 63, 64.
2h, see h, Sec. 78.   2i, after having received so great light, if a person murders, there is no forgiveness.   42: 18, 79.   2j, see c.
2k, ver. 37.   Luke 12 : 28.   2l, II. Nep. 3 : 7, 11, 12, 14—17.
2m, vers. 19, 31—37.

31. This promise is yours, also, because ye are of Abraham, and the promise was made unto Abraham; and by this law are the continuation of the works of my Father, wherein he glorifieth himself.

32. Go ye, therefore, and do the [2n]works of Abraham; enter ye into my law, and ye shall be saved.

33. But if ye enter not into my law ye cannot receive the promise of my Father, which he made unto Abraham.

34. God commanded Abraham, and Sarah [2o]gave Hagar to Abraham to wife. And why did she do it? Because this was the law, and from Hagar sprang many people. This, therefore, was fulfilling, among other things, the promises.

35. Was Abraham, therefore, under condemnation? Verily, I say unto you, Nay; for I, the Lord, commanded it.

36. Abraham was commanded to offer his son Isaac; nevertheless, it was written, thou shalt not kill. Abraham, however, did not refuse, and it was accounted unto him for righteousness.

37. Abraham received concubines, and they bear him children, and it was accounted unto him for righteousness, because they were [2p]given unto him, and he abode in my law, as Isaac also, and Jacob did none other things than that which they were commanded; and because they did none other things than that which they were commanded, they have entered into their exaltation, according to the promises, and sit upon thrones, and are not angels, but [2q]are Gods.

38. David also received many wives and concubines, as also Solomon and Moses my servants; as also many others of my servants, from the beginning of creation until this time; and in nothing did they sin, save in those things which they [2r]received not of me.

2n, John 8: 39   2o, Gen. 16.   25: 12—18.   2p, Gen. 25: 6.
2q, 133: 55. See v.   2r, vers. 7, 19, 39.

39. David's wives and concubines were [24]given unto him, of me, by the hand of Nathan, my servant, and others of the prophets who had the keys of this power; and in none of these things did he sin against me, save in the case of Uriah and his wife; and, therefore he hath fallen from his exaltation, and received his portion; and he shall [2t]not inherit them out of the world; for I gave them unto another, saith the Lord.

40. I am the Lord thy God, and I gave unto thee, my servant Joseph, an appointment, and restore all things; ask what ye will, and it shall be given unto you according to my word:

41. And as ye have asked concerning adultery— verily, verily I say unto you, if a man [2u]receiveth a wife in the new and everlasting covenant, and if she be with another man, and I have not appointed unto her by the holy anointing, she hath committed adultery, and shall be destroyed.

42. If she be not in the new and everlasting cove- nant, and she be with another man, she has [2v]com- mitted adultery;

43. And if her husband be with another woman, and he was under a vow, he hath broken his vow, and [2w]hath committed adultery,

44. And if she hath not committed adultery, but is innocent, and hath not broken her vow, and she know- eth it, and I reveal it unto you, my servant Joseph, then shall you have power, by the power of my Holy Priesthood, to take her, and give her unto him that [2x]hath not committed adultery, but hath been faithful; for he shall be made ruler over [2y]many:

45. For I have conferred upon you the keys and power of the Priesthood, wherein I restore [2z]all things, and make known unto you all things in due time.

2s, 7, 19, 33. II. Sam. 12: 8.   2t, II. Sam. 12: 11. 15: 16. 16:
20—23. 20: 3.   2u, vers. 4—7, 19.   2v, see m, Sec. 42.
2w, see m, Sec. 42.   2x, see m, Sec. 42.   2y, Luke 19: 15—26.
2z, Acts 3: 21. Isaiah 4: 1.

46. And verily, verily I say unto you, that [3a]whatsoever you seal on earth, shall be sealed in heaven; and whatsoever you [3b]bind on earth, in my name, and by my word, saith the Lord, it shall be eternally bound in the heavens; and whosesoever sins you [3c]remit on earth shall be remitted eternally in the heavens; and whosesoever sins you [3d]retain on earth, shall be retained in heaven.

47. And again, verily I say, [3e]whomsoever you bless, I will bless, and whomsoever you [3f]curse, I will curse, saith the Lord; for I, the Lord, am thy God.

48. And again, verily I say unto you, my servant Joseph, that whatsoever you give on earth, and to whomsoever you [3g]give any one on earth, by my word, and according to my law, it shall be visited with blessings, and not cursings, and with my power, saith the Lord, and shall be without condemnation on earth, and in heaven;

49. For I am the Lord thy God, and will be with thee even unto the end of the world, and through all eternity; for verily, I [3h]seal upon you your exaltation, and prepare a [3i]throne for you in the kingdom of my Father, with Abraham your father.

50. Behold, I have seen your sacrifices, and will forgive all your sins; I have seen your sacrifices, in obedience to that which I have told you; go, therefore, and I make a way for your escape, as I accepted the offering of Abraham, of his son Isaac.

51. Verily, I say unto you, a commandment I give unto mine handmaid, Emma Smith, your wife, whom I have given unto you, that she stay herself, and partake not of that which I commanded you to offer unto her; for I did it, saith the Lord, to prove you all, as I did Abraham; and that I might require an offering at your hand, by covenant and sacrifice;

3a, see d, Sec. 1.   3b, see d, Sec. 1.   Matt. 18 : 18.   3c, Matt.
16 : 19.   John 20 : 23.   3d, John 20 : 23.   3e, 124 : 93.
3f, 124 : 93.   3g, ver. 39.   3h, ver. 23.   3i, vers.
19, 37.

52. And let mine handmaid, Emma Smith, receive *ʲall those that have been given unto my servant Joseph, and who are virtuous and pure before me ; and those who are not pure, and have said they were pure, shall be destroyed, saith the Lord God ;

53. For I am the Lord thy God, and ye shall obey my voice ; and I give unto my servant Joseph, that he shall be made ruler over many things, for he hath been faithful over a few things, and from henceforth I will strengthen him.

54. And I command mine handmaid, Emma Smith, to abide and cleave unto my servant Joseph, and to none else. But if she will not abide this commandment, she shall be destroyed, saith the Lord ; for I am the Lord thy God, and will destroy her, if she abide not in my law ;

55. But if she will not abide this commandment, then shall my servant Joseph do all things for her, even as he hath said ; and I will bless him and multiply him, and give unto him an *ᵏhundred-fold in this world, of fathers and mothers, brothers and sisters, houses and lands, wives and children, and crowns of eternal lives in the eternal worlds.

56. And again, verily I say, let mine handmaid forgive my servant Joseph his trespasses ; and then shall she be forgiven her trespasses, wherein she has trespassed against me ; and I, the Lord thy God, will bless her, and multiply her, and make her heart to rejoice.

57. And again, I say, let not my servant Joseph put his property out of his hands, lest an enemy come and destroy him ; for Satan seeketh to destroy ; for I am the Lord thy God, and he is my servant ; and behold! and lo, I am with him, as I was with Abraham, thy father, even unto his exaltation and glory.

58. Now, as touching the law of the Priesthood, there are many things pertaining thereunto.

---

*ʲ, ver. 65.   *ᵏ, Mark 10 : 28—30.

59. Verily, if a man be called of my Father, as was Aaron, by mine own voice, and by the voice of him that sent me : and I have endowed him with the keys of the power of this Priesthood, if he do anything in my name, and according to my law, and by my word, he will not commit sin, and I will justify him.

60. Let no one, therefore, set on my servant Joseph ; for I will justify him ; for he shall do the sacrifice which I require at his hands, for his transgressions, saith the Lord your God.

61. And again, as pertaining to the law of the Priesthood : If any man espouse a virgin, and desire to espouse another, and the first give her consent ; and if he espouse the second, and they are virgins, and have vowed to no other man, then is he justified ; he cannot commit adultery, for they are [3l]given unto him ; for he cannot commit adultery with that that belongeth unto him and to no one else ;

62. And if he have ten virgins given unto him by this law, [3m]he cannot commit adultery, for they belong to him, and they are given unto him, therefore is he justified.

63. But if one or either of the ten virgins, after she is espoused, shall be with another man ; she has [3n]committed adultery, and shall be destroyed ; for they are given unto him to multiply and replenish the earth, according to my commandment, and to fulfill the promise which was given by my Father [3o]before the foundation of the world ; and for their exaltation in the eternal worlds, that they may bear [3p]the souls of men ; for herein is the work of my Father continued, that he may be glorified.

64. And again, verily, verily I say unto you, if any man have a wife, who holds the keys of this power, and he teaches unto her the [3q]law of my Priesthood, as

---

[3l], ver. 48.　　[3m], 19, 20, 48.　　[3n], ver. 41.　　[3o], Titus 1 : 2.　　[3p], that is, the souls or spirits of men to be born in heaven. Vers. 19, 30.　　[3q], ver. 52.

pertaining to these things, then shall she believe, and administer unto him, or she shall be destroyed, saith the Lord your God, for I will destroy her; for I will magnify my name upon all those who receive and abide in my law.

65. Therefore, it shall be lawful in me, if she receive not this law, for [37]him to receive all things, whatsoever I, the Lord his God, will give unto him, because she did not administer unto him according to my word; and she then becomes the transgressor; and he is exempt from the law of Sarah, who administered unto Abraham according to the law, when I [38]commanded Abraham to take Hagar to wife.

66. And now, as pertaining to this law, verily, verily I say unto you, I will reveal more unto you, hereafter; therefore, let this suffice for the present. Behold, I am Alpha and Omega. Amen.

3r, ver. 55.   3s, vers. 34—37.

APPENDIX.

SECTION 133.

Revelation, called the Appendix, given through Joseph, the Seer, at Hiram, Portage Co., Ohio.

1. Hearken, O ye people of ªmy church, saith the Lord your God, and hear the word of the Lord concerning you :

2. The Lord who shall suddenly come ᵇto his temple ; the Lord who shall come ᶜdown upon the world with a curse to judgment ; yea, upon all the nations that forget God, and upon all the ungodly among you.

3. For he shall make ᵈbear his holy arm in the eyes of all the nations, and all the ends of the earth shall see the salvation of their God.

4. Wherefore, prepare ye, prepare ye, O my people ; sanctify yourselves ; ᵉgather ye together, O ye people of my church, upon the land of Zion, all you that have not been commanded to tarry.

5. Go ye ᶠout from Babylon. Be ye clean that bear the vessels of the Lord.

6. Call your ᵍsolemn assemblies, and speak often one to another. And let every man call upon the name of the Lord ;

7. Yea, verily I say unto you again, the time has

---

a, see *a*, Sec. 1.   *b*, see *d*, Sec. 36.   *c*, see *e*, Sec. 1.   *d*, Isa. 52 : 10.   *e*, see *j*, Sec. 10.   *f*, see *j*, Sec. 10.   *g*, see 2r, Sec. 88.

come when the voice of the Lord is unto you, [h]go ye out of Babylon; [i]gather ye out from among the nations, from the four winds, from one end of heaven to the other.

8. Send forth the elders of [j]my church unto [k]the nations which are afar off; unto the islands of the sea; send forth unto foreign lands; call upon all nations; firstly, [l]upon the Gentiles, and then [m]upon the Jews.

9. And behold, and lo, this shall be their cry, and the voice of the Lord unto all people : [n]Go ye forth unto the land of Zion, that the borders of my people may be enlarged, and that her [o]Stakes may be strengthened, and that Zion may go forth unto the regions round about ;

10. Yea, let the cry go forth among all people: Awake and arise and go forth to [p]meet the Bridegroom : behold and lo, the Bridegroom cometh, go ye out to meet him. Prepare yourselves for the [q]great day of the Lord.

11. Watch, therefore, for ye know neither the day nor the hour.

12. Let them therefore, who are [r]among the Gentiles, flee unto Zion.

13. And let them who be of [s]Judah flee unto Jerusalem, unto the mountains of the Lord's house.

14. Go ye out from among the nations, [t]even from Babylon, from the midst of wickedness, which is spiritual Babylon.

15. But verily, thus saith the Lord, Let not your flight be in [u]haste, but let all things be prepared before you ; and he that goeth let him not [v]look back, lest sudden destruction shall come upon him.

---

h, see j, Sec. 10.   i, see j, Sec. 10.   j, see a, Sec. 1.   k, see b, Sec. 1.   l, see o, Sec. 18.   m, see o, Sec. 18.   n, see j, Sec. 10. o, see g, Sec. 87.   p, see e, Sec. 1.   q, see e, Sec. 1.   r, see j, Sec. 10.   s, see o, Sec. 45.   t, see j, Sec. 10.   u, see j, Sec. 10. v, Gen. 19 : 26.

16. Hearken and hear, O ye inhabitants of the earth. Listen ye elders of ᵂmy church together, and hear the voice of the Lord, for he calleth upon all men, and he commandeth ˣall men everywhere to repent ;

17. For, behold, the Lord God hath ʸsent forth the angel crying through the midst of heaven, saying, Prepare ye the way of the Lord, and make his paths straight, for the ᶻhour of his coming is nigh,

18. When the Lamb shall ²ᵃstand upon Mount Zion, and with him a hundred and forty-four thousand, having his Father's name written on their foreheads :

19. Wherefore, prepare ye for the ²ᵇcoming of the Bridegroom ; go ye, go ye out to meet him,

20. For behold, he shall ²ᶜstand upon the mount of Olivet, and upon the mighty ocean, even the great deep, and upon the islands of the sea, and ²ᵈupon the land of Zion ;

21. And he shall ²ᵉutter his voice out of Zion, and he shall ²ᶠspeak from Jerusalem, and his ²ᵍvoice shall be heard among all people,

22. And it shall be a voice as of the ²ʰvoice of many waters, and as the voice of a great thunder, which ²ⁱshall break down the mountains, and the ²ʲvalleys shall not be found ;

23. He shall command the great deep, and it shall be driven back into the north countries, and the ²ᵏislands shall become one land,

24. And the land of Jerusalem and the land of Zion shall be turned back into their own place, and the earth shall be like as it was in the days ²ˡbefore it was divided.

25. And the Lord, even the Saviour, shall stand in

---

w, see a, Sec. 1.   x, see b, Sec. 1.   y, see Sections 13, 27.
z, see e, Sec. 1.   2a, Rev. 14 : 1.   2b, see e, Sec. 1.   2c, 45 : 48.
2d, III. Nep. 20: 22.   21 : 25.   2e, Joel 3: 16.   2f, Joel 3: 16.
2g, 45 : 49.   2h, 110 : 3.   Rev. 19 : 6.   2i, ver. 40.   49 : 23.   Isaiah
40 : 4.   2j, see 2i.   2k, ver. 24.   Rev. 6 : 15.   2l, Gen.
10 : 25.   Isaiah 62 : 4.

the midst of his people, and shall [2m]reign over all flesh.

26. And they who are in the [2n]north countries shall come in remembrance before the Lord, and their prophets shall hear his voice, and shall no longer stay themselves, and they shall smite the rocks, and the ice shall flow down at their presence.

27. And an [2o]highway shall be cast up in the midst of the great deep.

28. Their enemies shall become a prey unto them,

29. And in the [2p]barren deserts there shall come forth pools of living water ; and the [2q]parched ground shall no longer be a thirsty land.

30. And they shall bring forth their rich treasures unto the children of Ephraim my servants.

31. And the boundaries of the [2r]everlasting hills shall tremble at their presence.

32. And there shall they fall down and be crowned with glory, even in Zion, by the hands of the servants of the Lord, even the [2s]children of Ephraim ;

33. And they shall be filled with [2t]songs of everlasting joy.

34. Behold, this is the blessing of the everlasting God upon the tribes of Israel, and the [2u]richer blessing upon the head of Ephraim and his fellows.

35. And they also of the tribe of Judah, [2v]after their pain, shall be sanctified in holiness before the Lord to dwell in his presence, day and night, for ever and ever.

36. And now, verily saith the Lord, That these things might be known among you, O inhabitants of the earth, I have [2w]sent forth mine angel, flying through the midst of heaven, having the everlasting gospel, who

2m, see e, Sec. 1.   2n, the ten tribes.   2o, Isaiah 51: 9—11.
35: 8—10.   2p, Isaiah 35: 6, 7.   2q, Isaiah 35: 6, 7.   2r, the great chain of the Rocky mountains.   2s, L Chron. 5: 1.   Gen. 48: 16, 19.   49: 22—26.   Deut. 33: 13—17.   2t, Isaiah 35: 10.   51: 11.
Jer. 31: 12.   2u, see 2s.   2v, 45: 51—53.   Zech. 12: 10—14.
2w, Rev. 14: 6.

hath appeared unto [2x]some, and hath committed it unto man, who shall appear unto [2y]many that dwell on the earth ;

37. And this gospel shall be preached [2z]unto every nation, and kindred, and tongue, and people,

38. And the servants of God shall go forth, saying, with a loud voice, Fear God and give glory to him, for the hour of his judgment is come :

39. And worship him that made heaven, and earth, and the sea, and the fountains of waters,

40. Calling upon the name of the Lord day and night, saying, O that thou wouldst [3a]rend the heavens, that thou wouldst come down, that the mountains might flow down at thy presence.

41. And it shall be answered upon their heads, for the presence of the Lord shall be as the [3b]melting fire that burneth, and as the fire which causeth the waters to boil.

42. O Lord thou shalt come down to make thy name known to thine adversaries, and all nations shall [3c]tremble at thy presence.

43. When thou doest [3d]terrible things—things they look not for ;

44. Yea, when thou comest down, and the [3e]mountains flow down at thy presence, thou shalt meet him who rejoiceth and worketh righteousness, who remembereth thee in thy ways ;

45. For since the beginning of the world have not men heard nor perceived by the ear, neither hath any eye seen, O God, besides thee, how [3f]great things thou hast prepared for him that waiteth for thee.

46. And it shall be said, [3g]Who is this that cometh down from God in heaven with dyed garments ; yea, from the regions which are not known, clothed in his

---

2x, 20: 6.　　See testimony of three witnesses, Book of Mormon.
2y, 77 : 8.　88 : 103, 104.　　　2z, Rev. 14 : 6.　　　3a, Isaiah 64 : 1.
3b, Isaiah 64 : 2.　　　3c, Isaiah 64 : 2.　　　3d, Isaiah 64 : 3.
3e, Isaiah 64 : 3.　　　3f, Isaiah 64 : 4.　　　3g, Isaiah 63 : 1.

glorious apparel, traveling in the greatness of his strength?

47. And he shall say, I am he who spake in righteousness, mighty to save.

48. And the Lord shall be [h]red in his apparel, and his garments like him that treadeth in the wine vat,

49. And so great shall be the [i]glory of his presence, that the sun shall hide [j]his face in shame; and the moon shall withhold its light; and the stars shall be [k]hurled from their places;

50. And his voice shall be heard, [l]I have trodden the wine-press alone, and have brought judgment upon all people; and none were with me;

51. And I have trampled them in my fury, and I did tread upon them in mine anger, and their blood have I sprinkled upon my garments, and stained all my raiment; for this was the [m]day of vengeance which was in my heart.

52. And now the [n]year of my redeemed is come, and they shall mention the loving kindness of their Lord, and all that he has bestowed upon them according to his goodness, and according to his loving kindness, for ever and ever.

53. In all their afflictions he was afflicted. And the angel of his presence saved them; and in his love, and in his pity, he redeemed them, and bear them, and carried them all the days of old;

54. Yea, and Enoch also, and they who were with him; the prophets who were before him; and Noah also, and they who were before him, and Moses also, and they who were before him;

55. And from Moses to [o]Elijah; and from [p]Elijah to John, who were with Christ in his resurrection, and

the holy apostles, with Abraham, Isaac, and Jacob, shall be in the presence of the Lamb.

56. And the [3q]graves of the saints shall be opened, and they shall come forth and stand on the right hand of the Lamb, when he shall [3r]stand upon Mount Zion, and upon the holy city, the New Jerusalem, and they shall sing the song of the Lamb, day and night, for ever and ever.

57. And for this cause, that men might be made partakers of the glories which were to be revealed, the Lord sent forth the fullness of his gospel, his [3s]everlasting covenant, reasoning in plainness and simplicity,

58. To prepare the [3t]weak for those things which are coming on the earth, and for the Lord's errand in the day when the weak should confound the wise, and [3u]the little one become a strong nation, and [3v]two should put their tens of thousands to flight;

59. And by the weak things of the earth the Lord should thresh the nations by the power of his Spirit.

60. And for this cause these commandments were given; they were commanded to be kept from the world in the day that they were given, but now are to [3w]go forth unto all flesh.

61. And this according to the mind and will of the Lord, who ruleth over all flesh.

62. And unto him that repenteth and sanctifieth himself before the Lord, shall be given eternal life;

63. And upon them that hearken not to the voice of the Lord, shall be fulfilled that which was written by the Prophet Moses, that they should be [3x]cut off from among the people.

64. And also that which was written by the [3y]pro-

3q, see m, Sec. 20.   3r, see 2d.   3s, see k, Sec. 1.   3t, see j, Sec. 1.   3u, Isaiah 60: 22.   3v, Deut. 32: 29, 30.   3w, see b, Sec. 1.   3x, I. Nep. 22: 20, 21.   III. Nep. 20: 23.   21: 11.   Acts 8: 22, 23.   3y, Mal. 4: 1.

phet Malachi ; for, behold, the day cometh that shall
burn as an oven, and all the proud, yea, and all that
do wickedly, shall be stubble ; and the day that cometh
shall burn them up, saith the Lord of hosts, that it
shall leave them neither root nor branch.

65. Wherefore, this shall be the answer of the Lord
unto them :—

66. In that day when I came unto my own, no man
among you received me, and you were driven out.

67. When I called again, there was none of you to
answer, yet my [3z]arm was not shortened at all, that I
could not redeem, neither my power to deliver.

68. Behold, at my rebuke I dry up the sea. I make
the rivers a wilderness ; their fish stinketh, and dieth
for thirst.

69. I clothe the heavens with blackness, and make
sackcloth their covering.

70. And this shall ye have of my hand,—[4a]ye shall
lay down in sorrow.

71. Behold and lo, there are none to deliver you,
for ye obeyed not my voice when I called to you out
of the heavens ; ye believed not my servants, and
[4b]when they were sent unto you ye received them not ;

72. Wherefore [4c]they sealed up the testimony and
bound up the law, and ye were delivered over unto
darkness ;

73. These shall go away into [4d]outer darkness,
where there is weeping, and wailing, and gnashing of
teeth.

74. Behold the Lord your God hath spoken it.
Amen.

3z, Isaiah 50 : 2.   4a, Isaiah 50 : 11   4b, II. Nep. 28 : 32.
4c, see d, Sec. 1.   4d, see c, Sec. 19.

SECTION 134.

OF GOVERNMENTS AND LAWS IN GENERAL.

That our belief with regard to earthly governments and laws in general may not be misinterpreted nor misunderstood, we have thought proper to present near the close of this volume our opinion concerning the same.

1. We believe that governments were instituted of God for the benefit of man, and that he holds men accountable for their acts in relation to them, either in making laws or administering them, for the good and safety of society.

2. We believe that no government can exist in peace, except such laws are framed and held inviolate as will secure to each individual the free exercise of conscience, the right and control of property, and the protection of life.

3. We believe that all governments necessarily require civil officers and magistrates to enforce the laws of the same, and that such as will administer the law in equity and justice, should be sought for and upheld by the voice of the people (if a republic,) or the will of the sovereign.

4. We believe that religion is instituted of God, and that men are amenable to him, and to him only, for the exercise of it, unless their religious opinions prompt them to infringe upon the rights and liberties of others ; but we do not believe that human law has a right to interfere in prescribing rules of worship to bind the consciences of men, nor. dictate forms for public or private devotion ; that the civil magistrate should restrain crime, but never control conscience ; should punish guilt, but never suppress the freedom of the soul.

5. We believe that all men are bound to sustain and uphold the respective governments in which they reside, while protected in their inherent and inalienable rights by the laws of such governments; and that sedition and rebellion are unbecoming every citizen thus protected, and should be punished accordingly; and that all governments have a right to enact such laws as in their own judgment are best calculated to secure the public interest, at the same time, however, holding sacred the freedom of conscience.

6. We believe that every man should be honored in his station : rulers and magistrates as such, being placed for the protection of the innocent, and the punishment of the guilty; and that to the laws, all men owe respect and deference, as without them peace and harmony would be supplanted by anarchy and terror ; human laws being instituted for the express purpose of regulating our interests as individuals and nations, between man and man, and divine laws given of heaven, prescribing rules on spiritual concerns, for faith and worship, both to be answered by man to his Maker.

7. We believe that rulers, states, and governments, have a right, and are bound to enact laws for the protection of all citizens in the free exercise of their religious belief; but we do not believe that they have a right in justice, to deprive citizens of this privilege, or proscribe them in their opinions, so long as a regard and reverence are shown to the laws, and such religious opinions do not justify sedition nor conspiracy.

8. We believe that the commission of crime should be punished according to the nature of the offence ; that murder, treason, robbery, theft, and the breach of the general peace, in all respects, should be punished according to their criminality, and their tendency to evil among men, by the laws of that government in which the offence is committed ; and for the public peace and tranquility, all men should step forward and

use their ability in bringing offenders against good laws to punishment.

9. We do not believe it just to mingle religious influence with civil government, whereby one religious society is fostered, and another proscribed in its spiritual privileges, and the individual rights of its members as citizens, denied.

10. We believe that all religious societies have a right to deal with their members for disorderly conduct according to the rules and regulations of such societies, provided that such dealings be for fellowship and good standing ; but we do not believe that any religious society has authority to try men on the right of property or life, to take from them this world's goods, or to put them in jeopardy of either life or limb, neither to inflict any physical punishment upon them, they can only excommunicate them from their society, and withdraw from them their fellowship.

11. We believe that men should appeal to the civil law for redress of all wrongs and grievances, where personal abuse is inflicted, or the right of property or character infringed, where such laws exist as will protect the same ; but we believe that all men are justified in defending themselves, their friends, and property, and the government, from the unlawful assaults and encroachments of all persons, in times of exigency, where immediate appeal cannot be made to the laws, and relief afforded.

12. We believe it just to preach the gospel to the nations of the earth, and warn the righteous to save themselves from the corruption of the world ; but we do not believe it right to interfere with bond servants, neither preach the gospel to, nor baptize them, contrary to the will and wish of their masters, nor to meddle with or influence them in the least, to cause them to be dissatisfied with their situations in this life, thereby jeopardizing the lives of men ; such interference we believe to be unlawful and unjust, and dangerous to the peace of every government allowing human beings to be held in servitude.

SECTION 135.

Martyrdom of Joseph Smith, the Prophet, and his brother Hyrum.

1. To seal the testimony of this book and the Book of Mormon, we announce the Martyrdom of Joseph Smith the Prophet, and Hyrum Smith the Patriarch. They were shot in Carthage jail, on the 27th of June, 1844, about five o'clock p.m., by an armed mob, painted black—of from 150 to 200 persons. Hyrum was shot first and fell calmly, exclaiming, "I am a dead man!" Joseph leaped from the window, and was shot dead in the attempt, exclaiming, "O Lord my God!" They were both shot after they were dead in a brutal manner, and both received four balls.

2. John Taylor, and Willard Richards, two of the Twelve, were the only persons in the room at the time; the former was wounded in a savage manner with four balls, but has since recovered; the latter, through the providence of God, escaped, "without even a hole in his robe."

3. Joseph Smith, the Prophet and Seer of the Lord, has done more (save Jesus only,) for the salvation of men in this world, than any other man that ever lived in it. In the short space of twenty years, he has brought forth the Book of Mormon, which he translated by the gift and power of God, and has been the means of publishing it on two continents; has sent the fullness of the everlasting gospel which it contained to the four quarters of the earth; has brought forth the revelations and commandments which compose this Book of Doctrine and Covenants, and many other wise documents and instructions for the benefit of the children of men; gathered many thousands of the Latter-day Saints, founded a great city; and left a fame and name that cannot be slain. He lived great, and he died great in the eyes of God and his people,

and like most of the Lord's anointed in ancient times, has sealed his mission and his works with his own blood—and so has his brother Hyrum. In life they were not divided, and in death they were not separated!

4. When Joseph went to Carthage to deliver himself up to the pretended requirements of the law, two or three days previous to his assassination, he said, "I am going like a lamb to the slaughter; but I am calm as a summer's morning; I have a conscience void of offence towards God, and towards all men. I SHALL DIE INNOCENT, AND IT SHALL YET BE SAID OF ME—HE WAS MURDERED IN COLD BLOOD." The same morning, after Hyrum had made ready to go—shall it be said to the slaughter? Yes, for so it was,—he read the following paragraph, near the close of the fifth chapter of Ether, in the Book of Mormon, and turned down the leaf upon it :—

5. "And it came to pass that I prayed unto the Lord that he would give unto the Gentiles grace, that they might have charity. And it came to pass that the Lord said unto me, if they have not charity, it mattereth not unto you, thou hast been faithful; wherefore thy garments are clean. And because thou hast seen thy weakness, thou shalt be made strong, even unto the sitting down in the place which I have prepared in the mansions of my Father. And now I ———bid farewell unto the Gentiles; yea and also unto my brethren whom I love, until we shall meet before the judgment-seat of Christ, where all men shall know that my garments are not spotted with your blood." The testators are now dead, and their testament is in force.

6. Hyrum Smith was 44 years old, February, 1844, and Joseph Smith was 38 in December, 1843; and henceforward their names will be classed among the martyrs of religion; and the reader in every nation will be reminded that the "Book of Mormon," and this book of Doctrine and Covenants of the church,

cost the best blood of the nineteenth century to bring them forth for the salvation of a ruined world : and that if the fire can scathe a *green tree* for the glory of God, how easy it will burn up the "dry trees" to purify the vineyard of corruption. They lived for glory ; they died for glory ; and glory is their eternal reward. From age to age shall their names go down to posterity as gems for the sanctified.

7. They were innocent of any crime, as they had often been proved before, and were only confined in jail by the conspiracy of traitors and wicked men ; and their *innocent blood* on the floor of Carthage jail, is a broad seal affixed to "Mormonism" that cannot be rejected by any court on earth ; and their *innocent blood* on the escutcheon of the State of Illinois, with the broken faith of the State as pledged by the Governor, is a witness to the truth of the everlasting gospel, that all the world cannot impeach ; and their *innocent blood* on the banner of liberty, and on the *magna charta* of the United States, is an ambassador for the religion of Jesus Christ, that will touch the hearts of honest men among all nations ; and their *innocent blood*, with the innocent blood of all the martyrs under the altar that John saw, will cry unto the Lord of hosts, till he avenges that blood on the earth. Amen.

SECTION 136.

The Word and Will of the Lord, given through President Brigham Young, at the Winter Quarters of the Camp of Israel, Omaha Nation, West Bank of Missouri River, near Council Bluffs, January 14th, 1847.

1. The word and will of the Lord concerning the Camp of Israel in their journeyings to the West.

2. Let all the people of the *Church of Jesus Christ of Latter-day Saints, and those who journey with them, be organized into companies, with a covenant and promise to keep all the commandments and statutes of the Lord our God.

3. Let the *companies be organized with captains of hundreds, captains of fifties, and captains of tens, with a president and his two counselors at their head, under the direction of the *Twelve Apostles;

4. And this shall be our covenant, that we will walk in all the ordinances of the Lord.

5. Let each company provide themselves with all the teams, wagons, provisions, clothing, and other necessaries for the journey that they can.

6. When the companies are organized, let them go to with their might, to prepare for those who are to tarry.

7. Let each company with their captains and presidents decide how many can go next spring; then choose out a sufficient number of able-bodied and expert men, to take teams, seeds, and farming utensils, to go as pioneers to prepare for putting in spring crops.

8. Let each company bear an *equal proportion, according to the dividend of their property, in taking the poor, the widows, the fatherless, and the families of those who have gone into the army, that the cries of the widow and the fatherless come not up into the ears of the Lord against this people.

9. Let each company prepare houses, and fields for raising grain, for those who are to remain behind this season, and this is the will of the Lord concerning his people.

10. Let every man use all his influence and property to remove this people to the place where the Lord shall locate a *Stake of Zion ;

---

a, see a, Sec. 1.   b, Exod. 18 : 21—27.   c, 107 : 24.   d, 38 :
24—27   42 : 30.   e, see g, Sec. 87.

11. And if ye do this with a pure heart, in all faithfulness, ye shall be blessed ; you shall be blessed in your flocks, and in your herds, and in your fields, and in your houses, and in your families.

12. Let my servants Ezra T. Benson and Erastus Snow organize a company ;

13. And let my servants Orson Pratt and Wilford Woodruff organize a company.

14. Also, let my servants Amasa Lyman and George A. Smith organize a company ;

15. And appoint presidents, and captains of hundreds, and of fifties, and of tens,

16. And let my servants that have been appointed go and teach this my will to the saints, that they may be ready to go to a land of peace.

17. Go thy way and do as I have told you, and fear not thine enemies ; for they shall not have power to stop my work.

18. Zion shall be ʃredeemed in mine own due time,

19. And if any man shall seek to build up himself, and seeketh not my counsel, he shall have no power, and his folly shall be made manifest.

20. Seek ye and keep all your pledges one with another, and covet not that which is thy brother's.

21. Keep yourselves from evil to take the ᵍname of the Lord in vain, for I am the Lord your God, even the God of your fathers, the God of Abraham, and of Isaac, and of Jacob.

22. I am he who led the children of Israel out of the land of Egypt, and my arm is stretched out in the last days to save my people Israel.

23. Cease to ʰcontend one with another, cease to ⁱspeak evil one of another.

24. Cease drunkenness, and let your words tend to edifying one another.

---

f, see *h*, Sec. 103.   *g*, 63 : 61—64.   *h*, III. Nep. 11 : 29, 30.
i, 20 : 54. 88 : 124.

25. If thou borrowest of thy neighbour, thou shalt return that which thou hast borrowed ; and if thou canst not repay, then go straightway and tell thy neighbor, lest he condemn thee.

26. If thou shalt find that which thy neighbor has lost, thou shalt make diligent search till thou shalt deliver it to him again.

27. Thou shalt be diligent in preserving what thou hast, that thou mayest be a *j*wise steward ; for it is the free gift of the Lord thy God, and thou art his steward.

28. If thou art merry, praise the Lord with singing, with music, with dancing, and with a prayer of praise and thanksgiving.

29. If thou art sorrowful, call on the Lord thy God with supplication, that your souls may be joyful.

30. Fear not thine enemies, for they are in mine hands, and I will do my pleasure with them.

31. My people must be tried in all things, that they may be prepared to receive the glory that I have for them, even the glory of Zion, and he that will not *k*bear chastisement, is not worthy of my kingdom.

32. Let him that is ignorant learn wisdom by humbling himself and calling upon the Lord his God, that his eyes may be opened that he may see, and his ears opened that he may hear,

33. For my Spirit is sent forth into the world to enlighten the humble and contrite, and to the condemnation of the ungodly.

34. Thy brethren have rejected you and your testimony, even the nation that has driven you out ;

35. And now cometh the day of their calamity, even the days of sorrow, like a woman that is taken in travail ; and their sorrow shall be great, unless they speedily repent ; yea, very speedily ;

---

j, see *o,* Sec. 42. *k,* 90 : 36. 97 : 26.

36. For they killed the prophets, and them that were sent unto them, and they have shed 'innocent blood, which crieth from the ground against them :

37. Therefore marvel not at these things, for ye are not pure; ye can not yet bear my glory; but ye shall behold it if ye are faithful in keeping all my words that I have given you from the days of Adam to Abraham ; from Abraham to Moses ; from Moses to Jesus and his apostles ; and from Jesus and his apostles to Joseph Smith, whom I did call upon by mine angels, my ministering servants; and by mine own voice out of the heavens to bring forth my work,

38. Which foundation he did lay, and was faithful and I took him to myself.

39. Many have marveled because of his death, but it was needful that he should ᵐseal his testimony with his blood, that he might be honored, and the wicked might be condemned.

40. Have I not delivered you from your enemies, only in that I have left a witness of my name?

41. Now, therefore, hearken, O ye people of my church; and ye elders listen together; you have received my kingdom.

42. Be diligent in keeping all my commandments, lest judgment come upon you, and your faith fail you, and your enemies triumph over you.—So no more at present. Amen, and Amen.

---

l, 58 : 53. 63 : 28—31. Rev. 18 : 24. 19 : 2. ᴜ Nep. 14 : 13. 22 : 14.
ɪɪ. Nep. 5 : 16. Mor. 8, 27, 40, 41. Ether 8 : 22—24. *m,* Sec. 135.

INDEX.

A.

B.

K K

R

S.

T.